SOCIAL PROBLEM SOLVING
AND OFFENDING

WILEY SERIES IN
FORENSIC CLINICAL PSYCHOLOGY

Edited by

Clive R. Hollin
Clinical Division of Psychiatry, University of Leicester, UK

and

Mary McMurran
School of Psychology, Cardiff University, UK

COGNITIVE BEHAVIOURAL TREATMENT OF SEXUAL OFFENDERS
William L. Marshall, Dana Anderson and Yolanda Fernandez

VIOLENCE, CRIME AND MENTALLY DISORDERED OFFENDERS:
Concepts and Methods for Effective Treatment and Prevention
Sheilagh Hodgins and Rudiger Müller-Isberner (*Editors*)

OFFENDER REHABILITATION IN PRACTICE:
Implementing and Evaluating Effective Programs
Gary A. Bernfeld, David P. Farrington and Alan W. Leschied (*Editors*)

MOTIVATING OFFENDERS TO CHANGE:
A Guide to Enhancing Engagement in therapy
Mary McMurran (*Editor*)

THE PSYCHOLOGY OF GROUP AGGRESSION
Arnold P. Goldstein

OFFENDER REHABILITATION AND TREATMENT:
Effective Programmes and Policies to Reduce Re-offending
James McGuire (*Editor*)

OFFENDERS WITH DEVELOPMENTAL DISABILITIES
William R. Lindsay, John L. Taylor and Peter Sturmey (*Editors*)

NEW PERSPECTIVES ON AGGRESSION REPLACEMENT TRAINING:
Practice, Research and Application
Arnold P. Goldstein, Rune Nensén, Bengt Daleflod and Mikael Kalt (*Editors*)

SOCIAL PROBLEM SOLVING AND OFFENDING:
Evidence, Evaluation and Evolution
Mary McMurran and James McGuire (*Editors*)

SOCIAL PROBLEM SOLVING AND OFFENDING

Evidence, Evaluation and Evolution

Edited by

Mary McMurran
Cardiff University, UK

and

James McGuire
University of Liverpool, UK

John Wiley & Sons, Ltd

Other Wiley Editorial Offices

John Wiley & Sons Inc., 111 River Street, Hoboken, NJ 07030, USA

Jossey-Bass, 989 Market Street, San Francisco, CA 94103-1741, USA

Wiley–VCH Verlag GmbH, Boschstr. 12, D-69469 Weinheim, Germany

John Wiley & Sons Australia Ltd, 42 McDougall Street, Milton, Queensland 4064, Australia

John Wiley & Sons (Asia) Pte Ltd, 2 Clementi Loop #02-01, Jin Xing Distripark, Singapore 129809

John Wiley & Sons Canada Ltd, 22 Worcester Road, Etobicoke, Ontario, Canada M9W 1L1

Wiley also publishes its books in a variety of electronic formats. Some content that appears in print may not be
available in electronic books.

Library of Congress Cataloging-in-Publication Data

Social problem solving and offending: evidence, evaluation, and evoluation/edited by
    Mary McMurran and James McGuire.
        p. cm.—(Wiley series in forensic clinical psychology)
    Includes bibligraphical references and index.
    ISBN-13 978-0-470-86406-7 (cloth: alk.paper)–978-0-470-86407-4 (pbk. : alk.)
    ISBN-10-0-470-86406-0 (cloth: alk.paper)–0-470-86407-9 (pbk.: alk.paper)
    1. Criminals—Rehabilitation. 2. Correctional psychology. 3. Social intelligence.
    4. Problem-solving therapy. 5. Cognitive therapy. I. McMurran, Mary. II. McGuire, James, 1948-   III. Series.
    HV9275..S53 2005
    364.3—dc22   2005005165

British Library Cataloguing in Publication Data

A catalogue record for this book is available from the British Library

    ISBN-13 978-0-470-86406-7 (hbk) 978-0-470-86407-4 (pbk)
    ISBN-10 0-470-86406-0 (hbk) 0-470-86407-9 (pbk)

Typeset in 10/12pt Palatino by Thomson Press (India) Limited, New Delhi
Printed and bound in Great Britain by Antony Rowe Ltd, Chippenham, Wiltshire
This book is printed on acid-free paper responsibly manufactured from sustainable forestry
in which at least two trees are planted for each one used for paper production.

In memory of Mark Williams, former psychologist with HM Prison Service, who died on 27 November 2004.

MM

CONTENTS

ABOUT THE EDITORS

Mary McMurran is consultant clinical and forensic psychologist at Llanarth Court Hospital, Wales, and Senior Research Fellow in the School of Psychology, Cardiff University. She has worked with offenders in a young offenders centre, a maximum-security psychiatric hospital, a regional secure unit, and in the community. In 1999, she was awarded a five-year Senior Baxter Research Fellowship by the National Health Service's National Programme on Forensic Mental Health Research and Development. Her research interests are the assessment and treatment of intoxicated aggression, social problem-solving therapy for personality-disordered offenders, and understanding and enhancing offenders' motivation to change. She is the author, with Philip Priestley, of Addressing Substance-Related Offending (ASRO), an accredited group treatment programme used in HM Prison and Probation Services, and Control of Violence for Angry Impulsive Drinkers (COVAID), an individual treatment programme. She is a Fellow of the British Psychological Society and former Chair of the Society's Division of Forensic Psychology. She is founding editor, with Sally Lloyd-Bostock, of the journal *Legal & Criminological Psychology*, and is joint editor of *Criminal Behaviour and Mental Health*. She is a former member of the Scottish Prison Service's Offender Treatment Programme Accreditation Panel, and is currently a member of Her Majesty's Prison and Probation Services Correctional Services Accreditation Panel.

James McGuire is Professor of Forensic Clinical Psychology at the University of Liverpool, UK, Director of Studies for the Doctorate in Clinical Psychology programme, and an honorary consultant clinical psychologist in Mersey Care NHS Trust. A chartered clinical and forensic psychologist, he carries out psycho-legal work involving assessment of offenders and has prepared reports on young offenders charged with offences of violence, for hearings of the Mental Health Review Tribunal on adults detained in secure hospitals, and for the Criminal Cases Review Commission. He has conducted research in prisons, probation services, and other settings on aspects of the effectiveness of treatment with offenders and allied topics. He has engaged in a range of consultative work with criminal justice agencies in the United Kingdom, Sweden, Canada, Australia and Hong Kong. He was co-organizer of the *What Works* series of conferences, and has written or edited 12 books and numerous other publications on this and related areas.

LIST OF CONTRIBUTORS

Daniel H. Antonowicz

Assistant Professor, Department of Criminology, Wilfrid Laurier University—Brantford, Grand River Hall, Room 125, Brantford, Ontario, N3T 2Y3, Canada

Andreas Beelmann

Professor of Psychology, Institute of Psychology, University of Jena, Am Steiger 3/Haus 1, Jena 07743, Germany

Fiona H. Biggam

Lecturer in Psychology, Department of Psychology, Glasgow Caledonian University, City Campus, Cowcaddens Road, Glasgow G4 0BA, and clinical psychologist, The State Hospital, Carstairs, ML11 8RP, UK

Shelley L. Brown

Research Manager, Research Branch, Correctional Service Canada, 340 Laurier Ave. W., Ontario K1A 0P9, Canada

Laura E. Dreer

NIH Rehabilitation Research Fellow, Department of Psychology, 415 Campbell Hall, Room 233, 1300 University Boulevard, University of Alabama at Birmingham, Birmingham, AL 35294-1170, USA

Conor Duggan

Professor of Forensic Mental Health, Department of Psychiatry, University of Nottingham, Duncan MacMillan House, Porchester Road, Nottingham NG3 6AA, UK

Thomas J. D'Zurilla

Professor of Psychology, Department of Psychology, Stony Brook University, Stony Brook, New York, NY 11794-2500, USA

Vincent Egan

Professor of Psychology, Department of Psychology, Glasgow Caledonian University, City Campus, Cowcaddens Road, Glasgow G4 0BA, UK

Timothy R. Elliott

Professor of Psychology, Department of Psychology, 415 Campbell Hall, 1300 University Boulevard, University of Alabama at Birmingham, Birmingham, AL 35294-1170, USA

Theresa A. Gannon

Postdoctorate Fellow, Department of Psychology, Victoria University of Wellington, PO Box 600, Wellington 6001, New Zealand

Robin Harvey

Research Fellow, School of Psychology, University of Western Australia, 35 Stirling Highway, Crawley 6609, Australia

Warren T. Jackson

Associate Professor, Department of Psychiatry and Behavioral Neurobiology, School of Medicine, University of Alabama at Birmingham, SPC 409 1530, 3rd Avenue South, Birmingham, AL 35294-0018, USA

Liisa Keltikangas-Järvinen

Professor of Psychology, Department of Psychology, University of Helsinki, PO Box 9 (Siltavuorenpenger 20 D), Helsinki FIN-00014, Finland

John E. Lochman

Professor of Psychology, Department of Psychology, University of Alabama, Box 870348, Tuscaloosa, AL 35487-0348, USA

Friedrich Lösel

Professor of Psychology and Director of the Institute of Psychology, University of Erlangen-Nuremberg, Bismarckstr. 1, Erlangen 91054, Germany

Walter Matthys

Professor of Aggression in Children, Department of Child and Adolescent Psychiatry, University Medical Centre Utrecht, PO Box 8550, 3508 GA Utrecht, The Netherlands

James McGuire

Professor of Forensic Clinical Psychology, Division of Clinical Psychology, University of Liverpool, The Whelan Building, Quadrangle, Brownlow Hill, Liverpool L69 3GB, UK

Mary McMurran

Consultant Clinical and Forensic Psychologist, Llanarth Court Hospital, Raglan NP5 2YD, and Senior Research Fellow, Cardiff University, Cardiff CF10 3AT, UK

Arthur M. Nezu

Professor of Psychology, Medicine, and Public Health, and Director of the Center for Behavioral Medicine and Mind/Body Studies, Department of Psychology, Drexel University, 245 N 15th Street, Philadelphia, PA 19102-1192, USA

Christine Maguth Nezu

Professor of Psychology, Associate Professor of Medicine, Co-Director for the Center for Behavioral Medicine and Mind/Body Studies, and Director for Assessment and Treatment Services for Sexual Aggression, Department of Psychology, Drexel University, 245 N 15th Street, Philadelphia, PA 19102-1192, USA

Devon L.L. Polaschek

Senior Lecturer in Psychology, Department of Psychology, Victoria University of Wellington, PO Box 600, Wellington 6001, New Zealand

Kevin G. Power

Honorary Professor of Clinical Psychology, Department of Psychology, University of Stirling, Stirling FK9 4LA, and Head of Psychology Services, Tayside Primary Healthcare NHS Trust, UK

Robert R. Ross

Professor, Department of Criminology, University of Ottawa, Ottawa, Ontario K1N 6N5, Canada

Ralph C. Serin

Assistant Professor of Psychology, Department of Psychology, Carleton University, 1125 Colonel By Drive, Ottawa, Ontario K1S 5B6, Canada

Tony Ward

Professor of Psychology, Department of Psychology, Victoria University of Wellington, PO Box 600, Wellington 6001, New Zealand

SERIES EDITORS' PREFACE

ABOUT THE SERIES

At the time of writing it is clear that we live in a time, certainly in the UK and other parts of Europe, if perhaps less so in other areas of the world, when there is renewed enthusiasm for constructive approaches to working with offenders to prevent crime. What do we mean by this statement and what basis do we have for making it?

First, by "constructive approaches to working with offenders" we mean bringing the use of effective methods and techniques of behaviour change into work with offenders. Indeed, this view might pass as a definition of forensic clinical psychology. Thus, our focus is the application of theory and research in order to develop practice aimed at bringing about a change in the offender's functioning. The word *constructive* is important and can be set against approaches to behaviour change that seek to operate by destructive means. Such destructive approaches are typically based on the principles of deterrence and punishment, seeking to suppress the offender's actions through fear and intimidation. A constructive approach, on the other hand, seeks to bring about changes in an offender's functioning that will produce, say, enhanced possibilities of employment, greater levels of self-control, better family functioning, or increased awareness of the pain of victims.

A constructive approach faces the criticism of being a "soft" response to the damage caused by offenders, neither inflicting pain and punishment nor delivering retribution. This point raises a serious question for those involved in working with offenders. Should advocates of constructive approaches oppose retribution as a goal of the criminal justice system as a process that is incompatible with treatment and rehabilitation? Alternatively, should constructive work with offenders take place within a system given to retribution? We believe that this issue merits serious debate.

However, to return to our starting point, history shows that criminal justice systems are littered with many attempts at constructive work with offenders, not all of which have been successful. In raising the spectre of success, the second part of our opening sentence now merits attention: that is, "constructive approaches to working with offenders *to prevent crime*". In order to achieve the goal of preventing crime, interventions must focus on the right targets for behaviour change. In addressing this crucial point, Andrews and Bonta (1994) have formulated the *need principle*:

> Many offenders, especially high-risk offenders, have a variety of needs. They need places to live and work and/or they need to stop taking drugs. Some have poor self-esteem, chronic headaches or cavities in their teeth. These are all "needs". The need principle draws our attention to the distinction between *criminogenic* and *noncriminogenic* needs. Criminogenic needs are a subset of an offender's risk level. They are dynamic attributes of an offender that, when changed, are associated with changes in the probability of recidivism. Noncriminogenic needs are also dynamic and changeable, but these changes are not necessarily associated with the probability of recidivism. (p.176)

Thus, successful work with offenders can be judged in terms of bringing about change in noncriminogenic need *or* in terms of bringing about change in criminogenic need. While the former is important and, indeed, may be a necessary precursor to offence-focused work, it is changing criminogenic need that, we argue, should be the touchstone in working with offenders.

While, as noted above, the history of work with offenders is not replete with success, the research base developed since the early 1990s, particularly the meta-analyses (e.g. Lösel, 1995), now strongly supports the position that effective work with offenders to prevent further offending is possible. The parameters of such evidence-based practice have become well established and widely disseminated under the banner of "*What Works*" (McGuire, 1995).

It is important to state that we are not advocating that there is only one approach to preventing crime. Clearly, there are many approaches, with different theoretical underpinnings, that can be applied. Nonetheless, a tangible momentum has grown in the wake of the "*What Works*" movement as academics, practitioners, and policy-makers seek to capitalize on the possibilities that this research raises for preventing crime. The task now facing many service agencies lies in turning the research into effective practice.

Our aim in developing this Series in Forensic Clinical Psychology is to produce texts that review research and draw on clinical expertise to advance effective work with offenders. We are both committed to the ideal of evidence-based practice and we will encourage contributors to the Series to follow this approach. Thus, the books published in the Series will not be practice manuals or "cook books": they will offer readers authoritative and critical information through which forensic clinical practice can develop. We are both enthusiastic about the contribution to effective practice that this Series can make and look forward to continuing to develop it in the years to come.

ABOUT THIS BOOK

In the current enthusiasm for offending behaviour programmes, much is made of the need for such programmes to be cognitive-behavioural in orientation. However, when it comes to understanding what is meant by the term "cognitive-behavioural" there is perhaps rather less clarity than there is enthusiasm. If we begin to try to unpick the meaning of "cognitive-behavioural" we quickly stray into the realms of social learning theory and social-cognitive theory (Bandura, 1977, 1986) and the complexities of the interplay between the three domains of environment, cognition, and action. For those working with offenders, there is a research base that speaks to the specific individual aspects of each of environment, cognition, and action and their associations with crime and criminal conduct. However, if we focus on cognition, Ross and Fabiano (1985) have drawn the distinction between *im*personal cognition, such as solving mathematical puzzles or reading a map, and *inter*personal cognition which is that aspect of cognition that is concerned with how we think about ourselves and our relationships with other people. In the context of understanding a social act such as offending, the main concern is clearly with interpersonal cognition.

A body of empirical evidence has emerged since the 1980s that has, at least in part, illuminated our understanding of interpersonal cognition as it relates to offenders and offending. Thus, within the professional literature a familiarity has emerged with regard to those terms—such as self-control, impulsivity, locus of control, empathy, perspective-taking, role-taking, and moral reasoning—that refer explicitly to cognition. Alongside these terms, we see reference to social problem solving as another aspect of cognition associated with offending. Simply, we may think of social problem solving as the complex range of cognitions that we all use to deal effectively with the interpersonal issues that we all encounter in our daily lives. The contribution of the early studies in this area was to show that, compared to non-delinquents, offenders, both male and female, tend to give less socially competent responses to social problems than non-offenders (e.g., Freedman, Rosenthal, Donahoe, Schlundt, & McFall, 1978; Higgins & Thies, 1981). Of course, there are other populations that exhibit difficulties in social problem solving and hence techniques to enhance social problem-solving skills have been established in the broader clinical literature. These social problem-solving techniques, variously termed social problem-solving skills training or problem-solving therapy, were applied to work with offenders and eventually became a standard component of several offending behaviour programmes.

There are three points that arise from the broad issue of social problem solving and offending: first, how can we understanding the finer points of social problem solving in offender populations?; second, what is the nature of the relationship between social problem solving and other aspects of cognition?; third, what are the dynamics of the interaction between cognition, including social problem solving, and antisocial and criminal behaviour? This book addresses all three of these issues so that in the first part of the book there is consideration of the evidence on social problem solving, its relationship to offending, and changing problem-solving skills. The effectiveness of attempts to change social problem solving is a critical issue and the second part of the book looks in depth at the topic of evaluation. Finally, reminding us that this is a changing and developing field, the third part of the book addresses some of the conceptual, theoretical, and research topics that are of current concern.

Overall, this book presents a view of the "state of the art" in a developing area of forensic practice. We are confident that it will inform the work of both practitioners and researchers and is a welcome addition to the Series.

Clive Hollin and Mary McMurran

REFERENCES

Andrews, D. A. & Bonta, J. (1994). *The psychology of criminal conduct*. Cincinnati, OH: Anderson Publishing.

Bandura, A. (1977). *Social learning theory*. Englewood Cliffs, NJ: Prentice Hall.

Bandura, A. (1986). *Social foundations of thought and action: A social-cognitive theory*. Englewood Cliffs, NJ: Prentice Hall.

Freedman, B. J., Rosenthal, L., Donahoe, C. P., Schlundt, D. G., & McFall, R. M. (1978). A social-behavioral analysis of skills deficits in delinquent and non-delinquent adolescent boys. *Journal of Consulting and Clinical Psychology, 46*, 1448–1462.

Higgins, J. P. & Thies, A. P. (1981). Social effectiveness and problem-solving thinking of reformatory inmates. *Journal of Offender Counselling Services and Rehabilitation, 5*, 93–98.

Lösel, F. (1995). Increasing consensus in the evaluation of offender rehabilitation? *Psychology, Crime, & Law, 2*, 19–39.

McGuire, J. (ed.) (1995). *What works: Reducing reoffending*. Chichester: John Wiley & Sons, Ltd.

Ross, R. R. & Fabiano, E. A. (1985). *Time to think: A cognitive model of delinquency prevention and offender rehabilitation*. Johnson City, TN: Institute of Social Sciences and Arts.

PREFACE

In 2001, a conference on 'Problem Solving and Offenders' was held in Nottingham, UK. Speakers addressed theory, research, and practice, contributing to what turned out to be an inspiring event. The proceedings of that conference are published in a special issue of the journal *Criminal Behaviour and Mental Health*, 2001, Volume 11, No. 4 (http://www.whurr.co.uk).

The enthusiasm for the subject demonstrated at that conference led us to the decision to take the subject one step further forward by compiling an edited text. The joys of editing a book lie in a completely self-centred motivation. It is a great privilege to be able to choose a topic of personal interest, invite world-class researchers, academics, and practitioners to contribute, and be first to read their work. Each and every contribution to this text is a fascinating, incisive, and evidence-based account of offenders' social problem solving and issues relevant to it that will draw the field together and promote further development.

What is clear from this book is that evidence and practice regarding offenders' social problem solving are in good shape. One possible reason for this is that here is an area where theory–practice links are strong. The language and structure of social problem-solving research have a common-sense appeal to both practitioners and offender-clients. This permits the application of problem-solving therapies by practitioners of many different professional backgrounds with a wide range of clients. An active applied school enlivens and enriches research, which in turn informs and refines practice. This healthy symbiosis is one that should be nurtured and nourished, and we hope that this book will contribute to the continued development of both academic and applied aspects.

Mary McMurran and James McGuire
February 2005

ACKNOWLEDGEMENT

Mary McMurran would like to acknowledge funding from the NHS National Programme on Forensic Mental Health R&D, which gave the time needed to produce this book.

PART I

EVIDENCE

Chapter 1

SOCIAL PROBLEM SOLVING: BASIC CONCEPTS, RESEARCH, AND APPLICATIONS

JAMES MCGUIRE

University of Liverpool, UK

INTRODUCTION

The phrase "problem solving" has several levels of meaning in mental health and related fields. There is, first, a general sense in which it can be used metaphorically to describe any planned therapeutic effort. Given its function of alleviating distress, therapy by its very nature can be envisioned as helping to solve a problem. There is also a second, more focused, use of the term which arises in psychotherapy and counselling process research, in which problem solving is used to specify certain actions by counsellors or therapists during clinical sessions.

The sense in which it will be used in the present book is distinct from both of the foregoing definitions. In what follows, we will be considering a specific approach, method, or set of procedures within cognitive-behavioural therapy, which has evolved over the past 30 years and is now particularly influential in shaping the design of intervention programmes in a number of inter-related fields.

This opening chapter has three objectives. The first is to describe the origins of the concepts and theoretical underpinnings of a cluster of methods collectively known as social or interpersonal problem-solving training. The second is to provide a brief outline of these methods and an account of the empirical justification for their use. Other chapters will expand considerably upon this and will give illustrations of it in a range of settings. The third objective is to review ways in which the models and methods developed on this basis have

Revised and updated version of an article that originally appeared in *Criminal Behaviour and Mental Health* (2001), 11, 210–235. The author wishes to thank the journal editors and Whurr Publishers for permission to adapt the material for the present book.

been used in the design of intervention programmes, and applied in criminal justice and mental health settings.

There is, of course, another separate though overlapping use of the term "problem solving". This occurs primarily within cognitive psychology where it is employed mainly to designate processes that are involved in solving abstract or impersonal problems, connected with the manipulation of objects or ideas in fields such as logic, mathematics, or science. A large volume of research has been conducted on mental operations such as induction, deduction, syllogistic and analogical reasoning, and creativity (Eysenck, 2001). While studies of this type were traditionally performed in laboratory settings, cognitive psychologists have also extended their research to investigate the processes that underpin everyday reasoning (see, for example, Galotti, 1994). The subject matter nevertheless remains primarily the application of mental effort to the solution of problems in the impersonal, material, or abstract ideational world.

DEFINITIONS AND BASIC CONCEPTS

In the sense that will concern us here, problem solving has been defined as "the self-directed cognitive-behavioral process by which a person attempts to identify or discover effective or adaptive solutions for specific problems encountered in everyday living" (D'Zurilla & Nezu, 2001, p. 212). Alternatively it may be conceptualised as "a goal-directed sequence of cognitive and affective operations as well as behavioral responses for the purpose of adapting to internal or external demands or challenges" (Heppner & Krauskopf, 1987, p. 375). In this respect the terms *problem solving* and *coping* have sometimes been viewed as synonymous (Heppner & Hillerbrand, 1991). Engaging in this process inevitably activates some of the routines involved in other types of reasoning and typically studied in cognitive psychology research. It has been widely recognised, however, that there are additional activities involved in attempting to solve problems in the inter-personal domain. While practical, mechanical problem solving is an intrinsic part of healthy adjustment and everyday functioning, it may be insufficient for adaptive behaviour in complex social environments. Another way to characterise this difference is in terms of a distinction between the "well-structured" tasks that are customarily used in cognitive psychology experiments, versus the more "ill-structured" problems encountered in daily life (ibid.) In these contexts, therefore, other procedures are called into play.

Problem solving self-evidently links two elements: the problem with which the individual begins and which leads to engaging in the exercise; and the solution which presumably is an objective or desired outcome of that effort. It is important therefore to clarify what we mean by these terms. D'Zurilla and Nezu have described a *problem* as "any life situation or task (present or anticipated) that demands a response for adaptive functioning, but for which no effective response is immediately apparent or available to the person, due to the presence of some obstacle(s)" (2001, pp. 212–213). A *solution* is "a situation-specific coping response or response pattern (cognitive and/or behavioral) which is the product or outcome of the problem-solving process when it is applied to a specific problematic situation'' (ibid., p. 213). Put at its simplest, problem-solving training or therapy is designed to help individuals find their way from problems to solutions, using a systematised sequence of methods and steps. Perhaps more importantly, it is also designed to enable them to acquire the capacity to repeat this when necessary on subsequent occasions.

Within cognitive social learning theory, effective problem solving is regarded as a *skill*. To be more precise, it is made possible through the acquisition or development of some constituent types of skill. While this concept is firmly established in the behavioural domain, skilled activity at a cognitive level is more difficult to define. Skills are generally conceptualised as over-learned, automatic sequences of behaviour, which can be controlled and directed towards achievement of a goal. On a behavioural level, this includes motor skills (driving, speed-typing, playing tennis or the piano). On a cognitive level, skilled sequences of activity underpin many kinds of frequently recurring thought processes, as well as language and speech production. In the cognitive-interpersonal domain, individuals deploy skills in activities that range from communication, interaction, or building and maintaining relationships, to negotiation and resolving conflicts.

Origins of Research on Social Problem-Solving

A key question that arises is whether, like their counterparts on the behavioural level, skills for solving problems in the cognitive-interpersonal domain can be learned through conscious effort and repeated practice. The origins of this form of intervention are generally traced to two main approaches or traditions. While in practical terms they are very close and exhibit numerous similarities, there are also some important differences between them, primarily in terms of their conceptual and research origins.

In the first approach, formulated by D'Zurilla and Goldfried (1971), and later refined by D'Zurilla and Nezu (1982), problem-solving concepts were articulated as an extension of principles of behaviour modification. These authors specified a number of mediational stages in the process of behaviour change. Their proposals were initially made during the late 1960s, a period of rapid evolution in behaviourism when the importance of mediating events was beginning to be more broadly recognised. This was associated, among other changes, with the formal statement of cognitive social learning theory by Bandura (1977) and the emergence of the first integrated models of behavioural and cognitive therapies (Mahoney, 1974; Meichenbaum, 1977). A specific impetus for the advent of problem-solving concepts arose from the failure, in many studies of behaviour modification, to demonstrate adequate generalisation of intervention effects. In social skills training, for example, transfer and generalisation of acquired skills are facilitated by the inclusion of training elements focused on perceptual and cognitive aspects of social encounters (Akhtar & Bradley, 1991).

The second approach was derived from work in applied settings but from the outset had a strong developmental emphasis. Spivack and Levine (1963) discovered differences between normally adjusted and social-problem groups in the way they thought about problems. A group of adolescent boys resident in a reform school was compared with a "normal" control group on a large number of measures of various aspects of self-regulation. The latter were assessed by means of a series of specially designed tasks that called upon processes hypothesised to be necessary for the effective solution of problems in the interpersonal domain. Among them was one task in which participants were given the beginning and the end of a story and asked to make up a central, connecting section. A highly significant difference was found between the two populations both in the length and the quality of the stories they invented. The idea that impoverished "means–end thinking", as this skill was designated, might characterise the poorly-adjusted adolescent led to the broader notion that an individual's performance on measures such as this might have implications for other areas of his or her functioning.

In the model that emerged from this (Spivack, Platt, & Shure, 1976), it was hypothesised that some problems could result from the absence of, or failure to apply, certain cognitive-interpersonal abilities. Such problem-solving "deficits" might include repeated rigidity when a situation demanded flexibility of response; acting impulsively without considering the alternatives; or neglecting to look ahead and anticipate the ramifications of a particular decision or course of action.

There are numerous overlaps between these two approaches. But there has also been a tendency for them to be applied in different specialist areas. The D'Zurilla and Goldfried (1971) model has been more frequently used, or cited as a seminal source, in work on emotional and mental health problems (Nezu, D'Zurilla, Zwick, & Nezu, 2004; Nezu, Nezu, & Houts, 1993). Specific areas of focus have included anxiety-related problems (Nezu et al., 2004); depression (Nezu, Nezu, & Perri, 1989); closed head injury (Foxx, Martella, & Marchand-Martella, 1989c); obesity (Perri et al., 2001); and schizophrenia (Favrod, Caffaro, Grossenbacher, Rubio, & Von Turk, 2000). The approach has also been applied within psychological responses to cancer (Nezu, Nezu, Houts, Friedman, & Faddis, 1999) and a variety of other medical problems (Nezu et al., 2004). When the methods are used in healthcare services, they are most commonly designated as problem-solving *therapy*.

By contrast, the model of Spivack et al. (1976) has been more extensively applied in child development and educational settings. In this context it has sometimes formed part of a broader curriculum designed to teach thinking skills for application to social problems. This parallels methods such as those developed by Feuerstein (1980). It has also been used with other difficulties including conduct disorder, substance abuse, gambling, and criminal offending. In educational and criminal justice settings, work of this kind is more frequently entitled problem-solving *training*. Despite these differences in focus and nomenclature, to a large extent the fundamental methods remain the same.

Elements of Problem-Solving Training

In their initial conceptualisation, D'Zurilla and Goldfried (1971) envisaged problem solving as a progression through five stages. They were delineated as:

1. Problem orientation or "set";
2. Problem definition and formulation;
3. Generation of alternative solutions;
4. Decision-making;
5. Solution implementation and verification.

In advocating the view that the ability to secure ideas for solving problems is a skill that can be acquired, D'Zurilla and Goldfried (1971) cited research on the procedure of *brainstorming*. This was originally developed by Alex Osborn, an advertising executive, during the 1930s and described in his book *Applied Imagination* (Osborn, 1963). The term is derived from the metaphor of using the brain to storm a problem. D'Zurilla and Goldfried were impressed by studies which had suggested that producing more ideas led to producing better ideas. Although this expectation was fulfilled in their own experimental studies, it was not always fully confirmed by subsequent research (Stein, 1975). It has, however, been shown both that brainstorming leads to generating more ideas and that individuals can be trained to engage in it and produce more ideas than prior to such training. In problem-solving therapy, a collection of methods is employed for sequential development, practice, and application of each of the five skills in the D'Zurilla and Goldfried model.

By contrast, the work of Spivack et al. (1976) revolved around the following core propositions:

1. A number of separate cognitive skills can be isolated that are crucial for effective functioning in interpersonal situations. They include, for example, the ability to think of several options before acting, or to appreciate the likely consequences of an act.
2. Different combinations of these skills are important for adjustment during different phases of development (early and middle childhood, adolescence, adulthood).
3. These skills, though cognitive in nature, are directed towards the interpersonal domain and are psychometrically distinct from what we normally assume we assess by means of conventional intelligence tests.
4. Through specially developed methods of training it is possible to enable individuals deficient in those skills to acquire them, with consequent improvements in interpersonal adjustment.

It is a proposal common to both these approaches that the absence of effective problem-solving is associated with interpersonal difficulties and other mental health or behavioural problems. There are two possible causal pathways leading to this outcome.

In the first, poor problem solving is a result of *inhibition* of skill. Individuals have the ability to solve problems but they do not apply it. This is primarily a motivational issue and unlikely to be remedied by training. In the second, the problem derives from a *deficit* of skill. Individuals have not acquired adequate levels of skill for effective problem solving, most probably as a consequence of limited learning opportunities, constrained by parenting or other socialisation influences.

The manner in which interpersonal learning occurs is a function of its wider socio-cultural context. It is therefore often emphasised within problem-solving training procedures that the focus of intervention is upon the *how* rather than the *what* of problem-solving. Individuals are given assistance in acquiring or improving skills (changes in cognitive-behavioural capacities) without any presumptions regarding the ways in which those skills will be applied (the content of their thinking). This is based on the supposition that while culture has a profound influence on the dominant themes is individuals' thoughts (expressed through language, beliefs, values, personal goals), most aspects of cognitive processing show much less variation. However, more research is needed in order to determine the parameters of this.

Whatever its exact content, social problem-solving training is a comparatively distinct form of intervention within the broader cognitive-behavioural repertoire. Its application draws on methods of change including functional analysis of habitual reactions, skills practice, rehearsal, and feedback as used in behaviour modification. Additionally however, it draws on methods more familiar within cognitive and self-control therapies, such as self-monitoring, analysis of thinking patterns and distortions, Socratic questioning, guided discussion, and reflection. Thus, it occupies an intermediate point on a conceptual continuum between more behaviourally-oriented and cognitively-oriented therapies (McGuire, 2000a). Figure 1.1 depicts this relationship and locates problem-solving within a broader framework of connections between other cognitive-behavioural approaches.

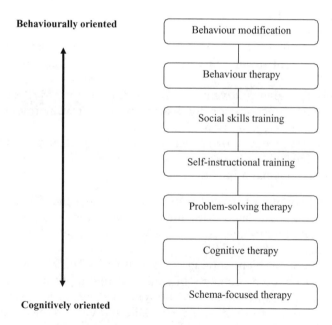

Figure 1.1   A continuum of methods in behavioural and cognitive therapy
Source: Adapted from McGuire, J. (2000a), *Cognitive-behavioural approaches: An introduction to theory and research.* London: Home Office.

The component skills isolated in the studies of D'Zurilla and Goldfried (1971) and Spivack et al. (1976) and in numerous subsequent studies, have also been incorporated within integrative information-processing models of social adjustment and responding (Akhtar & Bradley, 1991; Crick & Dodge, 1994). In these models, a sequence of events and processes is hypothesised to precede an observed behavioural response. They include the encoding of environmental cues, attribution of motives, the generation of alternative solutions, pursuit of appropriate social goals, and acquisition of skills for enactment of social behaviours. These may be modified by tendencies towards egocentrism or limited perspective-taking. Individuals vary in their level of or engagement in different phases of the above sequence, and their competencies within discrete elements should be assessed directly using a comprehensive procedure designed to probe each area of potential deficit in turn.

Assessment of Social Problem-Solving

The assessment of the activities and skills that can be circumscribed and separately defined in this area has posed recurrent difficulties, several of which remain to be solved. In an initial review of the field, Butler and Meichenbaum (1981) expressed concerns with regard to several aspects of the measures then in use. A central issue was the extent to which the various tasks employed genuinely tapped events or abilities that were activated in everyday problem situations. In addition, a number of the commonly used assessments posed instrumentation problems and were psychometrically weak. Butler and Meichenbaum proposed, among other things, that measures be developed that were based on behavioural observation rather than verbal assessment of problem-solving. They also recommended a focus on self-reflective, meta-cognitive processes in problem situations. In the intervening period several measures have become more firmly established for assessment of problem-solving and are conventionally divided into two sub-groups respectively associated with *process* and *outcome*.

Process measures are designed to access general cognitive and behavioural activities that facilitate solving problems. They rely mainly on self-report. They therefore evaluate typical patterns of responding when individuals address cognitive-interpersonal problems and provide information regarding their perceptions of how they approach such challenges. The two most widely used measures for this purpose are the *Social Problem-Solving Inventory* (available in a variety of forms; see D'Zurilla & Nezu, 1999), and the *Problem-Solving Inventory* (Heppner & Peterson, 1982).

Outcome measures, by contrast, entail the assessment of performance or problem-solving competence, as judged by the products of the activity. To a certain extent this entails the making of value judgements which will inevitably be informed by culturally prescribed expectations as to what is acceptable in a given context, what is a better quality response, or more likely to be effective, given presumed situational constraints. They include such measures as the *Alternative Thinking Test* (Spivack & Platt, 1980); *Means–End Problem-Solving*

(MEPS; Spivack & Platt, 1980); and the *Adolescent Problems Inventory* (Freedman, Rosenthal, Donahoe, Schlundt, & McFall, 1978; Palmer & Hollin, 1996).

Issues in the assessment of problem-solving orientation and skill are discussed in more detail by D'Zurilla and Maydeu-Olivares (1995) and a more recent, and wider-ranging list of available measures is provided by D'Zurilla, Nezu, and Maydeu-Olivares (2004). The latter authors also argue that probably the most valid approach to assessment of problem-solving is by the means of *self-monitoring* procedures. Here individuals are asked to record their everyday experiences of problems and their attempts to solve them. The record so maintained will bear a much closer relationship to their actual problem-solving in respect of both process and outcome. Its contents can subsequently be reviewed and solutions, or different components of their skills, can be rated for effectiveness and appropriate remedial strategies devised.

Interpersonal Cognitive Problem Solving (ICPS)

The model of problem-solving derived from the work of Spivack et al. (1976) has been particularly influential in the design of intervention programmes in offender services. Some further information will now be given on the way in which this approach was developed after its initial inception.

Following the work of Spivack and Levine (1963), a number of studies were made of differences in problem-solving ability between normal/adjusted and deviant/maladjusted groups. For example, Platt and Spivack (1972a) compared 53 short-stay psychiatric hospital patients with a staff control group matched in age and other criteria on the means–end stories test. Highly significant differences were found between the two; and a series of studies was initiated to explore the contrasts between patient and control samples in more depth (Platt, Siegel, & Spivack, 1975; Platt & Spivack, 1972b). This work was also extended to include other groups such as heroin users (Platt, Scura, & Hannon, 1973), and disturbed adolescents (Platt, Spivack, Altman, & Altman, 1974).

These findings were cast in terms of a developmental model of the acquisition and application of a range of abilities for solving problems in the interpersonal realm. The resulting conceptualisation, known as *Interpersonal Cognitive Problem Solving* (ICPS) (Spivack et al., 1976) envisaged such skills as emerging during child and adolescent development. The extent to which they matured was stimulated and fostered—or conversely inhibited—by aspects of child-rearing and other socialisation practices (Shure & Spivack, 1978). At the same time other projects were undertaken to establish the factorial purity of the MEPS and to determine its status as comparatively independent of intelligence (e.g. Siegel, Platt, & Peizer, 1976). Another strand of research involved exploration of the developmental processes involved in the accretion of social problem-solving abilities. Research was carried out with a number of age-groups, including 4-year-olds (Shure, Spivack, & Jaeger, 1972) and 10- to 12-year-olds (Shure & Spivack, 1972). Among all age cohorts studied, the MEPS test and other specially devised measures revealed significant differences between disturbed or maladjusted groups and their normative peers. Spivack et al. (1976) also collated evidence that at successive stages of development, a different selection of ICPS skill becomes vital in ensuring adjustment. In adolescence, when young people may become at risk of involvement in delinquency, the principal ICPS skills are held to include the following:

1. *Alternative-solution thinking*: "an individual's ability to generate in his or her own mind different options (solutions) that could potentially be put into action to solve a problem" (Spivack et al., 1976, p. 19).
2. *Means–end thinking*: "the ability to orient oneself to and conceptualise the step-by-step means of moving towards a goal" (ibid., p. 83).
3. *Consequential thinking*: "the ability to generate in one's own mind what might happen as a direct result of carrying out an interpersonal act" (ibid., p. 31).
4. *Social cause-and-effect thinking*: "the ability to relate one event to another over time with regard to the 'why' that might have precipitated an event" (ibid., pp. 38–39).
5. *Perspective taking*: "the ability to see interpersonal situations from the perspectives of other involved individuals" (ibid., p. 83).

Numerous studies have been conducted to examine the relationship between measures of interpersonal problem-solving skill and social adjustment. For example, Richard and Dodge (1982) obtained peer ratings on a sample of 24 children aged between 7 and 10 in an infant/junior school. Within each school grade, the children were thus classified as "isolated", "aggressive", or "cooperative"; ratings were also made by teachers of the children's popularity in their respective peer groups. The children were administered the Means–End Problem-Solving Stories (MEPS). There was a close relationship between children's peer status, their social adjustment, and their performance on the MEPS, confirming previous findings in this vein. Further confirmation of significant associations between sociometric status as an index of adjustment and social-cognitive skills came from studies such as those of Ford (1982) and Marsh (1982). Deluty (1981) found differences in social-cognitive skills between children respectively classified as predominantly assertive, aggressive or submissive in their interactional style.

Comparisons between deviant and non-deviant groups, or between members of groups varying in perceived status or behavioural ratings of adjustment, were undertaken in many settings and with regard to numerous kinds of psycho-social problem. The groups studied have included emotionally disturbed boys differing in popularity (Higgins & Thies, 1981a); prison inmates judged as "successful" or as "misfits" within their institution (Higgins & Thies, 1981b); university students varying in levels of depression (Gotlib & Asarnow, 1979); and narcotic drug abusers rated as having good versus poor prospects of recovery (Appel & Kaestner, 1979). Deficient problem-solving skills have also been shown to be associated with such diverse difficulties as unplanned pregnancies (Flaherty, Marecek, Olsen, & Wilcove, 1983; Steinlauf, 1979), suicide attempts (Asarnow, Carlson, & Guthrie, 1987; Schotte & Clum, 1987), agoraphobia (Brodbeck & Michelson, 1987), and depression among older adults (Kleftaras, 2000).

Several studies suggest that cognitive processes and difficulties in problem-solving skills such as perspective taking may influence factors that are associated with the likelihood of committing an offence. For example, in a meta-analysis of 41 studies Orobrio de Castro, Veerman, Koops, Bosch and Monshouwer (2002) found a strong relationship between aggressive behaviour and attribution of hostile intent. In a smaller-scale review, Jolliffe and Farrington (2003) found a significant association between violent offending and low cognitive empathy, though the possibility that this was a function of intelligence and socio-economic status could not be ruled out.

More specifically, social problem-solving skill deficits have been linked to aggression in several populations including children, adolescents, and adults. Lochman and Lampron (1986) found that aggressive boys generated fewer assertive solutions to conflicts than non-aggressive controls. Lochman and Dodge (1994) discovered differences between aggressive and non-aggressive boys on several social-cognitive processing tasks, with the more violent boys being marked by a larger number of such deficits. Among adolescents, Jaffee and D'Zurilla (2003) showed that several dimensions of social problem-solving were associated with aggression, juvenile delinquency, and other risk-taking behaviours. Working respectively with college students and with a non-offending adult sample, D'Zurilla, Chang, and Sanna (2003) and McMurran, Blair, and Egan (2002) found that poorer problem-solving skills mediated the links between other variables such as self-esteem, anger, hostility, heavy drinking, and aggression.

INTERVENTION STUDIES

From the accumulating evidence of the foregoing studies, the corollary proposition has emerged that those individuals who are deficient in skills such as means–end thinking can be given training to improve their abilities. If their limitations in respect of social problem-solving are partly responsible for their adjustment difficulties, such training should lead not only to enhanced social-cognitive skills but also to improvements in behaviour and mental health. In an early study Spohn and Wolk (1963) reported their work with psychiatric in-patients diagnosed as schizophrenic and showing marked withdrawal symptoms. Their research showed that group-based training sessions in which patients jointly worked on *impersonal* problems reduced their levels of social withdrawal and improved their rates of social contact. Given such a finding it might be expected that interventions based on specific social interaction or interpersonal problem-solving training could be similarly effective, if not more so.

Initial attempts to test such a proposition were made principally with kindergarten and elementary (primary) school children. Shure et al. (1972), for example, trained 22 four-year-old children by means of a 50-session training course covering basic communication, self-awareness, and problem-solving skills. The latter included the ability to verbalise alternative possible solutions to problems, and to think consequentially ("If this happens, what else will happen?"). By comparison with attention placebo and no-treatment control groups, trained children showed greater improvement in problem-solving scores and were more able to delay gratification following the sessions. There was also a close relationship between increased problem-solving skills and improved social behaviour. While not all of the findings were statistically significant, there were marked differences between the experimental and control groups on the majority of the indices used.

Results such as these led to further projects with the aim of designing and implementing preventive problem-solving training programmes for children aged from 4 years upwards. Follow-up evaluation of these programmes showed them to be an effective means of preventing and reducing behaviour problems in groups of at-risk children (Shure, 1993; Shure & Spivack, 1979, 1982). Recent studies have continued to provide support for the effectiveness of social problem-solving training for children with conduct problems even at a very early age (Webster-Stratton, Reid, & Hammond, 2001). Training programmes were also developed for parents of young children (Shure & Spivack, 1978), founded on the principle that the ability to solve interpersonal problems was fostered by a specific style of interaction with children in which they were encouraged to think situations through for themselves. Other versions of problem-solving training designed to improve general social awareness have also been extensively used in work with children in middle school, in the age range 8-11 (Frauenknecht & Black, 2004).

Reviewing the by then voluminous literature on problem-solving training and therapy, Heppner and Hillerbrand (1991) proposed a useful framework for classifying interventions in terms of three levels of complexity.

First, some studies were focused on evaluation of single components of problem-solving training, such as the ability to define problems or generate alternative solutions. Several studies along such lines were reported by Nezu and D'Zurilla (1979, 1981a, 1981b; D'Zurilla & Nezu, 1980). Thus, when individuals were given explicit instructions and training on the process of defining and formulating problems, there were significant improvements in both the quantity and quality of solutions they generated and in the effectiveness of their decision-making.

Second, other studies evaluated the use of problem-solving skills therapy as a single-modality package in its own right. This is illustrated in research by Nezu (1986; Nezu & Perri, 1989) on the treatment of depression. Individuals diagnosed as suffering from unipolar depression were randomly allocated to one of three conditions: (1) problem-solving therapy involving a structured, systematic approach; (2) problem-focused therapy which primarily entailed discussion without a sequential, skills-training focus; and (3) a waiting list control. Substantial reductions in depressive symptoms were observed only for clients in the first of these groups, and were maintained at a six-month follow-up.

This kind of study, of evaluating extended problem-solving training, is also exemplified in a paper by Yu, Harris, Solovitz, and Franklin (1986), employing the ICPS model. A group of child outpatients attending a psychiatric clinic was divided and assigned to either a problem-solving intervention or a control condition. The intervention was a 34-session course addressing problem-solving skills. In the control condition, subjects attended the clinic and took part in a typical range of other "ordinary" treatments. Subsequent comparisons showed significant differences in favour of the group trained in ICPS skills in terms of both improved behaviour and social competence.

Studies along these lines have been conducted with an impressively wide variety of problems, in the majority of cases with successful results. "Social development" and related packages drawing heavily upon ICPS materials have proven effective is improving the classroom adjustment and interactive skills of 8-to-10-year-old children (Elardo & Caldwell, 1979; McClure, Chinsky, & Larcen, 1978).

Other studies have found problem-solving training effective in enhancing the interactions of adult psychiatric patients (Coché & Douglas, 1977; Coché & Flick 1975; Edelstein, Couture, Cray, Dickens, & Lusebrink, 1980; Hansen, St. Lawrence, & Christoff, 1985). In most of these studies, skill training was shown to have generalised outside practice sessions and in some cases (such as the work of Hansen et al. and that of Edelstein et al.), training gains were maintained after modest follow-up intervals of four months. Problem-solving training has also been shown to be efficacious in improving the interactive skills of problem drinkers (Intagliata, 1978) and in the treatment of childhood obesity (Graves, Meyers, & Clark, 1988).

Methods of training employing the ICPS approach have been used preventively on a sizeable scale with children of varying ages, including those attending primary (elementary) school but also in pre-school settings such as nursery or kindergarten. The foremost example of this is the work of Shure (1993, 2001) in Philadelphia schools, applying a series of educational classes in which the acronym ICPS is used to denote "I can problem solve".

In the third and commonest format of interventions, problem solving is integrated with other types of training or therapy in a multi-modal programme. The range of permutations within this is fairly wide but the combinations have usually entailed some admixture of problem solving with self-instructional or self-management training, social skills training, values education, or relapse prevention. More elaborate versions have involved the application of such combined treatments within the context of family therapy, or alongside other types of intervention such as community support.

Considering this third tier of intervention, it is useful to draw on a distinction made by McFall (1982) and amplified by D'Zurilla et al. (2004) between *problem solution* and *implementation*. The first refers to the formal process of applying problem-solving training in order to identify solutions to problems with which individuals are faced. The second refers to other skills or capacities they will need to apply those solutions in practice, for example, in the areas of self-management or social and behavioural performance.

For example, Chaney, O'Leary, and Marlatt (1978) obtained reductions in alcohol consumption at one-year follow-up among problem drinkers who had participated in an integrated problem-solving and social skills training programme. This combination of methods, with the addition of relapse prevention, has also proved effective in work with individuals meeting the criteria for pathological gambling (Sylvain, Ladouceur, & Boisvert, 1997). Training interventions using ICPS methods or related kinds of approach have been combined with other cognitive-behavioural treatments. Examples of this are the work of Lochman and Curry (1986) and of Kazdin, Esveldt-Dawson, French, and Unis (1987) with impulsive, acting-out adolescents. In both these pieces of work, the combined treatment proved superior to other treatments (anger-control training and relationship therapy respectively), with which it was being compared. The literature on the applications of these methods with emotionally or behaviourally disturbed children and adolescents is sizeable, and a comprehensive review is beyond the scope of the present chapter. Three meta-analytic reviews (Baer & Nietzel, 1991; Denham & Almeida, 1987; Durlak, Fuhrman, & Lampman, 1991) provided firm support for the use of problem-solving training methods in these contexts. More recently, Kazdin (1998) has provided a review of problem-solving skills training as an ingredient in the search for empirically supported treatments. This training is one of four therapy modalities (together with parent training, functional family therapy, and multi-systemic therapy) which to date have accumulated substantial support from randomised controlled trials.

While it might be anticipated that a moderate-to-high level of verbal ability is a prerequisite of beneficial participation in problem-solving training, research has shown that the methods can have positive effects in work with clients with learning disabilities. Foxx, Kyle, Faw, and Bittle (1989b) adapted methods and materials to meet these clients' needs, for example, by working in small groups (n = 3) and using cue cards in training exercises. More recently, Loumidis and Hill (1997a, 1997b) have described the use of a problem-solving training package for adults with learning disabilities, and obtained significant changes in a number of target problem-solving measures.

Detailed guidelines for construction of problem-solving sessions and for individual work in mental health have been given by Bedell and Michael (1985; see also Bedell & Lennox, 1997). Pekala, Siegel, & Farrar (1985) described the use of structured problem-solving support groups, while Coché (1987) provided guidelines for the application of the methods in practice and reviewed evidence for the usefulness of this approach. Platt, Taube, Metzger, and Duome (1988) outlined the ingredients of a combined problem-solving and communication skill programme and forwarded evaluative evidence.

The contribution of problem-solving-based interventions to mental health care has continued to be recognised and advocated by authors reviewing these fields (Dixon, 1999; Kendrick, 1999; Timmerman, Emmelkamp, & Sanderman, 1998). This includes work with persons suffering from severe and enduring mental health problems, and more broadly for stress management in community settings. This coverage has been strengthened by a recent book re-stating and refining the theoretical basis of the approach and reviewing developments across the social problem-solving field (Chang, D'Zurilla, & Sanna, 2004).

APPLICATIONS WITH OFFENDER POPULATIONS

Problem Solving and Models of Criminal Offending

During the 1980s there was a growing recognition of the potential significance of cognitive-interpersonal skills in work with offenders. This was encompassed in proposals for interventions focused directly on *offending behaviour* (McGuire & Priestley, 1985) and also in a theoretical approach designated as the *cognitive model of offender rehabilitation* (Ross & Fabiano, 1985). Within the latter model, it is hypothesised that persistent offenders are likely to be found to lack, or to fail to apply, social problem-solving skills of one or more types. It is important to note that this does not entail the assumption that all offenders lack such skills, nor that their presence or absence differentiates between offender and non-offender populations. Such deficits are more likely to be found among persistent, repetitive, or chronic offenders. Similarly, it is not proposed that members of this category lack all component problem-solving skills. The aim of individualised assessment is to identify, in each case, which skills an individual possesses and which they do not, and the extent to which they make use of available skills.

In testing their model, Ross and Fabiano (1985) embarked upon a major review of evidence concerning problem solving and other skill deficits in persistent offenders. In a number of respects the evidence they sought was, perhaps not surprisingly, incomplete. Available findings were not wholly consistent with the hypothesis of cognitive skills deficits. However, significant differences emerged with sufficient consistency to suggest a need for intervention programmes that would focus attention on reducing impulsivity, cognitive rigidity, and other variables shown to be risk factors for criminal acts. Recent, more elaborate, versions of this model are based on *risk-need* concepts in which deficiencies of skill in problem solving, self-management, or social interaction have been empirically linked to greater risk of involvement in criminal activity (Andrews, 1995, 2001).

Further support for the proposition that limited or distorted cognitive processes may be a contributory factor in some offences, and may be a valid and promising target of intervention, has come from other studies on problem-solving difficulties amongst recidivist groups. They include the work of Zamble and Porporino (1988) on coping behaviour of adult prisoners in which more poorly adjusted prison inmates were found to have more limited problem-solving skills. Data relevant to this were also obtained by Zamble and Quinsey (1997) in their study of factors contributing to new offences among highly repetitive offenders. Offences were often preceded by difficulties in coping and by poor self-management, characterised by an absence of a positive problem-oriented approach, allowing problems to accumulate to intolerable levels. Deficits in problem-solving skills have been shown to be associated with homelessness among mentally disordered offenders (Morrison-Dyke, 1996).

Parallel findings have been obtained in studies with young offenders. Wesner (1996) found poorer problem-solving skills in offenders than among non-offending controls, with lowest levels of skill observed in a group classified as "under-socialised aggressive" offenders. Whitton and McGuire (2002) administered a problem checklist, the modified *Adolescent Problems Inventory* (API), and a self-report coping scale to a sample of 38 young offenders and compared them with a sample (n = 43) of non-offenders in a school setting. Young offenders reported a significantly higher frequency of serious problems than controls, higher rates of usage of non-productive coping, and lower rates of problem-focused coping. In addition, there was a low but significant correlation between level of criminality as measured by numbers of previous convictions and API scores.

Recently, there has been a growing recognition within criminology of the significant role played by cognitive processes in the genesis of criminal acts. This is exemplified in a recent paper by Foglia (2000), who examines several dimensions of problem-solving skills, and describes the inclusion of cognitive variables in sociological theories which is often assumed at an implicit level. Such a departure accords with viewpoints expressed by psychologists seeking a rapprochement between psychological and sociological models of criminal conduct (Andrews, 1995; McGuire, 2000c).

Intervention Studies

Problem solving is a pivotal component within the majority of the structured programmes of cognitive skills training currently in use in criminal justice agencies in several countries. However, some of the earliest studies in this field addressed single components of problem-solving skills or applied programmes with a virtually exclusive problem-solving focus. Chandler (1973) examined the cognitive skill of perspective-taking in a group of persistent young offenders aged 11-13 years. Using specially designed role-playing and story-telling techniques, he found first that the young offender group were significantly more 'egocentric', that is, they appeared less able to adopt other people's perspectives than a comparison group of non-offenders. The young offender sample (n = 45) was randomly assigned to one of three conditions. The first consisted of a series of training sessions involving role-reversal and perspective-taking exercises. The other conditions were placebo and non-treatment controls. Following the intervention, evaluation showed that the treated group improved significantly in their role-playing and perspective-taking abilities. Moreover, an 18-month follow-up showed a significant reduction in the recidivism rate of the experimental group alone.

In a later study conducted with adult offenders, Platt, Perry, and Metzger (1980) described results of the Wharton Tract Program, based in a 45-bed, open-door prison "satellite" unit. Residents of the unit were in transition from prison to the community; all participants were adult male offenders with lengthy histories of criminal behaviour and of heroin use. Platt and his colleagues combined two elements in a structured group intervention programme. The first was a form of guided group interaction, a specified pattern of activity in which the group leader took active role; there was an emphasis on the group and its development and on the creation of a supportive atmosphere. Members were to be seen as agents of change for others. The second was a focus on overt behaviour and on the learning of a series of communication and problem-solving skills. These included recognising problems, generating alternative ideas, consequential thinking, means–end thinking, decision-making, and perspective-taking. At the end of a two-year follow-up period, group participants were reported by parole officers to be significantly better adjusted than the comparison sample. They had a significantly lower re-arrest rate (49% vs. 66%), and, if re-convicted, had a lower rate of re-commitment to institutions, implying their re-offences were of a less serious nature. Also, if they were re-arrested, this occurred after a longer average arrest-free period (238 vs. 168 days) than for the control group members.

Hains and Hains (1988) used problem-solving training alongside impulse control training as an intensive intervention with a small group of five youths assessed as "conduct-disordered" and evaluated their progress by means of a multiple-baseline experimental design. Improvements in target skills were noted for four out of the five youths participating in this study. Koles and Jenson (1985) described the successful use of problem-solving training with a boy who manifested a number of severe behaviour problems including chronic fire-setting.

Claims regarding the possible importance of cognitive variables in attempting to reduce offender recidivism were consolidated by the outcome of a meta-analytic review by Izzo and Ross (1990). This study entailed a comparison of offender programmes with and without cognitive-training elements. Rather than computing a mean effect size, the authors reported the ratio of relative effectiveness of the two types of programme. Among the 46 interventions included in this review, the ratio of effect sizes for those with and without cognitive-training components was 2.5 to 1.

Two further meta-analytic reviews have confirmed cognitive-behavioural programmes as among the most consistently effective approaches to reduction of recidivism at the "tertiary prevention" level. Applying relatively broad inclusion criteria, Lipton, Pearson, Cleland, and Yee (2002) surveyed findings from 68 studies. Lipsey, Chapman, and Landenberger (2001) applied much stricter criteria and integrated results from 14 studies. In a more recent review, Wilson, Bouffard and MacKanzie (2005) focused their analysis on only the best designed outcome studies. All reviews obtained similar findings of positive effect sizes significantly different from zero. Problem-solving methods are a standard ingredient in programmes of this type, usually combined with other implementation elements in a "multi-modal" approach. The extent to which the use of cognitively-based intervention programmes had been pursued within criminal justice services even by the mid-1990s is amply illustrated in the two edited volumes by Ross, Antonowicz, and Dhaliwal (1995) and Ross and Ross (1995).

Whether problem-solving training is employed as a single therapeutic modality or conjoined with other methods, the essential process comprises a sequence of skills training exercises combining several types of activity. The precise series of skills included is likely to vary according to the age, assessed needs, and other features of the target participant group. Thus, there can be variations of emphasis between different programmes, and varying levels of elaboration, as some exercises or sessions may be formatted to impart different combinations of skills. Other chapters of this book illustrate some of the adaptations.

Beyond some of these common elements, there is considerable breadth in the manner in which problem-solving training has been applied. Klein and Bahr (1996) developed a family-centred problem-solving programme designed to help prisoners (male and female) who were about to leave institutions and rejoin their families. Structured problem-solving training yielded significant gains in the participants' ability to recognise problems, to generate solutions, and identify appropriate sources of help. Using a random-allocation design, Wells (2001) has described positive outcomes from the use of a 20-session programme combining problem solving, social perspective-taking, and moral reasoning training, with young offenders identified as suffering from conduct or oppositional-defiant disorders. Working with incarcerated adult women offenders, Baguena and Belena (1999) found positive effects using a 33-session intervention on a wide range of component ICPS skills. Rose, Duby, Olenick, and Weston (1996) have described an integrated programme of group and family treatment, incorporating problem-solving training as a vital component, in work with institutionalised young offenders. With a quite different focus, Platt, Husband, Iguchi, and Baxter (1993) devised a programme of problem-solving training for use in the reduction of high-risk behaviours among intravenous drug users.

Another permutation of problem-solving with other types of intervention is the *Coping Power Program* developed by Lochman and Wells (2002). This was designed for young people in the age range from late middle childhood to early adolescence manifesting problems of aggressiveness, substance abuse, and initial involvement in delinquency. It contains two main elements: (1) a combined social problem-solving and social skills training programme; and (2) a series of behavioural skills-training sessions for parents. In a one-year follow-up, Lochman and Wells (2003) found significant reductions in rates of occurrence of the three target problems.

Bakker, Ward, Cryer, and Hudson (1997) focused on offenders convicted of driving while disqualified and formulated a model of this type of offence which located a key contributory factor as being poor interpersonal problem-solving. On this basis they devised a multi-modal programme comprising four elements: (1) cognitive restructuring; (2) social skills; (3) anger management; and (4) problem solving. The programme was delivered to a sample of offenders with encouraging preliminary results. A subsequent evaluative report by Bakker, Hudson, and Ward (2000) showed the programme had positive effects. The treated group made gains in social competence, exhibited reduced levels of general offending, and had a significantly lower rate of unlicensed/illegal driving; though no difference was found for drink-driving convictions.

Treatment programmes based on problem-solving training have also been applied in secure forensic settings with groups of offenders detained under mental health legislation. Baker (1995) developed a ten-session group programme based on D'Zurilla and Goldfried's model of problem-solving and evaluated it in a study employing random assignment to the programme or to a no-treatment control group. Training resulted in significant gains in problem-solving skills (judged by both a process measure, the *Problem-Solving Inventory*, and an outcome measure, the *MEPS*). Donnelly and Scott (1999) outlined effects of the *Reasoning and Rehabilitation* programme in a high security hospital in Scotland. This study involved a non-random control sample; significant changes in some problem-solving skill components were noted for the trained group only. Encouraging results were also obtained by Hughes, Hogue, Hollin, and Champion (1997) in a study with personality-disordered offenders. McMurran and her colleagues (1999) devised a series of six 1½-hour sessions for use with a group of residents of a secure mental health unit. Significant pre- to post test changes were noted in total scores on the *Social Problem Solving Inventory* and two of its sub-scales. Finally, McGuire (1999) described the development of a 12-session programme of social problem-solving training which was provided to two groups of patients in a high-security psychiatric hospital. Preliminary results were not encouraging, however, probably as a result of numerous logistical difficulties in ensuring regular delivery of sessions.

Returning to the issue of cognitive-behavioural programmes more broadly defined, these have also emerged as holding promise in yielding therapeutic benefits for offenders diagnosed with personality disorders, a group hitherto regarded as highly resistant to change. In a meta-analytic review Salekin (2002) synthesised findings from 42 outcome studies. Many were single case studies, and only eight included control groups, thus, no firm conclusions can be drawn. However, five studies of cognitive-behavioural therapy incorporating a cumulative sample of 246 individuals produced moderately good effect sizes.

In the past few years, numerous manualised programmes have been developed for use in criminal justice services (e.g., Bourke & Van Hasselt, 2001) and in some instances disseminated widely. The latter include *Reasoning and Rehabilitation* (Ross & Ross, 1995; see Chapter 9 of this volume), and offence-focused programmes such as *Think First* (McGuire, 2000b; see Chapter 10 of this volume). The *Reasoning and Rehabilitation* programme was originally developed in Canada and initially evaluated in probation services with very positive short-term outcomes (Ross, Fabiano, & Ewles 1988). Implementation on a much larger scale within Canadian federal prisons with a very large sample ($n = 1,444$) and a lengthier follow-up also yielded positive results, though these were moderated by offence type (Robinson, 1995; Robinson & Porporino, 2001). The programme has been applied extensively in both prison (Williams, 1995) and probation (Raynor & Vanstone, 1996) settings in the United Kingdom.

The use of such programmes is now a central activity in these services, following the advent of a new *Key Performance Indicator* by the prison service in 1996, and the announcement by the Home Office of the Crime Reduction Programme in 1998. Three large-scale outcome evaluations have been conducted. Friendship, Blud, Erikson, and Travers (2002) reported a 14% reduction in recidivism among prisoners who completed the *Reasoning and Rehabilitation* and *Enhanced Thinking Skills* programmes as compared with those who did not attend. In later evaluations, however, treatment effects were weaker and in one study were as low as 4% (Cann, Falshaw, Nugent, & Friendship, 2003; Falshaw, Friendship, Travers, & Nugent, 2003).

CONCLUSIONS

In a few instances, implementation of problem-solving training has taken place on an individual basis and has been evaluated by means of single-case and multiple-baseline experimental designs (Buie-Hune, 1997; Edelstein et al., 1980; Foxx et al., 1989a, 1989c; Foxx & Faw, 1990; Hains & Hains, 1988; Hansen et al., 1985). However, the typical format for delivery of problem-solving training in most settings has been in small groups, usually of six–eight members and with group sizes up to ten. Kazdin (1998) has expressed reservations concerning the use of group-based treatment for certain populations such as delinquent youth where the influence of a deviant peer group may detract from the quality of the training, indeed, may create a risk of undermining it. While evidence pertaining to this remains equivocal, and there are numerous instances of successful group-based interventions with offenders, staff in criminal justice and secure mental health settings should beware of the possibility of contagion by anti-social attitudes. The provision of group activities within these services is a highly skilled and demanding task and within this context the use of "pro-social modelling" becomes particularly important, as does the establishment of ground rules regarding behaviour in groups.

Several other issues have perhaps not yet been adequately addressed (Denham & Almeida, 1987; Foxx & Faw, 2000) and therefore present questions for future research. First, the finding of cognitive skills deficits in client groups with behavioural or emotional problems has not been uniformly obtained. More searching investigation is required of the relationship between problem-solving component skills and patterns of mental disorder or criminal behaviour. Second, measured changes in problem-solving abilities as a product of training are not always accompanied by commensurate changes in behaviour or mental health status (e.g., Olexa & Forman, 1984). Even where this has been shown to occur, correlations between improved test performance and everyday problem-solving effectiveness may be low, casting doubt on the hypothesised link between these variables. Third, the relationship between apparent limitations of problem-solving skill and motivational factors remains unclear. This can be a serious obstacle in the selection of participants for cognitive skills interventions, and also a crucial influence on adherence versus attrition in programmes.

Overall, however, the development of problem-solving training is in many ways an excellent example of the value of the scientist–practitioner model at work. There has been a constant cycle of exchange between theory construction and the testing of hypotheses in applied settings. Furthermore, the majority of the studies carried out in this area from its inception have been with authentic clinical groups as opposed to analogue samples. The gradually extending use of the methods with offender populations provides invaluable opportunities for testing of more specific hypotheses and learning from practical experience.

REFERENCES

Akhtar, N. & Bradley, E. J. (1991). Social information processing deficits of aggressive children: present findings and implications for social skills training. *Clinical Psychology Review, 11*, 621–644.

Andrews, D. A. (1995). The psychology of criminal conduct and effective treatment. In J. McGuire (ed.), *What works: Reducing re-offending: guidelines from research and practice.* Chichester: John Wiley & Sons, Ltd.

Andrews, D. A. (2001). Principles of effective correctional programs. In L. L. Motiuk & R. C. Serin (eds), *Compendium 2000 on effective correctional programming.* Ottawa: Correctional Service Canada.

Appel, P. & Kaestner, E. (1979). Interpersonal and emotional problem solving among narcotic drug abusers. *Journal of Consulting and Clinical Psychology*, 47, 1125–1127.

Asarnow, J. R., Carlson, G. A., & Guthrie, D. (1987). Coping strategies, self-perceptions, hopelessness and perceived family environments in depressed and suicidal children. *Journal of Consulting and Clinical Psychology*, 55, 361–366.

Baer, R. A. & Nietzel, M. T. (1991). Cognitive and behavioral treatment of impulsivity in children: A meta-analytic review of the outcome literature. *Journal of Clinical Child Psychology*, 20, 400–412.

Baguena, M. J. & Belena, M. A. (1999). Interpersonal skills training program applied to incarcerated delinquent women: Effects of the training program on qualitative response criteria. *Análisis y Modificación de Conducta*, 25, 303–320.

Baker, L. (1995). Training mentally ill offenders in problem-solving. *Dissertation Abstracts International, 56(1–B)*, 0515.

Bakker, L., Hudson, S. M., & Ward, T. (2000). Reducing recidivism in driving while disqualified: A treatment evaluation. *Criminal Justice and Behavior*, 27, 531–560.

Bakker, L., Ward, T., Cryer, M., & Hudson, S. M. (1997). Out of the rut: A cognitive-behavioral treatment program for driving-while-disqualified offenders. *Behaviour Change, 14*, 29–38.

Bandura, A. (1977). *Social learning theory*. New York: Prentice-Hall.

Bedell, J. R. & Lennox, S. S. (1997). *Handbook for communication and problem-solving skills training: a cognitive-behavioral approach*. New York: John Wiley & Sons, Ltd.

Bedell, J. R. & Michael, D. (1985). Teaching problem-solving skills to chronic psychiatric patients. In D. Upper and S. Ross (eds), *Handbook of behavioral group therapy*. New York: Plenum Press.

Bourke, M. L. & Van Hasselt, V. B. (2001). Social problem-solving skills training for incarcerated offenders: A treatment manual. *Behavior Modification*, 25, 163–188.

Brodbeck, C. & Michelson, L. (1987). Problem-solving skills and attributional styles of agoraphobics. *Cognitive Therapy and Research*, 11, 593–610.

Buie-Hune, J. D. (1997). Effects of a problem-solving strategy on the alternative solutions of preschool children. *Dissertation Abstracts International, 58(6-A)*, 2157.

Butler, L. & Meichenbaum, D. (1981). The assessment of interpersonal problem-solving skills. In P. C. Kendall and S. D. Hollon (eds), *Assessment strategies for cognitive-behavioral interventions*. New York: Academic Press.

Cann, J., Falshaw, L., Nugent, F., & Friendship, C. (2003). *Understanding what works: Accredited Cognitive Skills Programmes for Adult Men and Young Offenders*. Findings' 226. London: Home Office Research, Development and Statistics Directorate.

Chandler, M. J. (1973). Egocentrism and anti-social behavior: the assessment and training of social perspective-taking skills. *Developmental Psychology*, 9, 326–332.

Chang, E. C., D'Zurilla, T. J., & Sanna, L. J. (eds) (2004). *Social problem solving: Theory, research, and training*. Washington, DC: American Psychological Association.

Chaney, E., O'Leary, M., & Marlatt, A. (1978). Skill training with alcoholics. *Journal of Consulting and Clinical Psychology*, 46, 1092–1104.

Coché, E. (1987). Problem-solving training: A cognitive group therapy modality. In A. Freeman and V. Greenwood (eds), *Cognitive therapy: Applications in psychiatric and medical settings*. New York: Human Sciences Press.

Coché, E. & Douglas, A. A. (1977). Therapeutic effects of problem-solving training and play-reading groups. *Journal of Clinical Psychology*, 33, 820–827.

Coché, E. & Flick, A. (1975). Problem-solving training groups for hospitalised psychiatric patients. *Journal of Psychology*, 91, 19–29.

Crick, N. R. & Dodge, K. A. (1994). A review and reformulation of social information-processing mechanisms in children's social adjustment. *Psychological Bulletin, 115*, 74–101.

Deluty, R. H. (1981). Alternative-thinking ability of aggressive, assertive, and submissive children. *Cognitive Therapy and Research, 5*, 309–312.

Denham, S. A. & Almeida, M. C. (1987). Children's social problem-solving skills, behavioral adjustment, and interventions: A meta-analysis evaluating theory and practice. *Journal of Applied Developmental Psychology, 8*, 391–409.

Dixon, L. (1999). Providing services to families of persons with schizophrenia: Present and future. *Journal of Mental Health Policy and Economics, 2*, 3–8.

Donnelly, J. P. & Scott, M. F. (1999). Evaluation of an offending behaviour programme with a mentally disordered offender population. *British Journal of Forensic Practice, 1*, 25–32.

Durlak, J. A., Fuhrman, T., & Lampman, C. (1991). Effectiveness of cognitive-behavioral therapy of maladapting children: A meta-analysis. *Psychological Bulletin, 110*, 204–214.

D'Zurilla, T. J., Chang, E. C., & Sanna, L. J. (2003). Self-esteem and social problem solving as predictors of aggression in college students. *Journal of Social and Clinical Psychology, 22*, 424–440.

D'Zurilla, T. J & Goldfried, M. R. (1971). Problem solving and behavior modification. *Journal of Abnormal Psychology, 78*, 107–126.

D'Zurilla, T. J. & Maydeu-Olivares, A. (1995). Conceptual and methodological issues in social problem-solving assessment. *Behavior Therapy, 26*, 409–432.

D'Zurilla, T. J. & Nezu, A. M. (1980). A study of the generation-of-alternatives process in social problem solving. *Cognitive Therapy and Research, 4*, 67–72.

D'Zurilla, T. J. & Nezu, A. (1982). Social problem-solving in adults. *Advances in Cognitive-Behavioral Research and Therapy, 1*, 201–274.

D'Zurilla, T. J. & Nezu, A. M. (1999). *Problem-solving therapy: A social competence approach to clinical intervention.* 2nd edn. New York: Springer.

D'Zurilla, T. J. & Nezu, A. M. (2001). Problem-solving therapies. In K. S. Dobson (ed.), *Handbook of cognitive-behavioral therapies.* 2nd edn. New York: Guilford Press.

D'Zurilla, T. J., Nezu, A. M, & Maydeu-Olivares, A. (2004). Social problem solving: Theory and assessment. In E. C. Chang, T. J. D'Zurilla and L. J. Sanna (eds), *Social problem solving: Theory, research, and training.* Washington, DC: American Psychological Association.

Edelstein, B. A., Couture, E., Cray, M., Dickens, P., & Lusebrink, N. (1980). Group training of problem-solving with psychiatric patients. In D. Upper and S. M. Ross (eds), *Behavioral group therapy: An annual review.* Champaign, IL: Research Press.

Elardo, P. T. & Caldwell, B. M. (1979). The effects of an experimental social development program on children in the middle childhood period. *Psychology in the Schools, 16*, 93–100.

Eysenck, M. W. (2001). *Principles of cognitive psychology.* Hove: Psychology Press.

Falshaw, L., Friendship, Travers, R., & Nugent, F. (2003). *Searching for 'What Works': An evaluation of cognitive skills programmes.* Findings 206. London: Home Office Research, Development and Statistics Directorate.

Favrod, J., Caffaro, M., Grossenbacher, B., Rubio, A., & Von Turk, A. (2000). Interpersonal problem-solving skills training with patients suffering from schizophrenia in different treatment settings. *Annales Medico Psychologiques, 158*, 302–311.

Feuerstein, R. (1980). *Instrumental enrichment.* Baltimore, MD: University Park Press.

Flaherty, E. W., Marecek, J., Olsen, K., & Wilcove, G. (1983). Preventing adolescent pregnancy: An interpersonal problem-solving approach. In R. Hess and J. A. Hermalin (eds), *Innovations in prevention.* Binghamton, NY: Haworth Press.

Foglia, W. D. (2000). Adding an explicit focus on cognition to criminological theory. In D. H. Fishbein (ed.), *The science, treatment, and prevention of antisocial behaviors: Application to the criminal justice system.* Kingston, NJ: Civic Research Institute.

Ford, M. E. (1982). Social cognition and social competence in adolescence. *Developmental Psychology, 18*, 323–340.

Foxx, R. M. & Faw, G. D. (1990). Problem-solving skills training for psychiatric inpatients: An analysis of generalization. *Behavioral Residential Treatment*, 5, 159–176.

Foxx, R. M. & Faw, G. D. (2000). The pursuit of actual problem-solving behavior: An opportunity for behavior analysis. *Behavior and Social Issues*, 10, 71–81.

Foxx, R. M., Kyle, M. S., Faw, G. D., & Bittle, R. G. (1989a). Teaching a problem solving strategy to inpatient adolescents: Social validation, maintenance, and generalization. *Child and Family Behavior Therapy*, 11, 71–88.

Foxx, R. M., Kyle, M. S., Faw, G. D., & Bittle, R. G. (1989b). Problem-solving skills training: Social validation and generalization. *Behavioral Residential Treatment*, 4, 269–288.

Foxx, R. M., Martella, R. C., & Marchand-Martella, N. E. (1989c). The acquisition, maintenance, and generalisation of problem-solving skills by closed head-injured adults. *Behavior Therapy*, 20, 61–76.

Frauenknecht, M. & Black, D. R. (2004). Problem-solving training for children and adolescents. In E. C. Chang, T. J. D'Zurilla and L. J. Sanna (eds), *Social problem solving: Theory, research, and training*. Washington, DC: American Psychological Association.

Freedman, B. J., Rosenthal, L., Donahoe, C. P., Schlundt, D. G., & McFall, R. M. (1978). A social-behavioral analysis of skill deficits in delinquent and non-delinquent adolescent boys. *Journal of Consulting and Clinical Psychology*, 46, 1448–1462.

Friendship, C., Blud, L., Erikson, M., & Travers, R. (2002). *An evaluation of cognitive-behavioural treatment for prisoners*. Findings 161. London: Home Office Research, Development and Statistics Directorate.

Galotti, K. (1994). *Cognitive psychology in and out of the laboratory*. Pacific Grove, CA: Brooks-Cole.

Gotlib, I. H. & Asarnow, R. F. (1979). Interpersonal and impersonal problem-solving skills in mildly and clinically depressed university students. *Journal of Consulting and Clinical Psychology*, 47, 86–95.

Graves, T., Meyers, A. W., & Clark, L. (1988). An evaluation of parental problem-solving training in the behavioral treatment of childhood obesity. *Journal of Consulting and Clinical Psychology*, 56, 246–250.

Hains, A. A. & Hains, A. H. (1988). Cognitive-behavioral training of problem-solving and impulse-control with delinquent adolescents. *Journal of Offender Counseling, Services and Rehabilitation*, 12, 95–113.

Hansen, D., St. Lawrence, J., & Christoff, K. (1985). Effects of interpersonal problem-solving training with chronic aftercare patients on problem-solving component skills and effectiveness of solutions. *Journal of Consulting and Clinical Psychology*, 53,167–174.

Heppner, P. P. & Hillerbrand, E. T. (1991). Problem-solving training: Implications for remedial and preventive training. In C. R. Snyder and D. R. Forsyth (eds), *Handbook of social and clinical psychology*. New York: Pergamon Press.

Heppner, P. P. & Krauskopf, C. J. (1987). An information processing approach to personal problem solving. *The Counseling Psychologist*, 15, 371–447.

Heppner, P. P. & Peterson, C. H. (1982). The development and implications of a personal problem solving inventory. *Journal of Counselling Psychology*, 29, 66–75.

Higgins, J. P. & Thies, A. P. (1981a). Problem solving and social position among emotionally disturbed boys. *American Journal of Orthopsychiatry*, 51, 356–358.

Higgins, J. P. & Thies, A. P. (1981b). Social effectiveness and problem-solving thinking of reformatory inmates. *Journal of Offender Services, Counseling and Rehabilitation*, 5, 93–98.

Hughes, G., Hogue, T., Hollin, C. R., & Champion, H. (1997). First-stage evaluation of a treatment programme for personality disordered offenders. *Journal of Forensic Psychiatry*, 8, 515–527.

Intagliata, J. (1978). Increasing the interpersonal problem-solving skills of an alcoholic population. *Journal of Consulting and Clinical Psychology*, 46, 489–498.

Izzo, R. L. & Ross, R. R. (1990). Meta-analysis of rehabilitation programmes for juvenile delinquents. *Criminal Justice and Behavior, 17*, 134–142.

Jaffee, W. B. & D'Zurilla, T. J. (2003). Adolescent problem solving, parent problem solving, and externalizing behavior in adolescents. *Behavior Therapy, 34*, 295–311.

Jolliffe D. & Farrington, D. P. (2003). Empathy and offending: A systematic review and meta-analysis. *Aggression and Violent Behaviour, 9*, 441–476.

Kazdin, A. E. (1998). Psychosocial treatments for conduct disorder in children. In P. E. Nathan & J. M. Gorman (eds), *A guide to treatments that work.* New York: Oxford University Press.

Kazdin, A. E., Esveldt-Dawson, K., French, N. H., & Unis, A. S. (1987). Problem-solving skills training and relationship therapy in the treatment of anti-social child behavior. *Journal of Consulting and Clinical Psychology, 55*, 76–85.

Kendrick, T. (1999). Primary care options to prevent mental illness. *Annals of Medicine, 311*, 359–363.

Kleftaras, G. (2000). Interpersonal problem-solving of means–end thinking, frequency and strength of pleasant and unpleasant activities and symptoms of depression in French older adults. *Physical and Occupational Therapy in Geriatrics, 17*, 43–66.

Klein, S. R. & Bahr, S. J. (1996). An evaluation of a family-centered cognitive skills program for prison inmates. *International Journal of Offender Therapy and Comparative Criminology, 40*, 334–346.

Koles, M. R. & Jenson, W. R. (1985). Comprehensive treatment of chronic fire setting in a severely disordered boy. *Journal of Behavior Therapy and Experimental Psychiatry, 16*, 81–85.

Lipsey, M. W., Chapman, G. L., & Landenberger, N. A. (2001). Cognitive-behavioral programs for offenders. *Annals of the American Academy of Political and Social Science, 578*, 144–157.

Lipton, D. S., Pearson, F. S., Cleland, C. M., & Yee, D. (2002). The effectiveness of cognitive-behavioural treatment methods on recidivism. In J. McGuire (ed.), *Offender rehabilitation and treatment: Effective programmes and policies to reduce re-offending.* Chichester: John Wiley & Sons, Ltd.

Lochman, J. E. & Curry, J. F. (1986). Effects of social problem-solving training and self-instruction training with aggressive boys. *Journal of Clinical Child Psychology, 15*, 159–164.

Lochman, J. E. & Dodge, K. A. (1994). Social cognitive processes of severely violent, moderately aggressive, and nonaggressive boys. *Journal of Consulting and Clinical Psychology, 62*, 366–374.

Lochman, J. E. & Lampron, L. B. (1986). Situational social problem-solving skills and self-esteem of aggressive and non-aggressive boys. *Journal of Abnormal Child Psychology, 14*, 605–617.

Lochman, J. E. & Wells, K. D. (2002). Contextual social-cognitive mediators and child outcome: A test of the theoretical model in the Coping Power Program. *Development and Psychopathology, 14*, 971–993.

Lochman, J. E. & Wells, K. D. (2003). Effectiveness of the Coping Power Program and of classroom intervention with aggressive children: Outcomes at a 1-year follow-up. *Behavior Therapy, 34*, 493–515.

Loumidis, K. & Hill, A. (1997a). Social problem-solving groups for adults with learning disabilities. In B. Stenfert-Kroese, D. Dagnan, & K. Loumidis (eds), *Cognitive-behaviour therapy for people with learning disabilities.* London: Routledge.

Loumidis, K. & Hill, A. (1997b). Training social problem-solving skill to reduce maladaptive behaviours in intellectual disability groups: The influence of individual difference factors. *Journal of Applied Research in Intellectual Disabilities, 10*, 217–237.

Mahoney, M. J. (1974). *Cognition and behavior modification.* Cambridge, MA: Ballinger.

Marsh, D. T. (1982). The development of interpersonal problem solving among elementary school children. *Journal of Genetic Psychology, 140*, 107–118.

McClure, L. F., Chinsky, J. M., & Larcen, S. W. (1978). Enhancing social problem-solving performance in an elementary school setting. *Journal of Educational Psychology, 70*, 504–513.

McFall, R. M. (1982). A review and reformulation of the concept of social skills. *Behavioral Assessment, 4*, 1–33.

McGuire, J. (1999). Problem-solving training: Pilot work with secure hospital patients. In D. Mercer, T. Mason, M. McKeown, & G. McCann (eds), *Forensic mental health care: A case study approach*. Edinburgh: Churchill Livingstone.

McGuire, J. (2000a). *Cognitive-behavioural approaches: An introduction to theory and research*. London: Home Office.

McGuire, J. (2000b). *Thinkfirst: Outline, programme manual, case managers' manual, and supplements*. London: Home Office Communications Unit.

McGuire, J. (2000c). Explanations of criminal behaviour. In J. McGuire, T. Mason, & A. O'Kane (eds), *Behaviour, crime and legal processes: A guide for forensic practitioners*. Chichester: John Wiley & Sons, Ltd.

McGuire, J. (2004). *Understanding psychology and crime: Perspectives on theory and action*. Buckingham: Open University Press/McGraw-Hill Education.

McGuire, J. & Priestley, P. (1985). *Offending behaviour: Skills and stratagems for going straight*. London: Batsford.

McMurran, M., Blair, M., & Egan, V. (2002). An investigation of the correlations between aggression, impulsiveness, social problem-solving, and alcohol use. *Aggressive Behavior, 28*, 439–445.

McMurran, M., Egan, V., Richardson, K., & Ahmadi, S. (1999). Social problem-solving in mentally disordered offenders: A brief report. *Criminal Behaviour and Mental Health, 9*, 315–322.

Meichenbaum, D. H. (1977). *Cognitive-behavior modification: An integrative approach*. New York: Plenum Press.

Morrison-Dyke, D. F. (1996). Interpersonal cognitive problem-solving skills and severity of criminal behavior among homeless mentally disordered criminal offenders. *Dissertation Abstracts International, 56(8-B)*, 4589.

Nezu, A. M. (1986). Efficacy of a social problem-solving therapy approach for unipolar depression. *Journal of Consulting and Clinical Psychology, 54*, 196–202.

Nezu, A. M. & D'Zurilla, T. J. (1979). An experimental evaluation of the decision-making process in social problem solving. *Cognitive Therapy and Research, 3*, 269–277.

Nezu, A. M. & D'Zurilla, T. J. (1981a). Effects of problem definition and formulation on the generation of alternatives in the social problem-solving process. *Cognitive Therapy and Research, 5*, 265–271.

Nezu, A. M. & D'Zurilla, T. J. (1981b). Effects of problem definition and formulation on decision making in the social problem-solving process. *Behavior Therapy, 12*, 100–106.

Nezu, A. M., D'Zurilla, T. J., Zwick, M. L., & Nezu, C. M. (2004). Problem-solving therapy for adults. In E. C. Chang, T. J. D'Zurilla, & L. J. Sanna (eds), *Social problem solving: Theory, research, and training*. Washington, DC: American Psychological Association.

Nezu, A. M., Nezu, C. M., Houts, P. S., Friedman, S. H., & Faddis, S. (1999). Relevance of problem-solving therapy to psychosocial oncology. *Journal of Psychosocial Oncology, 16*, 5–26.

Nezu, A. M., Nezu, C. M., & Perri, M. G. (1989). *Problem-solving therapy for depression: Theory, research and clinical guidelines*. New York: Wiley.

Nezu, A. M. & Perri, M. G. (1989). Social problem-solving therapy for unipolar depression: An initial dismantling investigation. *Journal of Consulting and Clinical Psychology, 57*, 408–413.

Nezu, C. M., Nezu, A. M., & Houts, P. S. (1993). Multiple applications of problem-solving principles in clinical practice. In K. T. Kuehlwein and H. Rosen (eds), *Cognitive therapies in action: Evolving innovative practice*. San Francisco, CA: Jossey-Bass.

Olexa, D. F. & Forman, S. G. (1984). Effects of social problem-solving training on classroom behavior of urban disadvantaged students. *Journal of School Psychology, 22*, 165–175.

Orobrio de Castro, B., Veerman, J.W., Koops, W., Bosch, J. D., & Monshouwer, H. (2002). Hostile attribution of intent and aggressive behavior: A meta-analysis. *Child Development, 73*, 916–934.

Osborn, A. (1963). *Applied imagination*. 3rd edn. New York: Scribner.

Palmer, E. J. & Hollin, C. R. (1996). Assessing adolescent problems: An overview of the Adolescent Problems Inventory. *Journal of Adolescence, 19*, 347–354.

Pekala, R. J., Siegel, J. M., & Farrar, D. M. (1985). The problem-solving support group: Structured group therapy with psychiatric inpatients. *International Journal of Group Psychotherapy, 35*, 391–409.

Perri, M. G., Nezu, A. M., McKelvey, W. F., Shermer, R. L., Renjilian, D. A., & Viegener, B. J. (2001). Relapse prevention training and problem-solving therapy in the long-term management of obesity. *Journal of Consulting and Clinical Psychology, 69*, 722–726.

Platt, J. J., Husband, S. D., Iguchi, M. Y., & Baxter, R. (1993). Problem-solving skills training: Addressing high-risk behaviors in Newark and Jersey City. In B. S. Brown & G. M. Beschner (eds), *Handbook of risk of AIDS: Injection drug users and sexual partners*. Westport, CT: Greenwood Press.

Platt, J. J., Perry, G., & Metzger, D. (1980). The evaluation of a heroin addiction treatment program within a correctional environment. In P. Gendreau & R. R. Ross (eds), *Effective correctional treatment*. Toronto: Butterworths.

Platt, J. J., Scura, W., & Hannon, J. (1973). Problem-solving thinking of youthful incarcerated heroin addicts. *Journal of Community Psychology, 1*, 278–291.

Platt, J. J., Siegel, J., & Spivack, G. (1975). Do psychiatric patients and normals see the same solutions as effective in solving interpersonal problems? *Journal of Consulting and Clinical Psychology, 43*, 279.

Platt, J. J. & Spivack, G. (1972a). Problem-solving thinking of psychiatric patients. *Journal of Consulting and Clinical Psychology, 39*, 148–151.

Platt, J. J. & Spivack, G. (1972b). Social competence and effective problem-solving thinking in psychiatric patients. *Journal of Clinical Psychology, 28*, 3–5.

Platt, J.J., Spivack, G., Altman, N., & Altman, D. (1974). Adolescent problem-solving thinking. *Journal of Consulting and Clinical Psychology, 42*, 787–793.

Platt, J. J., Taube, D., Metzger, D., & Duome, M. (1988). Training in Interpersonal Problem Solving (TIPS). *Journal of Cognitive Psychotherapy, 2*, 5–34.

Raynor, P. & Vanstone, M. (1996). Reasoning and rehabilitation in Britain: The results of the straight thinking on probation (STOP) programme. *International Journal of Offender Therapy and Comparative Criminology, 40*, 272–284.

Richard, B. A. & Dodge, K. A. (1982). Social maladjustment and problem solving in school-aged children. *Journal of Consulting and Clinical Psychology, 50*, 226–233.

Robinson, D. (1995). *The impact of cognitive skills training on post-release recidivism among Canadian federal offenders*. Ottawa: Correctional Services of Canada.

Robinson, D. & Porporino, F. J. (2001). Programming in cognitive skills: The reasoning and rehabilitation programme. In C. R. Hollin (ed.), *Handbook of offender assessment and treatment*. Chichester: John Wiley & Sons, Ltd.

Rose, S. D., Duby, P., Olenick, C., & Weston, T. (1996). Integrating family, group and residential treatment: A cognitive-behavioral approach. *Social Work with Groups, 19*, 35–48.

Ross, R. R., Antonowicz, D. H., & Dhaliwal, G. K. (eds), (1995). *Going straight: Effective delinquency prevention and offender rehabilitation*. Ottawa: Air Training and Publications.

Ross, R. R. & Fabiano, E. A. (1985). *Time to think: A cognitive model of delinquency prevention and offender rehabilitation.* Ottawa: Air Training and Publications.

Ross, R. R., Fabiano, E. A., & Ewles, C. D. (1988). Reasoning and rehabilitation. *International Journal of Offender Therapy and Comparative Criminology, 32,* 29–35.

Ross, R. R. & Ross, R. D. (eds) (1995). *Thinking straight: The reasoning and rehabilitation program for delinquency prevention and offender rehabilitation.* Ottawa: Air Training and Publications.

Salekin, R. T. (2002). Psychopathy and therapeutic pessimism: Clinical lore or clinical reality? *Clinical Psychology Review, 22,* 79–112.

Schotte, D. & Clum, G. (1987). Problem-solving skills in suicidal psychiatric patients. *Journal of Consulting and Clinical Psychology, 55,* 49–54.

Shure, M. B. (1993). I can problem solve (ICPS): Interpersonal cognitive problem solving for young children. *Early Child Development and Care, 96,* 49–64.

Shure, M. B. (2001). I can problem solve (ICPS): An interpersonal cognitive problem-solving program for children. *Residential Treatment for Children and Youth, 18,* 3–14.

Shure, M. B. & Spivack, G. (1972). Means–end thinking, adjustment, and social class among elementary-school-aged children. *Journal of Consulting and Clinical Psychology, 38,* 348–353.

Shure, M. B. & Spivack, G. (1978). *Problem-solving techniques in childrearing.* San Francisco, CA: Jossey-Bass.

Shure, M. B. & Spivack, G. (1979). Interpersonal cognitive problem solving and primary prevention: Programming for preschool and kindergarten children. *Journal of Clinical Child Psychology, 8,* 89–94.

Shure, M. B. & Spivack, G. (1982). Interpersonal problem solving in young children: A cognitive approach to prevention. *American Journal of Community Psychology, 10,* 341–356.

Shure, M. B., Spivack, G., & Jaeger, M. (1972). Problem-solving thinking and adjustment among disadvantaged preschool children. *Child Development, 42,* 1791–1803.

Siegel, J. M., Platt, J. J., & Peizer, S. B. (1976). Emotional and social real-life problem-solving thinking in adolescent and adult psychiatric patients. *Journal of Clinical Psychology, 32,* 230–232.

Spivack, G. & Levine, M. (1963). *Self-regulation in acting-out and normal adolescents.* Report No. M-4531. Washington, DC: National Institute of Health.

Spivack, G. & Platt, J. J. (1980). *Measures of social problem-solving for adolescents and adults.* Philadelphia, PA: Preventive Intervention Research Center, Hahnemann University.

Spivack, G., Platt, J. J., & Shure, M. B. (1976). *The problem-solving approach to adjustment.* San Francisco, CA: Jossey-Bass.

Spohn, H. & Wolk, W. (1963). Effect of group problem solving experience upon social withdrawal in chronic schizophrenics. *Journal of Abnormal and Social Psychology, 66,* 187–190.

Stein, M. I. (1975). *Stimulating creativity.* Vol. 2: *Group procedures.* New York: Academic Press.

Steinlauf, B. (1979). Problem-solving skills, locus of control, and the contraceptive effectiveness of young women. *Child Development, 50,* 268–271.

Sylvain, C., Ladouceur, R., & Boisvert, J. M. (1997). Cognitive and behavioral treatment of pathological gambling: A controlled study. *Journal of Consulting and Clinical Psychology, 65,* 727–732.

Timmerman, I. G. H., Emmelkamp, P. M. G., & Sanderman, R. (1998). The effects of a stress-management training program in individuals at risk in the community at large. *Behaviour Research and Therapy, 36,* 863–875.

Webster-Stratton, C., Reid, J., & Hammond, M. (2001). Social skills and problem-solving training for children with early-onset conduct problems: Who benefits? *Journal of Child Psychology and Psychiatry, 42,* 943–952.

Wells, C. (2001). The treatment of severe antisocial behaviour in young people. In G. Baruch (ed.), *Community-based psychotherapy with young people: Evidence and innovation in practice.* Philadelphia, PA: Brunner-Routledge.

Wesner, D. W. (1996). Cognitive factors mediating the social problem-solving ability of adolescent offenders. *Dissertation Abstracts International, 57(1-B),* 0768.

Whitton, A. & McGuire, J. (2005). Problems and coping skills in adolescent offenders. Manuscript submitted for publication.

Williams, N. (1995). Cognitive skills groupwork. *Issues in Criminological and Legal Psychology, 23,* 22–30.

Wilson, D. B., Bouffard, L. A. and Mackenzie, D. L. (2005). A quantitative review of structured, group-oriented, cognitive-behavioral programs for offenders. *Criminal Justice and Behavior, 32,* 172–204.

Yu, P., Harris, G. E., Solovitz, B. L., & Franklin, J. L. (1986). A social problem-solving intervention for children at high risk for later psychopathology. *Journal of Clinical Child Psychology, 15,* 30–40.

Zamble, E. & Porporino, F. J. (1988). *Coping, behavior and adaptation in prison inmates.* New York: Springer.

Zamble, E. & Quinsey, V. L. (1997). *The criminal recidivism process.* Cambridge: Cambridge University Press.

Chapter 2

SOCIAL PROBLEM SOLVING AND THE DEVELOPMENT OF AGGRESSION

Liisa Keltikangas-Järvinen
University of Helsinki, Finland

INTRODUCTION

Until the 1980s, developmental psychology was dominated by psychoanalytic theories. These theories see aggression as an indication of deep-rooted personality pathology. In psychodynamic terms, it is an attempt to re-establish the lost intrapsychic balance through destructive acting-out behaviour. Aggression becomes manifest when the ego cannot integrate and the superego cannot control the libidinal and aggressive drives of the id, and childhood grandiosity fails to become integrated into a reality-oriented ego (e.g., Kohut, 1966).

Since the 1980s, aggressive behaviour has increasingly been explained in terms of biases in social-cognitive information processing. The social-cognitive approach to the development of aggression has its origins in the observation that the characteristics and the development of aggressive behaviour reflect cognitive development (e.g., Hartup, 1974), i.e., they reflect a child's ability to distinguish different activities of their social world, to recognise aggression, to understand causalities and others' intentions, and to adopt moral cognitions. From this perspective, aggressive behaviour is seen as a deficiency of social-cognitive development. More specifically, it is seen as a maladaptive way of solving social problems that result from deficient and aggressively biased social problem-solving strategies.

Based on social information processing theories, in the late 1970s and early 1980s researchers proposed a comprehensive theory of human cognitions to explain the development of aggression from this social-cognitive perspective (Crick & Dodge, 1994; Huesmann, 1988; Huesmann & Eron, 1989). According to

Social Problem Solving and Offending: Evidence, Evaluation and Evolution.
Edited by Mary McMurran and James McGuire © 2005 John Wiley & Sons, Ltd.

this theory, social behaviour is to a large extent controlled by programmes learned during a person's early development. These programmes can be described as cognitive scripts that are encoded, rehearsed, and stored in a person's memory and retrieved in much the same way as are other strategies for intellectual behaviour. They are learned through observation, reinforcement, and personal experiences in various situations and used as guides for behaviour. A script suggests what events happen in the environment, how the person should behave in response to these events, and what the likely outcome of those behaviours would be.

Social problem solving that utilises scripts can be described in terms of social strategies constructed of a sequence of steps. First, a person encodes and interprets the contextual information and social cues of the situation. Then she or he selects a goal or desired outcome, accesses possible responses from memory or, if the situation is novel, constructs new behaviours in response to immediate social cues, evaluates the solution generated, makes the decision to perform the most positively assessed act, and finally acts it out.

Empirical findings have shown that aggressive children and adolescents have numerous deficiencies in their social problem-solving strategies. They do not detect intention cues accurately: rather, they are likely to see situations as hostile, to interpret other people's intentions in a hostile way, to consider few facts and to select inappropriate behavioural goals aimed at aggressiveness (Lochman & Dodge, 1994; Quiggle, Garber, Panak, & Dodge, 1992; Richard & Dodge, 1982; Slaby & Guerra, 1988). They produce fewer problem-solving solutions. These solutions are qualitatively poor or ineffective, usually aggressive and at least not prosocial (Evans & Short, 1991; Lochman & Dodge, 1994; Mize & Cox, 1990; Quiggle et al., 1992; Slaby & Guerra, 1988).

They have difficulties co-ordinating multiple goals, they evaluate responses inadequately, and they feel effective in performing aggressive behaviour (Crick & Dodge, 1994; Quiggle et al., 1992; Slaby & Guerra, 1988). They also evaluate aggressive responses as favourable (Evans & Short, 1991; Mize & Cox, 1990; Richard & Dodge, 1982), and express a moral approval of aggression (Lochman & Dodge, 1994, Quiggle et al., 1992).

As a rule, aggressive children and adolescents have a high number of aggressive problem-solving strategies stored in their social-cognitive memory structures. Once incompetent scripts have been established, they are resistant to change and may even persist into adulthood (Huesmann, 1988). Thus, it is of vital importance to investigate how aggressive behaviour is initially formed and transmitted within different contexts.

However, it has been suggested that the strategies of aggressive children and adolescents are not generally more aggressive, except when reactively aggressive (Dodge & Coie, 1987) or severely violent adolescents are concerned (Lochman & Dodge, 1994). Furthermore, high levels of aggressive problem-solving strategies are also found among isolated or rejected children (Richard & Dodge, 1982) and among depressed children (Quiggle et al., 1992). Thus, in spite of a great amount of empirical research supporting a link, the association between aggressive problem-solving strategies and aggressive behaviour is somewhat controversial.

IMPORTANCE OF ROLES

Parents' Role

Deficient information-processing resulting in aggressive behaviour might be learned through observation, reinforcement, and personal experience in various situations (Huesmann, 1988; Huesmann & Eron, 1989). This process starts early in life, usually within the children's family. Parents may serve as behavioural models and reinforcers. Parents' aggressiveness and the indifference or punitiveness of their child-rearing practices serve as models for children to observe and as opportunities to incorporate aggressiveness into their own behavioural repertoires (Dodge, Pettit, & Bates, 1994; Huesmann & Eron, 1989; Parke & Slaby, 1983).

Children's cognitive processes may also be influenced directly by their parents' own cognitive processes. It is suggested that parents of aggressive children themselves lack the social problem-solving skills needed in social situations (Dodge et al., 1994).

However, surprisingly little research has been carried out when considering the great deal of interest there is in adolescent–parent conflicts as a whole. Existing research has tended to focus on behavioural models to resolve conflict between adolescents and parents, not on ways of solving problems outside the family. Consequently, our knowledge about the agreement between parents' and adolescents' scripts, manifesting themselves in the form of social problem-solving strategies, is rather slim.

In addition, the parent–child relationship is influenced by the gender of the parent. The father is the more important model for the boy, and the mother for the girl (Huston, 1983). It has also been shown that the parental practices the children expect from their mothers are different from those they expect from their fathers. Mothers are the people whom children perceive to be the best providers of social support, while fathers are perceived to be excellent sources of informational support but less satisfactory in their availability for and provision of direct help (e.g., Huston, 1983; Reid, Landesman, Treder, & Jaccard, 1989).

However, it has been suggested that father–child interaction rather than the mother–child relationship predicts children's aggressiveness (e.g., East, 1991). It has been shown, for example, that fathers use more forceful child-rearing practices than mothers (Power & Shanks, 1989) and that mothers use more information-seeking strategies in reaction to children's aggression than do fathers (Mills & Rubin, 1990).

Further, the child's own gender plays a role. It has been shown that parents perceive girls and boys differently and may expose them to different socialisation processes (e.g., Huston, 1983; Power & Shanks, 1989), which is likely to show up later as differences in children's problem-solving strategies and behaviour of the children (Parke & Slaby, 1983). Parents emphasise the appropriateness of the behaviour of boys more and use harsher disciplinary practices and more aggressive problem-solving strategies when raising them (Dodge et al., 1994; Huston, 1983; Parke & Slaby, 1983). However, parents react more negatively to the aggressive acts of daughters than to those of sons (e.g., Mills & Rubin, 1990; Parke & Slaby, 1983).

Peers' Role

Social problem-solving strategies are encoded and maintained by an active and observational learning, with social feedback being an important agent. During adolescence, peers are the major providers of social feedback, and the adoption of adequate social skills is very dependent on peer-group experiences (e.g., Rubin, Bukowski & Parker, 1998). Social acceptance by peers, that is, whether one is accepted or rejected by a peer group, is especially influential (Pombeni, Kirchler, & Palmonari, 1990).

Previous studies indicate that social acceptance, meaning social preference, especially social popularity, or positive social characteristics that peers attribute to an adolescent, are related to aggressive behaviour and aggressive problem-solving strategies. Low social acceptance and low social status have been shown to be related to aggressive behaviour and cognition, while high social acceptance is related to non-aggressive behaviour and cognitions (Newcomb, Bukowski, & Pattee, 1993). The findings, however, are not indisputable. It has been shown that aggressive adolescents may also be socially accepted (Bierman, Smoot, & Aumiller, 1993). This means that the relationship between aggressive problem-solving strategies, aggressive behaviour, and social acceptance is far from clear. Depending on the social characteristics that peers attribute to adolescents, they may receive congruent or incongruent social feedback for aggressive behaviour.

Social problem-solving strategies are included in a person's more general knowledge about the self (Crick & Dodge, 1994), and an individual's self-concept, in turn, is largely derived from their social status in a group (Tajfel, 1978; Turner, Hogg, Oakes, Reicher, & Wetherell, 1987). Thus, feedback in terms of social acceptance that peers attribute to an adolescent is an important source of self-validitional information (Boivin & Hymel, 1997; Pombeni et al., 1990). Positive correlation between behaviour and social feedback is likely to lead to a reliable self-image concerning one's behaviour because the information is based on facts, but ambiguous information may yield varying interpretations. Incongruent social feedback has even been shown to change interpretations of self (e.g., Street, 1988). Evidence exists that an exaggerated positive self-concept reflects deficiencies in social cognitions and may impede socially appropriate behaviour (Aspinwall & Taylor, 1997).

RESEARCH EVIDENCE

Based on social cognitive information-processing theories, our study group examined the development of aggression in two large studies. In the first study, a sample of 120 highly aggressive and 120 non-aggressive young people (the most and least aggressive in one age-cohort in a medium-sized town in Western Finland, a total of 1,017 youngsters, peer ratings being the tool for assessing aggression) were followed for seven years, from childhood to late adolescence. The participants were assessed three times, at age 10 to 11 years old, at 13-14 years old and at 17-18 years old. In addition, their parents were also interviewed during the first follow-up (when the children were 13 to 14 years

old). This study focused on the stability of aggression over different developmental periods, on the differences in social cognitive strategies of aggressive and
non-aggressive children, on childhood strategies as predictors of late adolescence
aggressiveness, and, finally, on parents' role in the development of children's
social strategies.

Problem-solving strategies, both of the children and of their parents, were
assessed by describing to them stories about children's ordinary life (details are
given in Keltikangas-Järvinen & Kangas, 1988). The stories involved frustrating
and aggression-provocative elements, i.e., the main person behaved aggressively
or was the victim of an aggressive act. The children analysed the stories, and their
social information processes, i.e., causal thinking, alternative thinking (aggressive
vs. constructive coping), and consequential thinking were assessed on the basis of
these analyses.

In addition, the parents and children were presented with three stories in
which the protagonist was pressured by his or her peers into immoral, illegal, or
criminal behaviour. The children were asked how they would behave in this
situation, why they would behave that way, and what kind of advice they
thought their parents would give for solving this situation. The parents were
asked how they thought their children would behave in this same situation, why
they thought their children would behave that way, and how they would advise
their children to solve the problem.

In the second study, school registers were used to identify all students in three
age-cohorts, one of 11-, one of 14- and one of 17-year-olds, in five towns in
Western Finland. A total of 2,714 students were assessed for the purpose of
studying the relationship between aggressive problem-solving strategies and
aggressive behaviour, the role of peer feedback and moral cognitions, and the
age- and gender-related variance in those parameters (see Figure 2.1).

The students' aggressive and sociable behaviours and social acceptance, their
social problem-solving strategies and their moral evaluations were assessed
using the following questionnaires: the Social Behaviours and Social Status

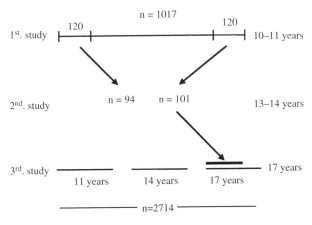

Figure 2.1 Participants and study phases of the present study

Questionnaire (Pakaslahti & Keltikangas-Järvinen, 2000), the Social Problem-Solving Strategies Questionnaire (Keltikangas-Järvinen & Pakaslahti, 2000a), and the Questionnaire on Moral Cognitions (Keltikangas-Järvinen & Pakaslahti, 2000b). The following steps of cognitive strategies were used: (1) perceiving the cues (situational orientation); (2) associating the cause and the consequence (causal thinking); (3) identifying alternative responses (alternative thinking); (4) response evaluation meaning internal standards and moral rules; and (5) prognosticating the consequences (consequential thinking).

The Relationship between Aggressive Problem-Solving Strategies and Aggressive Behaviour

Our series of findings (Keltikangas-Järvinen, 2002; Pakaslahti & Keltikangas-Järvinen, 1996) showed a significant although not very high correlation between aggressive problem-solving strategies and aggressive behaviour. This correlation was slightly stronger for boys than for girls. With respect to age, our findings suggest a curvilinear relationship. In 14-year-olds, aggressive problem-solving strategies correlated significantly with aggressive behaviour, explaining almost 6% of its variance. In contrast, the corresponding correlation among 11- and 17-year-olds was lower, the shared proportion of the variance being only 2% (see Table 2.1).

Social Problem-Solving Strategies of Aggressive and Non-Aggressive Children

The steps of social problem-solving strategies were analysed in our first study of 196 10-year-olds. The findings showed that the non-aggressive children, especially non-aggressive girls, were systematically superior in all phases of the problem-solving sequence, but that the only statistically significant difference between aggressive and non-aggressive participants was non-aggressive children's better

Table 2.1 Correlations (Pearson's r) between aggressive strategies, aggressive behaviour and social acceptance

	Aggressive behaviour	Social acceptance
Aggressive strategies		
11–year	0.15***	−0.11**
14–year	0.24***	−0.25***
17–year	0.13***	−0.09**
Aggressive behaviour		
11–year		−0.21***
14–year		0.02
17–year		0.04

Note: *$p < 0.05$; **$p < 0.01$; ***$p < 0.001$

ability to find constructive alternatives to aggressive behaviour in aggression-provoking situations. Thus, in conflict situations, it was not the level of aggression in problem-solving strategies that differentiated the aggressive and non-aggressive children, but the lack of constructive strategies among the aggressive ones (Keltikangas-Järvinen & Kangas, 1988).

The children's information-processing styles were very consistent even in childhood. The children had strategies that typified them and that they adopted in different kinds of conflict situations. They also used the same strategy across the problem solving: they selected either constructive or aggressive strategies throughout the situations, and if constructive coping was selected, then they used constructive interpretation of situational cues, and constructive consequences and constructive outcomes were also expected.

In the second study, i.e., 11-, 14- and 17-year-olds ($n = 2,714$), the different steps of social information processing were not examined, but a tendency to choose aggressive problem solving from a list of different alternatives was investigated. This approach made the difference between aggressive and non-aggressive young people still more apparent. Aggressive youngsters applied aggressive strategies systematically in different social situations, independently of the provocativeness of the situation. It was their personal trait, not the situational characteristic.

Among the 14-year-olds, the most obvious difference was shown in motives. Aggressive students approved of the use of aggression. More than 5% of 14-year-old students reported that they behaved aggressively, for instance, teased their classmates just because it was fun. Thus, with age, aggression was likely to become more rewarding.

Stability of Aggressive Behaviour and Problem-Solving Strategies

In line with the previous literature, aggressive behaviour was found to be very stable over different developmental periods. In our study, peer ratings were used to assess aggressive behaviour at baseline when the children were 10-years-old, while teacher and peer ratings were used seven years later. Based on those ratings, two categories (aggressive vs. non-aggressive) were adopted at both study levels. It was found that over 80% of the children stayed in their original categories. This was especially true with aggressive children: only six (all were girls) out of 89 who were originally assessed as aggressive moved to the non-aggressive category during the follow-up period of seven years, while the opposite was more common, with 12 out of 107 non-aggressive children moving to the aggressive category (Keltikangas-Järvinen & Pakaslahti, 1999).

Childhood Strategies and Their Changes as Predictors of Changes in Behaviours

Our study focused especially on questions of whether: (1) childhood strategies predicted later behaviour; or (2) changes in strategies were likely to be reflected in changes in behaviour. First, a stability of aggressive behaviour over seven years was predicted both by aggressive childhood problem-solving strategies and by a lack of alternative strategies, i.e., a lack of constructive and submissive strategies in childhood. In addition, it was possible to predict the stability of aggressive behaviour with a combination of aggressive strategies and a lack of constructive alternatives in childhood, and aggressive strategies in adolescence. Especially in boys, aggressive and incompetent childhood strategies were likely to turn later into aggressive strategies, a combination that increasingly predicted a stability of aggressive behaviour.

Second, a movement from aggressive to non-aggressive behaviour was seen only among girls. For them, low levels of aggressive and withdrawal strategies and a high level of submissive strategies in childhood predicted a move from the aggressive to the non-aggressive category. High levels of childhood sub-missive and adolescent withdrawal strategies were likely to combine with a low level of adolescent aggressive strategies, and this combination predicted the move from the aggressive to the non-aggressive category. This means that moving from the aggressive to the non-aggressive category was possible for girls who had never used aggressive strategies, i.e., whose aggressive behaviour in childhood was not consistent with their non-aggressive strategies. The effect could not be gauged among boys because of the lack of boys in this category, i.e., there were no boys who had moved from the aggressive to the non-aggressive category.

Third, the movement from the non-aggressive to the aggressive category was also found only among girls. This movement was consistent with the strategies used: non-aggressive girls who in childhood used withdrawal instead of aggres-sive strategies, but who used aggressive strategies in late adolescence, also behaved aggressively in adolescence. Thus, boys' behaviour was found to be more stable than that of girls.

Fourth, non-aggressive behaviour was also very stable. For boys, the stability of non-aggressiveness could not be predicted on the basis of problem-solving strategies, while for girls, constant non-aggressiveness was predicted by child-hood submissiveness as well as by combinations of high childhood submissive-ness and low adolescent aggressiveness, and of low childhood aggressiveness and high adolescent prosociality. That is, the same constellation both explained the stability of sociable behaviour, and predicted a positive change (Keltikangas-Järvinen & Pakaslahti, 1999).

The Role of Parents

Throughout the stories, parents of aggressive adolescents were more indifferent: they would do nothing to help their children, but they punished if the child got into trouble, and they also diverted responsibility to others, for example, to the teacher. The parents of non-aggressive adolescents gave more help, super-vision and advice (Pakaslahti, Asplund-Peltola, & Keltikangas-Järvinen, 1996; Pakaslahti, Spoof, Asplund-Peltola, & Keltikangas-Järvinen, 1998).

In both the families with aggressive children and families with non-aggressive children, mothers took more active roles than fathers in solving the problems described in the stories. Actually, fathers took an active role only in situations in which pressure came from outside such as when a son was pressured by his peers to take part in some illegal activity, or when an authority figure reported that a son had done something illegal or immoral. Then the fathers got more involved than the mothers in the situation. This was especially true with the fathers of the aggressive boys, who took more passive roles throughout the stories and offered less alternatives for problem solving than did the fathers of non-aggressive boys. The fathers of aggressive boys said that they would discuss the situation with their sons. Actually, these discussions were indefinite consisting of free-floating comments that had no focus or solution regarding the particular problem.

As a rule, these findings are not very informative because they mostly replicate the previous findings that have widely documented an indifference by the parents of aggressive children, and more active and supportive role by the parents of sociable children. Previous studies have not, however, compared the problem-solving strategies of children with those of their parents for the same hypothetical situations. This was done here.

Adolescents (aged 13 to 14 years at that time) and their parents were presented with three stories from the adolescents' daily social life (details are given in Pakaslahti et al., 1996), and their problem-solving strategies were assessed. Correspondence between the parents' and their children's problem solving was very low. Generally, correspondence was higher between classmates than between children and their parents. The parents interpreted the causal relations in the situations differently from the children, the parents offered behavioural alternatives which did not appear in the children's answers, and the parents did not anticipate social consequences among peers in the same way as their children did.

Further, the strategies of the parents of aggressive adolescents were different from those of parents of non-aggressive adolescents. Interestingly, the fathers of aggressive boys and those of non-aggressive boys used strategies which have been shown in the literature to characterise aggressive boys and non-aggressive boys, respectively. This means that although there was low congruence, if any, between the fathers' and their sons' strategies, the fathers of aggressive boys used strategies which have been shown to be typical of aggressive boys (Pakaslahti et al., 1996).

Although the similarity between the adolescents' and their parents' strategies was minimal, the parents' evaluations of their children's strategies were consistent with peer ratings; those adolescents who were rated as aggressive by their peers were expected by their parents to use aggressive strategies, and those who were rated as non-aggressive were expected to choose non-aggressive strategies. This concordance was especially true with the dyads of aggressive boys and their fathers.

Parents' assessments, however, conflicted with the adolescents' own descriptions. Actually, an essential finding was that parents' expectations were in accordance with a child's peer-rated behaviour, but did not agree with a child's

own thinking, motives and goals. Contrary to the aggressive boys' own suggestions, their parents did not expect them to solve problems in a constructive way,
but instead expected their sons to concede to immoral behaviour, even to commit
crimes.

Similarly, parents did not expect sociable girls to capitulate to peer pressure,
while this was often true with the girls themselves. Further, sociable boys were
always expected to solve the social problems actively and in a constructive way,
again against the boys' own suggestions (Keltikangas-Järvinen & Asplund-
Peltola, 1995).

The same was true with motivation. If a sociable girl was thought to
misbehave, her parents suggested that this would happen because of fear
or peer pressure, never intentionally and because of social benefit, while the
girls themselves saw acceding to peer pressure as a possible alternative because
it would result in better status in the peer group. Sociable boys who thought
they would go along with peer pressure saw fear as a primary reason,
while their parents suggested that it was because of an occasional lack of
self-control.

The biggest controversy came in the theme "telling the parents". The parents of
non-aggressive girls were quite sure that the girls would tell them everything,
while the girls themselves said they were unlikely to do this. Aggressive boys, in
contrast, wanted to tell their problems to their parents, but the parents did not
expect this. Further, aggressive girls were often left without help from their
parents, again against the girls' own wishes (Keltikangas-Järvinen & Asplund-
Peltola, 1995).

This may indicate that adolescents do not yet know themselves, so that there is
a gap between how they are and how they think they are. Another possibility
is that parents think stereotypically: they assume that aggressive children's
thoughts are also aggressive. At least, our findings suggest that aggressive
children do not necessarily have a low cognitive capacity for solving social
problems, but that they may have a biased reinforcement history.

The same-sex parent effect, i.e., the phenomenon that the same-sex parent is of
higher importance, was apparent. In addition, sex-role expectations were present.
The boys were not expected to ask for help from their parents, although the boys
themselves expressed this wish. Conversely, the parents expected their girls,
especially the non-aggressive ones, to ask them for help, even though this idea
was not confirmed by the girls themselves. It is known that socialisation
experiences of boys and girls are different: boys are encouraged to be active
and independent, while more passivity is expected from girls.

Finally, an important finding is of the existence of a deep gap between the
parents' and their children' worlds. The situations described in the stories were
chosen in a pilot study by interviewing a randomised sample of adolescents of
the same age as the present sample. The adolescents in the present study said that
the situations described their daily lives well, while the parents said that something like this described in the stories could never happen in their children's real
lives. This, perhaps, made the parents feel helpless and prevented them from
understanding how complicated the situations really were from the point of view
of their children.

The Role of Peers

The correlation between aggressive behaviour and social acceptance was found only among early adolescents. Aggressive 11-year-olds were disliked by their peers, while aggressiveness was unrelated to social popularity among 14- and 17-year-olds. This suggests that aggressive behaviour is used as a criterion for social acceptance in early adolescence only (see Table 2.1).

With respect to cognitions, aggressive problem-solving strategies were inversely, but only marginally, correlated with social acceptance among 11- and 17-year-olds, but significantly among 14-year-olds. Thus, the relationship was curvilinear: weak in early adolescence, strong in middle adolescence, and likely to decrease in late adolescence. It seems that of these three phases of adolescence, the middle period is when adolescents are most sensitive to peer feedback as far as adopting aggression as their self-image is concerned. Further, in all age groups the correlation between social acceptance and aggressive problem-solving strategies was stronger for boys than for girls. This is in line with suggestions that in adolescence, boys have a higher dependence on acceptance among larger peer groups, and girls resort to more intimate dyadic relationships (e.g., Cross & Madson, 1997).

Peer acceptance was discovered to play an essential role in the young person's self-reported strategies. Non-aggressive adolescents with low social acceptance and aggressive adolescents with high social acceptance had equally high levels of aggressive problem-solving strategies. Even though both aggressive behaviour and social acceptance in these two groups were significantly different, the levels of their aggressive problem-solving strategies were equal. The highest level of aggressive problem-solving strategies was found among aggressive, non-accepted youngsters, and the lowest level of aggressive strategies was expressed by non-aggressive, accepted youngsters, while the non-aggressive, non-accepted, and aggressive, accepted levels fell between these two groups expressing equal level of aggressive problem-solving strategies (see Figures 2.2 and 2.3).

Thus, those who received congruent feedback for their behaviour, i.e., were rated as being aggressive and were socially rejected, or were rated as being non-aggressive and were socially approved by their peers, had self-rated problem-solving strategies in line with their behaviour. This means that aggressive, rejected adolescents saw aggression as typical of themselves. In contrast, those who received incongruent feedback showed strategies that were in conflict with their actual behaviour, i.e., aggressive, accepted adolescents perceived themselves as non-aggressive, and non-aggressive, non-accepted adolescents saw themselves as aggressive.

Peer acceptance had, however, an influence on both aggressive and non-aggressive students in middle adolescence only (see Figure 2.2), this effect being replicated in early (see Figure 2.2) and late adolescence (see Figure 2.3) only among the aggressive ones. In early and late adolescence, aggressive non-accepted students, i.e., aggressive youngsters who received congruent feedback for their aggressiveness had the highest levels of aggressive problem-solving strategies, i.e., saw themselves as aggressive, while the aggressive youngsters accepted, i.e., aggressive ones who received incongruent feedback, had levels of

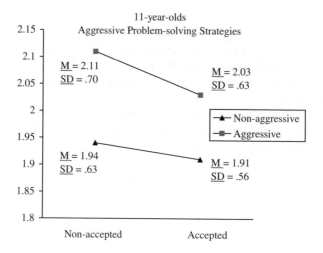

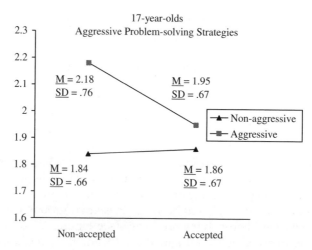

Figure 2.2 ANOVA Aggressive Behaviour × Social Acceptance × Age on aggressive strategies

Source: Reproduced with permission from Keltikangas-Järvinen, L. (2002). Aggressive problem-solving strategies, aggressive behavior, and social acceptance in early and late adolescence. *Journal of Youth and Adolescence*, 31, 279–287. Copyright © 2002 by Kluwer Academic/Plenum Publishers.

aggressive strategies equal to those of non-aggressive, accepted and non-aggressive unaccepted children. This was true although it was confirmed that both the 11- and 17-year-old aggressive adolescents had higher scores than their non-aggressive age mates on actual aggressive behaviour, and the accepted ones had higher scores than the unaccepted ones on social acceptance.

As has been suggested previously (Tajfel, 1978; Turner, 1978; Turner et al., 1987), it seems that an individual's self-concept, evaluated here through social strategies, is influenced by his or her social status in a group. Peers played a role

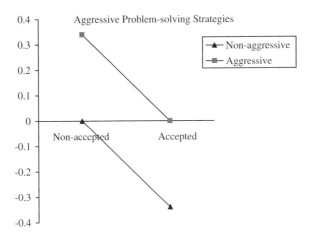

Figure 2.3   ANOVA Aggressive Behaviour × Social Acceptance on aggressive problem-solving strategies
Source: Reproduced with permission from Pakaslahti, L. and Keltikangas-Järvinen, L. (1996). Social acceptance and the relationship between aggressive problem-solving strategies and aggressive behaviour in 14-year-old adolescents. *European Journal of Personality, 10,* 249–261. Copyright © 1996 by John Wiley & Sons, Ltd.

in how the students perceived themselves and how they interpreted their own problem solving. In early and late adolescence, peer acceptance determined how the aggressive adolescents saw their own aggressiveness, i.e., whether they adopted aggressiveness as their self-image or not. Unaccepted aggressive adolescents recognised their own aggressiveness, while accepted aggressive ones underestimated it. Contrary to the middle adolescents, social acceptance played no role in the self-ratings of non-aggressive early and late adolescents; the non-aggressive unaccepted early and late adolescents did not see themselves as aggressively biased, unlike the non-aggressive unaccepted middle adolescents (Pakaslahti & Keltikangas-Järvinen, 1996).

In accordance with self-perception theory, it is possible that non-aggressive early and late adolescents are more able to use their own observations of their behaviour as a source of self-knowledge than are middle adolescents who, instead, are age-specifically affected by negative peer feedback. Supporting this claim, it has been shown that sensitivity to negative peer evaluations peaks in middle adolescence (e.g., Gavin & Furman, 1989), which might explain the present influence of peer feedback also on non-aggressive youngsters.

Because social feedback was so important, we asked whether acceptance is related to the type of aggression so that the level of aggression would be unimportant. It was revealed that at the same levels of aggression, non-accepted aggressive students used intriguing and bullying, while accepted aggressive ones used open aggression, that is, arguing and fighting (Pakaslahti & Keltikangas-Järvinen, 1998). This additionally emphasises the effectiveness of peer feedback. Accepted aggressive students used open aggression but, however, saw non-aggressive strategies as typical of themselves. It might be expected that open aggression would be easy to perceive, also by the young person him- or herself, but the results suggest that biased feedback was likely to distort this observation.

Moral Evaluations

The last step in social information processing is response evaluation, which is evaluation of the moral and ethical aspects of problem solving (Crick & Dodge, 1994). In our study, moral evaluations focused on approval and disapproval of aggression. Moral approval was assessed at two levels: general and applied, and both levels included two factors. Items assessing approval or disapproval of aggression at the general level focused on a universal rightness or wrongness of aggression, i.e., aggression is always wrong regardless of explanations or causes vs. it cannot be said that aggression as a rule is wrong. The applied level referred to a person's own coping with social problems, i.e. to a person's proneness to use aggression as a way to solve social problems

The factors of the general level of approval were "Relativism" and "Absolutism". The content of "Relativism" was that one can never say whether a deed as such is wrong or not because of the need to consider so many aspects such as causes, motives, consequences. "Absolutism" consisted of completely negative attitudes towards aggression, regardless of excuses for it.

Factors at the applied level of approval were "Legitimisation" and "Disapproval". "Legitimisation" refers to the approval of aggression as an actual way of coping with social problems because of existing excuses (such as situation, degree, intention, consequence: hitting is right if someone else starts the fighting, spanking is not wrong if you know to stop in time, aggression is not wrong if you do not mean it, aggression is not wrong if nothing serious happens). "Disapproval" refers to the view that aggression is an unaccepted way to behave, independent of the situational circumstances (Pakaslahti & Keltikangas-Järvinen, 1997).

It was found that, generally, approval of aggression was likely to increase aggressive behaviour, while disapproval decreased it, as could be expected. More specifically, "Legitimisation" correlated positively and "Absolutism" negatively with aggression (Pakaslahti & Keltikangas-Järvinen, 1997). As a rule, moral cognitions were statistically significantly related to behaviour, but did not explain very much of its variance (max. 4.5%). However, moral cognitions in combination with problem- solving strategies explained the variance of behaviour significantly more than strategies alone (max. 9%). Especially significant was a combination of low "Absolutism" and a high level of aggressive strategies. This combination was highly prognostic of aggressive behaviour (Pakaslahti & Keltikangas-Järvinen, 1997).

CONCLUSION

Aggression has been previously shown to be relatively stable, self-perpetuating behaviour that is rather resistant to change. Its harmful consequences and negative effects are far-reaching. A very recent 30-year follow-up demonstrated that childhood aggression was the most important predictor of adulthood long-term unemployment with its accompanying mental and social consequences, including criminality (Kokko, 2001). Thus, early intervention for aggressive behaviour is of fundamental importance.

Although aggression as such is rather resistant to change, studies have, however, demonstrated that aggressive adolescents' maladjusted behaviour can be altered and made more sociable by teaching them more sociable cognitions to replace the above-mentioned aggression-biased cognitions (e.g., Guerra & Slaby, 1990).

Our studies showed that aggressive behaviour was never used without the existence of aggressive strategies. In childhood, aggressive behaviour, especially in aggression-provoking situations, was likely to be related to an inability to find sociable alternatives to aggressive problem-solving. In middle and late adolescence, the difference in problem-solving strategies between aggressive and non-aggressive young people increased to involve all the steps in information processing, including moral cognitions. This may suggest that intervention is "easiest" in childhood or in early adolescence: when teaching a child, focusing on refraining from aggressive cognitions and teaching him or her alternative social cognitions might be effective, while with older adolescents, any intervention programme should cover the whole social cognitive repertoire.

It has previously been asked whether changes in problem-solving strategies can predict the development of aggressive behaviour in natural settings. Our follow-up study showed that changes in problem solving-strategies predicted aggressive behaviour in natural settings, but less than what has been documented in intervention programmes. Spontaneous positive changes were not forthcoming, which emphasises the need for interventions.

From the point of view of intervention, two of our findings are particularly important: the role of peer feedback in the formation of an adolescent's self-image, and the combined effect of social and moral cognitions. Parents are, of course, of primary importance, but biased self-perceptions and moral cognitions can easily be modified in adolescents' ordinary school settings.

Although congruence between parents' and their children's scripts was low, this does not mean that parental scripts do not play a role in the development of children's scripts. On the contrary, the fathers of aggressive boys used strategies which, according to the literature, are typical of aggressive persons.

It is not known how parent–child agreement about the supportiveness of their relationship is related to children's social competence, although the importance of this knowledge has been emphasised (e.g., East, 1991). The present data, however, provided convergent evidence that aggressive children, especially aggressive boys, feel they have less supportive relationships with their parents, especially with their fathers, than do non-aggressive children. As a rule, parents' stereotypical thinking that aggressive boys have unethical motives and immoral cognitions in addition to aggressive behaviour, is not a good starting point for reinforcement of aggressive boys' social skills. The biggest problem was that the parents were completely ignorant of the adolescents' daily life. The parents did not know about the real-life problems of their children, and did not themselves know how to solve such problems.

As mentioned earlier, aggressive behaviour can be altered by modifying problem-solving strategies. This modification, however, is not possible if the youngster does not recognise his or her strategies, i.e., has an inaccurate or biased self-concept. Our findings showed that incongruent social feedback in the form of social acceptance had a significant effect on biased self-perception, the phenomenon where the person attributes to himself or herself mental scripts which disagree with his or her actual behaviour and decrease an adolescent's recognition of his or her aggressiveness. This raises the question of whether adequate peer feedback could be of benefit in modifying aggressive behaviour through the modification of the self-concept. At least, this finding suggests that the young person's social status among his or her classmates should be taken into account in interventions.

The role of social feedback as such was not unexpected, but the strength of its effect was. In adolescence, social feedback is one of the most important information sources from which individuals obtain self-validitional knowledge, and peers are perceived to be of functional importance with respect to needs related to identity (Hortacsu, Gencoez, & Oral, 1995).

In our research, the intervening role of peer feedback was most effective in middle adolescence. It has previously been shown that the social acceptance that peers confer upon an adolescent is relatively stable throughout adolescence (Bukowski & Newcomb, 1984; Coie & Dodge, 1983), but the adolescent's own fear of peer non-acceptance peaks in middle adolescence. Group membership, conformity, and popularity are more valued and peer feedback is more influential during early and middle than during late adolescence (Gavin & Furman, 1989). In addition, it has been shown that middle adolescents live in an identity vacuum (Pombeni et al., 1990) and seek a lof of information about themselves from their peers (Adams & Gullotta, 1989). Consequently, it may be hypothesised that middle adolescence is an especially appropriate time for aggression interventions in terms of biased self-perceptions. Social feedback played a slightly more evident role among boys than among girls. This is not unexpected because adolescent boys have been shown to be more dependent on larger peer groups, while girls spend time with only a few close friends (Lagerspetz, Björkqvist, & Peltonen, 1988).

Although information processing for problem solving includes moral cognitions as the last step of the sequence cycle, they are not usually included in studies on aggression. As far as we know, this is the first study that has included both social and moral cognitions in the prediction of actual behaviour. It was shown that by combining moral and social cognitions, a two- to three-fold proportion of the variance of the actual behaviour was explained as compared with the variance explained by social cognitions alone. The moral cognitions discussed here can easily be taught and, thus, included in intervention programmes.

Our study showed that aggressive behaviour was evident if aggressiveness was morally accepted, or at least not rejected outright. This finding is of importance as far as the effect of the media is concerned. TV programmes that offer excuses for aggressive behaviour or show aggressiveness as an understandable and acceptable model for problem solving may increase actual aggressiveness (Huesmann, Moise-Titus, Podolski, & Eron, 2003).

In summary, aggressive behaviour is not likely to decrease spontaneously in adolescence. Instead, with age it is likely to become more stable and rewarding. Thus, early interventions are needed. Our findings suggest that aggressiveness could be decreased through modifying a person's social cognitive strategies.

REFERENCES

Adams, G. R. & Gullotta, T. (1989). *Adolescent life experiences* 2nd edn. Belmont, CA: Brooks/ Cole Publishing Co.

Aspinwall, L. G. & Taylor, S. E. (1997). A stitch in time: Self-regulation and proactive coping. *Psychological Bulletin, 121*, 417–436.

Bierman, K. L., Smoot, D. L., & Aumiller, K. (1993). Characteristics of aggressive-rejected, aggressive (nonrejected), and rejected (nonaggressive) boys. *Child Development, 64*, 139– 151.

Boivin, M. & Hymel, S. (1997). Peer experiences and social self-perceptions: A sequential model. *Developmental Psychology, 33*, 135–145.

Bukowski, W. M. & Newcomb, A. F. (1984). Stability and determinants of sociometric status and friendship choice: A longitudinal perspective. *Developmental Psychology, 20*, 941–952.

Coie, J. D. & Dodge, K. A. (1983). Continuities and changes in children's social status: A five-year longitudinal study. *Merrill-Palmer Quarterly, 29*, 261–282.

Crick, N. R. & Dodge, K. A. (1994). A review and reformulation of social information-processing mechanisms in children's social adjustment. *Psychological Bulletin, 115*, 74– 101.

Cross, S. E. & Madson, L. (1997). Models of the self: Self-construals and gender. *Psychological Bulletin, 122*, 5–37.

Dodge, K. A. & Coie, J. D. (1987). Social-information-processing factors in reactive and proactive aggression in children's peer groups. *Journal of Personality and Social Psychology, 53*, 1146–1158.

Dodge, K. A., Pettit, G. S., & Bates, J. E. (1994). Socialization mediators of the relation between socioeconomic status and child conduct problems. *Child Development, 65*, 649– 665.

East, P. L. (1991). The parent–child relationships of withdrawn, aggressive, and sociable children: Child and parent perspectives. *Merrill-Palmer Quarterly, 37*, 425–444.

Evans, S. W. & Short, E. J. (1991). A qualitative and serial analyses of social problem solving in aggressive boys. *Journal of Abnormal Psychology, 19*, 331–340.

Gavin, L. A. & Furman, W. (1989). Age differences in adolescents' perceptions of their peer groups. *Developmental Psychology, 25*, 827–834.

Guerra, N. G. & Slaby, R. G. (1990). Cognitive mediators of aggression in adolescent offenders: 2. Intervention. *Developmental Psychology, 26*, 269–277.

Hartup, W. W. (1974). Aggression in childhood. Developmental perspectives. *American Psychologist, 29*, 336–341.

Hortacsu, N., Gencoez, T., & Oral, A. (1995). Perceived functions of family and friends during childhood, adolescence, and youth: Developmental theories of two Turkish groups. *International Journal of Psychology, 30*, 591–606.

Huesmann, L. R. (1988). An information processing model for the development of aggression. *Aggressive Behavior, 14*, 13–24.

Huesmann, L. R. & Eron, L. D. (1989). Individual differences and the trait of aggression. *European Journal of Personality, 3*, 95–106.

Huesmann, L. R., Moise-Titus, J., Podolski, C. L., & Eron, L. D. (2003). Longitudinal relations between children's exposure to TV violence and their aggressive and violent behavior in young adulthood: 1977–1992. *Developmental Psychology, 39*, 201–221.

Huston, A. C. (1983). Sex-typing. In P. H. Mussen & E. M. Hetherington (eds). *Handbook of child psychology*: vol. 4. *Socialization, personality, and social development* (pp. 387–467). New York: Wiley.

Keltikangas-Järvinen, L. (2002). Aggressive problem-solving strategies, aggressive behavior and social acceptance in early and late adolescence. *Journal of Youth and Adolescence, 31*, 279–287.

Keltikangas-Järvinen, L. & Asplund-Peltola, R. L. (1995). Agreement between social problem-solving scripts of aggressive and sociable adolescents and their parents. *Aggressive Behavior, 21*, 419–429.

Keltikangas-Järvinen, L. & Kangas, P. (1988). Problem-solving strategies in aggressive and nonaggressive children. *Aggressive Behavior, 14*, 255–264.

Keltikangas-Järvinen, L. & Pakaslahti, L. (1999). Development of social problem-solving strategies and changes in aggressive behavior: A 7-year follow-up from childhood to late adolescence. *Aggressive Behavior, 25*, 269–279.

Keltikangas-Järvinen, L. & Pakaslahti, L. (2000a). Social problem-solving strategies questionnaire. In J. Maltby, C. A. Lewis, & A. Hill (eds) *A Handbook of psychological tests*: vol. 1. (pp. 234–237). Lampeter, Wales: Edwin Mellen Press.

Keltikangas-Järvinen, L. & Pakaslahti, L. (2000b). Questionnaire on moral cognitions. In J. Maltby, C. A. Lewis, & A. Hill (eds), *A Handbook of psychological tests*: vol. 1. (pp. 218–221) Lampeter, Wales: Edwin Mellen Press.

Kohut, H. (1966). Forms and transformations of narcissism. *Journal of American Psychoanalytic Assessment, 14*, 243–272.

Kokko, K. (2001). Antecedents and consequences of long-term unemployment. Doctoral thesis, Department of Psychology, University of Jyväskylä, Finland.

Lagerspetz, K. M., Björkqvist, K., & Peltonen, T. (1988). Is indirect aggression typical of females? Gender differences in aggressiveness in 11- to 12-year-old children. *Aggressive Behavior, 14*, 403–414.

Lochman, J. E. & Dodge, K. A. (1994). Social-cognitive processes of severely violent, moderately aggressive, and nonaggressive boys. *Journal of Consulting and Clinical Psychology, 62*, 366–374.

Mills, R. S. & Rubin, K. H. (1990). Parental beliefs about problematic social behaviors in early childhood. *Child Development, 61*, 138–151.

Mize, J. & Cox, R. A. (1990). Social knowledge and social competence: Number and quality of strategies as predictors of peer behavior. *Journal of Genetic Psychology, 151*, 117–127.

Newcomb, A. F., Bukowski, W. M., & Pattee, L. (1993). Children's peer relations: a meta-analytic review of popular, rejected, neglected, controversial, and average sociometric status. *Psychological Bulletin, 113*, 99–128.

Pakaslahti, L., Asplund-Peltola, R., & Keltikangas-Järvinen, L. (1996). Parents' social problem-solving strategies in families with aggressive and non-aggressive boys. *Aggressive Behavior, 22*, 345–356.

Pakaslahti, L. & Keltikangas-Järvinen, L. (1996). Social acceptance and the relationship between aggressive problem-solving strategies and aggressive behaviour in 14-year-old adolescents. *European Journal of Personality, 10*, 249–261.

Pakaslahti, L. & Keltikangas-Järvinen, L. (1997). The relationships between moral approval of aggression, aggressive problem-solving strategies, and aggressive behavior in 14-year-old adolescents. *Journal of Social Behavior and Personality, 12*, 905–924.

Pakaslahti, L. & Keltikangas-Järvinen, L. (1998). Types of aggressive behavior among aggressive preferred, aggressive non-preferred, non-aggressive preferred and non-aggressive non-preferred 14-year-old adolescents. *Personality and Individual Differences*, *24*, 821–828.

Pakaslahti, L. & Keltikangas-Järvinen, L. (2000). Social behavior and social status questionnaire. In J. Maltby, C. A. Lewis, & A. Hill (eds) *A handbook of psychological tests*: vol. 1. (pp. 246–249). Lampeter, Wales: Edwin Mellen Press.

Pakaslahti, L., Spoof, I., Asplund-Peltola, R., & Keltikangas-Järvinen, L. (1998). Parents' social problem-solving strategies in families with aggressive and non-aggressive girls. *Aggressive Behavior*, *24*, 37–51.

Parke, R. D. & Slaby, R. G. (1983). The development of aggression. In P. H. Mussen & E. M. Hetherington (eds), *Handbook of child psychology*: vol. 4. *Socialization, personality, and social development* (pp. 547-641). New York: John Wiley & Sons, Ltd.

Pombeni, M. L., Kirchler, E., & Palmonari, A. (1990). Identification with peers as a strategy to muddle through the troubles of the adolescent years. *Journal of Adolescence*, *13*, 351–369.

Power, T. G. & Shanks, J. A. (1989). Parents as socializers: Maternal and paternal views. *Journal of Youth and Adolescence*, *18*, 203–220.

Quiggle, N. L., Garber, J., Panak, W. F., & Dodge, K. A. (1992). Social information processing in aggressive and depressed children. *Child Development*, *63*, 1305–1320.

Reid, M., Landesman, S., Treder, R., & Jaccard, J. (1989). ''My family and friends'': Six- to twelve-year-old children's perceptions of social support. *Child Development*, *60*, 896–910.

Richard, B. A. & Dodge, K. A. (1982). Social maladjustment and problem solving in school-aged children. *Journal of Consulting and Clinical Psychology*, *50*, 226–233.

Rubin, K. H., Bukowski, W., & Parker, J. G. (1998). Peer interactions, relationships, and groups. In W. Damon & N. Eisenberg (eds) *Handbook of child psychology: vol. 3. Social, emotional, and personality development* 5th edn. (pp. 619–700). New York: John Wiley & Sons, Ltd.

Slaby, R. G. & Guerra, N. G. (1988). Cognitive mediators of aggression in adolescent offenders: I. assessment. *Developmental Psychology*, *24*, 580–588.

Street, S. (1988). Feedback and self-concept in high school students. *Adolescence*, *23*, 449–456.

Tajfel, H. (1978). Social categorization, social identity and social comparison. In H. Tajfel (ed.) *Differentiation between social groups: Studies in the social psychology of intergroup relations* (pp. 61–76). London: Academic Press.

Turner, J. C. (1978). Social comparison, similarity and ingroup favoritism. In H. Tajfel (ed.), *Differentiation between social groups: Studies in the social psychology of intergroup relations* (pp. 235–250). London: Academic Press.

Turner, J. C., Hogg, M. A., Oakes, P. J., Reicher, S. D., & Wetherell, M. S. (1987). *Rediscovering the social group: A self-categorization theory*. Worcester: Billing and Sons.

Chapter 3

SOCIAL PROBLEM SOLVING IN AGGRESSIVE CHILDREN

WALTER MATTHYS[1] and JOHN E. LOCHMAN[2]

[1]University Medical Centre Utrecht, The Netherlands
[2]University of Alabama, USA

INTRODUCTION

In clinical child psychology, the term aggression refers to children who manifest various forms of oppositional, aggressive, and antisocial behaviours, such as arguing with adults, initiating fights, and stealing. In child psychiatry, children with severe forms of these behaviours are diagnosed as suffering from one of the two Disruptive Behaviour Disorders according to DSM-IV (American Psychiatric Association, 1994), i.e. Oppositional Defiant Disorder (ODD), or Conduct Disorder (CD). Also, in children with Attention Deficit Hyperactivity Disorder (ADHD), mild forms of oppositional and aggressive behaviours frequently are observed. Moreover, ODD or CD and ADHD often co-occur.

Aggressive children are likely to evince poor interpersonal relations as is reflected in high levels of peer rejection (Coie, Dodge, & Kupersmidt, 1990) and in coercive parent–child interactions (Reid, Patterson, & Snyder, 2002). Therefore, intervention strategies have been developed that focus on the child's social problem solving skills. Several outcome studies have shown that this method can effect change in aggressive children. Moreover, there is a growing body of basic research in these children's social problem-solving skills that supports the conceptualisation of this treatment method. In this chapter we will provide an overview of the deficiencies of aggressive (disruptive behaviour disordered) children's social problem solving skills and related cognitions and emotions. We also will review the interventions that are based on their characteristic social problem-solving skills.

Social Problem Solving and Offending: Evidence, Evaluation and Evolution.
Edited by Mary McMurran and James McGuire © 2005 John Wiley & Sons, Ltd.

PATHOGENESIS OF DISRUPTIVE BEHAVIOUR DISORDERS

In developmental psychopathology and child psychiatry, it is thought that disruptive behaviour disorders originate from the interaction of early childhood characteristics, such as impulsivity and irritability, with non-optimal characteristics of the child's environment, such as parental conflict and inadequate parenting skills. According to this biopsychosocial approach, the child's temperamental characteristics evoke coercive, inconsistent, and negative parenting behaviours that transform these characteristics into aggressive and antisocial behaviours. Coercive parent–child interactions not only sustain the child's aggressive and antisocial behaviours but also contribute to distortions in the child's social problem-solving skills and emotion-regulating capabilities. Thus, along with the negative, coercive parent–child interactions that occur in the preschool years (Kiesner, Dishion & Poulin, 2001; Snyder & Patterson, 1995), it is assumed that characteristic cognitions in the young child develop. For example, it has been demonstrated that early physical abuse, being an extreme form of negative parent–child interaction, over time in the child leads to the attribution of hostile intentions to others which is responsible for the child's later aggressive behaviour (Dodge, Lochman, & Colder, 1997).

SOCIAL INFORMATION PROCESSING MODEL

In problem-solving theories (D'Zurilla, 1986; Goldfried & D'Zurilla, 1969), it is assumed that persons in everyday situations are faced again and again with problems, and that they are motivated to solve these problems. For this purpose they have at their disposal a series of cognitive skills such as defining the problem, generating possible solutions, and deciding which solution will be implemented. Social information processing models describe in detail how these cognitive skills can be applied to social problems.

In 1986, Dodge described a model according to which children, when faced with a situational cue, engage in four mental steps before enacting competent social behaviours:

1. encoding of situational cues;
2. representation and interpretation of these cues;
3. mental search for possible responses to the situation;
4. evaluation and selection of a response.

The first steps involve cognitive processing of the problem event, and the next steps involve cognitive processing about responses. Skilful processing at each step will lead to competent performance within the situation, whereas deficient or biased processing will lead to deviant behaviour. This model has formed the basis for empirical studies of aggressive children, which we will now review. Only in a few studies did the children involved meet the criteria of one or more psychiatric disorders (e.g. ODD and/or ADHD); in most of the studies children were defined in terms of scores on rating scales of aggressive behaviour.

SOCIAL PROBLEM-SOLVING SKILLS IN AGGRESSIVE CHILDREN

In the encoding of information, aggressive children have been found to recall fewer relevant cues about events (Lochman & Dodge, 1994) and to base interpretations of events on fewer cues (Dodge & Newman, 1981; Dodge, Petit, McClaskey, & Brown, 1986). The latter not only has been found in boys with ODD or CD, but also in boys with ADHD and in boys with both ADHD and ODD or CD (Matthys, Cuperus, & van Engeland, 1999). Thus, a deficit in the encoding of the number of cues appears not to be specific for aggressive children with Disruptive Behaviour Disorders, but also occurs in children with ADHD. Aggressive children have been found to selectively attend to hostile rather than neutral cues (Gouze, 1987; Milich & Dodge, 1984), and to recall the most recent cues in a sequence, with selective inattention to earlier presented cues (Milich & Dodge, 1984). McKinnon, Lamb, Belsky, and Baum (1990) have suggested that these biases at the encoding phase, which involves selective attention to particular cues in the environment, are a direct result of prior social interactions and in fact are a logical outcome of the aggressive child's early relationships which are affectively toned. Accordingly, the child learns to pay attention to interaction patterns and social cues that are similar to cues previously experienced; if a child has experienced primarily negative or aggressive interactions with the parent, he/she will more likely attend to, and process, aggressively toned cues.

At the interpretation stage, aggressive children have been shown to have a hostile attributional bias, as they tend excessively to infer that others are acting towards them in a provocative and hostile manner (e.g. Feldman & Dodge, 1987; Guerra & Slaby, 1989; Lochman & Dodge, 1994; Sancilio, Plumert, & Hartup, 1989; Waas, 1988; for a meta-analysis, see Orobio de Castro, Veerman, Koops, Bosch, & Monshouwer, 2002). Moreover, aggressive boys have been shown to have underperceptions of their own aggressive behaviour, as well as distorted overperceptions of others' aggression (Lochman & Dodge, 1998). As a result, aggressive boys develop attributions that their peers have relative responsibility for conflict rather than assuming responsibility themselves.

The third information processing stage involves a generative process whereby potential solutions for coping with a perceived problem are recalled from memory. At this stage, aggressive children demonstrate deficiencies in both the quantity and the quality of their problem-solving solutions. Aggressive boys have been found to generate fewer responses than popular boys (Richard & Dodge, 1982) or non-aggressive boys (Lochman & Dodge, 1994). Matthys et al. (1999) found that, when compared with normal controls, not only boys with an ODD or CD but also boys with ADHD and boys with both ADHD and ODD or CD generated fewer responses. Thus, a deficit in generating possible responses appears not to be specific for aggressive children or children with a Disruptive

Behaviour Disorder but does also occur in children with ADHD. As to the quality of the responses generated, aggressive children have been shown to offer fewer verbal assertion solutions (Asarnow & Callan, 1985; Joffe, Dobson, Fine, Marriage, & Haley, 1990; Lochman & Lampron, 1986), fewer compromise solutions (Lochman & Dodge, 1994), more direct action solutions (Lochman & Lamprom, 1986), a greater number of help-seeking or adult intervention responses (Asher & Renshaw, 1981; Dodge, Murphy, & Buschbaum, 1984; Lochman, Lampron, & Rabiner, 1989; Rabiner, Lenhart, & Lochman, 1990), and more physically aggressive responses (Pepler, Craig, & Roberts, 1998; Slaby & Guerra, 1988; Waas, 1988; Waas & French, 1989) to hypothetical vignettes describing interpersonal conflicts. Finally, it has been shown that boys with CD produce more aggressive/antisocial solutions in vignettes about conflicts with parents and teachers, and fewer verbal/nonaggressive solutions in peer conflicts, in comparison to boys with ODD (Dunn, Lochman, & Colder, 1997).

The fourth processing step involves evaluation of the previously accessed responses and selection of the most positively evaluated response for enactment. A number of factors are involved in children's evaluations of responses, including the moral ("good" versus "bad") acceptability of a response and the degree of confidence children have in their ability to enact each response (self-efficacy). Aggressive children judge aggression to be less morally "bad" than do other children (Deluty, 1983); by contrast, aggressive children evaluate aggressive behaviour as more positive (Crick & Werner, 1998). Aggressive children also are more confident in their ability to aggress than are non-aggressive children, i.e. they are more likely than others to expect that engaging in aggression will come easily for them (Perry, Perry, & Rasmussen, 1986). Similarly, boys with ODD or CD and boys with both ODD or CD and ADHD, but not boys with ADHD only, have been found to be more confident in their ability to enact an aggressive response when compared with normal controls (Matthys et al., 1999). Children's beliefs about the utility of aggression and about their ability to successfully enact an aggressive response can operate to increase the likelihood of aggression being displayed, as children who hold these beliefs will be more likely to also believe that this type of behaviour will help them to achieve the desired goals which then influences response evaluation (Lochman & Dodge, 1994; Perry, Perry, & Rasmussen, 1986). Recent research has found that these beliefs about the acceptability of aggressive behaviour lead to deviant processing of social cues, which in turn then lead to children's aggressive behaviour (Zelli, Dodge, Lochman, Laird, & The Conduct Problems Prevention Research Group, 1999), indicating that these information processing steps have recursive effects, rather than strictly linear effects on each other.

The final step, response selection, has received little attention in research. Matthys et al. (1999) found that when boys were given the opportunity to select a response among various responses shown, boys with ODD or CD and boys with both ODD or CD and ADHD, but not boys with ADHD only, when compared with normal controls, more often selected an aggressive response and less often selected a prosocial response.

Although in the past two decades research has shown that there are deficiencies in aggressive children's social problem-solving skills, many issues need to be addressed in order to obtain a more specific and deeper insight. We now go on to discuss these issues.

FURTHER DIFFERENTIATION OF AGGRESSIVE CHILDREN INTO SUB-TYPES

It is generally acknowledged that aggressive children and children with dis-ruptive behaviour disorders form a heterogeneous group. The above-mentioned studies in aggressive children defined in terms of psychiatric diagnoses support the usefulness of sub-classifying these children: such studies generate informa-tion on the specificity of the social problem-solving deviances in the various sub-groups. Indeed, next to children with ODD and children with CD, children with ADHD also show deviances in social problem-solving skills (Matthys et al., 1999). However, in children with ADHD, social problem solving was affected only in encoding and in the generation of responses, whereas in children with ODD or CD, with or without ADHD, social problem solving was also affected in evaluation of responses and in selection of the response for enactment (Matthys et al., 1999). In addition, children with the more severe of two Disruptive Behaviour Disorders, i.e. CD, show more deviances in response generation than children with ODD (Dunn, Lochman, & Colder, 1997).

Other ways of subtyping aggressive children have been successful in the further specification of deviant social problem-solving skills. For example, Dodge and Coie (1987) differentiated proactive aggressive children, who engage in aggressive behaviour in a relatively planful, unemotional way, from reactive aggressive children, who become impulsively aggressive when they are anger-aroused, following perceived provocations. Reactive aggression has been found to be specifically correlated with problems in the first steps of social problem solving, whereas proactive aggression has been found to be related to the last steps of social problem solving. Specifically, reactive aggressive children have been shown to be overly sensitive to hostile cues and to have higher rates of hostile attributional biases, whereas proactive aggressive children have been shown to have higher expectations that aggressive behaviour will work for them (Crick & Dodge, 1996).

Another perspective of subtyping aggressive children is defining them in the presence or absence of callous/unemotional traits (Pardini, Lochman, & Frick, 2003). It has been demonstrated that children with these traits show various deficiencies in response evaluation. Indeed, these traits were positively related with the outcome expectation and the outcome values of tangible rewards and dominance, and negatively related to expectations that aggression would result in punishment (Pardini, Lochman, & Frick, 2003).

THE SPECIFICITY OF THE SOCIAL PROBLEM

In both theory and research, the general issue of the extent to which children's problem behaviour is generalised across situations and to what it is situation-specific has been neglected. This issue has also received little attention in research on children's social problem solving, yet it has been suggested that children's appropriate and inappropriate social behaviours can be considered to be responses to specific situations (Goldfried & D'Zurilla, 1969; Mischel, 1968). According to such a behavioural-analytic approach, it is necessary to identify the specific situations that are critical for particular populations, e.g. primary school children.

Dodge, McClaskey, & Feldman (1985) developed the Taxonomy of Problematic Social Situations (TOPS) for primary school children. This questionnaire for teachers lists problem situations that can possibly lead to peer conflicts. In a replication study with a larger number of participants than in the original study, Matthys, Maassen, Cuperus, & van Engeland (2001) found four instead of six factors to underlie the TOPS scores. These were: (1) Being Disadvantaged; (2) Coping with Competition; (3) Social Expectations of Peers; and (4) Teacher Expectations. Because of the high internal consistency of the four factor scores in the first sample of this study, TOPS was abbreviated to a TOPS-Short Form. The four-factor model was cross-validated by means of a second sample. A model with only one general problem behaviour factor did not fit the data of both samples. When the four specific factors were added, a satisfactory fit resulted. Moreover, it was found that in the first sample 52% of the variance is explained by the general factor, whereas 18% is explained by the four specific factors together. Thus, the extent to which problem behaviour is situation-specific should not be disregarded.

Matthys et al. (1999) included the specificity of problem situations in their study on social problem-solving in boys with ODD or CD, in boys with ADHD, and in boys with both disorders. In this study, with social problem-solving measures as dependent variables and problem domains (Being Disadvantaged, Coping with Competition, Social Expectations of Peers) and psychiatric diagnosis as independent variables, an interaction effect between diagnosis and problem domains was shown. The data of this study thus support the situation-specificity of social problem solving.

PROBLEM RECOGNITION

Problem recognition has received little attention in the research on aggressive children's social problem solving. Nevertheless, the whole process of reflective social problem solving starts with the recognition that there is a problem. Problem recognition needs to be distinguished from problem identification. Problem recognition precedes problem identification and consists of becoming aware whether there is a problem, whereas problem identification consists of defining the problem. Problem recognition seems difficult to investigate. In fact, a direct question that examines whether the child recognises the situation as problematic is inadequate, the issue being whether the child spontaneously perceives the situation as problematic. In their study, Matthys et al. (1999) used a more indirect way by asking whether the child would be upset if the situation occurred, but did not find differences between Disruptive Behaviour

Disordered boys and normal controls. As these disordered children do show more problems in the various situations than normal controls (Matthys et al., 2001), one might expect that they would feel more upset in these situations, which was not the case. It might be that these children tend to deny the existence of problems. Sensitivity to problems, however, is an important prerequisite for effective problem solving (D'Zurilla, 1986): it sets in motion reflective problem-solving activity. In other words, without problem recognition there can be no reflective problem solving.

Biological research on children with Disruptive Behaviour Disorders has shown low autonomic nervous system (ANS) activity (low heart rate and low skin conductance level) and a decreased functioning of the hypothalamic-pituitary-adrenal (HPA) axis (low cortisol levels when exposed to frustration and provocation) (van Goozen, Matthys, Cohen-Kettersis, Gisper-de Wied, Weigont, & van Engeland, 1998; van Goozen, Matthys, Cohen-Kettenis, Buitelaar, & van Engeland, 2000; Snoek, van Goozen, Matthys, Buitelaar, & van Engeland, 2004; Williams, Lochman, Phillips, & Barry, 2003). These findings are consistent with the hypothesis of a lack of fear in individuals with antisocial behaviour (Raine, 1997). One can speculate that fearlessness is related to a low sensitivity to problems, which, as mentioned above, is a prerequisite for effective problem solving. It might be that in children with Disruptive Behaviour Disorders reflective problem-solving activity is less often set in motion because of their fearlessness.

RELATED COGNITIONS

Person perception, perspective-taking, and empathy are part of the encoding and representation steps of social problem solving. Person perception is the active process of selecting, interpreting, and arranging information about others (Schneider, Hastorf, & Ellsworth, 1979). Just as younger boys when compared with older ones, boys with a Disruptive Behaviour Disorder when compared with normal controls have been found to perceive their peers more from an egocentric point of view and to pay less attention to their peers' inner, personal worlds (Matthys et al., 1995). Instead, they have been found to attend more to the peers' external qualities, specifically to the peers' activities with others (ibid.). Also, aggressive children and children with externalising symptomatology have been found to have immature abilities in perspective-taking (Chandler, 1973; Chandler et al., 1974; Cohen et al., 1985; Neale, 1966) and in empathy (Miller & Eisenberg, 1988). Person perception, perspective-taking, and empathy are related to each other. Indeed, in order to identify accurately the thoughts, emotions, and intentions of their peers through perspective-taking, children need to attend to their peers' thoughts, emotions, and intentions, which is one aspect of person perception. Also, a precondition of empathy is to attend to the peers' emotions. Boys with a Disruptive Behaviour Disorder, just as younger boys, seem to be more action-oriented and less likely to pay attention to the inner features of their peers. As a consequence, it might be that they are less inclined to make inferences about their peers' thoughts, emotions, and intentions (i.e. perspective-taking), and are less inclined to share in another's emotional state (i.e. empathy).

Moreover, impairments in empathic responses to sadness and anger (but not to happiness) have been shown in boys with a Disruptive Behaviour Disorder (De Wied, Goudena, & Matthys, in press). In addition, in adolescents with CD deficits in empathy have been demonstrated (Cohen & Strayer, 1996).

ANGER

Emotions are part and parcel of social problem solving. Of the various emotions, anger is specifically relevant for aggressive behaviour. Although angry behaviour is characteristic for many children with aggressive behaviour, especially those with reactive aggression, it is unclear whether these children experience more anger than other children. In their study of social information processing in aggressive and depressed children, Quiggle, Garber, Panak, and Dodge (1992) included affect (anger, sadness, happiness): depressed children reported more anger than controls, but aggressive children did not. It might be that some aggressive children have difficulty in experiencing anger. One can speculate that low stress reactivity in these children, as shown by a low increase in cortisol (van Goozen et al., 1998; Snoek et al., in press), is related to their difficulty in experiencing anger. When negative cues from the environment do not lead to an increase in physiological arousal and muscle tension, these children do not become aware of their anger. On the other hand, in emotionally sensitive aggressive children, emotional activation may produce impairments in their information processing and in their anger control. Increases in aggressive children's heart rates following a perceived threat, which can be considered to be a physiological marker of emotional activation, have been found to significantly correlate with these children's increases in hostile attributions (Williams et al., 2003). Thus, some aggressive children may have problems in becoming aware of their anger, whereas others may have problems in controlling their rising anger. As to anger control, Orobrio de Castro, Bosch, Veerman, and Koops (2003) have shown that monitoring and regulation of own emotions reduced aggressiveness in aggressive boys.

SCHEMAS

Recent revisions of social-cognitive models have more explicitly stressed the role that children's cognitive schemas have on their information processing (Crick & Dodge, 1994, Lochman, Whidby, & FitzGerald, 2000). Schemas account for how organisms actively construct their perceptions and experiences, rather than merely being passive receivers and processors of social information. Schemas have been defined in somewhat different ways by various theoreticians and researchers, but they are commonly regarded as consistent, core beliefs, and patterns of thinking. The strength of a given schema can often be gauged by the degree of emotional activation that occurs when that schema is accessed. Schemas have been proposed to have a significant impact on the information processing steps for aggressive children (Lochman, et al., 2000).

Schemas can play a significant role in the solution-generation stage of information processing, as the child anticipates consequences for different problem solutions available to him or her, and as the child decides which strategy will be enacted. Social goals and outcome expectations are schemas, which, from a Social Learning Theory view (Rotter, Chance, & Phares, 1972), combine to produce children's potential for behaving in specific ways. When the child places a higher value on certain goals or reinforcements, the child then will engage in behaviors that he or she expects will have a high probability of meeting his or her goal. Aggressive adolescent boys have been found to place higher value on social goals for dominance and revenge, and lower value on social goals for affiliation, than do nonaggressive boys (Lochman, Wayland, & White, 1993). In this study, there was a clear relation between social goal choice and problem solving, indicating a direct effect of cognitive schemas on information processing. Aggressive boys proposed using fewer bargaining solutions and more aggressive solutions, in comparison to nonaggressive boys, but this problem-solving difference was only evident when the boys' main social goals were taken into account. Thus, children's schemas about social goals and outcome expectations can affect their response decisions in the fourth stage of information processing.

Schemas can also have effects on information processing through the influence of schemas on children's expectations for their own behaviour and for other's behaviour in specific situations, through the associated affect and arousal when schemas are activated, and through the influence of schemas on the style and speed of processing. Schemas about attributes of self and of others, such as aggressiveness or dominance, produce expectations about the anticipated presence or absence of these attributes as individuals prepare to interact with people in specific situations. Research by Lochman and Dodge (1998) has indicated that aggressive boys' perceptions of their own aggressive behaviour was primarily affected by their prior expectations, while nonaggressive boys relied more on their actual behaviour to form their perceptions. These results indicate that the schemas of aggressive boys about their aggressive behaviour are strong and compelling, leading the aggressive boys to display cognitive rigidity between their expectations and perceptions. The aggressive boys' perceptions of their behaviour, driven by their schemas, were relatively impermeable to actual behaviour, and instead were heavily governed by the boys' preconceptions.

AUTOMATIC VERSUS DELIBERATE PROCESSING

Because of their impulsive style and anger activation, aggressive children rely excessively on information processing that is automatic rather than deliberate, and this further contributes to their problem-solving difficulties. Lochman, Lampron, and Rabiner (1989) found that children responding to a hypothetical vignette measure of social problem solving in the usual open-middle format, which simulates automatic retrieval processes, had different patterns of responses than did children responding to these stories with a multiple-choice format. The multiple-choice format simulated more deliberate, comparative retrieval processes, similar to the cognitive process of carefully sifting through stored solutions in "memory bins". In the open-middle condition, aggressive children produced significantly more direct action solutions and fewer verbal assertion solutions than did nonaggressive children. However, in the deliberate processing, multiple-choice condition, both aggressive and nonaggressive boys had higher rates of competent verbal assertion solutions and lower rates of direct action solutions than they did in the automatic processing, open-middle condition. Thus, when aggressive children responded automatically, they quickly selected the most salient idea which was at the top of the memory bin. When the aggressive children processed information more deliberately, they were able to select more competent solutions from among the ideas that they had previously stored away in memory. The implication for intervention is that aggressive children, through frequent practice and activation of these more competent ideas, may be able to move their more competent ideas to the top of their memory bins, and therefore be more likely to retrieve them automatically during future social interactions. In a subsequent study, Rabiner, Lenhart, and Lochman (1990) replicated these findings while using a more direct paradigm in which automatic retrieval processes were guided by requiring children to respond to hypothetical vignette stories immediately. In contrast, deliberate processing was guided by requiring children to wait 20 seconds after hearing the problem vignette before responding.

COGNITIVE BEHAVIOURAL THERAPY

Cognitive behavioural methods have been developed that target aggressive children's characteristic social problem-solving skills and related cognitions and emotions. Children learn and practise, either in small groups or individually, to identify and adequately solve social problems, and to identify and control feelings of anger.

In the *Problem Solving Skills Training* developed by Kazdin and colleagues (1989) school-aged children individually learn five problem-solving steps and their application in everyday situations. The steps serve as verbal prompts the children deliver to themselves to engage in thoughts and actions that guide behaviour. Role playing is used extensively to give the children the opportunity to enact what they would do in a situation. Critical to treatment is use of the skills outside of treatment. The parents are trained to help the child practise assignments at home. Problem Solving Skills Training has been found to reduce disruptive behaviours and increase prosocial behaviours at both home and school in comparison to non-directive therapy (ibid.). The combination of Problem Solving Skills Training with a parent management training was found to lead to more marked, pervasive, and durable changes than either constituent treatment alone (Kazdin, Siegel, & Bass, 1992).

Dinosaur School is a social skills and problem-solving training intervention for children aged 4 to 7 years that has been shown to lead to a reduction in the amount of conduct problems in comparison to controls (Webster-Stratton &

Hammond, 1997). This videotape-assisted modelling programme includes friendship skills, communication skills, problem-solving training, anger control, and empathy training. As in the case of Problem Solving Skills Training, the combination with a parent management training proved superior to each of the components (ibid.).

The *Anger Coping Program* has been used with children in the 4th to 6th grades in school settings for prevention and early intervention purposes (Lochman, Lampron, Gemmer, & Harris, 1987). Anger management training is addressed by assisting children in recognising the level of arousal and anger they experience in difficult interpersonal situations, the triggers that lead to these high arousal reactions, and then in assisting children to use several coping techniques to manage the arousal and to avoid an impulsive rage-filled response. The coping techniques that children are introduced to include distraction, relaxation, and self-talk. The largest section of the Anger Coping Program focuses on social problem solving, which also includes integrating in work from other sections of the programme on anger management and perspective-taking. Children practise brainstorming multiple possible solutions to social problems, and then evaluate the long-term and short-term consequences of each solution. The effectiveness of this programme has been demonstrated in various studies. For example, it has been found that aggressive boys who receive the Anger Coping Program displayed less parent-reported aggressive behaviour, fewer problems associated with disruptive and aggressive behaviour in the classroom, and higher levels of self-esteem at post-treatment in comparison to children assigned to minimal treatment and no treatment conditions (Lochman, Burch, Curry, & Lampron, 1984), and some of these gains have been found to persist to a follow-up assessment three years later (Lochman, 1992).

In order to enhance outcome effects and to provide for better maintenance of gains over time, a parent management training has been added to the Anger Coping Program, leading to the *Coping Power Program* (Lochman & Wells, 1996). The effectiveness of the Coping Power Program has been demonstrated in a set of studies (Lochman & Wells, 2002a, 2002b, 2003, in press) which have found that aggressive children receiving the Coping Power intervention have lower rates of delinquency, substance use, and school behaviour problems one year after the intervention. The Coping Power intervention has also been effectively disseminated to new settings and populations, such as aggressive deaf children in residential settings (Lochman, FitzGerald, Gage, Kanaly, Whidby, Barry, Pardini, & McElroy, 2001). Perhaps most importantly, intervention effects have been found to be mediated by changes in children's social-cognitive processes and parental disciplinary practices (Lochman & Wells, 2002a), thus supporting the validity of the social-cognitive model. Finally, the Coping Power Program has been adapted for use in the treatment of children with Disruptive Behaviour Disorders with or without ADHD in everyday clinical practice, i.e. the Utrecht Coping Power Program. It has been shown that this programme was effective in decreasing inappropriate behaviours whereas the costs to obtain the same improvement as in usual care were 42% lower (van de Wiel, Matthys, Cohen-Kettenis, & van Engeland, 2003).

CONCLUSION

Research in the past few decades has convincingly shown that aggressive children have systematic deficiencies in their social problem-solving skills. These deficits include under-generation of verbal assertion solutions, excessive generation of action-oriented and aggressive solutions, expectations that aggressive solutions will work in resolving interpersonal problems, and beliefs that aggressive solutions are acceptable strategies. This chapter has explored recent research on the nature of these social problem-solving deficits, and of factors that influence them. These research efforts have clarified: (1) the types of social problems that children attempt to resolve; (2) children's abilities to recognise whether situations were problematic; (3) aggressive children's impaired empathic reactions to others' sadness and anger; (4) children's awareness and control of their anger; (5) how children's schemas can influence their perceptions of themselves and of others in conflict situations; and (6) how children's problem-solving deficiencies can be most apparent during automatic information processing. These refinements in our understanding of the nature of aggressive children's social problem-solving deficiencies can lead to new extensions of cognitive behavioural therapies with aggressive children. Intervention research has shown that the current generation of cognitive behavioural therapies designed to address aggressive children's social problem-solving deficiencies have been effective in reducing their conduct problem behaviours.

REFERENCES

American Psychiatric Association (1994). *The diagnostic and statistical manual of mental disorders*. 4th edn. Washington, DC: American Psychiatric Association.

Asarnow, J. R. & Callan, J. W. (1985). Boys with peer adjustment problems: Social cognitive processes. *Journal of Consulting and Clinical Psychology, 53*, 80–87.

Asher, S. R. & Renshaw, P. D. (1981). Children without friends: Social knowledge and social skills training. In S. R. Asher & J. M. Gottman (eds) *The development of children's friendships* (pp. 273–296). New York: Cambridge University Press.

Chandler, M. (1973). Egocentrism and antisocial behaviour: The assessment and training of social perspective-taking skills. *Developmental Psychology, 9*, 326–332.

Chandler, M., Greenspan, S., & Barenboim, C. (1974). Assessment and training of role-taking and referential communication skills in institutionalized emotionally disturbed children. *Developmental Psychology, 10*, 546–553.

Cohen, N., Kershner, J., & Wehrspann, W. (1985). Characteristics of social cognition in children with different symptom patterns. *Journal of Applied Developmental Psychology, 6*, 277–290.

Cohen, D. & Strayer, J. (1996). Empathy in conduct-disordered and comparison youth. *Developmental Psychology, 32*, 988–998.

Coie, J. D., Dodge, K. A., & Kupersmidt, J. B. (1990). Peer group behavior and social status. In S. R. Asher and J. D. Coie (eds) *Peer rejection in childhood* (pp. 17–59). Cambridge: Cambridge University Press.

Crick, N. R. & Dodge, K. A. (1994). A review and reformulation of social-information processing mechanisms in children's social adjustment. *Psychological Bulletin, 115*, 74–101.

Crick, N. R. & Dodge, K. A. (1996). Social information-processing mechanisms in reactive and proactive aggression. *Child Development, 67,* 993–1002.

Crick, N. R. & Werner, N. E. (1998). Response decision processes in relational and overt aggression. *Child Development, 69,* 1630–1639.

Deluty, R. H. (1983). Children's evaluation of aggressive, assertive, and submissive responses. *Journal of Consulting and Clinical Psychology, 51,* 124–129.

De Wied, M., Goudena, P., & Matthys, W. (in press). Empathy in boys with disruptive behaviour disorders. *Journal of Child Psychology and Psychiatry.*

Dodge, K. A. (1986). A social information processing model of social competence in children. In M. Perlmutter (ed.), *Minnesota Symposium on Child Psychology* (pp. 77–125) Hillsdale, NJ: Erlbaum.

Dodge, K. A., Bates, J. E., Pettit, G. S., & Valente, E. (1997). Social information-processing patterns partially mediate the effect of early physical abuse on later conduct problems. *Journal of Abnormal Child Psychology, 104,* 632–643.

Dodge, K. A. & Coie, J. D. (1987). Social information processing factors in reactive and proactive aggression in children's peer groups. *Journal of Personality and Social Psychology, 53,* 1146–1158.

Dodge, K. A., McClaskey, C., & Feldman, E. (1985). Situational approach to the assessment of social competence in children. *Journal of Consulting and Clinical Psychology, 53,* 344–353.

Dodge, K. A., Murphy, R. R., & Buchsbaum, K. (1984). The assessment of intention-cue detection skills in children: Implications for developmental psychopathology. *Child Development, 55,* 163–173.

Dodge, K. A. & Newman, J. P. (1981). Biased decision making processes in aggressive boys. *Journal of Abnormal Psychology, 90,* 375–390.

Dodge, K. A., Petit, G. S., McClaskey, C. L., & Brown, M. M. (1986). *Social competence in children.* Monographs of the Society for Research in Child Development, 51.

Dunn, S. E., Lochman, J. E., & Colder, C. R. (1997). Social problem-solving skills in boys with Conduct and Oppositional Defiant Disorders. *Aggressive Behavior, 23,* 457–469.

D'Zurilla, T. J. (1986). *Problem-solving therapy: A social competence approach to clinical intervention.* New York: Springer.

Feindler, E. A., Ecton, R. B., Kingsley, D., & Dubey, D. R. (1986). Group anger-control training for institutionalized psychiatric male adults. *Behavior Therapy, 17,* 109–123.

Feindler, E. A., Marriott, S. A., & Iwata, M. (1984). Group anger control training for junior high school delinquents. *Cognitive Therapy and Research, 8,* 299–311.

Feldman, E. & Dodge, K. A. (1987). Social information processing and sociometric status: Sex, age, and situational effects. *Journal of Abnormal Child Psychology, 15,* 211–227.

Goldfried, M. R. & D'Zurilla, T. J. (1969). A behavioral-analytic model for assessing competence. In C. Speilberger (ed.) *Current topics in clinical and community psychology,* Vol. 1 (pp. 151–169). New York: Academic Press.

Gouze, K. R. (1987). Attention and Social problem solving as correlates of aggression in preschool males. *Journal of Abnormal Child Psychology, 15,* 181–197.

Guerra, N. G. & Slaby, R. G. (1989). Evaluative factors in social problem solving by aggressive boys. *Journal of Abnormal Child Psychology, 17,* 277–289.

Joffe, R. D., Dobson, K. S., Fine, S., Marriage, K., & Haley, G. (1990). Social problem-solving in depressed, conduct-disordered, and normal adolescents. *Journal of Abnormal Child Psychology, 18,* 565–575.

Kazdin, A. E., Bass, D., Siegel, T. et al. (1989) Cognitive-behavioral therapy and relationship therapy in the treatment of children referred for antisocial behavior. *Journal of Consulting and Clinical Psychology, 57,* 522–535.

Kazdin, A. E., Siegel, T. C., & Bass, D. (1992). Cognitive problem-solving skills training and parent-management training in the treatment of antisocial behavior in children. *Journal of Consultancy and Clinical Psychology*, 60, 733–747.

Kiesner, J., Dishion, T. J., & Poulin, F. (2001). A reinforcement model of conduct problems in children and adolescents: Advances in theory and intervention. In J. Hill & B. Maugham (eds) *Conduct disorders in childhood and adolescence*. (pp. 264–291). Cambridge: Cambridge University Press.

Lochman, J. E. (1992). Cognitive-behavioral intervention with aggressive boys: Three-year follow-up and preventive effects. *Journal of Consulting and Clinical Psychology*, 60, 426–432.

Lochman, J. E. & Dodge, K. A. (1994). Social cognitive processes of severely violent, moderately aggressive, and nonaggressive boys. *Journal of Consulting and Clinical Psychology*, 62, 366–374.

Lochman, J. E. & Dodge, K. A. (1998). Distorted perceptions in dyadic interactions of aggressive and nonaggressive boys: Effects of prior expectations, context, and boys' age. *Development and Psychopathology*, 10, 495–512.

Lochman, J. E., FitzGerald, D. P., Gage, S. M., Kannaly, M. K., Whidby, J. M., Barry, T. D., Pardini, D. A., & McElroy, H. (2001). Effects of social-cognitive intervention for aggressive deaf children: The Coping Power Program. *Journal of the American Deafness and Rehabilitation Association*, 35, 39–61.

Lochman, J. E. & Lampron, L. B. (1986). Situational social problem solving skills and self-esteem of aggressive and non-aggressive boys. *Journal of Abnormal Child Psychology*, 14, 605–617.

Lochman, J. E., Lampron, L. B., Burch, P. R., & Curry, J. E. (1985). Client characteristics associated with behavior change for treated and untreated boys. *Journal of Abnormal Child Psychology*, 13, 527–538.

Lochman, J. E., Lampron, L. B., & Rabiner, D. L. (1989). Format and salience effects in the social problem-solving of aggressive and nonaggressive boys. *Journal of Clinical Child Psychology*, 18, 230–236.

Lochman, J. E., Wayland, K. K., & White, K. J. (1993). Social goals: Relationship to adolescent adjustment and to social problem solving. *Journal of Abnormal Child Psychology*, 21, 135–151.

Lochman, J. E. & Wells, K. C. (1996). A social-cognitive intervention with aggressive children: Prevention effects and contextual implementation issues. In R. D. Peters & R. J. McMahon (eds) *Prevention and early intervention: Childhood disorders, substance use and delinquency* (pp. 111–143). Thousand Oaks, CA: Sage.

Lochman, J. E. & Wells, K. C. (2002a). Contextual social-cognitive mediators and child outcome: A test of the theoretical model in the Coping Power Program. *Development and Psychopathology*, 14, 971–993.

Lochman, J. E. & Wells, K. C. (2002b). The Coping Power Program at the middle school transition: Universal and indicated prevention effects. *Psychology of Addictive Behaviors*, 16, S40–S54.

Lochman, J. E. & Wells, K. C. (2003). Effectiveness study of Coping Power and classroom intervention with aggressive children: Outcomes at a one-year follow-up. *Behavior Therapy*, 34, 493–515.

Lochman, J. E. & Wells, K. C. (in press). The Coping Power program for preadolescent aggressive boys and their parents: Outcome effects at the one-year follow-up. *Journal of Consulting and Clinical Psychology*.

Lochman, J. E., Whidby, J. M., & FitzGerald, D. P. (2000). Cognitive-behavioral assessment and treatment. In P. C. Kendall (ed.) *Child and adolescent therapy*. 2nd edn. (pp. 31–87). New York: Guilford Press.

Mackinnon, C. E., Lamb, M. E., Belsky, J., & Baum, C. (1990). An affective-cognitive model of mother–child aggression. *Development and Psychopathology, 2*, 1–13.

Matthys, W., Cuperus, J., & van Engeland, H. (1999). Deficient social problem-solving in boys with ODD/CD, with ADHD, and with both disorders. *Journal of the American Academy of Child and Adolescent Psychiatry, 38*, 311–321.

Matthys, W., Maassen, G. H., Cuperus, J. M., & van Engeland, H. (2001). The assessment of the situational specificity of children's problem behaviour in peer–peer context. *Journal of Child Psychology and Psychiatry, 42*, 413–420.

Matthys, W., Walterbos, W., van Engeland, H., & Koops, W. (1995). Conduct disordered boys' perceptions of their liked peers. *Cognitive Therapy and Research, 19*, 357–372.

Milich, R. & Dodge, K. A. (1984). Social information processing in child psychiatric populations. *Journal of Abnormal Child Psychology, 12*, 471–490.

Miller, P. A. & Esenberg, N. (1988). The relation of empathy to aggressive and externalizing/antisocial behavior. *Psychological Bulletin, 103*, 324–344.

Mischel, W. (1968). *Personality and assessment*. New York: Wiley.

Neale, J. (1966). Egocentrism in institutionalized and non-institutionalized children. *Child Development, 37*, 97–101.

Orobio de Castro, B., Bosch, J. D, Veerman, J. W., & Koops, W. (2003). The effects of emotion regulation, attribution, and delay prompts on aggressive boys' social problem solving. *Cognitive Therapy and Research, 27*, 153–166.

Orobio de Castro, B., Veerman, J. W., Koops, W., Bosch, J. D., & Monshouwer, H. J. (2002). Hostile attribution of intent and aggressive behavior: a meta-analysis. *Child Development, 73*, 916–934.

Pardini, D. A., Lochman, J. E., & Frick, P. J. (2003). Callous/unemotional traits and social-cognitive processes in adjudicated youths. *Journal of the American Academy of Child and Adolescent Psychiatry, 42*, 364–371.

Pepler, D. J., Craig, W. M., & Roberts, W. I. (1998). Observations of aggressive and nonaggressive children on the school playground. *Merrill Palmer Quarterly, 44*, 55–76.

Perry, D. G., Perry, L. C., & Rasmussen, P. (1986). Cognitive social learning mediators of aggression. *Child Development, 57*, 700–711.

Quiggle, N. L., Garber, J., Panak, W., & Dodge, K. A. (1992). Social information-processing in aggressive and depressed children. *Child Development, 63*, 1305–1320.

Rabiner, D. L., Lenhart, L., & Lochman, J. E. (1990). Automatic vs. reflective problem solving in relation to children's sociometric status. *Developmental Psychology, 71*, 535–543.

Raine, A. (1997). Antisocial behavior and psychophysiology: A biosocial perspective and a prefrontal dysfunction hypothesis. In D. Stoff, J. Breiling, & J. D. Maser (eds) *Handbook of antisocial behavior* (pp. 289–304). New York: Wiley.

Reid, J. B., Patterson, G. R., & Snyder, J. (2002). *Antisocial behavior in children and adolescents*. Washington, DC: American Psychological Association.

Richard, B. & Dodge, K. A. (1982). Social maladjustment and problem solving in school-aged children. *Journal of Consulting and Clinical Psychology, 50*, 226–233.

Rotter, J. B., Chance, J. E., & Phares, E. J. (1972). *Applications of a social learning theory of personality*. New York: Holt, Rinehart, and Winston.

Sancilio, M., Plumert, J. M., & Hartup, W. W. (1989). Friendship and aggressiveness as determinants of conflict outcomes in middle childhood. *Developmental Psychology, 25*, 812–819.

Schneider, D., Hastorf, A., & Ellsworth, P. (1979). *Person perception*. Reading, MA: Addison-Wesley.

Slaby, R. G. & Guerra, N. G. (1988). Cognitive mediators of aggression in adolescent offenders: An assessment. *Developmental Psychology, 24*, 580–588.

Snoek, H., van Goozen, S. H. M., Matthys, W., Buitelaar, J. K., & van Engeland, H. (2004). Stress responsivity in children with externalizing behavior disorders. *Development and Psychopathology, 16*, 389–406.

Snyder, J. J. & Patterson, G. R. (1995). Individual differences in social aggression: A test of a reinforcement model of socialization in the natural environment. *Behavior Therapy, 26*, 371–391.

van de Wiel, N. M. H., Matthys, W., Cohen-Kettenis, P., & van Engeland, H. (2003). Application of the Utrecht Coping Power Program and Care as Usual to children with disuptive behavior disorders in outpatient clinics: A comparative study of cost and course of treatment. *Behavior Therapy, 34*, 421–436.

van Goozen, S., Matthys, W., Cohen-Kettenis, P. T., Buitelaar, J. K., & van Engeland, H. (2000). Hypothylamic-pituitary-adrenal axis and antonomic nervous system activity in disruptive children and matched controls. *Journal of the American Academy of Child and Adolescent Psychiatry, 39*, 1438–1445.

van Goozen, S., Matthys, W., Cohen-Kettenis, P., Gispen-de Wied, C., Wiegant, V. & van Engeland, H. (1998). Salivary cortisol and cardiovascular activity during stress in oppositional-defiant disorder boys and normal controls. *Biological Psychiatry, 43*, 531–539.

Waas, G. A. (1988). Social attributional biases of peer-rejected and aggressive children. *Child Development, 59*, 969–975.

Waas, G. A. & French, D. C. (1989). Children's social problem solving: Comparison of the open middle interview and children's assertive behavior scale. *Behavioral Assessment, 11*, 219–230.

Webster-Stratton, C. & Hammond, M. (1997). Treating children with early onset conduct problems: A comparison of child and parent training interventions. *Journal of Consulting and Clinical Psychology, 65*, 93–109.

Williams, S. C., Lochman, J. E., Phillips, N. C., & Barry, T. D. (2003). Aggressive and non-aggressive boys' physiological and cognitive processes in response to peer provocations. *Journal of Clinical Child and Adolescent Psychology, 32*, 568–576.

Zelli, A., Dodge, K. A., Lochman, J. E., Laird, R. D., & The Conduct Problems Prevention Research Group (1999). The distinction between beliefs legitimizing aggression and deviant processing of social cues: Testing measurement validity and the hypothesis that biased processing mediates the effects of beliefs on aggression. *Journal of Personality and Social Psychology, 77*, 150–166.

Chapter 4

SOCIAL PROBLEM SOLVING, PERSONALITY DISORDER, AND SUBSTANCE ABUSE

LAURA E. DREER, WARREN T. JACKSON, and TIMOTHY R. ELLIOTT
University of Alabama at Birmingham, USA

INTRODUCTION

Empirical support for the interrelation between substance abuse, personality disorders, and criminal activity is well summarized in the literature (Brooner, Kidorf, King, & Stoller, 1998; Cottler, Compton, Ridenour, Abdallah, & Gallagher, 1998; Crowley, Mikulich, MacDonald, Young, & Zerbe, 1998; Friedman, 1998; Hernandez-Avila et al., 2000; Kaye, Darke, & Finlay-Jones, 1998; McMurran, Blair, & Egan, 2002; van den Bree, Svikis, & Pickens, 1998). Foremost, substance abuse and personality disorders are highly comorbid, particularly when Antisocial Personality Disorder (APD) is considered (Abram, 1989; Armstrong & Costello, 2002; Carey & Carey, 1990; Kessler et al., 1996; Longato-Stadler, von-Knorring, & Hallman, 2002; Lynam, Leukefeld, & Clayton, 2003; Messina, Wish, Hoffman, & Nemes, 2002; Woody, McLellan, Luborsky, & O'Brien, 1985). The estimated frequency of substance abuse co-occurring with personality disorders ranges from 57–91% across personality disorders (Nace, Davis, & Gaspari, 1991). Furthermore, research suggests that coexisting APD and substance abuse decreases success rates for many different forms of substance abuse treatment (Alterman, Rutherford, Cacciola, McKay, & Boardman, 1998; Goldstein et al., 1999; Rutherford, Alterman, & Cacciola, 2000). These findings are somewhat disheartening given that dual-diagnosis patients have been poorly conceptualized and underserved by traditional mental health (Carey & Carey, 1990).

Substance abuse and personality disorders are pervasive and developmentally comorbid. Numerous studies have found that these variables consistently co-occur during the transition from adolescence to young adulthood (Anderson, Mahoney, Wennberg, Kuehlhorn, & Magnusson, 1999; Crowley et al., 1998;

Social Problem Solving and Offending: Evidence, Evaluation and Evolution.
Edited by Mary McMurran and James McGuire © 2005 John Wiley & Sons, Ltd.

Kjelsberg, 1999; Marks, Stewart, & Brown, 1998; McCord, 1995; Myers, Stewart, & Brown, 1998; Stattin, & Romelsjoe, 1995). These relations have been identified in many countries including the United States, Finland, Hong Kong, Germany, Sweden, Denmark, and Britain (Byqvist, 1999; Hodgins, Mednick, Brennan, Schulsinger, & Engberg, 1996; Kerner, Weitekamp, & Thomas, 1997; Longato-Stadler et al., 2002; McMurran et al., 2002; McMurran, Egan, Blair, & Richardson, 2001; Pulkkinen, Virtanen, Klinteberg, & Magnusson, 2000; Sandell & Bertling, 1999; Sass, Erkwoh, & Rodon, 1998; Segest, Mygind, & Bay, 1989; Tiihonen, Isohanni, Raesaenen, Koiranen, & Moring, 1997; Timonen et al., 2002). Despite these data, our understanding regarding their relation and the overlap between variables remains poorly understood. This is particularly unfortunate given the clinical challenge in treating these problems as well as the financial costs, rehabilitation efforts, and negative consequences experienced by patients with dual diagnosis, by their families, and the greater community.

A major limitation in our understanding of these relationships pertains to disagreement regarding causal pathways among these variables. One hypothesis suggests that APD may lead to substance use and abuse. Support for this hypothesis has come from several longitudinal studies. For example, Kratzer and Hodgins (1997) found that 17.5% of boys with serious childhood conduct problems had been hospitalized for severe substance abuse by age 30 compared to only 1.6% of boys without conduct problems. Other studies have found that early conduct problems are related to early substance use and later abuse (Brook, Cohen, Whiteman, & Gordon, 1992; Dobkin, Trembley, Masse, & Vitaro, 1995; Ferguson & Lynskey, 1998). Evidence has also been found, however, for an alternative hypothesis: substance abuse leads to antisocial behavior (Allen, Leadbeater, & Aber, 1994; Mason & Windle, 2002). Antisocial behavior and substance abuse may be related because they share common antecedents or causes. In a recent study, Lynam et al. (2003) tested the ability of the Five Factor Model, a general model of personality structure, to account for the temporal stability of antisocial behavior and substance use/abuse and the correlation between the two variables at points in time. Results indicate that personality traits account for relatively large proportions of the variance in both factors, with R^2 ranging from 0.19 for early substance misuse to 0.30 for early antisocial behavior. Personality profiles were also highly similar with correlation coefficients ranging from 0.87 to 0.97.

These relationships are further confused by a lack of understanding of the variables that may be embedded within these relations. A number of models have been developed to explain these relationships and include, but are not limited to, biological, behavioral, cognitive, and social learning approaches. One social-cognitive variable in particular that has been implicated to underlie such relationships is social problem-solving skills. This approach to understanding the relations between substance abuse, personality disorders, and criminal behavior has come from social-cognitive models that stipulate that substance abuse, personality disorders, and criminal behaviors are likely to exist when an individual possesses inadequate coping skills or cognitive skill deficits (Bijttebier & Vertommen, 1999; Foglia, 2000; Marlatt, Baer, Donovan, & Kivlahan, 1988). Empirical support for these variables has consistently shown an association between each of the variables and dysfunctional interpersonal relationships. This is consistent with both cognitive social learning theory and cognitive behavioral therapy which emphasize the interaction between the individual and their environment in order to understand behavior. Thus, the hypothesis that social problem-solving skills might be implicated as an underlying factor is worthy of further examination.

Real-life problem-solving skills can be operationally defined as the ability to work towards a successful resolution of real-life situations. Successful problem solvers typically generate a higher proportion of relevant problem-solving responses and plan a strategy for achieving the stated goals (Platt, Scura, & Hannon, 1973). Platt and Husband (1993) assert that effective problem-solving skills are essential to successful functioning in everyday life. That is, most individuals inevitably encounter problems or situations that arise in the course of daily living, and adjustment is related to making appropriate responses and decisions. Social problem solving involves the cognitive-behavioral process in which an individual engages in identifying effective strategies of coping with real-life problematic situations (D'Zurilla & Nezu, 1982; Nezu & Ronan, 1988). In particular, D'Zurilla and Goldfried (1971) proposed that social problem-solving skills are an essential part of one's ability to cope effectively. They further identified five specific components involved in the problem-solving process: (1) problem orientation; (2) problem definition; (3) generation of alternative solutions; (4) decision-making; and (5) solution implementation and verification of the selected solution. Empirical support for deficits in social problem-solving skills have been associated with adjustment to stressful situations (Bonner & Rich, 1988), depression (Kant, D'Zurilla, & Maydeu-Olivares, 1997), obesity (Perri et al., 2001) substance abuse (Intagliata, 1978; Platt & Husband, 1993), cancer (Nezu, Nezu, Houts, Friedman, & Faddis, 1999), and behavioral health issues, generally (Elliott, Grant, & Miller, 2004).

Empirical support for the role of social problem-solving as a causal factor in the conceptual constellation of substance abuse, personality disorders, and criminality has been demonstrated between each of these variables independently and to a lesser extent among these relationships (McMurran et al., 2002; McMurran, Egan, et al., 2001). The reason why poor social problem-solving skills may influence these relationships is believed to be related to: (1) an inhibition of problem solving skills; (2) lack of skills; and/or (3) deficits in these skills. That is, individuals may have the ability to carry out effective problem-solving skills, but they do not apply such skills, and/or individuals may not have acquired adequate levels of particular skills to engage in effective problem solving. Absence of or deficits in effective problem-solving skills are associated with interpersonal difficulties and other mental health and behavioral problems. McGuire (2001) contends that individuals may demonstrate ineffective problem-solving strategies as a consequence of limited learning opportunities, constrained by parenting or other socialization influences.

Another reason why social problem solving is believed to influence these relationships pertains to the similar behaviors found in personality disorders (APD in particular), substance abuse (Gerstley, Alterman, McLellan, & Woody, 1990), and criminality. For example, personality disorders, substance abuse, and criminality all have been associated with impulsivity, irresponsibility, sensation seeking, escape/avoidance, and criminal behavior. As in APD, individuals with Borderline Personality Disorder (BPD) are often at risk for the development of substance abuse. Estimates of the prevalence of substance abuse among individuals with BPD reach as high as two-thirds (Drake & Wallach, 1989; Dulit, Fyer, & Haas, 1990). Substance abuse in the context of BPD may also lead to aggravated symptomatology, including more self-destructive behaviors and suicidal thoughts (Links, Heslegrave, Mitton, van Reekum, & Patrick, 1995).

In sum, the extant literature clearly documents a strong association between substance abuse, personality disorders, and criminal behavior; however, a full understanding of these "mega-variables" is obscured by their conceptual overlap and the existence of competing causal models. Social problem-solving has been identified as an important variable to study when dismantling the mega-variables and their interrelations. The remainder of the chapter reviews studies involving social problem solving and each of the mega-variables, summarizes methodological problems inherent in such studies, and outlines directions for future research.

SOCIAL PROBLEM SOLVING AND SUBSTANCE ABUSE

The influence of social problem-solving skills on substance use has been examined most extensively in clinical populations at high risk for substance abuse. One proposed hypothesis for understanding why poor problem solving might be related to substance abuse is that individuals with social problem-solving deficits may find themselves lacking the specific skills necessary to negotiate their way out of risky situations involving substances or they may be unable to identify high risk situations until it is too late (Platt & Husband, 1993). Another hypothesis is that these individuals may have deficiencies in these skill areas, leading to failures or unsatisfactory outcomes in interpersonal situations and tasks, thereby leading to negative moods or affective states that lead back to substance use (Marlatt & Gordon, 1980; Platt & Metzger, 1987). In fact, it has been found that substance abusers demonstrate deficits in these types of skills (Appel & Kaestner, 1979; Frank, 1993; Hermalin, Husband, & Platt, 1990; Intagliata, 1978; Laine & Butters, 1982; Patterson, Parsons, Schaeffer, & Errico, 1988; Platt et al., 1973) and that persons progressing well in recovery programs evidence more effective skills in problem-solving scenarios (Appel & Kaestner, 1979; Intagliata, 1978). Carey and Carey (1990) also demonstrated that dually-diagnosed patients and psychiatric controls in comparison to community controls engage in significantly poorer problem solving and give verbal solutions that are poorly elaborated and generally less effective. Furthermore, research supports an association between a tendency to avoid coping with life problems and greater alcohol use among young adults (Cooper, Russell, Skinner, & Frone, 1992; Fromme & Rivet, 1994), older problem drinkers (Moos, Brennan, Fondacaro, & Moos, 1990), and college students (Evans & Dunn, 1995). Links between self-appraised ineffective problem solving and retrospective accounts of substance abuse have been found among undergraduates (Dreer, Ronan, Ronan, Dush, & Elliott, 2004; Godshall & Elliott, 1997; Heppner, Hibel, Neal, Weinstein, & Rabinowitz, 1982; Williams & Kleinfelter, 1989) and among adult children of alcoholics (Wright & Heppner, 1991).

Other support for the notion that poor problem-solving skills are associated with substance abuse in social situations comes from the cognitive social-learning literature on alcohol abuse which suggests that a failure to generate appropriate alternative behaviors to drinking may serve as a salient predictor of relapse to drinking (Williams & Kleinfelter, 1989). For example, Marlatt and Gordon (1980) found that following six months of initial abstinence for problem drinkers, 70–80% reported a relapse. Relapse was found to be related to interpersonal conflict, social pressure to drink, and negative emotional states. In an earlier study, Marlatt (1978) also found similar reported antecedents to relapse such as interpersonal conflict or social pressure to drink in more than 50% of problem drinkers who relapsed.

Impulsivity, which has been associated with ineffective problem solving, has also been implicated in alcohol use. For example, McMurran et al. (2002) investigated the associations among impulsiveness, social problem-solving, aggression, and alcohol use in a non-offender sample of 70 British men. Higher impulsivity was found to be related to poorer social problem solving, and poorer social problem solving was related to greater aggression. Combining impulsivity and social problem solving in the analyses indicated that poor social problem solving, not impulsivity, was the variable that exerted the most influence over aggression. Ineffective social problem-solving abilities may also be associated with risk-taking tendencies in a fashion that contributes to other detrimental consequences. Persons who incurred a severe physical disability and who were using substances at the time of injury reported a more negative problem orientation and more risk-taking tendencies than persons who were not using substances at injury (Dreer, Elliott, & Tucker, 2004). Although these data do not reflect any causal relationship, they do suggest a constellation of behaviors that compromise personal health and well-being.

Finally, research examining the neurocognitive abilities of chronic alcoholics, particularly on tasks involving problem-solving abilities (concept formation, mental shifting, disinhibition, flexibility in thinking, generation of solutions, and profit from feedback) and memory functioning supports the relations between substance abuse and social problem-solving skills (Beatty, Katzung, Nixon, & Moreland, 1993; Butters & Laine, 1982; Cynn, 1992; Schaeffer, Parsons, & Errico, 1989). These particular studies document the effect of chronic alcohol use on the frontal lobes, an area of brain functioning associated with problem solving.

Despite this accumulating evidence, other research has found contradictions in the purported relationship between social problem solving and addictive behavior. For example, Larson and Heppner (1989) found that men receiving inpatient treatment for alcohol addiction were more negative than comparison groups in their self-report of problem-solving abilities, but these reports were unrelated to severity of alcohol abuse. Preliminary research of problem-solving interventions for persons receiving treatment for dually-diagnosed disorders (e.g., people dually diagnosed with alcohol addiction and mental illness) has not been promising (Carey, Carey, & Meisler, 1990).

SOCIAL PROBLEM SOLVING AND PERSONALITY DISORDERS

The role of social problem-solving skills has been examined to a lesser extent in personality disorders (Harlow & Cantor, 1994; Platt & Siegel, 1976; Sutker, Winstead, Galina, & Allain, 1991; Wang, Heppner, & Berry, 1997). According to McMurran, Fyffe, McCarthy, Duggan, and Latham (2001), poor social problem solving is hypothesized to be both a cause and a consequence of dysfunction. In one study conducted by McMurran and colleagues (2001) that examined the relationship between personality and social problem solving in 38 mentally ill and 14 personality-disordered participants detained in a regional secure unit, no differences between the mentally ill and personality-disordered groups were found (McMurran, Egan, et al., 2001). The groups were then pooled into a single sample. Correlations revealed that high neuroticism (N) was related to poor social problem solving and high scores on the other five traits were related to good social problem solving. N was also negatively correlated with extraversion (E), conscientiousness (C), and agreeableness (A). McMurran, Egan, et al. (2001) suggest that a high N may signal emotional reactivity which compromises effective social problem solving. A positive correlation between E and a more positive problem-solving orientation remained, probably because optimism is a defining feature of high E.

In another study, Herrick and Elliott (2001) examined the relation of self-appraised social problem-solving abilities and personality disorder characteristics to the personal adjustment and treatment adherence of 117 persons with dual diagnoses undergoing inpatient substance abuse treatment. Results indicated that elements of the problem orientation component significantly contributed to the prediction of depressive behavior and distress after controlling for personality disorder characteristics among the participants. Self-appraised problem-solving abilities predicted the occurrence of "dirty" drug and alcohol screens during treatment and attendance in a predicted fashion. However, a low sense of control over emotions when solving problems was associated with compliance with the first scheduled community visit following discharge. This confusing pattern of results implies that little may be known concerning the real-life aspects of problem-solving abilities among persons with dual disorders.

Other studies have also supported a link between social problem solving and personality disorders. For example, Else, Wonderlich, Beatty, Christie, and Staton (1993) compared a group of 21 batterers with a group of nonbatterers and found that:

1. Batterers scored higher for characteristics associated with Borderline and Antisocial Personality Disorders.
2. Batterers were also more likely to have experienced physical or emotional abuse.
3. Their problem-solving skills were significantly worse than published norms for both of the groups.

The authors concluded that borderline-antisocial personality traits, certain types of hostility, and previous histories of abuse during youth may be predisposing factors for spousal abuse.

Ingram, Marchioni, Hill, Caraveo-Ramos, and McNeil (1985) examined recidivism, perceived problem-solving abilities, type of offense, and personality characteristics of an incarcerated male population. Twenty African-Americans and 32 Caucasians were selected systematically from inmate populations. Results revealed significant elevations on MMPI F (confusion), L (lie), Re (social responsibility), and Do (dominance) scales. However, the interpretation of this finding is limited because the scale score means fell within the normal ranges of the MMPI scores. Recidivists scored significantly higher than nonrecidivists on the Impulsive Scale which was obtained from an earlier version of the Problem Solving Inventory (PSI; Heppner, 1988). African-American recidivists generated significantly higher scores on the MMPI F Scale than did African-American or Caucasian nonrecidivists. The Psychopathic Deviate (Pd) Scale demonstrated a significant main effect for type of offense, with offenders incarcerated for violent crimes scoring higher than nonviolent criminals. In another study that examined coping strategies, stress, and emotion as predictors of personality disorder pathology in 154 university students, results showed strong correlations between the presence of personality disorder features and the coping strategies of escape-avoidance and accepting responsibility (Watson & Sinha, 1999-2000). Weak or negative associations were present between problem-solving and positive reappraisal strategies. Further, personality disorder was associated with stress, negative emotions, and low control and efficacy.

Finally, Kehrer and Linehan (1996) investigated the predictive relationship between interpersonal and emotional problem-solving skills and parasuicidal behavior in female outpatients with BPD. Results indicated that inappropriate problem solving measured at four and eight months significantly predicted subsequent parasuicidal behavior. Parasuicidal behavior was predicted by both suicidal and nonsuicidal inappropriate responses but not by active, passive, and self-soothing problem-solving strategies.

In contrast to the limited number of studies that have provided support for a relationship between social problem-solving and personality disorders, one published study did not provide support for such a relationship. Bijttebier and Vertommen (1999) investigated the relationship between personality and three basic coping modes (Social Support Seeking, Avoidance, and Problem-Solving) in a sample of 137 psychiatric inpatients. In general, results revealed a negative association between the Social Support Seeking coping mode and the dimensional personality disorder scores for Paranoid, Schizoid, Schizotypal, Avoidant, and Passive-Aggressive Personality Disorder scales. To a lesser extent, this pattern was also the case for Antisocial, Depressive, and Borderline Personality Disorder scales. For the Avoidance mode, a significant positive relationship was found for Paranoid, Schizoid, Schizotypal, Borderline, Avoidant, Depressive, Dependent, and Passive-Aggressive Personality Disorder scales. However, a general negative association between personality disorders and the Problem-Solving mode were not observed. The authors hypothesized that this lack of relationship may have been attributed to the nature of the coping instrument used which may not have captured specific problem-solving strategies and skills.

SOCIAL PROBLEM SOLVING AND CRIMINAL BEHAVIOR

The relationship between social problem solving and criminal behavior has been thoroughly examined in the literature (Ireland, 2001; McGuire, 2001; McMurran et al., 2002; McMurran, Richardson, Egan, & Ahmadi, 1999; McNamara, Ertl, & Neufeld, 1998). Poor social problem-solving abilities have been hypothesized to lead to criminal behaviors as maladaptive attempts to solve personal or interpersonal problems (McMurran et al., 1999). One of the explanations why poor social problem-solving skills may be implicated in criminality is based on how an individual processes information in relation to a social problem, including encoding social cues in the environment, interpreting these cues, identifying the problem(s), generating responses, deciding on responses, and implementing a response. These steps are consistent with the social problem-solving model that incorporates five components:

1. problem orientation;
2. problem definition and formulation;
3. generation of solutions;
4. decision-making;
5. solution implementation and verification.

McGuire (2001) emphasizes that it should not be assumed that all offenders lack such skills, rather, an objective individualized assessment is needed to identify existing skills and determine those not yet developed.

Research has demonstrated deficits in social problem-solving skills among those engaging in criminal and/or aggressive behavior. Such individuals have difficulty generating solutions to hypothetical problems and those solutions produced are generally not very effective (Ireland, 2001; Richard & Dodge, 1982; Slee, 1993). Mahoney and Arnoff (1978) reviewed evidence from research conducted on problem-solving skills in deviant and normal populations and concluded that: (1) those classified as deviants were deficient in their ability to generate solutions to problems; (2) solutions that were suggested were often antisocial; and (3) their predictions of the probable consequences of different options were highly inaccurate. A considerable body of evidence shows an association between poor problem-solving skills and hostility and aggression in children/adolescents (Akhtar & Bradley, 1991; Lochman & Dodge, 1994; Slaby & Guerra, 1988) and in young adult offender populations (Biggam & Power, 1996, 1999; Keltikangas-Järvinen & Pakaslahti, 1999; McMurran et al., 1999; McMurran, Egan, et al., 2001; McMurran, Fyffe et al., 2001). Further support for the argument that limited or distorted cognitive processes may be a contributory factor in some offenses has been found from studies on problem-solving difficulties and recidivist groups and this may be a useful point of intervention (Ross & Fabiano, 1985; Zamble & Porporino, 1990; Zamble & Quinsey, 1997).

Along similar lines, poor verbal information processing ability has been proposed as a basis for impulsive aggression. Hypothesized mechanisms purport that poor verbal information processing leads to impulsive aggression associated with frustration caused by verbal deficits, poor assimilation of prosocial rules, and a lack of internalized verbal orders to inhibit behavior (Barratt, Stanford, Kent, & Felthous, 1997). Studies that have investigated social problem-solving skills in children and adolescents have found that aggressive youngsters seek less information, generate fewer potential solutions, and choose more aggressive solutions in comparison with their non-aggressive counterparts (Akhtar & Bradley, 1991; Keltikangas-Järvinen & Pakaslahti, 1999; Perry, Perry, & Rasmussen, 1986; Slaby & Guerra, 1988).

Other studies have examined the relationship between social problem solving and criminality. Grier (1988) investigated whether 30 male incarcerated sexual offenders differed in means–ends thinking when compared with 30 nonoffender controls. Results indicated no differences between the two groups on problem-solving skills as measured by the Means–End Problem-Solving instrument (MEPS; Platt & Spivack, 1975). On one dependent measure, a task requiring conceptualizing a means of reconciling a heterosexual relationship, sexual offenders generated fewer means for solving problems than nonoffender controls.

Biggam and Power (1999) examined the relationship between means–end thinking and psychological distress in 100 young incarcerated Scottish offenders who exhibited difficulties in adjusting to the prison regimen. Four groups were evaluated and results suggested a hierarchy of problem-solving deficits and psychological distress that were most pronounced in the inmates placed in suicidal supervision. Deficits in problem solving were also found to correlate with higher levels of distress. Analyses of covariance revealed important relations between the status of the individuals and their adjustment to prison after controlling for age and the total amount of time incarcerated.

In contrast to other studies that have demonstrated deficits in problem-solving skills, Pugh (1993) found different results. Pugh examined the effect of incarceration on locus of control and problem-solving skills in a sample of 168 adult male prisoners and evaluated a program, called Decisions, designed to increase internal locus of control by improving problem-solving skills. Participants were assessed and then divided into treatment and control groups. In contrast to a priori hypotheses, a substantial number of participants were found to have an internal locus of control and adequate problem solving skills.

METHODOLOGICAL PROBLEMS

Despite the growing support for social problem solving as a factor that influences the relationships between substance misuse, personality disorders, and criminality, methodological problems pose obstacles to gaining a clear understanding these relations. For several reasons, these variables and their relations are difficult to study. One of the major difficulties lies in the reliability of psychiatric diagnosis (Cottler et al., 1998; Perry, 1992; Spitzer & Fleiss, 1974). Cottler and colleagues (1998) emphasize problems with low interrater and test–retest agreement between researchers regarding the psychiatric diagnosis of patient study participants. In response to this, attempts have been made to systematize and standardize the assessment and definition of psychiatric status. Most efforts have focused on developing and refining standardized nosology and decision criteria. Two widely used systems are the *Diagnostic and Statistical Manual of Mental Disorders*, fourth edition, text revision (DSM-IV-TR; American Psychiatric Association, 2000) which is a multiaxial system and the 10th revision of the International Classification of Diseases and Related Health Problems (ICD-10; World Health Organization, 1993). Both systems incorporate biopsychosocial factors as contributing to observed clinical syndromes. Other advancements in methods have included structured interviews such as the Diagnostic Interview Schedule (DIS; Robins, Helzer, Croughan, & Ratcliff, 1981) and objective self-report formats. As these assessment methods have evolved and been refined, the reliability of diagnoses has slowly improved.

Another methodological concern involves a reliance upon self-report instruments. A number of advantages to using self-report measures have been noted (i.e., time efficiency, low cost, brevity, ease of administration); however, concerns about the accuracy of individuals' perceptions of their symptoms, behaviors, cognitions, and emotions, continue to be raised. Previous arguments against using self-report measures over performance-based measures relate to concerns regarding face validity, specifically that individuals may: (1) tend to inaccurately estimate their true abilities; (2) intentionally attempt to inflate their actual abilities for secondary gain or avoidance of punishment; and/or (3) believe that they actually hold such abilities, but when confronted with problematic situations, fail to implement such skills. Thus, concerns have been raised when relying primarily upon self-report measures when evaluating skill deficits of individuals with a history of or suspected substance abuse problem/criminal behavior when motivation to avoid punishment and/or negative consequences is high. Given that antisocial personality disorder is characterized by a tendency to manipulate, deceive, and/or lie, the veracity of self-report data is questionable. However, some investigations that have examined reliability and validity of self-reported drug use and criminality have concluded that self-reported behaviors when compared to biomarkers, criminal records, and collateral interviews, show respectable reliability and validity (Darke, 1998). As a result, a lack of consensus exists regarding the best means to assess such variables.

Yet another methodological problem that arises is the fundamental difficulty in defining and conceptualizing constructs. Difficulties with conceptualization may be more challenging than reliably diagnosing personality disorders (Coid, 2003; Cottler et al., 1998; Mellsop, Varghese, Joshua, & Hicks, 1982; Spitzer, Forman, & Nee, 1979). Clinicians may at times place little value on distinctions between personality disorder categories. For example, in the Herrick and Elliott (2001) study of problem-solving abilities among persons in a dual-disordered (primary Axis I or Axis II diagnosis [*Diagnostic and Statistical Manual of Mental Disorders*, third edition, revised; DSM-III-R; American Psychiatric Association, 1987] indicating a major behavioral disorder substance abuse/dependence problem and a coexisting Axis I or Axis II diagnosis) treatment program, 77% of the participants were diagnosed by clinic staff as having a Personality Disorder Not Otherwise Specified. Responses to the Millon Clinical Multiaxial Inventory-Second Edition (MCMI-II; Millon, 1987) revealed a preponderance of individuals between Cluster B (37%) and Cluster C characteristics (22%), and very few with Cluster A characteristics (4%).

Descriptions of personality disorders have varied throughout the literature; however, advances have been made toward developing models that make personality disorders more understandable (Miller, Lynam, & Leukefeld, 2003). One of the more widely accepted trait models of personality is the five-factor model which outlines five coping styles in relation to the 'Big Five' personality dimensions: Neuroticism (N), Extraversion (E), Openness (O), Agreeableness (A), and Conscientiousness (C) (Costa & Widiger, 1994). Matthews, Saklofske, Costa, Deary, and Zeidner (1998) have suggested that coping with problems in everyday living is determined by dispositional factors and that a high N may dispose an individual to maladaptive coping by focusing on emotions, self-blame, escapist fantasy, withdrawal, and indecisiveness. However, high E may indicate coping through an active and optimistic approach to problems. High O, on the other hand, may predict a willingness to rethink problems from different perspectives and high C may be associated with a strong task-focus. High A has had no specific relation. Thus, McMurran, Egan, et al. (2001) speculate that the five personality factors may be linked to specific modes of social problem solving and have further identified the scales in which the factors might correlate with the Social Problem-Solving Inventory-Revised (SPSI-R; D'Zurilla, Nezu, & Maydeu-Olivares, 2002). Other models of personality have paved the way to better understand and conceptualize personality (e.g., Cloninger's Temperament and Character model; Eyesenck's P-E-N model; Tellegen's three factor model). Finally, there have been empirical advancements in self-report methods to evaluate personality constructs in response to criticisms that self-report instruments show a tendency towards overdiagnosis of personality disorders. For example, several of the most widely researched and empirically supported measures include the Personality Assessment Inventory (PAI; Morey, 1991), the Minnesota Multiphasic Personality Inventory-Second Edition (MMPI-2; Butcher, Dahlstrom, Graham, Tellegen, & Kaemmer, 1989), and the Millon Clinical Multiaxial Inventory-Third Edition (MCMI-III; Millon, 1994).

SOCIAL PROBLEM SOLVING AND EMPIRICALLY SUPPORTED TREATMENTS

Despite these methodological concerns, a number of empirically-supported prevention and treatment interventions have been developed in response to the research that supports a social problem-solving influence. Social problem solving has been a core part of the major cognitive-behavioral therapies that have targeted offender, substance abuse, and personality disorder treatment. Many of the social problem-solving therapies that have been developed employ a social problem-solving approach as the primary intervention or as a component to develop more effective cognitive problem-solving skills. In general, problem-solving training or therapy is designed to help individuals find ways to deal more effectively with problems using a systematized sequence and steps (McGuire, 2001). Problem-solving techniques typically focus on improving cognitive and behavioral processes that enable the individual to deal more rationally and effectively with problems in living (Mahoney & Arnkoff, 1978; Spivack, Platt, & Shure, 1976). Application utilizes various methods of change in both cognitive and behavioral realms including functional analysis of habitual reactions, skills practice, rehearsal and feedback, self-monitoring, analysis of thought patterns, Socratic questioning, and guided discussion.

Social Problem Solving as a Primary Intervention

Several major social problem-solving approaches have been developed as a primary intervention. In most of these approaches, the primary focus of intervention is to assist individuals in acquiring or improving skills. Some approaches have focused on a single component of problem-solving training (Chandler, 1973), whereas, others have emphasized all aspects of the problem-solving model (Nezu, 1986; Nezu & Perri, 1989). For example, D'Zurilla and Nezu's (1999) Problem Solving Therapy (PST) emphasizes the essential role of problem-solving skills in coping and in increasing the likelihood of selecting the best behavior to achieve goals. The objective is to teach the five critical components of problem-solving.

A related approach, known as Interpersonal Cognitive Problem-Solving (ICPS) therapy (Spivack et al., 1976), was developed from work in applied settings with a developmental emphasis. This approach is based upon the premise that some problems can result from the absence of or failure to apply existing cognitive-interpersonal skills. Emphasis is placed on the importance of the cognitive process of identifying, appraising, and resolving interpersonal problems. The training focuses on six skills: (1) recognition that a problem exists; (2) generation of alternative solutions to a problem; (3) appraisal of the likely consequences of different possible actions; (4) utilization of a logical, sequential process to reach a goal; (5) an understanding of the causal relationships in behavior; and (6) assessing the perspective of other people in a given situation (Platt & Husband, 1993). Spivack et al. (1976) also maintain that at successive stages of development, a different selection of ICPS skills becomes vital in promoting adjustment. This approach has been effective with a number of populations including drug users (Platt, Labate, & Wicks, 1977) and psychiatric patients (Platt, 1975; Platt & Spivack, 1972).

Related to ICPS is a similar approach known as Training in Personal Problem Solving (TIPS; Platt, Taube, Metzger, & Duome, 1988). This approach is targeted to drug-abusing populations and focuses on interpersonal problem-solving skills. The program consists of eight core sessions designed to remediate specific, empirically defined, cognitive-behavioral deficits. The eight core units essentially consist of the following: (1) problem recognition; (2) problem definition; (3) non-verbal communication skills; (4) verbal communication skills; (5) generating alternatives; (6) consequences; (7) assertiveness training; and (8) practice/

review/feedback. Preliminary evidence supporting this approach has been found (Platt, Perry, & Metzger, 1980).

Another empirically-supported social problem-solving intervention with personality-disordered offenders is called 'Stop & Think'! (McMurran, Fyffe, et al., 2001; see also Chapter 11), which is based on the work of D'Zurilla and Goldfried (1971).

One of the most widely used primary problem-solving interventions is known as the *Reasoning and Rehabilitation* (R & R) program (Ross, Fabiano, & Ross, 1986). This program involves problem-solving training and teaching cognitive skills that are required for adequate social adjustment. In an evaluation of the program's effectiveness, 11 male mentally disordered offender patients were provided with five months of treatment at two sessions per week. Results indicate that the program was successful in bringing about an improvement in problem-solving abilities and social adjustment.

Finally, another program with a problem-solving emphasis is known as *Vocational Problem-Solving Skills* (VPSS; Metzger, Platt, Zanis, & Fureman, 1992). VPSS is a cognitive-behavioral intervention designed to assist chronically unemployed drug-treatment patients in the transition to work. The sessions were designed to run approximately 30 to 60 minutes in length and to be delivered within a maximum of a 12-week period. There are five objectives of the VPSS intervention: (1) to help patients understand why they want to work; (2) to help patients understand how to overcome current barriers to work; (3) to set realistic vocational goals; (4) to identify realistic resources to help locate job opportunities; and (5) to take appropriate actions to obtain work. Preliminary research examining this intervention has suggested that VPSS alone is not a strong independent predictor of improved employment functioning, but improvements in employment functioning were detected at one of the two sites as a function of VPSS training (Zanis, Coviello, Alterman, & Appling, 2001).

Social Problem Solving as a Component of a Multi-Modal Intervention

Some widely studied psychotherapeutic interventions combine a problem-solving skills component with other treatment modalities. Combinations have typically included problem-solving with self-instructional or self-management training, social skills training, and/or relapse prevention. Dialectical Behavior Therapy (DBT; Linehan, 1993a, 1993b) is one example of such an approach. DBT is an empirically-supported cognitive-behavioral approach that emphasizes skills training to reduce self-destructive, impulsive, and aggressive behaviors. This approach is based on the proposal that the core difficulty of these patients is one of emotion dysregulation and that this dysregulation is exacerbated and maintained in part by being invalidated by others. This type of intervention focuses on the application of skills and coaching in all aspects of treatment and attends to the patient's skills deficits as well as to motivational obstacles to skills use. This approach has been widely studied and found to be effective in treating adult women with Borderline Personality Disorder, as well as incarcerated juvenile offenders evidencing emotional dysregulation (Trupin, Stewart, Beach, & Boesky, 2002).

Cognitive approaches that utilize components of a problem-solving intervention as a secondary emphasis have also been applied to the successful rehabilitation programs for prisoners (Ross et al., 1986), drinking and driving offenders (Bakker, Hudson, & Ward, 1997; Bakker, Ward, Cryer, & Hudson, 2000), personality-disordered offenders (Hughes, Hogue, Hollin, & Champion, 1997; Hurdle, 2001; McMurran et al., 1999), gambling (Sylvain, Ladouceur, & Boisvert, 1997), and problem drinkers (Chaney, O'Leary, & Marlatt, 1978; Hermalin et al., 1990).

FUTURE DIRECTIONS

Further explorations investigating the overlap between substance abuse, personality disorders, social problem-solving, and criminal behavior are warranted given the co-occurrence of these factors has been found to complicate treatment and that they have been linked to chronic criminality and mental health problems. While the links between these variables have been supported in the literature, further elucidation of the influence of social problem solving as a mediating factor and an investigation of the mechanisms of change is also warranted. For example, longitudinal studies would be informative. Investigations that identify possible problem-solving skill deficit profiles according to diagnoses are needed (McMurran, Fyffe, et al., 2001). Treatment dismantling studies examining the effectiveness of different approaches are also suggested. There is also a need for rigorous randomized clinical trials designed to help identify which treatment is effective in which particular combination of variables. Only when more comprehensive studies with methodologically solid designs are implemented and evaluated will progress be made.

The role of social problem solving has been documented in substance abuse, personality disorders, and criminal behavior; however, the majority of empirical studies have evaluated social problem-solving skill deficits based upon clients' self-perception of their social problem-solving abilities. Two of the most widely used social problem-solving inventories are the Problem Solving Inventory (PSI; Heppner, 1988) and the Social Problem Solving Inventory-Revised (SPSI-R; D'Zurilla et al., 2002). Both instruments rely upon Likert-type self-ratings. An alternative social problem-solving measure that comes closer to evaluating problem-solving performance is known as the Means–End Problem Solving (MEPS) procedure (Spivack et al., 1976). However, limitations regarding poor reliability in rating responses have been noted (House & Scott, 1996). It may be more useful to develop performance-based observational methods to assess an individual's actual real-life problem-solving skills as well as their thought processes, emotions, and behaviors. Carey and Carey (1990) also argue that because problem solving is a multidimensional construct, the development of different methods of assessment may potentially capture different aspects of the process that may be missed when relying upon self-report accounts. Such methods, first, are thought to more accurately reflect how one actually behaves when confronted with specific situations; second, are less biased by one's metacognitions, and, finally, allow for a process approach to exploring social cognition. Finally, other researchers have begun to focus on developing population and/or situation-specific measures of problem-solving (Chaney et al., 1978; Dreer, 2001; Patterson et al., 1988). Improving assessment instruments will help identify population-specific skill deficits to target for intervention.

Essentially, there is a dearth of empirical data to guide our understanding of personality disorders and social problem-solving abilities. Herrick and Elliott (2001) found Cluster A and Cluster C characteristics were associated with ineffective social problem-solving abilities (as measured by the PSI); no relations were found between Cluster B characteristics and problem-solving abilities. Intuitively, persons who have problems with symptoms associated with Cluster A or C would be more likely to give negative appraisals of their problem-solving abilities. In contrast, those with Cluster B characteristics may be more likely to misrepresent their skills, or be manipulative and exaggerate their abilities, depending upon their mood, level of stress, and immediate circumstances. These patterns have yet to be replicated in other research. Relevant studies have not taken into account personality-disorder characteristics, which could potentially elucidate discrepancies between observed and self-reported abilities, particularly among persons receiving treatment for substance abuse (e.g., Larson & Heppner, 1989). Continued improvement is needed in conceptualizing and identifying specific characteristics that may be implicated in treatment outcomes with dual-diagnosed populations. It should be emphasized that Herrick and Elliott (2001) found self-reported problem-solving abilities were better predictors of clinical outcomes and adherence to a substance abuse treatment program among persons in a dual-diagnosis (primary Axis I or Axis II diagnosis [DSM-III-R; American Psychiatric Association, 1987] indicating a major behavioral disorder substance abuse/dependence problem and a coexisting Axis I or Axis II diagnosis) program; despite the limitations of self-report measurement, it appears that these tools can provide unique and enlightening information that have clear directives for therapy.

While advancements have been made to better understand and explain these complex relationships, continued work is required. Better understanding of the variables that best respond to particular interventions is critical, given that: (1) many comorbid conditions exist and manifest in mild to severe forms of pathology; and (2) regardless of the diagnostic categories and the type of substance abused, dually diagnosed persons have been found to have poor treatment responses (Brady et al., 1990). This overlap makes treating these problems quite a challenging task. Studies have shown that dually diagnosed persons do poorer than others on measures related to rehospitalization and treatment noncompliance (Drake & Wallach, 1989; McCarrick, Manderschied, & Bertolucci, 1985). While this may seem like a daunting task to undertake, future research is needed to design more appropriate and effective treatment interventions that are more likely to succeed and more successfully minimize problematic behaviors and relapse.

REFERENCES

Abram, K. M. (1989). The effect of co-occurring disorders on criminal careers: Interaction of antisocial personality, alcoholism, and drug disorders. *International Journal of Law and Psychiatry, 12*, 133–148.

Akhtar, N. & Bradley, E. J. (1991). Social information processing deficits of aggressive children. *Clinical Psychology Review, 11*, 621–644.

Allen, J. P., Leadbeater, B. J., & Aber, J. L. (1994). The development of problem behavior syndromes in at-risk adolescents. *Development Psychopathology, 6*, 323–342.

Alterman, A. I., Rutherford, M. J., Cacciola, J. S., McKay, J. R., & Boardman, C. R. (1998). Prediction of 7 months methadone maintenance treatment response by four measures of antisociality. *Drug and Alcohol Dependence, 49*, 217–223.

American Psychiatric Association (1987). *Diagnostic and statistical manual of mental disorders.* 3rd edn, revised. Washington, DC: American Psychiatric Association.

American Psychiatric Association (2000). *Diagnostic and statistical manual of mental disorders* 4th edn, revision. Washington, DC: American Psychiatric Association.

Anderson, T., Mahoney, J. L., Wennberg, P., Kuehlhorn, E., & Magnusson, D (1999). The co-occurrence of alcohol problems and criminality in the transition from adolescence to young adulthood: A prospective longitudinal study on young men. *Studies on Crime and Prevention, 8*, 169–188.

Appel, P. W. & Kaestner, E. (1979). Interpersonal and emotional problem solving among narcotic drug abusers. *Journal of Consulting and Clinical Psychology, 47*, 1125–1127.

Armstrong, T. D. & Costello, J. E. (2002). Community studies of adolescent substance use, abuse, or dependence, and psychiatric comorbidity. *Journal of Consulting and Clinical Psychology, 70*, 1224–1239.

Bakker, L. W., Hudson, S. M., & Ward, T. (2000). Reducing recidivism in driving while disqualified: A treatment evaluation. *Criminal Justice and Behavior, 27*, 531–560.

Bakker, L. W., Ward, T., Cryer, M., & Hudson, S. M. (1997). Out of the rut: A cognitive-behavioural treatment program for driving-while-disqualified offenders. *Behaviour Change, 14*, 29–38.

Barratt, E. S., Stanford, M. S., Kent, T. A., & Felthous, A. (1997). Neuropsychological and cognitive psychophysiological substrates of impulsive aggression. *Biological Psychiatry, 41*, 1045–1061.

Beatty, W. W., Katzung, V. M, Nixon, S. J., & Moreland, V. J. (1993). Problem-solving deficits in alcoholics: Evidence from the California Card Sorting Test. *Journal of Studies on Alcohol, 54*, 687–692.

Biggam, F. H. & Power, K. G. (1996). Social problem-solving skills and psychological distress among incarcerated young offenders: The issue of bullying and victimization. *Cognitive Therapy and Research, 23*, 307–326.

Biggam, F. H. & Power, K. G. (1999). A comparison of the problem solving abilities and psychological distress of suicidal, bullied, and protected prisoners. *Criminal Justice and Behavior, 26*, 196–216.

Bijttebier, P. & Vertommen, H. (1999). Coping strategies in relation to personality disorders. *Personality and Individual Differences, 26*, 847–856.

Bonner, R. L. & Rich, A. R. (1988). Negative life stress, social problem-solving self-appraisal, and hopelessness: Implications for suicide research. *Cognitive Therapy and Research, 12*, 549–556.

Brady, K., Anton, R., Ballenger, J. C., Lydiard, B., Adinoff, B., & Selander, J. (1990). Cocaine abuse among schizophrenic patients. *American Journal of Psychiatry, 147*, 1164–1167.

Brook, J. S., Cohen, P., Whiteman, M., & Gordon, A. S. (1992). Psychosocial risk factors in the transition from moderate to heavy use or abuse of drugs. In M. D. Glantz & R. W. Pickens (eds) *Vulnerability to drug abuse*, (pp. 359–388). Washington, DC: American Psychological Association.

Brooner, R. K., Kidorf, M., King, V. L., & Stoller, K. (1998). Preliminary evidence of good treatment response in antisocial drug abusers. *Drug and Alcohol Dependence*, 49, 249–260.

Butcher, J. N., Dahlstrom, W. G., Graham, J. R., Tellegen, A. M., & Kaemmer, B. (1989). *MMPI-2: Manual for administration and scoring*. Minneapolis: University of Minnesota Press.

Butters, N. & Laine, M. (1982). Preliminary study of problem-solving strategies of detoxified long-term alcoholics. *Drug and Alcohol Dependence*, 10, 235–242.

Byqvist, S. (1999). Criminality among female drug abusers. *Journal of Psychoactive Drugs*, 31, 353–362.

Carey, K. B. & Carey, M. P. (1990). Social problem-solving in dual diagnosis patients. *Journal of Psychopathology and Behavioral Assessment*, 12, 247–254.

Carey, M. P., Carey, K. B., & Meisler, A. (1990). Training mentally ill chemical abusers in social problem solving. *Behavior Therapy*, 21, 511–519.

Chandler, M. J. (1973). Egocentrism and anti-social behaviour: The assessment and training of social perspective-taking skills. *Developmental Psychology*, 9, 326–332.

Chaney, E., O'Leary, M., & Marlatt, A. (1978). Skill training with alcoholics. *Journal of Consulting and Clinical Psychology*, 46, 1092–1104.

Coid, J. (2003). Epidemiology, public health and the problem of personality. *British Journal of Psychiatry*, 182 (Supp. 44), s3–s10.

Cooper, M. L., Russell, M., Skinner, J. B., & Frone, M. R. (1992). Stress and alcohol use: Moderating effects of gender, coping, and alcohol expectancies. *Journal of Abnormal Psychology*, 101, 139–152.

Costa, P. T. & Widiger, T. A. (1994). *Personality disorders and the five-factor model of personality*. Washington, DC: American Psychological Association.

Cottler, L. B., Compton, W. M., Ridenour, T. A., Abdallah, A. B., & Gallagher, T. (1998). Reliability of self-reported Antisocial Personality Disorder symptoms among substance abusers. *Drug and Alcohol Dependence*, 49, 189–199.

Crowley, T. J., Mikulich, S. K., MacDonald, M., Young, S. E., & Zerbe, G. O. (1998). Substance-dependent, conduct-disordered adolescent males: Severity of diagnosis predicts 2-year outcome. *Drug and Alcohol Dependence*, 49, 225–237.

Cynn, V. E. H. (1992). Persistence and problem-solving skills in young male alcoholics. *Journal of Studies on Alcohol*, 53, 57–62.

Darke, S. (1998). Self-report among injecting drug users: A review. *Drug and Alcohol Dependence*, 51, 253–263.

Dobkin, P. L., Tremblay, R. E., Masse, L. C., & Viatro, F. (1995). Individual and peer characteristics in predicting boys' early onset of substance abuse: A seven-year longitudinal study. *Child Development*, 66, 1198–1214.

Drake, R. E. & Wallach, M. A. (1989). Substance abuse among the chronic mentally ill. *Hospital and Community Psychiatry*, 40, 1041–1046.

Dreer, L. E. (2001). Relative utility of global self-report versus domain-specific performance-based measures of social problem solving in college drinkers. Symposium presented at the World Congress of Behavioral and Cognitive Therapies, Vancouver, BC.

Dreer, L. E., Elliott, T., & Tucker, E. (2004). Social problem-solving abilities and health behaviors among persons with recent spinal cord injuries. *Journal of Clinical Psychology in Medical Settings*, 11, 7–13.

Dreer, L. E., Ronan, G. F., Ronan, D. W., Dush, D. W., & Elliott, T. R. (2004). Binge drinking and college students: An investigation of social problem-abilities. *Journal of College Student Development*, 45, 303–315.

Dulit, R. A., Fyer, M. R., & Haas, G. L. (1990). Substance use in borderline personality disorder. *American Journal of Psychiatry*, 147, 1002–1007.

D'Zurilla, T. J. & Goldfried, M. R. (1971). Problem solving and behavior modification. *Journal of Abnormal Psychology, 78*, 107–126.

D'Zurilla, T. J. & Nezu, A. (1982). Social problem-solving in adults. *Advances in Cognitive-Behavioural Research and Therapy, 1*, 201–274.

D'Zurilla, T. J. & Nezu, A. M. (1999). *Problem-solving therapy: A social competence approach to clinical intervention*. New York: Springer Publishing.

D'Zurilla, T. J., Nezu, A. M., & Maydeu-Olivares, A. (2002). *Social problem-solving inventory-revised*. North Tonawanda, NY: Multi-Health Systems Inc.

Elliott, T., Grant, J., & Miller, D. (2004). Social problem solving abilities and behavioral health. In E. Chang, T. J. D'Zurilla, & L. J. Sanna (eds) *Social problem solving: Theory, research, and training* (pp. 117–133). Washington, DC: American Psychological Association.

Else, L. T., Wonderlich, S. A., Beatty, W. W., Christie, D. W., & Staton, R. D. (1993). Personality characteristics of men who physically abuse women. *Hospital and Community Psychiatry, 44*, 54–58.

Evans, D. M. & Dunn, N. J. (1995). Alcohol expectancies, coping responses and self-efficacy judgments: A replication and extension of Cooper et al.'s 1988 study in a college sample. *Journal of Studies in Alcohol, 56*, 186–193.

Ferguson, D. M. & Lynskey, M. T. (1998). Conduct problems in childhood and psychosocial outcomes in young adulthood: A prospective study. *Journal of Emotional and Behavioral Disorders, 6*, 2–18.

Foglia, W. D. (2000). Adding an explicit focus on cognition to criminological theory. In D. H. Fishbein (ed.) *The science, treatment, and prevention of antisocial behaviors: Application to the criminal justice system*. Kingston, NJ: Civic Research Institute.

Frank, A. (1993). Adolescent substance users: Problem-solving abilities. *Journal of Substance Abuse, 5*, 85–92.

Friedman, A. S. (1998). Substance use/abuse as a predictor to illegal and violent behavior: A review of the relevant literature. *Aggression and Violent Behavior, 3*, 339–355.

Fromme, K. & Rivet, K. (1994). Young adults' coping style as a predictor of their alcohol use and response to daily events. *Journal of Youth and Adolescence, 23*, 85–97.

Gerstley, L. J., Alterman, A. I., McLellan, A. T., & Woody, G. E. (1990). Antisocial personality disorder in patients with substance abuse disorders: A problematic diagnosis? *American Journal of Psychiatry, 147*, 173–178.

Godshall, F. & Elliott, T. (1997). Behavioral correlates of self-appraised problem-solving ability: Problem-solving skills and health-compromising behaviors. *Journal of Applied Social Psychology, 27*, 929–944.

Goldstein, R. B., Powers, S. I., McCusker, J., Lewis, B. F., Bigelow, C., & Mundo, A. (1999). Antisocial behavioral syndromes among residential drug abuse treatment clients. *Drug and Alcohol Dependence, 53*, 171–187.

Grier, P. E. (1988). Cognitive problem-solving skills in antisocial rapists. *Criminal Justice and Behavior, 15*, 501–514.

Harlow, R. E. & Cantor, N. (1994). Personality as problem solving: A framework for the analysis of change in daily-life behavior. *Journal of Psychotherapy Integration, 4*, 355–385.

Heppner, P. P. (1988). *Manual for the problem solving inventory (PSI)*. Palo Alto, CA: Consulting Psychologists Press.

Heppner, P. P., Hibel, J., Neal, G. W., Weinstein, C. L., & Rabinowitz, F. E. (1982). Personal problem solving: A descriptive study of individual differences. *Journal of Counseling Psychology, 29*, 580–590.

Hermalin, J., Husband, S. D., & Platt, J. J. (1990). Reducing costs of employee alcohol and drug abuse: Problem-solving and social skills training for relapse prevention. *Employee Assistance Quarterly, 6*, 11–25.

Hernandez-Avila, C. A., Burleson, J. A., Poling, J., Tennen, H., Rounsaville, B. J., & Kranzler, H. R. (2000). Personality and substance use disorders as predictors of criminality. *Comprehensive Psychiatry*, *41*, 276–283.

Herrick, S. M. & Elliott, T. R. (2001). Social problem-solving abilities and personality disorder characteristics among dual-diagnosed persons in substance abuse treatment. *Journal of Clinical Psychology*, *51*, 75–92.

Hodgins, S., Mednick, S. A., Brennan, P. A., Schulsinger, F., & Engberg, M. (1996). Mental disorder and crime: Evidence from a Danish birth cohort. *Archives of General Psychiatry*, *53*, 489–496.

Hughes, G., Hogue, T., Hollin, C., & Champion, H. (1997). First-stage evaluation of a treatment programme for personality disordered offenders. *Journal of Forensic Psychiatry*, *8*, 515–527.

House, R. & Scott, J. (1996). Problems in measuring problem-solving: The suitability of the Means-Ends Problem Solving (MEPS) procedure. *International Journal of Methods in Psychiatric Research*, *6*, 1–9.

Hurdle, D. (2001). ''Less is best''—A group-based treatment program for persons with personality disorders. *Social Work with Groups*, *23*, 71–80.

Ingram, J. C., Marchioni, P., Hill, G., Caraveo-Ramos, E., & McNeil, B. (1985). Recidivism perceived problem-solving abilities, MMPI characteristics, and violence: A study of black and white incarcerated male adult offenders. *Journal of Clinical Psychology*, *41*, 425–432.

Intagliata, J. (1978). Increasing the interpersonal problem-solving skills for an alcoholic population. *Journal of Consulting and Clinical Psychology*, *46*, 489–498.

Ireland, J. L. (2001). The relationship between social problem-solving and bullying behaviour among male and female adult prisoners. *Aggressive Behavior*, *27*, 297–312.

Kant, G. L., D'Zurilla, T. J., & Maydeu-Olivares, A. (1997). Social problem solving as a mediator of stress-related depression and anxiety in middle-aged and elderly community residents. *Cognitive Therapy and Research*, *21*, 73–96.

Kaye, S., Darke, S., & Finlay-Jones, R. (1998). The onset of heroin use and criminal behaviour: Does order make a difference? *Drug and Alcohol Dependence*, *53*, 79–86.

Kehrer, C. & Linehan, M. M. (1996). Interpersonal and emotional problem-solving skills and parasuicide among women with borderline personality disorder. *Journal of Personality Disorders*, *10*, 153–163.

Keltikangas-Järvinen, L., & Pakaslahti, L. (1999). Development of social problem-solving strategies and changes in aggressive behavior: A 7-year follow-up from childhood to late adolescence. *Aggressive Behavior*, *25*, 269–279.

Kerner, H. J., Weitekamp, E. G. M., & Thomas, J. (1997). Patterns of criminality and alcohol abuse: Results of the Tübingen Criminal Behaviour Development Study. *Criminal Behaviour and Mental Health*, *7*, 401–420.

Kessler, R. C., Nelson, C. B., McGonagle, K. A., Edlund, M. J., Frank, R. G., & Leaf, P. J. (1996). The epidemiology of co-occurring addictive and mental disorders: Implications for prevention and service utilization. *American Journal of Orthopsychiatry*, *66*, 17–31.

Kjelsberg, E. (1999). Adolescence-limited versus life-course-persistent criminal behavior in adolescent psychiatric inpatients. *European Child and Adolescent Psychiatry*, *8*, 276–282.

Kratzer, L. & Hodgins, S. (1997). Adult outcomes of child conduct problems: A cohort study. *Journal Abnormal Child Psychology*, *25*, 65–81.

Laine, M. & Butters, N. (1982). A preliminary study of the problem-solving strategies of detoxified long-term alcoholics. *Drug and Alcohol Dependence*, *10*, 235–242.

Larson, L. M. & Heppner, P. P. (1989). Problem-solving appraisal in an alcoholic population. *Journal of Counseling Psychology*, *36*, 73–78.

Linehan, M. M. (1993a). *Cognitive-behavioral treatment of borderline personality disorder*. New York: Guilford Press.

Linehan, M. M. (1993b). *Skills training manual for treating borderline personality disorder.* New York: Guilford Press.

Links, P. S., Heslegrave, R. J., Mitton, J. E., van Reekum, R., & Patrick, J. (1995). Borderline personality disorder and substance abuse: Consequences of comorbidity. *Canadian Journal of Psychiatry, 40,* 9–14.

Lochman, J. E. & Dodge, K. A. (1994). Social-cognitive processes of severely violent, moderately aggressive, and non-aggressive boys. *Journal of Consulting and Clinical Psychology, 62,* 366–374.

Longato-Stadler, E., von-Knorring, L., & Hallman, J. (2002). Mental and personality disorders as well as personality traits in a Swedish male criminal population. *Nordic-Journal of Psychiatry, 56,* 137–144.

Lynam, D. R., Leukefeld, C., & Clayton, R. R. (2003). The contribution of personality to the overlap between antisocial behavior and substance use/misuse. *Aggressive Behavior, 29,* 316–331.

Mahoney, M. J. & Arnkoff, D. B. (1978). Cognitive and self-control therapies. In S. L. Garfield & A. E. Bergin (eds) *Handbook of psychotherapy and behaviour change* (pp. 689–722). New York: Wiley.

Marks, M. G., Stewart, D. G., & Brown, S. A. (1998). Progression from conduct disorder to antisocial personality disorder following treatment for adolescent substance abuse. *American Journal of Psychiatry, 155,* 479–485.

Marlatt, G. A. (1978). Craving for alcohol, loss of control, and relapse: A cognitive-behavioral analysis. In P. E. Nathan, G. A. Marlatt, and T. Loberg (eds) *Alcoholism: New directions in behavioral research and treatment.* New York: Plenum Press.

Marlatt, G. A., Baer, J. S., Donovan, D. M., & Kivlahan, D. R. (1988). Addictive behaviors: Etiology and treatment. *Annual Review of Psychology, 35,* 223–252.

Marlatt, G. A. & Gordon, J. R. (1980). Determinants of relapse prevention: Implications for the maintenance of behavior change. In P. O. Davidson and S. M. Davidson (eds) *Behavioral medicine: Changing health lifestyles.* New York: Brunner/Mazel.

Mason, W. A. & Windle, M. (2002). Reciprocal relations between adolescent substance use and delinquency: A longitudinal latent variable analysis. *Journal of Abnormal Psychology, 111,* 63–76.

Matthews, G., Saklofske, D. H., Costa, P. T., Deary, I. J., & Zeidner, M. (1998). Dimensional models of personality: A framework for systematic clinical assessment. *European Journal of Psychological Assessment, 14,* 35–48.

McCarrick, A. K., Manderscheid, R. W., & Bertolucci, D. E. (1985). Correlates of acting-out behaviors among young adult chronic patients. *Hospital and Community Psychiatry, 35,* 848–853.

McCord, J. (1995). Relationship between alcoholism and crime over the life course. In H. B. Kaplan (ed.) *Drugs, crime, and other deviant adaptations: Longitudinal studies* (pp. 129–141). New York: Plenum Press.

McGuire, J. (2001). What is problem solving? A review of theory, research, and applications. *Criminal Behaviour and Mental Health, 11,* 210–235.

McMurran, M., Blair, M., & Egan, V. (2002). An investigation of the correlations between aggression, impulsiveness, social problem-solving, and alcohol use. *Aggressive Behavior, 28,* 439–445.

McMurran, M., Egan, V., Blair, M., & Richardson, C. (2001). The relationship between social problem-solving and personality in mentally disordered offenders. *Personality and Individual Differences, 30,* 517–524.

McMurran, M., Fyffe, S., McCarthy, L., Duggan, C., & Latham, A. (2001). "Stop & Think!" Social problem solving therapy with personality disordered offenders. *Criminal Behaviour and Mental Health, 11,* 273–285.

McMurran, M., Richardson, C., Egan, V., & Ahmadi, S. (1999). Social problem-solving in mentally disordered offenders: A brief report. *Criminal Behaviour and Mental Health, 9*, 315–322.

McNamara, J. R., Ertl, M., & Neufeld, J. (1998). Problem-solving in relation to abuse by a partner. *Psychological Reports, 83*, 943–946.

Mellsop, G., Varghese, F., Joshua, S., & Hicks, A. (1982). The reliability of Axis II of DSM-II. *American Journal of Psychiatry, 139*, 1360–1361.

Messina, N. P., Wish, E. D., Hoffman, J. A., & Nemes, S. (2002). Antisocial personality disorder and TC treatment outcomes. *American Journal of Drug and Alcohol Abuse, 28*, 197–212.

Metzger, D. S., Platt, J. J., Zanis, D., & Fureman, I. (1992). *Vocational problem-solving skills: A structured intervention for unemployed substance abuse treatment clients.* Philadelphia, PA: University of Pennsylvania.

Miller, J. D., Lynam, D., & Leukefeld, C. (2003). Examining antisocial behavior through the lens of the five factor model of personality. *Aggressive Behavior, 29*, 497–514.

Millon, T. (1987). *Manual for the MCMI-II.* 2nd edn. Minneapolis, MN: National Computer Systems.

Millon, T. (1994). *Manual for the MCMI-III.* 3rd edn. Minneapolis, MN: National Computer Systems.

Moos, R. H., Brennan, P. L., Fondacaro, M. R., & Moos, B. S. (1990). Approach and avoidance coping responses among older problem and non-problem drinkers. *Psychology and Aging, 5*, 31–40.

Morey, L. C. (1991). *Personality assessment inventory: Professional manual.* Odessa, FL: PAR.

Myers, M. G., Stewart, D. G., & Brown, S. A. (1998). Progression from conduct disorder to antisocial personality following treatment for adolescent substance abuse. *American Journal of Psychiatry, 155*, 479–485.

Nace, E. P., Davis, C. W., & Gaspari, J. P. (1991). Axis II comorbidity in substance abusers. *American Journal of Psychiatry, 148*, 118–120.

Nezu, A. M. (1986). Efficacy of a social problem-solving therapy approach for unipolar depression. *Journal of Consulting and Clinical Psychology, 54*, 196–202.

Nezu, A. M., Nezu, C. M., Houts, P. S., Friedman, S. H., & Faddis, S. (1999). Relevance of problem-solving therapy to psychosocial oncology. *Journal of Psychosocial Oncology, 16*, 5–26.

Nezu, A. M. & Perri, M. G. (1989). Social problem-solving therapy for unipolar depression: An initial dismantling investigation. *Journal of Consulting and Clinical Psychology, 57*, 408–413.

Nezu, A. M. & Ronan, G. F. (1988). Social problem solving as a moderator of stress-related depressive symptoms: A prospective analysis. *Journal of Counseling Psychology, 35*, 134–138.

Patterson, B. W., Parsons, O. A., Schaeffer, K. W., & Errico, A. L. (1988). Interpersonal problem solving in alcoholics. *Journal of Nervous and Mental Disease, 176*, 707–713.

Perri, M. G., Nezu, A. M., McKelvey, W. F., Shermer, R. L. Renjilian, D. A., & Viegener, B. J. (2001). Relapse prevention training and problem-solving therapy in the long-term management of obesity. *Journal of Consulting and Clinical Psychology, 69*, 722–726.

Perry, D. G., Perry, L. C., & Rasmussen, P. (1986). Cognitive social learning mediators of aggression. *Child Development, 57*, 700–711.

Perry, J. C. (1992). Problems and considerations in the valid assessment of personality disorders. *American Journal of Psychiatry, 149*, 1645–1653.

Platt, J. J. (1975). Adolescent problem-solving thinking. *Journal of Consulting and Clinical Psychology, 42*, 787–793.

Platt, J. J. & Husband, S. D. (1993). An overview of problem-solving and social skills approaches in substance abuse treatment. *Psychotherapy, 30*, 276–283.

Platt, J. J., Labate, C., & Wicks, R. J. (1977). Evaluation of the Wharton Tract narcotics treatment program. In J. J. Platt, C. Labate, & R. J. Wicks (eds) *Evaluate research in correctional drug abuse treatment* pp. 149–170. Lexington, MA: Lexington Books/D. C. Heath.

Platt, J. J. & Metzger, D. S. (1987). Cognitive interpersonal problem-solving skills and the maintenance of treatment success in heroin addicts. *Psychology of Addictive Behaviors, 1*, 5–13.

Platt, J. J., Perry, G., & Metzger, D. (1980). Evaluation of a heroin addiction treatment program within a correctional environment. In R. R. Ross and P. Gendreau (eds) *Effective correctional treatment* (pp. 421–435). Toronto: Butterworths.

Platt, J. J., Scura, W., & Hannon, J. (1973). Problem-solving thinking of youthful incarcerated heroin addicts. *Journal of Community Psychology, 1*, 278–281.

Platt, J. J. & Siegel, J. M. (1976). MMPI characteristics of good and poor social problem-solvers among psychiatric patients. *Journal of Psychology, 94*, 245–251.

Platt, J. J. & Spivack, G. (1972). Problem-solving thinking of psychiatric patients. *Journal of Consulting and Clinical Psychology, 39*, 148–151.

Platt, J. J. & Spivack, G. (1975). *Means–end problem-solving procedures (MEPS): Manual*. Philadelphia, PA: Hahnemann Medical College.

Platt, J. J., Taube, D. O., Metzger, D. S., & Duome, M. J. (1988). Training in Interpersonal Problem Solving (TIPS). *Journal of Cognitive Psychotherapy: An International Quarterly, 2*, 5–31.

Pugh, D. N. (1993). The effects of problem-solving ability and locus of control on prisoner adjustment. *International Journal of Offender Therapy and Comparative Criminology, 37*, 163–176.

Pulkkinen, L., Virtanen, T., afKlinteberg, B. A., & Magnusson, D. (2000). Child behaviour and adult personality: comparisons between criminality groups in Finland and Sweden. *Criminal Behaviour and Mental Health, 10*, 155–169.

Richard, B. A. & Dodge, K. A. (1982). Social maladjustment and problem-solving in school-aged children. *Journal of Consulting and Clinical Psychology, 50*, 226–233.

Robins, L. N., Helzer, J. E., Croughan, J. L., & Ratcliff, K. S. (1981). National Institute of Mental Health diagnostic interview schedule: Its history, characteristics, and validity. *Archives of General Psychiatry, 38*, 381–389.

Ross, R. R. & Fabiano, E. A. (1985). *Time to think: A cognitive model of delinquency prevention and offender rehabilitation*. Ottawa: Air Training and Publications.

Ross, R. R., Fabiano, E. A., & Ross, R. D. (1986). *Reasoning and rehabilitation*. Ottawa: University of Ottawa Press.

Rutherford, M., Alterman, A., & Cacciola, J. (2000). Psychopathy and substance abuse: A bad mix. In C. B. Gacomo (Ed.), *The clinical and forensic assessment of psychopathy: A practitioner's guide*. (pp. 351–388). Mahwah, NJ: Erlbaum.

Sandell, R. & Bertling, U. (1999). Heaviness of abuse, drug preferences, and personality organization among drug abusers in Sweden. *Journal of Clinical Psychology, 55*, 99–107.

Sass, H., Erkwoh, R., & Rodon, A. (1998). Medico-legal aspects of alcohol, drugs, and criminality in Germany. *Alcohol and Alcoholism, 33*, 26–32.

Schaeffer, K. W., Parsons, O. A., & Errico, A. L. (1989). Performance deficits on tests of problem solving in alcoholics: Cognitive or motivational impairment? *Journal of Substance Abuse, 1*, 381–392.

Segest, E., Mygind, O., & Bay, H. (1989). The allocation of drug addicts to different types of treatment: An evaluation and a two-year follow-up. *American Journal of Drug and Alcohol Abuse, 15*, 41–53.

Slaby, R. G. & Guerra, N. G. (1988). Cognitive mediators of aggression in adolescent offenders: I. Assessment. *Developmental Psychology, 24*, 580–588.

Slee, P. T. (1993). Bullying: A preliminary investigation of its nature and the effects of social cognition. *Early Child Development Care, 87*, 47–57.

Spitzer, R. L. & Fleiss, J. L. (1974). A re-analysis of the reliability of psychiatric diagnosis. *British Journal of Psychiatry, 125*, 341–347.

Spitzer, R. L., Forman, J. B., & Nee, J. (1979). DSM-III field trials: I. Initial interrater diagnostic reliability. *American Journal of Psychiatry, 136*, 815–817.

Spivack, G., Platt, J. J., & Shure, M. B. (1976). The problem-solving approach to adjustment. In B. Lahey and A. Kazdin (eds) *Advances in clinical psychology*, vol. 5. New York: Plenum Press.

Stattin, H. & Romelsjoe, A. (1995). Adult mortality in the light of criminality, substance abuse, and behavioural and family-risk factors in adolescence. *Criminal Behaviour and Mental Health, 5*, 279–311.

Sutker, P. B., Winstead, D. K., Galina, Z. H., & Allain, A. N. (1991). Cognitive deficits and psychopathology among former prisoners of war and combat veterans of the Korean conflict. *American Journal of Psychiatry, 148*, 67–72.

Sylvain, C., Ladouceur, R., & Boisvert, J. M. (1997). Cognitive and behavioural treatment of pathological gambling: A controlled study. *Journal of Consulting and Clinical Psychology, 65*, 727–732.

Tiihonen, J., Isohanni, M., Raesaenen, P., Koiranen, M., & Moring, J. (1997). Specific major mental disorders and criminality: A 26-year prospective study of the 1996 Northern Finland Birth Cohort. *American Journal of Psychiatry, 154*, 840–845.

Timonen, M., Miettunen, J., Hakko, H., Zitting, P., Veijola, J., von-Wendt, L., & Raesaenen, P. (2002). The association of preceding traumatic brain injury with mental disorders, alcoholism, and criminality: The Northern Finland 1966 Birth Cohort study. *Psychiatry Research, 113*, 217–226.

Trupin, E. W., Stewart, D. G., Beach, B., & Boesky, L. (2002). Effectiveness of a Dialectical Behaviour Therapy Program for incarcerated female juvenile offenders. *Child and Adolescent Mental Health, 7*, 121–127.

van den Bree, M. B. M., Svikis, D. S., & Pickens, R. W. (1998). Genetic influences in antisocial personality and drug use disorders. *Drug and Alcohol Dependence, 49*, 177–187.

Wang, L. F., Heppner, P. P., & Berry, T. R. (1997). Role of gender-related personality traits, problem-solving appraisal, and perceived social support in developing a mediational model of psychological adjustment. *Journal of Counseling Psychology, 44*, 245–255.

Watson, D. C. & Sinha, B. K. (1999–2000). Stress, emotion, and coping strategies as predictors of personality disorder pathology. *Imagination, Cognition, and Personality, 19*, 279–294.

Williams, J. G. & Kleinfelter, K. J. (1989). Perceived problem solving skills and drinking patterns among college students. *Psychological Reports, 65*, 1235–1244.

Woody, G. E., McLellan, A., Luborsky, L., & O'Brien, C. P. (1985). Sociopathy and psychotherapy outcome. *Archives of General Psychiatry, 42*, 1081–1086.

World Health Organization (1993). *The ICD-10-classification of mental and behavioral disorders: Diagnostic criteria for research.* Geneva: World Health Organization.

Wright, D. M. & Heppner, P. P. (1991). Coping among nonclinical college age children of alcoholics. *Journal of Counseling Psychology, 38*, 465–472.

Zamble, E. & Porporino, F. J. (1990). Coping, imprisonment, and rehabilitation: Some data and their implications. *Criminal Justice and Behavior, 17*, 53–70.

Zamble, E. & Quinsey, V. L. (1997). *The criminal recidivism process.* Cambridge: Cambridge University Press.

Zanis, D. A., Coviello, D., Alterman, A. I., & Appling, S. E. (2001). A community-based trial of vocational problem-solving to increase employment among methadone patients. *Journal of Substance Abuse Treatment, 21*, 19–26.

Chapter 5

SOCIAL PROBLEM-SOLVING DEFICITS IN OFFENDERS

Daniel H. Antonowicz[1] and Robert R. Ross[2]

[1]Wilfrid Laurier University–Brantford, Canada
[2]University of Ottawa, Canada

INTRODUCTION

Research has yielded some evidence to indicate that a number of social cognitive skill deficits are associated with criminal offending (McGuire, 2002; Ross & Fabiano, 1985). In a book entitled *Time to Think*, Ross and Fabiano (1985) reviewed the empirical research literature to examine the link between a variety of cognitive skill variables and offending: social or interpersonal problem-solving, self-control/impulsivity, locus of control, concrete versus abstract reasoning, social perspective-taking, role-taking, and empathy. It is beyond the scope of this chapter to review the recent empirical research studies for all of the cognitive skill deficits examined by Ross and Fabiano in 1985. A review of the post-1985 literature can be found in a new edition of *Time to Think* (Ross & Hilborn, 2005). This chapter will focus on reviewing the empirical evidence of the link between one specific cognitive skill and offending—social problem-solving. In this chapter, empirical research studies conducted to examine this relationship will be reviewed and some of the more commonly used measures of social problem-solving will be described. Following this, there will be a brief description of some social problem-solving interventions for offenders such as Platt's Wharton Tract program and the *Reasoning and Rehabilitation (R&R)* program. Finally, conclusions and directions for future research will be provided. However, first, some background will be provided on the general literature pertaining to social problem-solving skills.

Over the years, considerable attention has been devoted to studying social problem-solving deficits in individuals. Deficits in social problem-solving have

Social Problem Solving and Offending: Evidence, Evaluation and Evolution.
Edited by Mary McMurran and James McGuire © 2005 John Wiley & Sons, Ltd.

been associated with a number of emotional and behavioural problems in both children and adults (D'Zurilla & Nezu, 1982; D'Zurilla, Nezu, & Maydeu-Olivares, 2002; Shure and Spivack, 1972; Shure & Spivack, 1982; Tisdelle & St. Lawrence, 1986). Some more recent examples include contributions made to this book by Keltikangas-Jàrvinen on social problem solving and the development of aggression (Chapter 2) and by Matthys and Lochman on social problem solving and childhood maladjustment (Chapter 3). In the present chapter, we will focus on the relationship between social problem-solving deficits and criminal offending.

Social problem-solving skills have been identified as being crucial to social competency which is related to successful life adjustment. Several researchers have found that knowledge and use of social problem-solving skills are important aspects of mental health and behavioural adjustment (see Tisdelle & St. Lawrence, 1986).

As detailed by James McGuire in Chapter 1, there are two models of social problem solving that have been developed and empirically tested: interpersonal cognitive problem solving (ICPS; Spivack et al., 1976); and problem-solving therapy (PST; D'Zurilla & Goldfried, 1971). Both models assert that individuals can be trained to be more competent problem solvers. The D'Zurilla and Goldfried model has frequently been cited in work with individuals on emotional and mental health problems whereas the model developed by Spivack et al. has been extensively applied in child development and educational settings. Spivack, Shure and their colleagues have been instrumental in designing and implementing social problem-solving programs for children aged 4 years and older.

Both models advocate teaching skills such as awareness of interpersonal problems, defining problems, causal thinking, consequential or alternative thinking, means–end thinking, and perspective-taking (Husband & Platt, 1993). For a more detailed description of the ICPS problem-solving model and evidence supporting its efficacy please, see Platt and Hermalin (1989), Platt, Prout, and Metzger (1986), and Spivack, Platt, and Shure (1976). The PST model and a description of the growing body of research that supports its efficacy for a range of psychological and behavioral disorders are addressed by Nezu, D'Zurilla, and Nezu in Chapter 6 of this volume, and also in Chang, D'Zurilla, and Sanna (2004), D'Zurilla and Goldfried (1971), D'Zurilla and Nezu (1982), and D'Zurilla and Nezu (1999).

Less attention has been devoted to examining social problem-solving in criminal offenders. In the next sections we will briefly review two of the more commonly used measures of social problem solving as well as the empirical studies on the link between social problem solving deficits and offending.

MOST COMMONLY USED MEASURES OF SOCIAL PROBLEM SOLVING

In this section, we will describe two measures that have been commonly used in the social problem-solving literature: the Means–Ends Problem-Solving

Procedure (MEPS; Platt & Spivack, 1975) and the Social Problem-Solving Inventory – Revised (SPSI-R; D'Zurilla, Nezu, & Maydeu-Olivares, 2002). Other measures that have been used by researchers, that will not be described here, include the Problem-Solving Inventory (Heppner & Petersen, 1982), the Interpersonal Problem-Solving Assessment Technique (Getter & Nowinski, 1981), and the Adolescent Problems Inventory (Freedman, Rosenthal, Donahoe, Schlundt, & McFall, 1978; Palmer & Hollin, 1996). For a more detailed review of these measures of social problem-solving, see D'Zurilla and Maydeu-Olivares (1995).

The MEPS procedure (Platt & Spivack, 1975) has been used in a number of studies since it was first developed. According to Platt and Spivack, this instrument measures the ability to plan step-by-step means to achieve a stated goal in a given situation. The individual is required to conceptualize appropriate and effective means of reaching a specified goal in order to satisfy a need in a situation. This measure may be either administered to individuals using an interview or a pencil-and-paper format. A series of ten hypothetical interpersonal problems of incomplete stories that are comprised of only a beginning and an ending are presented to individuals. Individuals are asked to make up the middle part of the story that links the beginning of the story to the end. A quantitative scoring system is then used that computes separate frequency scores for relevant means, obstacles, and time. Support for the reliability and validity of MEPS can be found in Nezu & D'Zurilla (1989), Platt and Spivack (1975), and Spivack et al. (1976).

The second measure represents a more recent development - the Social Problem-Solving Inventory-Revised (SPSI-R; D'Zurilla, Nezu, & Maydeu-Olivares, 2002). The SPSI-R is a 52-item self-report measure that reflects the multidimensional nature of social problem-solving (Nezu, in press). According to Nezu (in press), social problem-solving consists of a variety of cognitive, affective, and behavioural skill components. This measure has five subscales: (1) Positive Problem Orientation (PPO), an optimistic attitude to tackling problems; (2) Negative Problem Orientation (NPO), a pessimistic attitude to solving problems; (3) Rational Problem Solving (RPS), a systematic approach to solving problems, including problem definition, problem analysis, and generation of alternative solutions; (4) Impulsive/Careless Style (ICS), an ill-thought-out and hurried approach to solving problems; and (5) Avoidance Style (AS), a tendency to procrastinate, blame others, or depend on others to solve one's problems. Problem-solving orientation is measured by two subscales—PPO and NPO—while the other three subscales measure problem-solving styles, i.e. RPS, ICS, and AS. Support for the reliability and validity of this measure is documented by D'Zurilla, Nezu and Maydeu-Olivares (2002). Next, we will review the empirical studies that have incorporated some of these measures.

EMPIRICAL STUDIES

Ross and Fabiano (1985) undertook a comprehensive search of the literature to determine: (1) if there was any empirical evidence to indicate that offenders differ from non-offenders in cognitive skill functioning; and (2) whether there was any evidence that antisocial behaviour is associated with inadequate cognitive functioning. Despite the fact that they found a considerable body of evidence of cognitive deficits among offenders, a number of shortcomings in the quality of the research limit what can be concluded about both the nature and the strength of the link. For instance, different researchers employed similar terms to refer to different cognitive functions and some do not define the cognitive functions they purport to have measured. Furthermore, a wide variety of tests has been used; this makes it difficult to synthesize the results since it is not known whether all the tests are measuring the same concept. In their review of a number of cognitive skills such as social problem solving, perspective-taking, and empathy, Ross and Fabiano (1985) found that there was sufficient evidence to support the link between social problem solving and offending. In the rest of this section, studies that were included in the Ross and Fabiano (1985) review and those conducted subsequent to it will be reviewed.

In one of the earliest studies on the social problem-solving abilities of offenders, Platt, Scura, and Hannon (1973) compared 28 young prisoners addicted to heroin with 31 non-addicted controls from a state reformatory in the United States. Using the MEPS procedure, these researchers found that those addicted to heroin were less able to provide solutions to problematic life situations, had fewer step-by-step means toward reaching problem resolution stages of the stories, and had a lower ratio of relevant responses than those not addicted.

In another study, Hains and Ryan (1983) investigated whether there were differences between delinquents and non-delinquents on knowledge of social problem solving and on a social problem-solving task. Two measures were developed specifically for the purposes of this study and were administered to 35 10–11-year-old and 40 14–25-year-old male delinquents and non-delinquents. Knowledge of social and self-control strategies for social problem solving was assessed using a five-item social metacognition questionnaire. Participants were asked to indicate ways of: (1) meeting a new girl in school; (2) avoiding the temptation of going to the movies with friends when homework needs to be done; and (3) staying out of a fight with another youth. For the final two items, they were asked to indicate strategies that non-delinquents used to avoid trouble and strategies that might be taught to delinquents to help them stay out of trouble. A strategic social thinking measure was created to assess the five different dimensions of social problem solving, namely:

1. antecedents to the problem;
2. alternative decisions to resolve the problem;
3. consequences for these decisions;
4. importance of the consequences;
5. likelihood of these consequences (Hains & Ryan, 1983).

Individuals were asked to consider the five problem-solving dimensions in solving four social dilemmas. In terms of knowledge of strategies to solve social problems, the results revealed that all groups were found to display comparable knowledge with the exception of younger delinquents. In regards to the social problem-solving task, older non-delinquents were found to be more comprehensive in considering the various problem-solving dimensions than the other groups.

In another study with offenders, Costello, Cohen, Goldstein, and Almanta (1983, as cited in Tisdelle & St. Lawrence, 1986) found that incarcerated delinquents showed significant deficits in social problem-solving skills when compared to controls. Unfortunately, no other details were provided about the nature of the study. As a result, we do not know which measure of social problem solving was employed in this study, how the samples were derived, or the sample size.

Two studies conducted by Guerra examined social problem-solving skills. In the first study, Slaby and Guerra (1988) investigated six information-processing components of social problem-solving:

1. seeking information;
2. defining the problem;
3. selecting a goal;
4. generating alternative solutions;
5. anticipating consequences;
6. prioritizing responses.

The skills in solving social problems of adolescent males and females incarcerated for antisocial aggression offences were compared to those of high school students who were rated as either high or low in aggression. The antisocial aggressive group was selected from a sample of adolescents incarcerated in a juvenile correctional facility in the United States for having committed one or more violent offences (i.e., assault and battery, robbery, rape, attempted murder, murder). The individuals in the high-aggressive and low-aggressive groups were selected from a sample of Grade 11 and 12 students from one public high school. The school was chosen since it was similar to the correctional facility in terms of geographic location, high percentage of lower- and middle-class youth, and high percentage of minority youth (African-American and Hispanics). The study sample was comprised of 56 violent juvenile offenders (antisocial aggressive) and 68 high aggressive and 70 low aggressive students. In general, the results indicated that high levels of aggression were associated with low levels of social problem-solving skills. In addition, antisocial aggressive individuals were most likely to solve social problems by:

1. defining problems in hostile ways;
2. adopting hostile goals;
3. seeking few additional facts;
4. generating few alternative solutions;
5. anticipating few consequences for aggression;
6. choosing few "best" and "second-best" solutions that were rated as "effective".

In contrast, low-aggressive individuals were least likely to solve problems in this manner.

In the second study, Guerra (1989) examined the consequential thinking of high-and low-level delinquent adolescents. Consequential thinking has generally been defined as an information-processing skill reflecting an individual's ability to generate a variety of consequences of responses to social problem situations (Shure, 1982). The sample included 245 African-American Grade 9 and 10 students (124 males and 121 females) attending a public high school in an inner-city neighbourhood of a large city in the midwestern United States. Male and female high school students were classified as either high and low delinquent, based on their responses to a self-report measure that assessed delinquent behaviour that had occurred one year prior to the time of testing.

Drawing upon hypothetical-reflective measures available in the literature (Marsh, 1982; Slaby & Guerra, 1988), Guerra developed a measure of consequential thinking for the purposes of this study. Her measure consisted of three hypothetical situations which required individuals to imagine that they were considering whether to commit an offence. These included: (1) a rule-breaking situation (non-violent); (2) a potentially violent situation; and (3) a violent situation. Following the presentation of each of the situations, six possible consequences were offered to the individual. Of the six consequences, two represented legal consequences, two represented moral consequences, and two represented social consequences. More specifically, the legal consequences involved being apprehended and punished; the moral consequences involved causing injury to others; and the social consequences involved the responses of the individual's peers to how the individual acted. The individuals were asked to rate the importance of each consequence, the probability of each consequence, and finally, the severity of each legal and moral consequence and for each social consequence the severity of their peers' reactions. The results of the study indicated that high-delinquents were found to be significantly more likely than their low-delinquent peers to minimize the importance, probability, and severity of the consequences of the rule breaking situation (cheating in an exam). However, these differences were not found for the situations involving potential violence or violence.

As part of a larger study on high-risk youth, Leadbeater, Hellner, Allen, and Aber (1989) examined the social problem-solving skills of 150 males and 121 females who had come to the attention of agencies that offer services to youth who engage in problem behaviours (e.g., delinquency, substance abuse). Leadbeater et al. administered the Adolescent Problem Inventory for Boys (Freedman et al., 1978) and the Problem Inventory for Adolescent Girls (Gaffney & McFall, 1981). They found that social problem-solving skills were moderately correlated with problem behaviours such as delinquency.

In another study involving adolescents, Greening (1997) examined the social problem-solving skills of 11 adolescent stealers in a court-ordered treatment program at a county mental health centre in the United States. This group of stealers was compared to 11 high school students who did not have a history of stealing. The individuals in the stealers group demonstrated a tendency not to consider the passage of time necessary for solving social problems on the MEPS test. In other words, they showed a tendency to become frustrated by the length of time it takes to achieve a goal or objective. The individuals with a history of stealing also demonstrated a bias for generating ineffective solutions to hypothetical social problems.

Two other studies cited in McGuire (2002) that examined young offenders will also be reviewed. In the first study, Wesner (1996) examined the social problem-solving skills of three groups of young offenders classified as Undersocialized Aggressive (UA), Socialized Aggressive (SA), and Anxiety-Withdrawal-Dysphoria (A-W-D) and a matched non-offender control group. The results of this study indicated that the problem-solving skills of non-offenders were superior to that of offenders. In terms of the offender group comparisons, the UA group presented with the least proficient problem-solving ability. Unfortunately, there were few methodological details provided in the description of the study.

In the second study cited in McGuire (2002), Whitton and McGuire (2002) compared a group of 38 young offenders to a group of 43 non-offenders in a school setting, using a problem checklist and a modified version of the Adolescent Problems Inventory (Freedman et al., 1978) to assess problem-solving competency. In relation to the control group, the young offenders were found to have a significantly higher frequency of serious problems. Furthermore, there was a significant inverse correlation between number of previous convictions and scores on the Adolescent Problems Inventory.

In a more recent study focusing on adolescents, Jaffee and D'Zurilla (2003) examined the social problem-solving abilities of adolescents and their parents and aggression and delinquency. Some 117 high school students, 83 of their mothers, and 73 of their fathers completed D'Zurilla et al.'s (2002) SPSI-R and measures of adolescent aggression and delinquency. The results indicated that adolescents' problem-solving ability was significantly lower than that of their parents. In addition, three dysfunctional problem-solving dimensions were found to be positively related to aggression and/or delinquency for the adolescent group. More specifically, avoidance style was found to be related to both aggression and delinquency; negative problem orientation was correlated with aggression; and impulsivity/carelessness style was related to delinquency.

Two studies have dealt with the social problem-solving abilities of adult offenders. In the first study, McMurran, Egan, Blair, and Richardson (2001) examined the relationship between the social problem-solving skill approaches and personality of 52 mentally disordered offenders detained in a regional secure unit in the United Kingdom. They found that high neuroticism was related to poor social problem solving as measured by the SPSI-R. McMurran et al. (2001) suggest that high scorers on neuroticism are not optimistic about their ability to solve problems, and tend to avoid problems or are careless in their approach to problem-solving. These researchers found that poor social problem-solving acted as a mediator between personality and criminal behaviour.

Second, Nezu, Nezu, Dudek, Peacock, and Stoll (2003, as cited in Nezu, D'Zurilla, & Nezu, Chapter 6 in this volume) assessed the relationship between various social problem-solving variables and sex offending and aggression among child molesters using the SPSI-R (D'Zurilla, Nezu, & Maydeu-Olivares, 2002). The results suggest that several components of social problem-solving appear to be significantly related to sexual offending among child molesters. The specific components were negative problem orientation, impulsivity/carelessness style, and avoidance style. However, no significant relationship was discovered between rational problem solving and sex offending. Unfortunately, few other methodological details were provided about the study.

Additional support for the link between problem solving and offending stems from studies on the coping behaviour of prisoners (e.g., Higgins & Thies, 1981; Zamble & Porporino, 1988). Both studies found that poor problem-solving skills were found in maladjusted incarcerated offenders.

Overall, the evidence from a number of empirical studies presented and reviewed in this chapter indicates that there is a link between social problem solving and offending. These studies suggest that deficits in social problem-solving skills may lead to criminal activities or offending. In the next section we will briefly describe interventions that target social problem-solving deficits.

COGNITIVE-BEHAVIOURAL AND SOCIAL PROBLEM-SOLVING INTERVENTIONS

There is a large body of literature on outcome evaluations of cognitive behavioural and cognitive skills treatment programmes for offenders that has shown these interventions to have beneficial effects (see Lipsey, Chapman, & Landenberger, 2001; Pearson, Lipton, Cleland, & Yee, 2002; Ross, Antonowicz, & Dhaliwal, 1995; Ross & Ross, 1995). McGuire (2002) indicated that problem-solving is a common component of many of these cognitive-behavioural programmes. More specifically, meta-analyses and component analyses have consistently found found that programmes that incorporated approaches to address social problem-solving, empathy, social perspective-taking, or social skills were significantly more effective than those that did not (Antonowicz & Ross, 1994; Izzo & Ross, 1990; Ross & Fabiano, 1985).

Two programmes that have incorporated approaches to address social problem-solving deficits in offenders are the *Wharton Tract Program*, developed by Platt and his colleagues (Platt et al., 1980), and *Reasoning and Rehabilitation*, developed by Ross, Fabiano, and Ross (1986). In one of the earliest evaluations of a social problem-solving intervention for offenders, Platt and his colleagues (Platt et al., 1980; Platt, Labate, & Wicks, 1977) conducted a study of incarcerated male heroin addicts who were participating in the *Wharton Tract Program* in the United States. The programme was a structured group intervention that combined elements of guided group interaction and Interpersonal Cognitive Problem-Solving Skills (ICPS) training. The problem-solving skills that were addressed in this programme included recognizing problems, generating alternatives, consequential thinking, means–end thinking, and perspective-taking. The results revealed that programme participants had significantly lower arrest and recommitment rates than controls at a two-year follow-up.

Drawing on Platt's work on social problem solving and the work of others on a number of other cognitive skills including perspective-taking and empathy, Ross, Fabiano, and Ross (1986) developed the *Reasoning and Rehabilitation (R&R)* programme for offenders. R&R is a multi-modal programme that has incorporated components of problem-solving training with other elements of cognitive skills training. A number of evaluations have been conducted over the years. Another chapter prepared by the senior author in this volume describes the outcome evaluations of *R&R* that have been conducted to date (Antonowicz, Chapter 9 in this volume).

Ross and Ross (1995) indicated that many offenders lack skills in interpersonal cognitive problem solving that are essential for solving problems when interacting with people. In their interpersonal relations, they may fail to recognize that a problem, exists or is about to occur. If they do recognize a problem they may not be able to understand it and therefore are unable to solve it. If they do understand it, they may not be able to conceptualize alternative solutions to it. They may not stop to think of another solution or try another approach. They may experience difficulty in calculating the consequences of their behaviour on other people.

Other more recent examples of problem-solving interventions for offenders include a programme developed for probation settings in the United Kingdom (McGuire & Hatcher, 2001) and a programme for sex offenders on parole in the United States (Nezu et al., 2003, cited in Nezu, D'Zurilla, & Nezu, Chapter 6 in this volume). Both programmes will have recidivism outcome results available in the near future. Nezu et al. (2003) are currently conducting a randomized outcome study in which programme participants will be compared to a waiting-list control. Furthermore, another programme has been developed to address social problem-solving deficits in mentally-disordered offenders located in a secure psychiatric unit in the United Kingdom, as described by McMurran et al. (Chapter 11 in this volume).

DISCUSSION

Social problem-solving deficits have been related to a number of emotional and adjustment difficulties in individuals (Chang et al., 2004). More specifically, it is often claimed that many offenders are characterized by deficits in social problem solving. The evidence from a number of empirical studies presented and reviewed in this chapter indicates that there is a link between social problem solving and offending. Studies suggest that deficits in social problem-solving skills may lead to criminal activities or offending. The findings from more recent studies are consistent with earlier studies.

The multidimensional nature of social problem solving should be taken into consideration in both assessment of offenders and in the design and development of interventions for offenders. The selection of offenders for programmes should be based on sound psychometric measures that tap into the various dimensions of social problem solving. This would assist programme managers in assigning offenders to interventions that target the relevant dimensions and hopefully, as a result, would maximize the effects of the available interventions.

Future directions for research include examining:

1. gender differences in social problem-solving abilities of offenders;
2. differences between subtypes of offenders;

3. the link between various personality characteristics and social problem-solving;

4. the differential impact of targeting the various components of social problem solving on post-intervention offending.

The evidence reviewed in this chapter provides further support for the growing number of researchers who promote social problem-solving skills training with offenders (Cullen & Gendreau, 1989; McGuire, 2002; McMurran, et al., 1999); Ross & Ross, 1995). As indicated in this chapter, recent years have witnessed an increasing number of programmes being developed to target social problem-solving deficits in offenders. While some problem-solving programmes are producing consistent reductions in antisocial behaviour (Durlak, Fuhrman & Lampman, 1991; Guerra, Attar, & Weissberg, 1997; Kazdin, Bass, Siegel, & Thomas, 1989; Kazdin & Crowley, 1997), the effects of most of those programmes have been small and many of those treated remain more antisocial than their same-age peers (e.g., Kazdin et al., 1989; Kazdin & Crowley, 1997). This may be due to the fact that most of these programmes have been limited to training in problem-solving skills and have not focused on the development of the other social reasoning skills, emotional skills, and values. Problem-solving skills may be essential but they are not sufficient for the acquisition of prosocial competence.

REFERENCES

Antonowicz, D. H. & Ross, R. R. (1994). Essential components of successful rehabilitation programs for offenders. *International Journal of Offender Therapy and Comparative Criminology, 38,* 97-104.

Chang, E. C., D'Zurilla, T. J., & Sanna, L. J. (eds) (2004). *Social problem solving: Theory, research, and training.* Washington, DC: American Psychological Association.

Clark, D. (2000). *Theory manual for enhanced thinking skills.* Prepared for the Joint Prison Probation Service Accreditation Panel.

Cullen, F. T. & Gendreau, P. (1989). The effectiveness of correctional rehabilitation: Reconsidering the "Nothing Works" doctrine. In L. Goodstein & D. L. MacKenzie (eds) *The American prison: Issues in research policy* (pp. 23-44). New York: Plenum Press.

D'Zurilla, T. J. & Goldfried, M. R. (1971). Problem solving and behavior modification. *Journal of Abnormal Psychology, 78,* 107–126.

D'Zurilla, T. J. & Maydeu-Olivares, A. (1995). Conceptual and methodological issues in social problem-solving assessment. *Behavior Therapy, 26,* 409–432.

D'Zurilla T. J. & Nezu, A. M. (1982). Social problem-solving therapy in adults. In P. C. Kendall (ed.) *Advances in cognitive-behavioral research and therapy* Vol. 1. (pp. 201–274). New York: Academic Press.

D'Zurilla T. J. & Nezu, A. M. (1999). *Problem-solving therapy: A social competence approach to clinical intervention.* 2nd edn. New York: Springer.

D'Zurilla, T. J., Nezu, A. M., & Maydeu-Olivares, A. (2002). *Social Problem-Solving Inventory – Revised (SPSI-R): Technical manual.* North Tonawanda, NY: Multi-Health Systems.

Durlak, J. A., Fuhrman, T., & Lampman, C. (1991). Effectiveness of cognitive-behavior therapy for maladapting children: A meta-analysis. *Psychological Bulletin, 110,* 204–214.

Freedman, B. I., Rosenthal, L., Donahue, C. P. Jr., Schlundt, D. G., & McFall, R. M. (1978). A social-behavioral analysis of skill deficits in delinquent and non-delinquent boys. *Journal of Consulting and Clinical Psychology, 46* ,1448–1462.

Gaffney, L. R. & McFall, R. M. (1981). A comparison of social skills in delinquent and nondelinquent adolescent girls using a behavioral role playing inventory. *Journal of Consulting and Clinical Psychology, 49*, 959–967.

Getter, H. & Nowinski, J. K. (1981). A free response test of interpersonal effectiveness. *Journal of Personality Assessment, 45*, 301–308.

Greening, L. (1997). Adolescent stealers' and nonstealers' social problem-solving skills. *Adolescence, 32*, 51–55.

Guerra, N. G. (1989). Consequential thinking and self-reported delinquency in high-school youth. *Criminal Justice and Behavior, 16*, 440–454.

Guerra, N. G., Attar, B., & Weissberg, R. P. (1997). Prevention of aggression and violence among inner-city youths. In D. M. Stoff, J. Breiling, & J. D. Maser (eds) *Handbook of antisocial behavior* (pp. 375–383). New York: John Wiley & Sons, Ltd.

Hains, A. A. & Ryan, E. B. (1983). The development of social cognitive processes among juvenile delinquents and nondelinquent peers. *Child Development, 54*, 1536–1544.

Heppner, P. P., & Petersen, C. H. (1982). The development and implications of a personal problem-solving inventory. *Journal of Counseling Psychology, 29*, 166–175.

Higgins, J. P. & Thies, A. P. (1981). Social effectiveness and problem-solving thinking of reformatory inmates. *Journal of Offender Services, Counseling and Rehabilitation, 5*, 93–98.

Husband, S. D. & Platt, J. J. (1993). The cognitive skills component in substance abuse treatment in correctional settings: A brief review. *Journal of Drug Issues, 23*, 31–42.

Izzo, R. L. & Ross, R. R. (1990). Meta-analysis of rehabilitation programs for juvenile delinquents: A brief report. *Criminal Justice and Behavior, 17*, 134–142.

Jaffee, W. B. & D'Zurilla, T. J. (2003). Adolescent problem solving, parent problem solving, and externalizing behavior in adolescents. *Behavior Therapy, 34*, 295–311.

Kazdin, A. E., Bass, D., Siegel, T., & Thomas, C. (1989). Cognitive-behavioral therapy and relationship therapy in the treatment of children referred for antisocial behavior. *Journal of Consulting and Clinical Psychology, 57*, 522–535.

Kazdin, A. E. & Crowley, M. J. (1997). Moderators of treatment outcome in cognitively based treatment of antisocial children. *Cognitive Therapy and Research, 21*, 185–207.

Leadbeater, B. J., Hellner, I., Allen, J. P., & Aber, J. L. (1989). Assessment of interpersonal negotiation strategies in youth engaged in problem behaviors. *Developmental Psychology, 25*, 465–472.

Lipsey, M. W., Chapman, G. L., & Landenberger, N. A. (2001). Cognitive-behavioral programs for offenders. *Annals of the American Academy of Political and Social Science, 578*, 144–157.

Marsh, D. T. (1982). The development of interpersonal problem-solving among elementary school children. *Journal of Genetic Psychology, 140*, 107–118.

McGuire, J. (2002). What is problem-solving? A review of theory, research and applications. *Criminal Behaviour and Mental Health, 11*, 210–235.

McGuire, J. & Hatcher, R. (2001). Offence-focused problem solving: Preliminary evaluation of a cognitive skills program. *Criminal Justice and Behavior, 28*, 564–587.

McMurran, M., Egan, V., Blair, M., & Richardson, C. (2001). The relationship between social problem-solving and personality in mentally disordered offenders. *Personality and Individual Differences, 30*, 517–524.

McMurran, M., Egan, V., Richardson, C., & Ahmadi, S. (1999). Social problem-solving in mentally disordered offenders: A brief report. *Criminal Behaviour and Mental Health, 9*, 315–322.

Nezu, A. M. (in press). Problem-solving and behavior therapy revisited. *Behavior Therapy.*

Palmer, E. J. & Hollin, C. R. (1996). Assessing adolescent problems: An overview of the Adolescent Problems Inventory. *Journal of Adolescence, 19*, 347–354.

Pearson, F. S., Lipton, D. S., Cleland, C. M., & Yee, D. S. (2002). The effects of behavioral/cognitive-behavioral programs on recidivism. *Crime and Delinquency, 48*, 476–496.

Platt, J. J. & Hermalin, J. (1989). Social skill deficit interventions for substance abusers. *Psychology of Addictive Behaviors, 3*, 114–133.

Platt, J.J., Labate, C., & Wicks, R. J. (1977). Evaluation of the Wharton Tract narcotics treatment program. In J.J. Platt, C. Labate, & R. J. Wicks (eds) *Evaluation research in correctional drug abuse treatment* (pp. 149-170). Lexington, MA: Lexington Books/D.C. Heath.

Platt, J. J., Perry, G., & Metzger, D. (1980). The evaluation of a heroin addiction treatment program within a correctional environment. In R.R. Ross & P. Gendreau (eds) *Effective correctional treatment* (pp. 421–437). Toronto: Butterworths.

Platt, J. J., Prout, M. F., & Metzger, D. S. (1986). Interpersonal cognitive problem-solving therapy. In W. Dryden & N. Gordon (eds) *Cognitive-behavioural approaches to psychotherapy* (pp. 261–289). London: Pergamon.

Platt, J.J. Scura, W., & Hannon, J. R. (1973). Problem-solving thinking of youthful incarcerated heroin addicts. *Journal of Community Psychology, 1*, 278–281.

Platt, J.J. & Spivack, G. (1975). *Manual for the Means–Ends Problem-Solving Procedure (MEPS): A measure of interpersonal cognitive problem-solving skills.* Philadelphia, PA: Hahnemann Community Mental Health/Mental Retardation Center.

Ross, R. R., Antonowicz, D. H., & Dhaliwal, G. K. (eds) (1995). *Going straight: Effective delinquency prevention and offender rehabilitation.* Ottawa: AIR Training and Publications.

Ross, R. R. & Fabiano, E. A. (1985). *Time to think: A cognitive model of delinquency prevention and offender rehabilitation.* Johnson City, TN: Institute of Social Sciences and Arts.

Ross, R. R., Fabiano, E. A., & Ross, R. D. (1986). *Reasoning and rehabilitation: A handbook for teaching cognitive skills.* Ottawa: Center for Cognitive Development.

Ross, R. R. & Ross, R. D. (eds) (1995). *Thinking straight: The Reasoning and Rehabilitation Program for delinquency prevention and offender rehabilitation.* Ottawa: AIR Training and Publications.

Ross, R. R. & Hilborn, J. (2005). *Time to think again: A prosocial competence approach to the prevention and treatment of antisocial behaviour.* Ottawa: Cognitive Centre of Canada.

Shure, M. B. (1982). Interpersonal problem-solving: A cog in the wheel of social cognition. In F. C. Serafica (ed) *Social cognitive development in context* (pp. 133–166). New York: Guilford, Press.

Shure, M. B. & Spivack, G. (1972). Means–end thinking, adjustment, and social class among elementary school-aged children. *Journal of Consulting and Clinical Psychology, 38*, 348–353.

Shure, M. B. & Spivack, G. (1982). Interpersonal problem solving in young children: A cognitive approach to prevention. *American Journal of Community Psychology, 10*, 341–356.

Slaby, R. G. & Guerra, N. G. (1988). Cognitive mediators of aggression in adolescent offenders: 1. Assessment. *Developmental Psychology, 24*, 580–588.

Spivack, G., Platt, J. J., & Shure, M. B. (1976). *The problem solving approach to adjustment.* San Francisco, CA: Jossey-Bass.

Tisdelle, D. A. & St. Lawrence, J. S. (1986). Interpersonal problem-solving competency: Review and critique of the literature. *Clinical Psychology Review, 6*, 337–356.

Zamble, E. & Porporino, F. J. (1988). *Coping behavior and adaptation in prison inmates.* New York: Springer.

Chapter 6

PROBLEM-SOLVING THERAPY: THEORY, PRACTICE, AND APPLICATION TO SEX OFFENDERS

CHRISTINE MAGUTH NEZU,[1] THOMAS J. D'ZURILLA,[2] and ARTHUR M. NEZU[1]
[1]Drexel University, Philadelphia, USA
[2]Stony Brook University, New York, USA

The term "Problem-Solving Therapy" (PST) refers to the application of training in constructive problem-solving attitudes and skills to the treatment and prevention of psychological and behavioral disorders (D'Zurilla & Goldfried, 1971; D'Zurilla & Nezu, 1999; A. M. Nezu, 2004). The aims of this chapter are: (1) to describe the theory underlying PST; (2) to discuss the relationship between problem solving and sex offending; (3) to provide a brief overview of general guidelines for conducting problem-solving therapy; and (4) to describe Project CBT, an outcome study currently in progress that involves the evaluation of a PST intervention for the treatment of sex offenders.

THE THEORY OF PST

The goal of PST is to reduce and prevent psychopathology by helping individuals cope more effectively with stressful problems. Effective coping may involve changing the problematic situation for the better (e.g., achieving a positive goal, removing an aversive condition), reducing the emotional distress generated by the problem (e.g., accepting an uncontrollable situation, making something good come from the problem), or both of these outcomes. The use of PST for this purpose is based on two conceptual models: (1) the social problem-solving model and (2) the relational/problem-solving model of stress.

Social Problem Solving and Offending: Evidence, Evaluation and Evolution.
Edited by Mary McMurran and James McGuire   © 2005 John Wiley & Sons, Ltd.

The Social Problem-Solving Model

The term "social problem solving" refers to problem solving as it occurs in the natural social environment (D'Zurilla & Nezu, 1982). The social problem-solving model presented here was originally introduced by D'Zurilla and Goldfried (1971) and later expanded and refined by D'Zurilla, Nezu, and Maydeu-Olivares (2002; D'Zurilla & Nezu, 1982, 1990, 1999; Maydeu-Olivares & D'Zurilla, 1995, 1996).

Definitions of Major Concepts

The three major concepts in social problem solving theory are: (1) problem solving; (2) problem; and (3) solution. *Problem solving* may be defined as the self-directed cognitive-behavioral process by which an individual, couple, or group attempts to identify or discover effective solutions for specific problems encountered in everyday life. As this definition implies, social problem solving is conceived here as a conscious, rational, effortful, and purposeful activity. Depending on the nature of the problematic situation (e.g., controllable vs. uncontrollable), this process may be aimed at changing the situation, reducing or modifying the emotions produced by the situation, or both. Social problem solving deals with all kinds of problems in living, including impersonal problems (e.g., insufficient finances, property damage), personal/intrapersonal problems (cognitive, emotional, behavioral, health), and interpersonal problems (e.g., interpersonal disputes, marital conflicts).

A *problem* (or problematic situation) is defined as any life situation or task (present or anticipated) that demands a response for adaptive functioning, but no effective response is immediately apparent or available to the person confronted with the situation due to the presence of one or more obstacles. The demands in a problematic situation may originate in the environment (e.g., objective task demands) or within the person (e.g., a personal goal, need, or commitment). The obstacles might include novelty, ambiguity, unpredictability, conflicting demands, performance skill deficits, or lack of resources. A specific problem might be a single time-limited event (e.g., forgetting an important appointment, an acute illness), a series of similar or related events (e.g., repeated unreasonable demands from a boss, repeated substance use by an adolescent daughter), or a chronic, ongoing situation (e.g., continuous pain or loneliness).

A *solution* is a situation-specific coping response or response pattern (cognitive and/or behavioral) that is the product or outcome of the problem-solving process when it is applied to a specific problematic situation. An *effective* solution is one that achieves the problem-solving goal (e.g., changing the situation for the better, reducing negative emotions, increasing positive emotions), while at the same time maximizing other positive consequences and minimizing negative consequences. The relevant consequences include both personal and social outcomes, long-term as well as short-term.

Problem solving, as it has been defined above, should be distinguished from *solution implementation*. These two processes are conceptually different and require different sets of skills. Problem solving refers to the process of *finding* solutions to specific problems, whereas solution implementation refers to the process of *carrying out* those solutions in the actual problematic situations. Problem-solving skills are assumed to be general, whereas solution-implementation skills are expected to vary across situations depending on the type of problem and solution. Because they are different, problem-solving skills and solution-implementation skills are not always correlated. Hence, some individuals might possess poor problem-solving skills but good solution-implementation skills, or vice versa. Because both sets of skills are required for effective functioning or social competence, it is often necessary in PST to combine training in problem-solving skills with training in other social and behavioral performance skills in order to maximize positive outcomes (D'Zurilla & Nezu, 1999).

Major Problem-Solving Dimensions

A major assumption of the social problem-solving model is that problem-solving outcomes in the real world are largely determined by two general, partially independent processes: (1) problem orientation; and (2) problem-solving style (also referred to as "problem-solving proper", e.g., D'Zurilla & Nezu, 1999). *Problem orientation* is a metacognitive process that primarily serves a motivational function in social problem solving. It involves the operation of a set of relatively stable cognitive-emotional schemas that reflect a person's general beliefs and feelings about problems in living, as well as his or her own problem-solving ability. *Problem-solving style*, on the other hand, refers to the cognitive and behavioral activities by which a person attempts to understand problems in everyday living and find effective "solutions" or ways of coping with them.

   During the past two decades or so, the collective research of D'Zurilla, Nezu, and Maydeu-Olivares on these two general problem-solving processes has culminated in a five-dimensional model of social problem solving consisting of two different, albeit related, problem orientation dimensions and three different problem-solving styles (see D'Zurilla et al., 2002). The two problem orientation dimensions are *positive problem orientation* and *negative problem orientation*, whereas the three problem-solving styles are *rational problem solving*, *impulsivity/carelessness style*, and *avoidance style*. Positive problem orientation and rational problem solving are constructive dimensions that increase the likelihood of positive problem-solving outcomes, whereas negative problem orientation, impulsivity/carelessness style and avoidance style are dysfunctional dimensions that disrupt or inhibit effective problem solving, resulting in negative personal and social outcomes.

   Positive problem orientation is a constructive problem-solving cognitive set that involves the general disposition:

1. to appraise a problem as a "challenge" (i.e., opportunity for benefit or gain);
2. to believe that problems are solvable ("optimism");
3. to believe in one's personal ability to solve problems successfully ("self-efficacy");
4. to believe that successful problem solving takes time, effort, and persistence;
5. to commit oneself to solving problems with dispatch rather than avoiding them.

In contrast, *negative problem orientation* is a dysfunctional or inhibitive cognitive-emotional set that involves the general tendency: (1) to view a problem as a significant threat to well-being (psychological, social, economic); (2) to doubt one's personal ability to solve problems successfully ("low self-efficacy"); and (3) to easily become frustrated and upset when confronted with problems in living ("low frustration tolerance").

Rational problem solving is a constructive problem-solving style that is defined as the rational, deliberate, and systematic application of effective problem-solving skills. In the present model, four major problem-solving skills are identified: (1) problem definition and formulation; (2) generation of alternative solutions; (3) decision-making; and (4) solution implementation and verification (D'Zurilla & Goldfried, 1971). Specifically, the rational problem solver carefully and systematically gathers facts and information about a problem, identifies demands and obstacles, sets realistic problem-solving goals, generates a variety of possible solutions, anticipates the consequences of the different solutions, judges and compares the alternatives, and then chooses and implements a solution while carefully monitoring and evaluating the outcome.

Impulsivity/carelessness style is a dysfunctional problem-solving pattern characterized by active attempts to apply problem-solving strategies and techniques, but these attempts are narrow, impulsive, careless, hurried, and incomplete. A person with this problem-solving style typically considers only a few solution alternatives, often impulsively going with the first idea that comes to mind. In addition, he or she scans alternative solutions and consequences quickly, carelessly, and unsystematically, and monitors solution outcomes carelessly and inadequately.

Avoidance style is another dysfunctional problem-solving pattern characterized by procrastination, passivity or inaction, and dependency. The avoidant problem solver prefers to avoid problems rather than confronting them immediately, puts off problem solving for as long as possible, waits for problems to resolve themselves, and attempts to shift the responsibility for solving his or her problems to other people.

The five problem-solving dimensions described above can be measured by the Social Problem-Solving Inventory-Revised (SPSI-R; D'Zurilla et al., 2002). Using this instrument, "good" social problem-solving ability is indicated by high scores on positive problem orientation and rational problem solving and low scores on negative problem orientation, impulsivity/carelessness style, and avoidance style, whereas "poor" social problem-ability is indicated by low scores on positive problem orientation and rational problem solving and high scores on negative problem orientation, impulsivity/carelessness style, and avoidance style.

A Relational/Problem-Solving Model of Stress

The major assumption underlying the use of PST is that symptoms of "psychopathology" (e.g., behavior deficits and deviations, interpersonal dysfunction, excessive negative affect) can often be understood and effectively treated or prevented by viewing them as ineffective, inappropriate, or maladaptive coping behavior and its negative personal and social consequences (D'Zurilla & Goldfried, 1971). Based on this assumption, the conceptual framework underlying PST is a relational/problem-solving model of stress in which the concept of social problem solving is given a central role as a general coping strategy that increases adaptive functioning while reducing and preventing the negative impact of stress on psychological and physical well-being (D'Zurilla, 1990; D'Zurilla & Nezu, 1999; A. M. Nezu, 1987; 2004, A. M. Nezu & D'Zurilla, 1989).

The relational/problem-solving model integrates Richard Lazarus' relational model of stress (Lazarus, 1999; Lazarus & Folkman, 1984) with the social problem-solving model presented above. In Lazarus' model, "stress" is defined as a particular type of person–environment relationship in which demands are appraised by the person as taxing or exceeding coping resources and threatening his or her well-being (Lazarus & Folkman, 1984). Comparing this relational definition of stress to the definition of a "problem" described earlier, it can be concluded that a problem is also a "stressor" if it is at all difficult and significant for well-being. Hence, within the relational/problem-solving model, stress is viewed as a function of the reciprocal relations among three major variables: (1) stressful life events, with an emphasis on everyday problems; (2) emotional stress responses; and (3) problem-solving coping.

Stressful life events are life experiences that present a person with strong demands for personal, social, or biological readjustment (Bloom, 1985). Two major types of stressful life events are major negative events and daily problems. A *major negative event* is a broad life experience, such as a major negative life change, which often requires sweeping readjustments in a person's life (e.g., divorce, death of a loved one, job loss, major illness or injury). In contrast, a *daily problem* (or problematic situation) is a more narrow and specific life experience defined by the existence of a perceived discrepancy between situational demands and coping response availability. Although major negative events and daily problems may develop independently in a person's life, they are often causally related (A. M. Nezu & D'Zurilla, 1989). A major negative event, such as a divorce, or imprisonment, usually creates many new stressful problems (e.g., financial, social, sexual, parenting). Conversely, an accumulation of unresolved daily problems may eventually cause or contribute to a major negative event (e.g., job loss, cardiac disease, criminal behavior). Some research suggests that the number of daily problems in one's life may have a greater negative impact on well-being than the number of major negative events (Kanner, Coyne, Schaefer, & Lazarus, 1981; A. M. Nezu, 1986; A. M. Nezu & Ronan, 1985; Weinberger, Hiner, & Tierney, 1987).

The concept of *emotional stress* refers to the immediate emotional responses of a person to stressful life events, as modified or transformed by cognitive appraisal and coping processes (Lazarus, 1999). Although emotional stress responses are often negative (e.g., anxiety, anger, depression), they can also be positive in nature (e.g., hope, relief, exhilaration). Negative affect is likely to predominate when the person (1) appraises a problem as harmful or threatening to well-being; (2) doubts his or her ability to cope effectively; and/or (3) performs ineffective or maladaptive coping responses. On the other hand, positive affect may occur and compete with negative affect when the person (1) appraises the problem as a challenge or opportunity for benefit; (2) believes that he or she is capable of coping with the problem effectively; and (3) performs coping responses that are successful in resolving the problem satisfactorily.

The most important concept in the relational/problem-solving model is *problem-solving coping*, a process that integrates all cognitive appraisal and coping activities within a general social problem-solving framework. A person who applies the problem-solving coping strategy effectively (1) perceives a stress situation as a "problem-to-be-solved"; (2) believes that he/she is capable of resolving the problem successfully; (3) generates a variety of alternative "solutions" or coping responses; (4) chooses the "best" solution; (5) implements the solution effectively; and (6) carefully observes and evaluates the outcome. Depending on the nature of the situation and how it is appraised (e.g., controllable vs. uncontrollable), the problem-solving goals may be problem-focused (i.e., aimed at altering the situation), emotion-focused (i.e., aimed at reducing or modifying one's emotions), or both.

In addition to providing a theoretical rationale for PST, the relational/problem-solving model of stress also provides a useful cognitive-behavioral framework for assessing clinical problems prior to treatment. During assessment, the problem-solving therapist identifies and pinpoints major negative life events, current daily problems, emotional stress responses, problem orientation deficits and distortions, problem-solving style deficits, and solution implementation deficits. Based on this assessment, PST is then applied:

1. to increase one's positive problem orientation;
2. to reduce one's negative problem orientation;
3. to improve rational problem-solving skills;
4. to reduce or prevent impulsive/careless problem solving;
5. to minimize the tendency to avoid problem solving.

If necessary, effective solution implementation skills (e.g., assertiveness skills, communication skills) are also taught. The successful achievement of these goals is expected to increase adaptive situational coping, general competence, and positive psychological and physical well-being, while reducing and preventing the negative effects of stress on personal-social functioning and well-being.

During the past two decades, a growing body of empirical research has provided support for the theory underlying PST. In addition, there is also a growing body of outcome research that supports the efficacy of PST for a variety of psychological and behavioral disorders. For recent reviews of this research, the reader is referred to Chang, D'Zurilla, and Sanna (2004), D'Zurilla and Nezu (1999), and A. M. Nezu (2004).

PROBLEM SOLVING AND SEX OFFENDING

The research and clinical literature addressing the association between problem solving and sex offending is somewhat misleading with specific regard to the level of interest afforded the etiological and treatment roles this psychological variable plays in sex-offending behaviors. On one hand, when conducting a literature search for the link between problem solving and sex offending, very little is directly identified. For example, in searching both PsychINFO and MEDLINE databases, there are only a handful of published citations are identified when looking for combinations between (social) problem solving and sex offenders. However, aspects of this psychosocial variable have frequently been invoked *indirectly* by researchers and clinicians in this field as both an explanatory variable and as an important treatment target (C. M. Nezu, 2003; C. M. Nezu, Nezu, & Dudek, 1998).

Problem Solving, Social Skills, and Sex Offending

One factor contributing to this confusion is the overlap between social skills and problem-solving skills. Social skills training is often a common approach to psychological treatment for sex offenders (McFall, 1990). However, research has collectively failed to identify a clear pattern of behavioral deficits for either rapists or child molesters, thus questioning the empirical basis underlying the popularity of such treatments for these individuals. To help explain this discrepancy, McFall argued that researchers need to better define what is termed "social skills". For example (McFall 1982 McFall & Dodge, 1982) developed an information-processing model of social skills in which three sequentially-staged component processes are identified as helping an individual transform incoming stimulus information, or the task demands in a given situation, into the actual behaviors that are enacted which are judged to be competent or incompetent. These include decoding skills, decision skills, and enactment skills. *Decoding skills* include the processes involved in the reception, perception, and interpretation of incoming information within a given situation. Herein lies some of the confusion regarding which constructs are actually under investigation with regard to sex offenders. More specifically, looking to the previously described problem-solving model, decoding skills appear to overlap with aspects of problem orientation and problem definition.

Decision skills, according to McFall's (1990) model, are the central processes by which the situation is subsequently transformed into the behavioral program to be carried out in the next stage. In noting the specific skills included in this process, the reader can further recognize the overlap between McFall's social skills model and our definitions of rational problem solving. Specifically, decision skills in his model include

> generating response options, matching these to task demands, selecting the best option, searching for that option in the behavioral repertoire, and evaluating the subjective utility of that option's likely outcomes relative to the likely outcomes of other options. If the person encounters a problem at any step, the decision process is recycled until it generates a behavioral program that the person considers appropriate, available, and acceptable. (ibid. p. 313).

Last, the third component process, that of *enactment skills*, involves the person executing the program, monitoring its impact on the environment, and making adjustments where necessary. Once again, the overlap between social skills and problem-solving skills is readily ascertained, as this set of skills mirror those included in the *solution implementation and verification* process of our problem-solving model.

Research regarding the link between this information-processing model of social skills and sex offending has focused mostly on decoding skills, indicating an association between sexual aggression and the inaccuracy of reading women's and children's cues in interpersonal situations. With regard to the "decision skills" component of this model, Goddard (1987, as reported by McFall, 1990) found that on a measure of heterosexual problem situations, peer-identified "competent" individuals scored better on a measure of decision-making as compared to their peer-identified "incompetent" counterparts. In addition, related unpublished research indicated that child molesters were equally as good as nonoffenders in recognizing the existence of a problem and at generating alternative solutions, but tended to choose socially unacceptable solutions and failed to recognize likely negative outcomes (Barbaree, Marshall, & Connor, 1988, as described by Stermac et al., 1990).

Problem Solving, Relapse Prevention, and Sex Offenders

Relapse Prevention (RP), a cognitive-behavioral treatment strategy, is another popular intervention for sex offenders (e.g., Laws, 1989). It was originally devised as a method of enhancing maintenance of change in substance abusers (e.g., Marlatt & Gordon, 1985) and modified by Pithers, Marques, Gibat, and Marlatt (1983) for application with sex offenders. The basic idea behind RP is that it represents a method of enhancing self-management skills by strengthening self-control in patients.

Relevant to the present discussion, the problem-solving model described previously also appears to share a major overlap with RP, thus creating additional confusion regarding the link between problem solving *per se* and sex offending. For example, according to Pithers (1990), in order to increase self-control in anticipation of encountering a high-risk situation (e.g., a child molester passing a schoolyard filled with children), individuals are directed to engage

> in a standard problem-solving process. Offenders follow a routine sequence of stages in problem solving: describe the problematic situation in detail, brainstorm potential coping responses, evaluate the likely outcome of each suggested coping strategy, and rate one's ability to enact the behavior. (p. 353)

However, similar to McFall's (1990) model of social skills, these problem-solving tasks are embedded in a differing conceptual model. As such, few investigators have attempted to isolate the link between the problem-solving skills as contained in the RP model and sex offending, thus limiting our ability to determine the exact nature and existence of a sex-offending association with problem solving *per se*.

Problem Solving and Sex Offenders

Although substantial clinical lore exists suggesting that sex offenders have poor problem-solving and decision-making skills (e.g., Jenkins-Hall, 1989), there is a dearth of published data to support this claim either directly (C. M. Nezu, Nezu, Dudek, Peacock, & Stoll, 2005) or indirectly as noted above. Despite this lack of an established empirical relationship between deficient problem solving and sex-offending behavior, many research and clinical programs incorporate aspects of problem-solving therapy within the context of a larger, multicomponent intervention for sex offenders (e.g., Friedman, Festinger, Nezu, McGuffin, & Nezu, 1999; Hains, Herrman, Baker, & Graber, 1986; Marshall & Barbaree, 1990; O'Connor, 1996).

Because sex offender-associated deficits in problem solving have not been clearly identified or empirically demonstrated, the validity of targeting such skills as meaningful offender-related mechanisms of action is questionable. To help bridge this gap in knowledge, Nezu and her colleagues (C. M. Nezu et al., 2005) recently assessed the relationship directly between various social problem-solving variables and sex-offending deviance and aggression among a population of child molesters using the Social Problem-Solving Inventory-Revised (SPSI-R; D'Zurilla, Nezu, & Maydeu-Olivares, 2002) as the major measure of problem solving.

The SPSI-R is a 52-item multi-dimensional measure of problem-solving ability derived from a factor analysis of the original theory-driven Social Problem-Solving Inventory (D'Zurilla & Nezu, 1990). In addition to a total score, it consists of five scales that measure two constructive dimensions (positive problem orientation, rational problem solving) and three dysfunctional dimensions (negative problem orientation, impulsivity/carelessness style, avoidance style). Respondents are asked to rate items (e.g., "I go out of my way to avoid having to deal with problems in my life"; "Before I try to solve a problem, I set a specific goal so that I know exactly what I want to accomplish") on a 5-point Likert-type scale ranging from 0 (*not at all true of me*) to 4 (*extremely true of me*). Higher scores on the constructive dimensions (e.g., rational problem solving) represent more effective problem solving, whereas higher scores on one of the dysfunctional dimensions (e.g., avoidance style) are indicative of more ineffective or maladaptive problem solving.

Research has found the SPSI-R to have strong internal consistency (range of alpha coefficients of 0.79–0.95 across the five scales) and test–retest reliability (estimates of 0.93 and 0.89 for the total score over a three-week period among two different samples), as well as strong structural, concurrent, predictive, convergent, and discriminant validity (D'Zurilla et al., 2002). It has also been found to be sensitive to the effects of treatment (e.g., A. M. Nezu, Nezu, Felgoise, McClure, & Houts, 2003).

To minimize the potential for biased self-reports in this study, criterion scores on a lie scale that is part of a greater self-report measure of sexual deviance (i.e., Multiphasic Sex Inventory, MSI; Nichols & Molinder, 1984) were employed to exclude individuals who might be prone to misrepresent their responses. This lie scale measures the openness verses dishonesty regarding a sexual offender's report of his deviant thoughts and behaviors. It has been standardized where at the low end of the scale (approaching zero), the offender is openly admitting his sexual deviance, whereas a score of 8 or more is indicative that the sex offender is likely to be dishonest about his deviant sexual interests. After all measures were administered and scored in this study, participants who received a score of greater than 7 on the MSI Child Molest Lie Scale were excluded from further consideration regarding data analysis. This led to a reduction of an original sample size of 124 incarcerated child molesters to 68 participants.

Initial results indicated that, in comparison to the norms provided in the SPSI-R manual (D'Zurilla et al., 2002), the sample of sexual offenders included in this study had mean scores on two problem-solving dimensions, negative problem orientation and impulsivity/carelessness style, that are significantly different from the general population in the direction of being more maladaptive. Further, their mean score on avoidance style showed a trend toward being 1 SD above the general population.

To assess the relationship between the various problem-solving dimensions and clinician-rated sexual aggression, a hierarchical multiple regression analysis was conducted. Results indicated that neither demographic variables nor variables measuring prior abuse were found to add significantly to the variance. The only statistically significant increase in the adjusted R^2 was associated with avoidance style.

To assess the association between problem solving and sexual deviancy among this sample of child molesters, a similar hierarchical regression was conducted as above, this time with the MSI serving as the dependent measure of current levels of sexual deviance. Overall, the model tested was found to account for 26% of the variance in statistically predicting self-reported sexual deviance ($p < 0.01$). Once again, neither demographic characteristics nor previous abuse were found to be significantly related to sexual aggression scores. However, impulsivity/carelessness style was found to add significantly to the R^2. Moreover, the regression analysis revealed that, beyond this amount, negative problem orientation added an additional increase to the R^2 value, was which also significant. The other three problem-solving dimensions (positive problem orientation, rational problem solving, avoidance style) were not significantly related to sexual aggression scores.

In general, these results suggest that several problem-solving variables appear to be significantly related to sexual-offending dimensions among child molesters (i.e., negative problem orientation, impulsivity/carelessness style, avoidance style). As such, given that such significant associations were identified, those interventions that have targeted problem solving as a meaningful mechanism of action would appear to be resting on solid and empirical grounding.

Of particular interest, however, is the lack of any significant association regarding rational problem solving as measured by the SPSI-R. As noted earlier, rational problem solving represents a series of skills, such as defining the problem, generating options, and decision-making, that collectively represent those behaviors that contribute to the discovery of an adaptive solution. Normatively, the sample of child molesters included in the C. M. Nezu et al. (2005) study scored close to the population mean regarding rational problem solving. Moreover, in the regression analyses, rational problem solving was not a significant predictor of either sexual aggression or sexual deviancy. This set of findings have important implications for designing treatment protocols for this population.

We have repeatedly emphasized the notion that social problem solving should *not* be viewed as a unitary construct, that it involves various cognitive, affective, and behavioral skill components (e.g., A. M. Nezu, 2004). As such, when developing interventions to improve one's problem-solving skills and abilities, clinicians and researchers need to take this multidimensional nature into account. Moreover, A. M. Nezu (2004) has noted that too often treatment programs that claim to include social problem-solving training, in fact, only include training in rational problem-solving skills. This helps to explain the variability in the efficacy of various problem-solving interventions in the literature (ibid.), as a dismantling study by A. M. Nezu and Perri (1989) found significant differences in outcome regarding an intervention based solely on training in rational problem solving as compared to one that included the "full model". Given the results from the C. M. Nezu et al. (2005) investigation, it would appear that child molesters may need less training in rational problem solving and more therapy addressing their negative problem orientation, impulsive-careless problem-solving style, and tendency to avoid problem solving. As such, we would advise future researchers to take the present findings into account (see, for example, the section on PST guidelines for sex offenders).

Although the C. M. Nezu et al. (2005) investigation does help establish the validity of a model of sex offending that includes social problem solving as one important vulnerability factor, it is unable to fully explain the causal mechanisms by which problem-solving variables impact upon sex offending. Future research should attempt to better elucidate these relationships in order to eventually obtain a more comprehensive and valid picture of the etiopathogenesis of this set of behaviors. Elsewhere, we have hypothesized that social problem-solving deficits might lead offenders to rely more heavily on denial, avoidance, and sexually deviant fantasies as habituated means of coping with life stress (C. M. Nezu et al., 1998). Research focusing on aggressive responding to perceived threats also has identified aggression-related deficits in problem solving (e.g., Basquill, Nezu, Nezu, & Klein, 2004; Hastings, Anderson, & Hemphill, 1997). Although the present results are consistent with such an hypothesis, additional research remains important.

GENERAL PST GUIDELINES

Although PST involves teaching individuals specific skills, similar to other CBT approaches, it should be conducted within a therapeutic context. Because PST does focus on skill building, it can easily be misunderstood by the novice therapist that it only entails a "teaching" process. However, it is important for the problem-solving therapist to be careful: (1) not to conduct PST in a mechanistic manner; (2) not to focus only on skills training and ignore the patient's emotional experiences; (3) not to deliver a "canned" treatment that does not address the unique strengths, weaknesses, and experiences of a given patient; and (4) not to assume that PST only focuses on superficial problems, rather than on more complex interpersonal, psychological, existential, and spiritual issues (if warranted). Thus, in addition to teaching the patient certain techniques to better cope with problems, effective PST requires the therapist to be competent in a variety of other assessment and intervention strategies, such as fostering a positive therapeutic relationship, assessing for complex clinical problems, modeling, behavioral rehearsal, assigning homework tasks, and appropriately providing corrective feedback.

Prior to teaching the specific PST components, the therapist should present an overall rationale describing the purpose, goals, and specific components of PST, emphasizing how it can be helpful to the unique circumstances of a given patient. Part of this rationale includes the notion that the experience of stressful events and difficult problems often leads to emotional distress and various behavioral problems. Moreover, PST is geared to teach people some new skills, as well as help them to apply previously acquired problem-solving skills to new problems and stressful situations. An emphasis is also provided in the rationale that the goal of effective problem solving may not always lead to changes in the situation itself (i.e., problem-focused goals), but can also encompass cognitive or emotional changes, such as acceptance, increased tolerance, and decreases in emotional reactions to unchangeable events (i.e., emotion-focused goals). Structurally, PST training can be broken into three major foci:

1. training in problem orientation;
2. training in the four specific rational problem-solving skills (i.e., problem definition and formulation, generation of alternatives, decision-making, solution implementation and verification);
3. practice of these skills across a variety of real-life problems.

Training in Problem Orientation

Training in problem orientation (PO) is geared to foster (1) positive self-efficacy beliefs; (2) acceptance of the notion that it is "normal" to experience a wide range of problems in life; (3) the ability to identify problems accurately when they occur; and (4) the ability to minimize the likelihood that negative emotional reactions lead to impulsive or avoidant reactions. To achieve such objectives, PO training can include several different techniques, as described below:

- *Reversed-Advocacy Role-Play.* According to this strategy, the problem-solving therapist pretends to adopt a particular belief about problems (i.e., ones that tend to reflect a negative orientation) and asks the patient to provide reasons why that belief is irrational, illogical, incorrect, or maladaptive. Such beliefs might include the following statements— "Problems are not common to everyone, if I have a problem, that means I'm crazy", "All my problems are caused by me", "There must be a perfect solution to this problem". At times when the patient has difficulty generating arguments against the therapist's position, the counselor then adopts a more extreme form of the belief, such as "no matter how long it takes, even if it takes forever, I will continue to try and find the perfect solution to my problem". This procedure is intended to help individuals identify alternative ways of thinking and then to dispute or contradict previously held negative beliefs with more adaptive perspectives. Moreover, this task permits the individual to provide arguments in his or her own words against previously expressed maladaptive thoughts.

- *ABC Method of Constructive Thinking.* In this technique, patients are taught to view emotional reactions from the "ABC" perspective, where $A =$ activating event (such as a problem), $B =$ beliefs about the event (including what people say to themselves), and $C =$ emotional and behavioral consequences. In other words, how individuals *feel and act* often are products of how they *think*. Using a current problem, the PST therapist can use this procedure to diagnose negative self-talk and thoughts that are likely to lead to distressing emotions for a given patient. Such cognitions often include highly evaluative words, such as "should" and "must", "catastrophic" words used to describe non-life-threatening events, and phrases that tend to be overgeneralizations (e.g., "*Nobody* understands me!"). By examining one's self-talk, the patient can learn to separate realistic statements (e.g., "I wish...") from maladaptive ones (e.g., "I must have...") as they pertain to problems in living. The patient can also be given a list of positive self-statements that can be used to substitute for or help dispute the negative self-talk (as in the reverse-advocacy role-play strategy).

- *Visualization.* As a means of enhancing patients' optimism, this technique is used to help them create the experience of successful problem resolution in their "mind's eye" and vicariously experience the reinforcement to be gained. Visualization in this context requests individuals to close their eyes and imagine that they have successfully solved a current problem. The focus is on the end point—not on "how one got to the goal", but rather "focusing on the feelings of having reached the goal". To foster this, additional questions include: "How would your life be different with this problem solved?", "How would you feel about yourself having solved this problem?" The central goal of this strategy is to have patients create and "experience" their own positive consequences related to solving a problem as a motivational step towards enhanced self-efficacy. In essence, it helps create a visual image of "the light at the end of the tunnel".

- *Identifying Problems When They Occur.* The purpose of this technique is to help "normalize" the experience of problems by discussing the wide range of possible problems that people in general can experience. The therapist can use existing problem checklists or create handouts that contain various categories of potential problems (e.g., work, relationships, sex, career) as a springboard to discuss such issues, as well as to begin to assess for the specific problems that a given patient is currently experiencing. In order to foster an individual's ability to recognize a problem, patients are taught to *use feelings as cues* (i.e., negative physical and emotional reactions) that a problem exists. In other words, rather than labeling one's negative emotions as "the problem", they are instructed to conceptualize such emotions as a "signal" that a problem exists and then to observe what is occurring in their environment in order to recognize the "real problem" that is causing such emotions. Once feelings such as depression, anger, muscle tension, nausea, or anxiety arise, the patient is then instructed to use the mnemonic *"STOP and THINK"* as a means of inhibiting avoidance or impulsive problem-solving behavior. A handout containing a visual depiction of a "stop sign" with this message can be helpful for patients to place in their environment (e.g., on their refrigerator or bathroom mirror) as an important reminder. The "think" aspect of this phrase refers to the use of the four specific rational problem-solving skills as described below. In addition, PST emphasizes that combining emotions and rational thinking (rather than relying solely on only one of these areas) leads to "wisdom", which represents effective real-life problem solving.

Training in Problem Definition and Formulation (PDF)

The importance of this first rational problem-solving skill can be expressed in the age-old proverb—"*A problem well defined is a problem half solved.*" In other words, with a clear understanding of what is "wrong", one can then make attempts to make circumstances "right". Problem definition and formulation include:

1. gathering information about the problem;
2. objectively and concisely defining the problem;
3. separating facts from assumptions;
4. identifying the features that make the situation problematic;
5. setting realistic goals.

In an effort to gain a comprehensive understanding of the problem, patients are instructed to use questions such as "*who, what, where, when, and how*" in order to gather important facts about a problem. Suggesting that the patient take on the role of "detective", "investigator reporter", or "scientist" can foster such efforts. When describing problems, patients are trained to separate *assumptions* (e.g., "I'm no good") from *facts* (e.g., "I reacted poorly to my boss' criticism"), as well as to use clear and unambiguous language (e.g., "I feel angry when I think about my father's death, which then makes me feel like getting in a fight", versus "I feel like losing it!"). In addition, patients are taught to identify why a given situation is a problem (i.e., What are the obstacles to goal attainment? What are the conflicting goals that make this a problem?) and to break larger problems into smaller ones in order to be able to articulate reasonably achievable goals.

Similar to all of the remaining problem-solving skills, training in PDF includes: (1) therapist modeling of appropriate responses; (2) in-session practice of the skills; (3) therapist feedback of the patient's responses; and (4) relevant homework assignments.

Training in Generation of Alternatives (GoA)

Patients are instructed to use various "brainstorming principles" to foster creativity and flexibility and to minimize the tendency to react to stressful problems in previously maladaptive habitual ways. These principles include: (1) the *quantity principle* (i.e., the more solution ideas that are identified, the more likely it is to develop an effective solution); (2) the *deferment-of-judgment principle* (i.e., refrain from evaluating solutions until a comprehensive list is generated); and (3) the *strategies-tactics principle* (i.e., ideas can be conceptualized as both general strategies and a variety of tactics or steps to carry out each of the strategies). If patients have difficulty developing such a list, they are instructed: (1) to combine ideas; (2) to modify existing ideas; (3) to identify how a role model (e.g., personal hero) may approach a similar problem; or (4) to use visualization. If severe emotional distress (e.g., anger or anxiety) interferes with one's ability to be creative, the therapist may wish to engage in relaxation training.

Training in Decision-Making (DM)

DM involves conducting a cost–benefit analysis with regard to the previously generated list of solutions as a means of identifying highly effective ones. Here, patients are first instructed to assess the likelihood that (1) a given solution will actually solve the problem (i.e., likelihood of success); and (2) they can actually carry it out in an optimal manner (i.e., likelihood of implementation). Second, they are taught to identify various positive and negative consequences related to each generated solution that are (1) *personal* (i.e., effects on themselves); (2) *social* (e.g., effects on family, co-workers, neighbors); (3) *short term*; and (4) *long term*. Next, using a simple rating scale (e.g., $-1 =$ negative; $0 =$ neutral; $+1 =$ positive), each of these criteria is then appraised. These ratings are then used as guidelines to evaluate the overall "effectiveness" for each alternative. Because most problems in real life are likely to be complex, patients are generally taught to combine various effective ideas into an overall "solution plan". Effective solution plans are defined as those that not only lead to successful problem resolution (i.e., achieve the relevant problem-solving goals), but additionally increase the likelihood of subsequent positive consequences and minimize the probability of related negative consequences.

Training in Solution Implementation and Verification (SIV)

This final rational problem-solving skill involves: (1) carrying out the solution plan; (2) monitoring its outcome; (3) evaluating its effectiveness; and (4) trouble-shooting if the solution is unsuccessful versus engaging in self-reinforcement if the problem is resolved. Initially, in an effort to enhance motivation and decrease avoidance, patients are instructed to conduct another cost-benefit analysis, this one assessing the advantages and disadvantages of *implementing versus not implementing* a solution plan. Visualization can be used to increase a patient's

self-efficacy related to executing the solution, identifying and overcoming obstacles, and increasing the effectiveness of solution implementation. In addition, if
relevant, the patient can practice, via role playing, actually carrying out the
chosen solution plan.

With regard to the "verification" aspect of this skill, patients are taught to assess
the success or effectiveness of a given implemented solution plan by gathering
relevant data to compare the actual to the desired outcome. If they are similar
(i.e., the problem-solving goals are being achieved), patients are encouraged to
reward themselves for their effort. If the problem is not adequately resolved,
individuals are taught to "recycle" back through each of the rational problem-
solving steps in order to identify "what went wrong?" (i.e., "Was the problem
not well defined?", "Were the goals unrealistic?" "Was the solution plan not
carried out optimally?", "Were not enough solution ideas generated?", etc.).

Guided Practice

After the majority of training has occurred, the remainder of the PST sessions
should be devoted to practicing the newly acquired skills and applying them to a
variety of stressful problems. The more an individual applies these skills to
various problem situations, the better he or she becomes at overall problem
resolution. Beyond actually solving stressful problems, continuous in-session
practice serves three additional purposes:

1. The patient can receive "professional" feedback from the therapist.
2. Increased facility with the overall PST model can decrease the amount of time
   and effort necessary to apply the entire model with each new problem.
3. Practice fosters maintenance and generalization of the skills.

The number of "practice" sessions required after formal PST training often is
dependent upon the competency level a patient achieves, as well as the actual
improvement in his or her overall quality of life. Of the research protocols that
have found PST to be an effective CBT intervention for non-offender populations,
the number of included sessions have ranged from 8 to 12 sessions.

In addition to focusing on resolving and coping with current problems, these
practice sessions should also allow for "future forecasting", whereby the patient
is encouraged to look to the future and anticipate where potential problems
might arise in order to apply such skills in a preventive manner (e.g., anticipated
geographic move, request for promotion, contemplating raising a family). Continuous application of these skills is encouraged to order to manage stressful
situations that might occur in the future.

PROJECT CBT: PST FOR SEXUAL OFFENDERS

PROJECT CBT is a randomized clinical outcome study that is currently being conducted at Drexel University to evaluate the efficacy of a PST-based intervention

for sex-offending men on parole (C. M. Nezu, 2005). Study participants are men who have been in prison for a minimum of two years for a sex offense and who are now living in the community. In addition to comparing PST to a wait-list control condition, a randomly selected group of participants undergoing PST will be provided further PST in a maintenance condition. The initial PST protocol involves 20 sessions of group treatment.

Rationale of PST as Intervention for Sex Offenders

Essentially, PST is offered as a potentially efficacious treatment approach for this population as it has been previously found to be an effective intervention to help people better cope with stressful events (A. M. Nezu, 2004). Conceptually, deficient problem-solving skills are viewed in this framework as one important dynamic factor that is related to sexual aggression and deviance (see section on problem solving and sex offending). PST helps sex offenders to better identify those stressful problems and situations that serve either distally or proximally as triggers for sex-offending behaviors, including aggression towards others. More importantly, it also is geared to help teach such individuals to engage in alternative ways of coping with these stressful situations that are more adaptive and have less negative consequences attached to them.

Identifying trigger situations, according to the PST model, also entails overcoming cognitive distortions, such as *justification* (e.g., "she wanted to have sex with me—she was wearing sexy lipstick") and *minimization* (e.g., "I was the only one who cared about loving that child"), as well as *denial* (e.g., "I didn't do anything"). Such deviant thought patterns are often well learned and serve as major obstacles to the offenders themselves to validly understand the chain of events that ultimately led them to engage in sex offenses. These cognitive factors are emphasized in problem-orientation training.

Application of PST to Sex Offenders

Based on years of clinical experience plus the research referred to earlier (e.g., C. M. Nezu et al., 2005), PST as it is being implemented in PROJECT CBT has been revised to be theoretically more relevant to a population of sex offenders. More specifically, while previous PST manuals (e.g., D'Zurilla & Nezu, 1999; A. M. Nezu, Nezu, & Perri, 1989; A. M. Nezu, Nezu, Friedman, Faddis, & Houts, 1998) served as the basis of the manual devised for PROJECT CBT, it was developed to be specifically relevant to a sample of sex offenders.

One major difference involves an increase in the length of the experimental protocol. In previous PST outcome studies, the number of sessions included ranged from 8–12. For the sex offender participants, it was felt that 20 sessions of group PST would be more realistic in terms of having a potentially efficacious effect. In addition, whereas the introductory and problem-orientation training sessions have typically involved two sessions, in PROJECT CBT, such content has been increased to be the focus for seven sessions. This is due to the intensity with which cognitive distortions are often paired with a stress response (e.g., anger or anxiety). The presence of such cognitive distortions, which are often focused on blaming stress for any experienced distress, serve as fuel for further physiological arousal, which then sets in motion a vicious cycle of impulsive behavioral attempts to reduce this distress (i.e., sex-offending behaviors).

In addition, a much greater emphasis on identifying consequences of one's behavior is included in PROJECT CBT as compared to other PST outcome studies. In this protocol, we are more interested in developing prosocial and adaptive alternatives in dealing with aggression-associated triggers as compared to fostering the ability to generate ideas *per se*. Finally, there are specific content areas that are programmed with regard to problem areas that serve as stimuli in practice sessions that are specific to sex offenders (e.g., high-risk situations). This offers participants the opportunity to learn additional skills that can foster the effectiveness of their behavioral performance when implementing solutions.

CONCLUSION

This chapter began with an overview of the constructs of problem solving, problems, and solutions, followed by a discussion of the five major problem-solving dimensions that are essential to our model. These include orientation processes (i.e., positive and negative problem orientation) and various problem-solving styles (i.e., rational problem solving, impulsivity/carelessness style, avoidance style). A major assumption underlying the relevance of PST as a clinical intervention involves the notion that psychopathology can be viewed as the results of ineffective and maladaptive coping. As such, training in a systematic model of PST is hypothesized to improve one's ability to cope various forms of stressful events and thus to reduce symptoms of psychopathology (e.g., depression, inappropriate behavior).

In looking to the literature to discuss the relevance of problem-solving constructs to sex offending, confusion over terms was identified, where such constructs were labeled in differing ways within differing models (i.e., social skills, relapse prevention). As such, the nature and existence of a relationship between problem solving and sex offending remain more an empirical question than a set of "facts". One study that was recently conducted to address this gap in the literature, despite the use of PST in various clinical programs, found strong associations between sex offending and a negative problem orientation, avoidance, and impulsivity. What was interesting to note was the lack of differences between offenders and non-offenders regarding their rational problem solving.

General guidelines for conducting PST were provided, followed by a brief description of PROJECT CBT, a randomized clinical trial of PST for adult male sex offenders on parole that is currently being conducted. Differences between a "standard" PST clinical protocol and that contained in PROJECT CBT were highlighted.

REFERENCES

Barbaree, H. E., Marshall, W. I. & Connor, J. (1988). The social problem solving of child molesters. Unpublished manuscript, Queen's University, Kingston, Ontario, Canada.

Basquill, M., Nezu, C. M., Nezu, A. M., & Klein, T. L. (2004). Aggression-related hostility bias and social problem-solving deficits in adult males with mental retardation. *American Journal on Mental Retardation, 109*, 255–263.

Bloom, B. L. (1985). *Stressful life event theory and research: Implications for primary prevention.* D. H. H. S. Publication No. (AMD) 85-1385. Rockville, MD: National Institute of Mental Health.

Chang, E. C., D'Zurilla, T. J., & Sanna, L. J. (eds) (2004). *Social problem solving: Theory, research, and training.* Washington, DC: American Psychological Association.

D'Zurilla, T. J. (1990). Problem-solving training for effective stress management and prevention. *Journal of Cognitive Psychotherapy: An International Quarterly, 4*, 327–355.

D'Zurilla, T. J. & Goldfried, M. R. (1971). Problem solving and behavior modification. *Journal of Abnormal Psychology, 78*, 107–126.

D'Zurilla, T. J. & Nezu, A. M. (1982). Social problem solving in adults. In P. C. Kendall (ed.) *Advances in cognitive-behavioral research and therapy.* Vol. 1 (pp. 201–274). New York: Academic Press.

D'Zurilla, T. J. & Nezu, A. M. (1990). Development and preliminary evaluation of the Social Problem-Solving Inventory (SPSI). *Psychological Assessment: A Journal of Consulting and Clinical Psychology, 2*, 156–163.

D'Zurilla, T. J. & Nezu, A. M. (1999). *Problem-solving therapy: A social competence approach to clinical intervention.* 2nd edn. New York: Springer.

D'Zurilla, T. J., Nezu, A. M., & Maydeu-Olivares, A. (2002). *Social Problem-Solving Inventory Revised (SPSI-R): Technical manual.* North Tonawanda, NY: Multi-Health Systems.

Freidman, S. H., Festinger, D. A., Nezu, C. M., McGuffin, P. W., & Nezu, A. M. (1999). Group therapy for mentally retarded sex offenders: A behavioral approach. *The Behavior Therapist, 22*, 32–33.

Hains, A. A., Herrman, L.P., Baker, K. L., & Graber, S. (1986). The development of a psychoeducational group program for adolescent sex offenders. *Journal of Offender Counseling, Services & Rehabilitation, 11*, 63–76.

Hastings, T., Anderson, S. J., & Hemphill, P. (1997). Comparisons of daily stress, coping, problem behavior, and cognitive distortions in adolescent sexual offenders and conduct disordered youth. *Sexual Abuse: A Journal of Research and Treatment, 9*, 29–42.

Jenkins-Hall, K. D. (1989). The decision matrix. In D. R. Laws (ed.) *Relapse prevention with sex offenders.* New York: Guilford Press.

Kanner, A. D., Coyne, J. C., Schaefer, C., & Lazarus, R. S. (1981). Comparison of two modes of stress measurement: Daily hassles and uplifts versus major life events. *Journal of Behavioral Medicine, 4*, 1–39.

Laws, D. R. (ed.) (1989). *Relapse prevention with sex offenders.* New York: Guilford Press.

Lazarus, R. S. (1999). *Stress and emotion: A new synthesis.* New York: Springer.

Lazarus, R. S. & Folkman, S. (1984). *Stress, appraisal, and coping.* New York: Springer.

Marlatt, G. A. & Gordon, J. R. (eds) (1985). *Relapse prevention: Maintenance strategies in the treatment of addictive disorders.* New York: Guilford Press.

Marshall, W. L. & Barbaree, H. E. (1990). Outcome of comprehensive cognitive-behavioral treatment programs, In W. L. Marshall, D. R. Laws, & H. E. Barbaree (eds) *Handbook of sexual assault: Issues, theories, and treatment of the offender* (pp. 363–385). New York: Plenum Press.

Maydeu-Olivares, A. & D'Zurilla, T. J. (1995). A factor analysis of the Social Problem-Solving Inventory using polychoric correlations. *European Journal of Psychological Assessment, 11*, 98–107.

Maydeu-Olivares, A. & D'Zurilla, T. J. (1996). A factor-analytic study of the Social Problem-Solving Inventory: An integration of theory and data. *Cognitive Therapy and Research, 20*, 115–133.

McFall, R. M. (1982). A review and reformulation of the concept of social skills. *Behavioral Assessment, 4*, 1–33.

McFall, R. M. (1990). The enhancement of social skills: An information-processing analysis. In W. L. Marshall, D. R. Laws, & H. E. Barbaree (eds) *Handbook of sexual assault: Issues, theories, and treatment of the offender* (pp. 311–330). New York: Plenum Press.

McFall, R. M. & Dodge, K. A. (1982). Self-management and interpersonal skills learning. In P. Karoly & F. Kanfer (eds) *Self-management and behavior change: From theory to practice* (pp. 353–392). New York: Pergamon Press.

Nezu, A. M. (1986). Effects of stress from current problems: Comparisons to major life events. *Journal of Clinical Psychology, 42*, 847–852.

Nezu, A. M. (1987). A problem-solving formulation of depression: A literature review and proposal of a pluralistic model. *Clinical Psychology Review, 7*, 122–144.

Nezu, A. M. (2004). Problem solving and behavior therapy revisited. *Behavior Therapy, 35*, 1–33.

Nezu, A. M. & D'Zurilla, T. J. (1989). Social problem solving and negative affective conditions. In P.C. Kendall & D. Watson (eds) *Anxiety and depression: Distinctive and overlapping features* (pp. 285–315). New York: Academic Press.

Nezu, A. M., Nezu, C. M., Felgoise, S., McClure, K. S., & Houts, P. S. (2003). Project Genesis: Assessing the efficacy of problem solving therapy for distressed adult cancer patients. *Journal of Consulting and Clinical Psychology, 71*, 1036–1048.

Nezu, A. M., Nezu, C. M., Friedman, S. H., Faddis, S., & Houts, P. S. (1998). *Helping cancer patients cope: A problem-solving approach*. Washington, DC: American Psychological Association.

Nezu, A. M., Nezu, C. M., & Perri, M. G. (1989). *Problem-solving therapy for depression: Theory, research and clinical guidelines*. New York: John Wiley & Sons, Ltd.

Nezu, A. M. & Perri, M. G. (1989). Problem-solving therapy for unipolar depression: An initial dismantling investigation. *Journal of Consulting and Clinical Psychology, 57*, 408–413.

Nezu, A. M. & Ronan, G. F. (1985). Life stress, current problems, problem solving, and depressive symptomatology: An integrative model. *Journal of Consulting and Clinical Psychology, 53*, 693–697.

Nezu, C. M. (2003). Cognitive behavior therapy for sexual offenders: Current status. *Japanese Journal of Behavior Therapy, 29*, 15–24.

Nezu, C. M., Nezu, A. M., & Dudek, J. A. (1998). A cognitive-behavioral model of assessment and treatment for intellectually disabled sexual offenders. *Cognitive and Behavioral Practice, 5*, 25–64.

Nezu, C. M., Nezu, A. M., Dudek, J. A., Peacock, M., & Stoll, J. (2005). Social problem-solving correlates of sexual deviancy and aggression among adult child molesters. *Journal of Sexual Aggression, 11*, 27–36.

Nichols, H. R. & Molinder, I. (1984). *Multiphasic sex inventory manual*. Tacoma, Washington: Authors.

O'Connor, W. (1996). A problem-solving intervention for sex offenders with an intellectual disability. *Journal of Intellectual and Developmental Disability, 21*, 219–235.

Pithers, W. D. (1990). Relapse prevention with sexual aggressors: A method for maintaining therapeutic gain and enhancing external supervision. In W. L. Marshall, D. R. Laws, & H. E. Barbaree (eds) *Handbook of sexual assault: Issues, theories, and treatment of the offender* (pp. 343–361). New York: Plenum Press.

Pithers, W. D., Marques, J. K., Gibat, C. C., and Marlatt, G. A. (1983). Relapse prevention with sexual aggressives: A self-control model of treatment and maintenance of change. In J. G. Greer & L. R. Stuart (eds) *The sexual aggressor: Current perspectives on treatment* (pp. 214–239). New York: Van Nostrand Reinhold.

Stermac, L. E., Segal, Z. V., & Gillis, R. (1990). Social and cultural factors in sexual assault. In W. L. Marshall, D. R. Laws, & H. E. Barbaree (eds) *Handbook of sexual assault: Issues, theories, and treatment of the offender* (pp. 143–159). New York: Plenum Press.

Weinberger, M., Hiner, S. L., & Tierney, W. M. (1987). In support of hassles as a measure of stress in predicting health outcomes. *Journal of Behavioral Medicine*, 10, 19–31.

PART II

EVALUATION

Chapter 7

SOCIAL PROBLEM-SOLVING PROGRAMS FOR PREVENTING ANTISOCIAL BEHAVIOR IN CHILDREN AND YOUTH

FRIEDRICH LÖSEL[1] and ANDREAS BEELMANN[2]

[1]University of Erlangen-Nuremberg, Germany
[2]University of Jena, Germany

INTRODUCTION

During the past decade, social problem-solving programs have become one of the most important areas in offender treatment and rehabilitation. Examining the "what-works" literature reveals a substantial body of positive outcomes in experimental and quasi-experimental evaluations of cognitive-behavioral programs designed to improve social problem-solving (Lösel, 1995; McGuire, 2002). Although effects are sometimes smaller in the widespread implementation in everyday practice compared with model projects (e.g., Harper & Chitty, 2004), programs focusing on competencies of social perception, means–ends thinking, generating alternative solutions, and reflection of consequences show much promise for treating various forms of criminality.

The social problem-solving approach is supported by cross-sectional and longitudinal studies on the origins of aggression (Loeber & Stouthamer-Loeber, 1998; Moffitt, 1993; Tremblay, 2000). This area of research has shown that specific modes of social information processing and deficits in social-cognitive competencies are among the early predictors of aggressive and other antisocial behavior (e.g., Akhtar & Bradley, 1991; Coie & Dodge, 1998; Coy, Speltz, DeKlyen, & Jones, 2001; Gifford-Smith & Rabiner, 2004; Huesman, 1997; Keltikangas-Järvinen & Pakaslahti, 1999). As a consequence, social problem-solving programs are indicated not only for the treatment of offending but also for early developmental approaches to prevention (Kazdin, 1998; Lösel & Beelmann, 2003a; Tremblay & Craig, 1995). Indeed, social problem-solving modules are important elements in

Social Problem Solving and Offending: Evidence, Evaluation and Evolution.
Edited by Mary McMurran and James McGuire © 2005 John Wiley & Sons, Ltd.

some of the largest and most important studies on the prevention of antisocial behavior (e.g., Conduct Problems Prevention Research Group, 1999; Tremblay, Pagani-Kurtz, Vitaro, Masse, & Pihl, 1995).

Against this background, in this chapter we focus on the preventive function of social problem-solving programs. The chapter starts with a brief introduction to the theoretical concepts, and then goes on to use one of our own projects to illustrate program implementation and evaluation. The third part of the chapter presents a systematic meta-analysis of experimental outcome studies. The chapter concludes with general effectiveness, differential outcomes, and suggestions for further research and practice in this field.

BASIC RESEARCH BACKGROUND

Social problem solving refers to the cognitions, emotions, and actions that are relevant to the outcome of social interactions and interpersonal conflicts (see the introduction to this volume). It overlaps with the broader concept of social information processing underlying social interactions and social behavior. Drawing on the social-cognitive learning theories of Bandura (1973) and Mischel (1973), this social information processing concept has become one of the most important constructs in the explanation of human aggression and other forms of antisocial behavior (Coie & Dodge, 1998). It assumes that individuals differ in how they process relevant information in social situations. Within the framing conditions of biological capacities, these differences develop through experience and learning processes from early childhood onward. The attendant cognitive mechanisms mediate between the influences of social contexts, biological dispositions, personality traits, and situational factors (e.g., Dodge, 2000; Lösel & Bliesener, 2003). Although there is still no single common theory of social information processing in aggressive individuals, the most important concepts do overlap (e.g., Dodge, 2000; Huesman, 1997). According to Crick and Dodge's (1994) integrative model, individuals in social situations do the following:

1. Perceive and encode the situational and social cues.
2. Form a mental representation and interpretation of the situation.
3. Clarify and set own goals for the interaction.
4. Recall or construct possible reactions to the situation.
5. Evaluate these reactions.
6. Initiate what they expect to be an adequate action.

Regarding the first phase, the *encoding of cues*, studies of aggressive children have shown a focus on aggression-relevant stimuli (Gouze, 1987). They remember more aggression-relevant details of a situation than other youngsters (e.g., Dodge & Frame, 1982) and perceive more aggression in their partners (e.g., Lochman & Dodge, 1998). In the phase of *stimulus interpretation*, aggressive children are less able to recognize the specific intentions and motivations of their interaction partners (e.g., Dodge, Price, Bachorowski, & Newman, 1990). For example, they exhibit a tendency to attribute hostile intentions to them (e.g., Coie, Dodge, Terry,

& Wright, 1991; Slaby & Guerra, 1988; Zelli, Dodge, Lochman, Laird, & Conduct Problems Prevention Research Group, 1999). In the phase of *goal clarifying*, more egocentric and antisocial goals have been found in aggressive youngsters. For example, thcy try more frequently to maximize to their own utility, even when this harms others, or they are more interested in dominating than maintaining a relationship (e.g., Coie et al., 1991; Crick & Ladd, 1990; Lochman, Wayland, & White, 1993; Slaby & Guerra, 1988). In the fourth phase, *response access or construction*, aggressive children retrieve and generate more aggressive and hostile alternatives (Beelmann & Lösel, 2004; Rubin, Bream, & Rose-Krasnor, 1991; Zelli et al., 1999). This is not due to a generally smaller number of stored response schemes, but to the dominance of aggressive, impulsive, and sometimes fanciful alternatives (Asarnow & Callan, 1985; Lösel & Bliesener, 1999, 2003). In the phase of *response evaluation and decision*, antisocial individuals take a more short-term orientation when estimating consequences (Gottfredson & Hirschi, 1990; Lösel, 1975; Nagin & Pogarsky, 2003). They also seem to expect more self-efficacy and relatively positive consequences for their aggressive behavior (e.g., Lösel & Bliesener, 1999; Perry, Perry, & Rasmussen, 1986; Zelli et al., 1999). These evaluations may be derived from enduring beliefs that have been learned in the family and in peer groups (e.g., Coie & Dodge, 1998). In the sixth phase, *behavioral enactment*, individuals initiate the reaction that seems to be most appropriate and in line with their goals. Here, studies suggest that aggressive children exhibit fewer skills for engaging in non-aggressive interactions (e.g., Dodge, Pettit, McClaskey, & Brown, 1986; Gottman, Gonso, & Rasmussen, 1975; Moffitt, 1993).

Models of social information processing assume that individuals go through these phases more or less automatically. Although the processes themselves may depend to some extent on dispositions regarding neuropsychological functioning and temperament (e.g., Moffitt, 1993), their content is attributed mainly to learning in social contexts (Bandura, 1973; Coie & Dodge, 1998). Experiences of aggression, conflict, abuse, and inappropriate parenting in the family may have a fundamental influence (e.g., Dodge, Pettit, Bates, & Valente, 1995; Patterson, Reid, & Dishion, 1992). Aggression-prone schemas, scripts and beliefs may also be learned via media consumption, at school, and particularly in peer groups (Coie & Dodge, 1998; Lösel, Bliesener & Bender, in press). The attendant cognitions influence interactions and are evaluated and reinforced cyclically by them (Crick & Dodge, 1994).

Relationships between social information processing and aggressive behavior have been confirmed by both cross-sectional and longitudinal studies from preschool age onward. However, relations are not equally well demonstrated across different forms of antisocial behavior. For example, some studies show that social information processing is more relevant for proactive than for reactive aggression (Crick & Dodge, 1996; Dodge, Lochman, Harnish, Bates, & Pettit, 1997). Other research suggests a broader relation to antisocial behavior (Lösel et al., in press).

Not all phases of information processing are equally well investigated, and they do not seem to be equally relevant for different outcomes (e.g., Lösel, Bliesener, & Bender, in press). Specific characteristics such as hostile attributions should not only be interpreted as a skill deficit or cognitive bias, but may well represent an effective approach to interactions in a given context (Sutton, Smith, & Swettenham, 1999). Furthermore, it must be taken into account that most studies have investigated features of social information processing retrospectively. In the prospective construction of behavior in concrete interactions, they may well have a different impact (Winstok & Enosh, in press). Last but not least, methodological differences can have a strong impact on findings (Bliesener & Lösel, 2001). For example, the assessment stimuli may be real-life or fictitious scenarios, presented on video or in a paper-and-pencil format, with more or less time for reflection, and so forth.

In spite of such needs for differentiation and gaps in research, concepts of social information form a relatively solid base for interventions. Because they refer to variables mediating between social experiences or biological dispositions and outcome behavior, they are dynamic, changeable risk factors. Less aggression-prone modes of social information processing even seem to protect against antisocial development when family and other risk factors are present (Beelmann & Lösel, 2004; Lösel & Bender, 2003). In general, changes in social information processing may be due to new social experiences, differentiations of cognitive schemas, and acquired social skills during development (Coie & Dodge, 1998; Huesman, 1997). Training programs for improving social problem solving represent a deliberate means of encouraging such change processes.

AN EXAMPLE OF RESEARCH AND PRACTICE

Social-cognitive training programs have a long tradition in the field of child-oriented prevention measures (see Guerra & Slaby, 1988; Urbain & Kendall, 1980). Within this context, we find that the social problem-solving approach is not only recommended for the improvement of social development in general (Durlak & Wells, 1997, 1998) but also for the early prevention and treatment of antisocial behavior problems (Kazdin, 1998, 2003). The approach can be traced back to Spivack and Shure (1974) and has now expanded into a variety of different programs (Frauenknecht & Black, 2004; Webster-Stratton & Taylor, 2001). In the following, we shall sketch one of our own studies that draws on this tradition. The aim is not only to illustrate typical program contents, implementation problems, and outcomes in this field, but also to provide an example of broader prevention approaches that combine child-oriented and parent-oriented programs.

The Erlangen-Nuremberg Development and Prevention Study contains both a prospective longitudinal analysis of the development of antisocial behavior in childhood and a controlled evaluation of two prevention programs (Lösel & Beelmann, 2003b; Lösel, Beelmann, Jaursch, & Stemmler, 2004). The study design is based on four groups: developmental study only, child program, parent program, and child-plus-parent program. Currently, we have completed the following assessments: Time 1 (pre-test), Time 2 (*circa* 3 months after training), and Time 3 (*circa* 14 months after training).

The core sample is a representative group of 675 kindergarten children from the southern German cities of Erlangen and Nuremberg. The study commenced when the children had a mean age of 4.7 years ($SD = 9.3$ months). Families were contacted through talks on education problems held at parent evenings in each kindergarten. More than half of the contacted families agreed to participate in the study. In addition to mothers, nearly 90% of fathers took part in the first wave of assessment. We also collected child behavior ratings from 180 preschool teachers or kindergarten educators.

The assessment at Time 1 used multiple methods and data sources: parent questionnaires on the child's behavior and family characteristics; home visits with interviews and behavior observations; child testing and physiological measures; kindergarten staff members' ratings of the child's behavior, and pediatric data. Assessments at Times 2 and 3 contained selected instruments from the Time 1 battery plus further data on the child's development between the two measurement points. We managed to keep the dropout rate from Time 1 to Time 3 at less than 5%. However, as expected, not all parents filled out all questionnaires, and more than one-third of the fathers dropped out over time.

The *child program* was a manual-based group training in social problem solving. It was adapted from Shure (1992) and modified for the German context. In addition to the core social-cognitive components of the program, it also placed strong emphasis on concrete behavioral exercises. The overview in Table 7.1 summarizes the key characteristics of training.

The program was tested and adapted during pilot studies for its application in a universal and selective prevention context (Beelmann, 2003, 2004). Process analyses revealed no serious implementation problems such as those that so often complicate everyday practice (e.g., Kazdin & Wassell, 1999). Short-term outcome analyses during the pilot studies suggested moderate effects on test measures of social problem solving and small effects on behavioral measures of problem behavior and social competence.

Table 7.1 Characteristics of the training "I Can Solve Problems"

Target group	Preschool and elementary school children (4–7 years)
Format	Manual-based group format; 6–10 children, 2 trainers
Duration/Intensity	15 sessions of 45–60 min per day over 3 weeks or 3 times a week over 5 weeks
Location	Group rooms in the kindergarten
Contents/Topics	1. *Basics of social-cognitive problem solving* Verbal meaning (e.g., some–all, equal–different) Identification of emotions (e.g., happy, angry) Reasons and origins of behavior (causality issues) 2. *Social-cognitive problem-solving skills* Alternative solutions Anticipation of consequences Evaluation of consequences
Methods/Materials	Model presentations, vignettes showing typical peer conflicts, question–answer rounds, action games, question games, painting and drawing, singing, role play with finger puppets, moderation by hand puppets, measures to promote identification with the program

The *parent program* addressed basic parenting skills in groups of approximately ten participants. We adapted some elements from Fisher et al. (1997) and Dishion and Patterson (1996) and added sessions designed for the German context. To avoid low participation and high dropout rates, the program was relatively short (5 weekly 2-hour sessions). It dealt with basic rules of positive parenting; perception and assessment of child behavior; modes of asking, demanding, and setting limits; family stress and parenting; and social relations in the family. Educational methods were group discussions, lectures, workshops, role-playing, homework, structured materials, and a phone hotline.

After the first wave of measurement, we used a randomized block design with stratification techniques (taking age, gender, and pre-test problem scores as control variables) for our outcome evaluation. The largest group of children remained in the developmental part of the study, that is, neither they nor their parents received a program. From this group, we selected three control groups that were matched to the various training groups in terms of the above-mentioned criteria. The child training was offered to 190 families. In 94% of the cases, the children participated in the program. Of these, 91% attended at least one-half of the sessions ($n = 158$). The parent program was offered to 226 families. In more than two-thirds of the families, at least one parent participated in the program. Three-quarters of the participants attended at least half of the sessions ($n = 143$, mainly mothers). In 74 families, both children and parents participated in a program (combined training).

These implementation data showed advantages for child-oriented programs compared with parent training, that is, they are able to reach their target groups more easily in order to practice prevention (e.g., Prinz & Miller, 1994; Spoth, Redmond, Hockaday, & Shin, 1996). Process evaluations revealed a relatively successful implementation for both programs. The on-task behavior of the children during the sessions was around 90% and parent satisfaction with various aspects of the training was generally high.

Because we used such a broad variety of quantitative and qualitative measures, the data analysis of our outcome evaluation is still incomplete. At Time 2 (approximately three months after training), we found a large variation of effect sizes in different measures (see also Conduct Problems Prevention Research Group, 2002; Sanders, Markie-Dadds, Tully, & Bor, 2000). Particularly important were the reports on child behavior from the kindergarten staff. We used the total score on the Preschool Social Behavior Questionnaire (Tremblay, Vitaro, Gagnon, Piché, & Royer, 1992) as a key indicator. A Group x Time ANOVA revealed a highly significant effect of measurement time and a significant interaction between time and group. Whereas the pre-test scores in all four groups were very similar, the control group had the highest problem scores at Time 2. The combination of child and parent training revealed the largest effect ($d = 0.39$). The effect of child training alone was also significant ($d = 0.26$), and the effect of the parent training was slightly above the 5% level ($d = 0.22$). Social-emotional problems revealed a larger effect than physical aggression. Children who showed more intensive problem behavior before the training benefited more than children with fewer problems.

Measures of social information processing and problem solving at Time 1 predicted antisocial behavior at Time 2. As expected, the child training had a significant impact on such variables. For example, the training group exhibited a more differentiated perception of social situations and produced more competent and less aggressive solutions. The parent training had no effect on such child characteristics.

The long-term follow-up data have not yet been analyzed completely. However, there seems to be a trend toward a slight decrease in effect sizes. Nonetheless, the combined child and parent training is still revealing a significantly positive effect on relatively hard outcome measures such as kindergarten staff ratings or (for the older children) behavior evaluations in teachers' school grades.

SYSTEMATIC REVIEW OF OUTCOME EVALUATIONS

A number of systematic research integrations have addressed the effects of social-cognitive skills trainings in childhood and adolescence. Generally, these are not restricted to a homogeneous class of social problem solving (e.g., conflict resolution), but address a broader range of the skills necessary for positive social interactions. In an early review, Denham and Almeida (1987) found that social problem-solving interventions promoted interpersonal cognitive problem-solving skills and had a significant impact on social behavior (measured through behavior observations and ratings). In a later meta-analysis, Beelmann, Pfingsten, and Lösel (1994) integrated a more comprehensive range of studies. Like Denham and Almeida (1987), they found a generally significant and substantial effect of social problem-solving programs on social-cognitive measures. However, so-called monomodal programs (i.e., programs focusing on social-cognitive competencies in artificial conflict situations) had no significant impact on measures of either social behavior (e.g., social skills) or general adjustment (e.g., peer acceptance, behavior problems). Multimodal programs, in contrast, showed broader effects. Such training combines learning social problem solving with intensive behavioral practice and other cognitive-behavioral interventions (e.g., to improve self-control).

Later reviews (e.g., Ang & Hughes, 2001; Taylor, Eddy & Biglan, 1999; Webster-Stratton & Taylor, 2001; Wilson, Lipsey, & Derzon, 2003) came to similar conclusions. They all indicated that children should not just be taught crucial social-cognitive competencies but also trained in applying these competencies in concrete behavioral settings.

Because of the great variety in the methodological quality of evaluations, we recently conducted a further meta-analysis concentrating on randomized studies alone. This meta-analysis is being conducted within the framework of the Campbell Collaboration Group on Crime and Justice (Farrington & Petrosino, 2001). First results have already been published or are currently in press (Lösel & Beelmann, 2003a, in press). In the following, we shall sketch the core results from these studies while adding some further data from new and more differentiated analyses.

This synthesis contained published and unpublished studies on child social competence training for the prevention of antisocial behavior. Although treatment programs for adjudicated juvenile delinquents were excluded, we did include selective prevention programs for children with some behavioral problems (conduct problems, impulsivity, hyperactivity) or from high-risk family backgrounds. After a literature search of more than 800 documents, we found 84 research reports that met our detailed eligibility criteria (see, for details, Lösel & Beelmann, 2003a). These reports contained 135 treatment-control comparisons and a total of 16,723 children and adolescents. Most studies came from the United States (85%), had small sample sizes ($n < 50:73\%$), and rather short time periods for measuring post-intervention effects (< 3 months: 85%). Less than 5% contained a follow-up period longer than 1 year. In accordance with the preventive approach, the main target groups were rather young (mean age $< 13: 87\%$). Typically, the programs had a group format (78%), lasted less than 30 sessions (75%), and were implemented within a school context (74%).

The comparisons contained 519 single post-intervention effect sizes (calculated from each dependent variable measured up to three months after training) and 125 single follow-up effect-sizes (calculated from each dependent variable measured three months after intervention or later). The outcome data could be classified into three main categories: (1) antisocial behavior (e.g., aggressive, oppositional, or delinquent); (2) social skills (e.g., social interaction skills, prosocial behavior); and (3) social-cognitive skills (e.g., social problem-solving skills, self-control). The various program types were subsumed under four categories: (1) behavioral programs (i.e., programs focusing particularly on role-play and other behavioral training methods for concrete social skills); (2) cognitive programs (i.e., programs focusing mainly on self-control, social problem-solving, and/or perspective taking without behavioral practice); (3) cognitive-behavioral programs (programs combining the two aforementioned orientations); and (4) approaches based on general counseling, psychotherapeutic, or other methods (e.g., Adlerian counseling, buddy programs). Table 7.2 presents an overview of the frequencies in each respective category.

Cognitive-behavioral programs were most prevalent; programs based on neither a cognitive nor a behavioral concept were less frequent among such high-quality studies. Cognitive-behavioral trainings also used the most and varied outcome criteria.

Although a substantial number of single effects were negative (i.e., control groups scored better than treatment groups), the majority did reveal a positive effect. Applying the inverse-variance random effect model (Hedges & Olkin, 1985; Lipsey & Wilson, 2001), the best estimate of a mean effect was $d = 0.38$ (post-intervention) and $d = 0.28$ (follow-up). Because the results showed significant heterogeneity (i.e., effect size variance could not be attributed to sample error alone), various moderator analyses were performed. For example, outcomes in antisocial behavior were smaller than the overall effects. Studies conducted by study authors, research staff, and/or supervised students produced significantly better outcomes than programs carried out by teachers or psychosocial professionals. Studies with smaller samples had higher effects than large studies. Both these results may help to determine which conditions contribute to higher

Table 7.2 Number and content of dependent measures by type of treatment

Treatment types	No. of comparisons	%	Number and content of single ES at post-intervention				Number and content of single ES at follow up			
			Total*	AS Beh	Soskills	Soc-cog	Total*	AS Beh	Soskills	Soc-cog
Behavioral	39	28.9	133(37)	55	51	27	18(5)	8	10	0
Cognitive	33	17.0	114(25)	45	17	52	30(9)	9	6	15
Cognitive-behavioral	53	39.3	225(47)	70	60	95	55(14)	22	18	15
Other	20	14.8	47(17)	20	18	9	22(6)	9	10	3
Total	135	100	519(126)	190	146	183	125(34)	48	44	33

Note: AS Beh = Antisocial behavior. Soskills = Social skills. Soc-cog = Social-cognitive skills. * Number of comparisons in parentheses.

Table 7.3 Effect sizes for different dependent measures by type of treatment

Dependent measures	Treatment types and results at post-intervention				Treatment types and results at follow-up			
	Behavioral	Cognitive	Cognitive-Behavioral	Other	Behavioral	Cognitive	Cognitive-Behavioral	Other
Overall ES	.37*(37)	.39*(25)	.39*(47)	.36*(17)	.17(5)	.36*(9)	.37*(14)	.17*(6)
Antisocial behavior	.15(25)	.13(15)	.50*(26)	.38*(16)	.12(4)	-.06(3)	.50*(7)	.18(6)
Social skills	.55*(21)	.22(8)	.30*(24)	.45*(8)	.42(4)	.73*(3)	.33(3)	.30(1)
Social-cognitive skills	.39*(6)	.50*(19)	.37*(28)	.20(4)	—	.23*(7)	.38*(5)	—

*$p < .05$. Numbers of comparisons in parentheses.

integrity in treatment implementation. There was also a tendency toward better outcomes in selective compared with universal prevention. Such moderator effects seem similar to those found in meta-analyses of young offender treatment (Lipsey & Wilson, 1998).

In contrast, we found no significant moderator effect of program type on general effect size. Therefore, we conducted a further analysis taking the kind of outcome criteria into account. These results are presented in Table 7.3.

Cognitive-behavioral approaches were the only programs with significant effects in terms of reducing *antisocial behavior* at post-intervention and follow-up assessment. As expected, behavioral or cognitive approaches had relatively high effect sizes in the domain on which the specific program focused (e.g., behavioral programs on social skills and cognitive programs on social-cognitive skills). However, this did not generalize to antisocial behavior. Only cognitive-behavioral approaches had significant effects of at least $d = 0.30$ on all outcome measures. These differential results became even more pronounced when we analysed the various indicators of antisocial behavior more specifically (see Table 7.4).

Table 7.4 Effect sizes for different types of antisocial behavior by type of treatment

Dependent measures	Treatment types: Results at post-intervention[a]			
(Types of antisocial behavior)	Behavioral	Cognitive	Cognitive-behavioral	Other
Total	.15(25)	.13(15)	.50*(26)	.38*(16)
Aggressive behavior	.04(13)	.08(11)	.39*(20)	.53*(8)
Oppositional/disruptive behavior	.22(11)	.22(7)	.75*(5)	.12(5)
Delinquent behavior	.09(3)	.00(2)	.37*(5)	.06(1)
Unspecified antisocial behavior	.17(10)	−.09(2)	.55*(7)	.64*(3)

Note: [a]Due to the small number of comparisons, only post-intervention results are presented here (see text). $p < .05$. Numbers of comparisons in parentheses.

Only cognitive-behavioral approaches had a significant short-term effect in all four categories (aggressive, oppositional/disruptive, delinquency, and unspecified antisocial behavior). This was particularly notable for delinquency, the only field in which we found official records data, which generally revealed low effect sizes (Lösel & Beelmann, in press). We were unable to perform a similar differentiation of the longer-term follow-up data because the number of studies in some subcategories was too small.

CONCLUSIONS

Training in social problem solving is a relatively well-investigated approach to the early developmental prevention of antisocial behavior. A substantial body of research shows that children with deficits in social information processing and related skills are at high risk for aggressive and other forms of antisocial behavior. Because styles of social information processing and interaction mediate between social or biosocial influences and outcome behavior, training in this area may interrupt chain reactions leading to antisocial careers (Lösel & Bender, 2003). The development of programs can also be derived from relatively differentiated basic theories.

The meta-analysis reveals that training in social problem solving has a positive effect in terms of preventing antisocial behavior—at least in short-term outcomes. However, our own study and other examples suggest that it may be more effective to combine child-oriented programs with parent training or more complex systemic approaches. This is plausible insofar as ongoing negative models and experiences within the family may counteract any positive changes in children's social information processing and skills. On the other hand, there is also a large variance in the effects of combined parent- and child training on antisocial behavior (Farrington & Welsh, 2003). One should also bear in mind that it is easier to reach the whole target group with child-focused programs, and that they are less expensive and easier to implement (e.g., group programs delivered by school or preschool teachers). In sum, social problem-solving training for children is an important focus for the practice of prevention.

As the meta-analytic data have shown, the overall effect is positive. However, a large proportion of studies address only short-term outcomes in social cognitions and skills, assessed in more or less artificial testing situations. Although positive effects in outcomes that are very close to the program content are not a trivial finding, generalization to everyday behavior is crucial. Such a broader impact has only been confirmed relatively well for multimodal cognitive-behavioral programs. Nonetheless, despite such positive results, we still face serious research deficits. More high-quality studies are needed that address long-term effects and "hard" behavioral outcomes. Existing studies with relatively long-term follow-ups (e.g., Dishion & Andrews, 1995; Hundert et al., 1999; Kazdin, Esveldt-Dawson, French, & Unis, 1987; Lochman, Coie, Underwood, & Terry, 1993; Michelson, Mannarino, Marchione, Stern, Figueroa, & Beck, 1983) reveal a mix of large, small, zero, and negative outcomes in antisocial behavior. We also need more well-controlled studies outside the United States.

Both our own research example and the systematic review suggest that one cannot expect high effects from a single training program in social problem solving. Typical effect sizes are small. This is particularly the case for universal prevention, in which the majority of children in the program and control groups will develop relatively unproblematically without any intervention. One should also take into account that most longitudinal correlations between the respective risk factors and antisocial outcome are also small (Lösel, 2002). However, from a public health perspective, even small effects may well pay off in reducing the prevalence of risk cases and behavioral problems (e.g., Rose, 1992). Similar to recent experiences in the practice of offender treatment, single programs should not be regarded in isolation (Maguire, 2004). For example, a more long-term and generalized impact of social problem-solving training can be expected if one is able to deliver booster programs and age-related extensions of previous trainings. Currently, we are investigating exactly this issue in our Erlangen-Nuremberg study.

ACKNOWLEDGEMENTS

The Erlangen-Nuremberg Development and Prevention Study and the systematic review of child social skills trainings were supported by grants from the German Federal Ministry for Family, Women, Seniors, and Juveniles and the Smith Richardson Foundation (USA).

REFERENCES

Akhtar, N. & Bradley, E. J. (1991). Social information processing deficits of aggressive children: Present findings and implications for social skills training. *Clinical Psychology Review, 11*, 621–644.

Ang, R. P. & Hughes, J. N. (2001). Differential benefits of skills training with antisocial youth based on group composition: A meta-analytic investigation. *School Psychology Review, 31*, 164–185.

Asarnow, J. R. & Callan, J. W. (1985). Boys with peer adjustment problems: Social cognitive processes. *Journal of Consulting and Clinical Psychology, 53*, 80–87.

Bandura, A. (1973). *Aggression: A social learning analysis.* New York: Prentice Hall.

Beelmann, A. (2003). Wirksamkeit eines sozialen Problemlösetrainings bei entwicklungs-verzögerten Vorschulkindern [Effects of a social problem-solving training with developmentally delayed preschool children]. *Zeitschrift für Pädagogische Psychologie, 17*, 27–41.

Beelmann, A. (2004). Förderung sozialer Kompetenzen im Kindergarten: Evaluation eines sozialen Problemlösetrainings zur universellen Prävention dissozialer Verhaltensprobleme [Promoting social competences in the kindergarten: Evaluation of a social problem-solving training for universal prevention of antisocial behavior]. *Kindheit und Entwicklung, 13*, 113–121.

Beelmann, A. & Lösel, F. (2004). Soziale Informationsverarbeitung und Verhaltensprobleme im Vorschulalter. [Social information processing and behavior problems in preschool children]. Paper presented at the Annual Conference on Clinical Psychology of the German Society of Psychology, Halle, Germany.

Beelmann, A., Pfingsten, U., & Lösel, F. (1994). Effects of training social competence in children: A meta-analysis of recent evaluation studies. *Journal of Clinical Child Psychology, 23*, 260–271.

Bliesener, T. & Lösel, F. (2001). Social information processing in bullies, victims, and competent adolescents. In G. Traverso & L. Bagnoli (eds.) *Psychology and law in a changing world* (pp. 65–85). London: Routledge.

Coie, J. D., Cillessen, A. H. N., Dodge, K. A., Hubbard, J. A., Schwartz, D., Lemerise, E. A., & Bateman, H. (1999). It takes two to fight: A test of relational factors and a method for assessing aggressive dyads. *Developmental Psychology, 35*, 1179–1188.

Coie, J. D. & Dodge, K. A. (1998). Aggression and antisocial behavior. In W. Damon & N. Eisenberg (eds) *Handbook of child psychology*: Vol. 3. *Social, emotional and personality development* 5th edn. (pp. 779–862). New York: John Wiley & Sons, Ltd.

Coie, J. D., Dodge, K. A., Terry, R., & Wright, V. (1991). The role of aggression in peer relations: An analysis of aggression episodes in boys' playgroups. *Child Development, 62*, 812–826.

Conduct Problems Prevention Research Group (1999). Initial impact of the fast track prevention trial for conduct problems: II. Classroom effects. *Journal of Consulting and Clinical Psychology, 67*, 648–657.

Conduct Problems Prevention Research Group (2002). Evaluation of the first 3 years of the Fast Track Prevention Trial with children at high risk for adolescent conduct problems. *Journal of Abnormal Child Psychology, 19*, 553–567.

Coy, K., Speltz, M. L., DeKlyen, M., & Jones, K. (2001). Social-cognitive processes in preschool boys with and without oppositional defiant disorder. *Journal of Abnormal Child Psychology, 29*, 107–119.

Crick, N. R. & Dodge, K. A. (1994). A review and reformulation of social information-processing mechanisms in children's social adjustment. *Psychological Bulletin, 115*, 74–101.

Crick, N. R. & Dodge, K. A. (1996). Social information-processing mechanisms in reactive and proactive aggression. *Child Development, 67*, 993–1002.

Crick, N. R. & Ladd, G. W. (1990). Children's perceptions of the outcomes of aggressive strategies: Do the ends justify being mean? *Developmental Psychology, 26*, 612–620.

Denham, S. A. & Almeida, M. C. (1987). Children's social problem-solving skills, behavioral adjustment, and interventions: A meta-analysis evaluating theory and practice. *Journal of Applied Developmental Psychology, 8*, 391–409.

Dishion, T. J. & Andrews, D. W. (1995). Preventing escalation in problem behaviors with high-risk young adolescents: Immediate and 1-year outcomes. *Journal of Consulting and Clinical Psychology, 63*, 538–548.

Dishion, T. J. & Patterson, S. G. (1996). *Preventive parenting with love, encouragement and limits. The preschool years.* Eugene, OR: Castalia.

Dodge, K. A. (2000). Conduct disorder. In A. J. Sameroff, M. Lewis, & S. M. Miller (eds) *Handbook of developmental psychopathology* 2nd edn. (pp. 447–463). New York: Kluwer/Plenum.

Dodge, K. A. & Frame, C. L., (1982). Social cognitive biases and deficits in aggressive boys. *Child Development, 53*, 620–635.

Dodge, K. A., Lochman, J. E., Harnish, J. D., Bates, J. E., & Pettit, G. S. (1997). Reactive and proactive aggression in school children and psychiatrically impaired chronically assaultive youth. *Journal of Abnormal Psychology, 106*, 37–51.

Dodge, K. A., Pettit, G. S., Bates, J. E., & Valente, E. (1995). Social-information-processing patterns partially mediate the effect of early physical abuse on later conduct problems. *Journal of Abnormal Psychology, 104*, 632–643.

Dodge, K. A., Pettit, G. S., McClaskey, C. L., & Brown, M. (1986). Social competence in children. *Monographs of the Society for Research in Child Development, 51* (2, No. 213).

Dodge, K. A., Price, J. M., Bachorowski, J. A., & Newman, J. P. (1990). Hostile attributional biases in severely aggressive adolescents. *Journal of Abnormal Psychology, 99*, 385–392.

Durlak, J. A. & Wells, A. M. (1997). Primary prevention mental health programs for children and adolescents: A meta-analytic review. *American Journal of Community Psychology, 25*, 115–152.

Durlak, J. A. & Wells, A. M. (1998). Evaluation of indicated preventive intervention (secondary prevention) mental health programs for children and adolescents. *American Journal of Community Psychology, 26*, 775–802.

Farrington, D. P. & Petrosino, A. (2001). The Campbell Collaboration Crime and Justice Group. *Annals of the American Academy of Political and Social Science, 578*, 35–49.

Farrington, D. P. & Welsh, B. C. (2003). Family-based prevention of offending: A meta-analysis. *Australian and New Zealand Journal of Criminology, 36*, 127–151.

Fisher, P. A., Ramsay, E., Antoine, K., Kavanagh, K., Winebarger, A., Eddy, J. M., & Reid, J. B. (1997). *Success in parenting: A curriculum for parents with challenging children.* Eugene, OR: Oregon Social Learning Center.

Frauenknecht, M. & Black, D. R. (2004). Problem-solving training for children and adolescents. In E. C. Chang, T. J. ĐZurilla, & L. T. Sanna (eds) *Social problem solving: Theory, research, and training* (pp. 153–170). Washington, DC: American Psychological Association.

Gifford-Smith, M. E. & Rabiner, D. L. (2004). Social information processing and children's social adjustment. In J. B. Kupersmidt & K. A. Dodge (eds) *Children's peer relations: From development to intervention* (pp. 61–79). Washington, DC: American Psychological Association.

Gottfredson, M. R. & Hirschi, T. (1990). *A general theory of crime*. Stanford, CA: Stanford University Press.

Gottman, J., Gonso, J., & Rasmussen, B. (1975). Social interaction, social competence, and friendship in children. *Child Development*, *46*, 709–718.

Gouze, K. R. (1987). Attention and social problem solving as correlates of aggression in preschool males. *Journal of Abnormal Child Psychology*, *15*, 181–197.

Guerra, N. & Slaby, R. (1988). Cognitive mediators of aggression in adolescent offenders: II. Intervention. *Developmental Psychology*, *26*, 269–277.

Harper, G. & Chitty, C. (eds) (2004). *The impact of corrections on re-offending: a review of 'What Works'*. Home Office Research Study 291. London: Home Office.

Hedges, L. V. & Olkin, I. (1985). *Statistical methods for meta-analysis*. New York: Academic Press.

Huesman, L. R. (1997). Observational learning of violent behavior: Social and biosocial processes. In A. Raine, D. P. Farrington, P. Brennan, & S. A. Mednick (eds) *Biosocial bases of violence* (pp. 69–88). New York: Plenum Press.

Hundert, J., Boyle, M. H., Cunningham, C. E., Duku, E., Heale, J., McDonald, J., Offord, D. R., & Racine, Y. (1999). Helping children adjust - a tri-ministry study: II. Program Effects. *Journal of Child Psychology and Psychiatry*, *40*, 1061–1073.

Kazdin, A. E. (1998). Psychosocial treatments for conduct disorder in children. In P. E. Nathan & J. M. Gorman (eds) *A guide to treatments that work* (pp. 65–89). New York: Oxford University Press.

Kazdin, A. E. (2003). Problem-solving skills training and parent management training for conduct disorder. In A. E. Kazdin & J. R. Weisz (eds) *Evidence-based psychotherapies for children and adolescents*. New York: Guilford Press.

Kazdin, A. E., Esveldt-Dawson, K., French, K., & Unis, A. (1987). Problem-solving skills training and relationship therapy in the treatment of antisocial child behavior. *Journal of Consulting and Clinical Psychology*, *55*, 76–85.

Kazdin, A. E. & Wassell, G. (1999). Barriers to treatment participation and therapeutic change among children referred for conduct disorder. *Journal of Clinical Child Psychology*, *28*, 160–172.

Keltikangas-Järvinen, L. & Pakaslahti, L. (1999). Development of social problem-solving strategies and changes in aggressive behavior: A 7-year follow-up from childhood to late adolescence. *Aggressive Behavior*, *25*, 267–279.

Lipsey, M. W. & Wilson, D. B. (1998). Effective intervention for serious juvenile offenders: A synthesis of research. In R. Loeber & D.P. Farrington (eds) *Serious and violent juvenile offenders* (pp. 313–345). Thousand Oaks, CA: Sage.

Lipsey, M. W. & Wilson, D. B. (2001). *Practical meta-analysis*. Thousand Oaks, CA: Sage.

Lochman, J. E., Coie, J. D., Underwood, M. K., & Terry, R. (1993). Effectiveness of a social relations intervention program for aggressive and nonaggressive, rejected children. *Journal of Consulting and Clinical Psychology*, *61*, 1053–1058.

Lochman, J. E. & Dodge, K. A. (1998). Distorted perceptions in dyadic interactions of aggressive and nonaggressive boys: Effects of prior expectations, context, and boys' age. *Development and Psychopathology*, *10*, 495–512.

Lochman, J. E., Wayland, K. K., & White, K. J. (1993). Social goals: Relationship to adolescent adjustment and social problem solving. *Journal of Abnormal Child Psychology*, *21*, 135–151.

Loeber, R. & Stouthamer-Loeber, M. (1998). Development of juvenile aggression and violence. *American Psychologist*, *53*, 242–259.

Lösel, F. (1975). *Handlungskontrolle und Jugenddelinquenz*. [Action control and juvenile delinquency]. Stuttgart: Enke.

Lösel, F. (1995) The efficacy of correctional treatment: A review and synthesis of meta-evaluations. In J. McGuire (ed) *What works: Reducing reoffending* (pp. 70–111). Chichester: John Wiley & Sons, Ltd.

Lösel, F. (2002). Risk/need assessment and prevention of antisocial development in young people: Basic issues from a perspective of cautionary optimism. In R. R. Corrado, R. Roesch, S. Hart & J. Gierowski (eds) *Multi-problem violent youth* (pp. 35–57). Amsterdam, NL: IOS Press/NATO Science Series.

Lösel, F. & Beelmann, A. (2003a). Effects of child skills training in preventing antisocial behavior: A systematic review of randomized evaluations. *Annals of the American Academy of Political and Social Science*, *587*, 84–109.

Lösel, F. & Beelmann, A. (2003b). Early developmental prevention of aggression and delinquency. In F. Dünkel & K. Drenkhahn (eds) *Youth violence: New patterns and local responses* (pp. 245–265). Mönchengladbach, Germany: Forum Verlag.

Lösel, F. & Beelmann, A. (in press). Child skills training. In B. C. Welsh & D. P. Farrington (eds) *Preventing crime: What works for children, offenders, victims, and places*. Doordrecht, NL: Springer.

Lösel, F. Beelmann, A., Jaursch, S., & Stemmler, M. (2004). *Soziale Kompetenz für Kinder und Familien: Ergebnisse der Erlangen-Nürnberger Entwicklungs- und Präventionsstudie* [Social competence for children and families: Results from the Erlangen-Nuremberg Development and Prevention Study]. Research report for the Federal Ministry for Families, Seniors, Women, and Youth. University of Erlangen-Nuremberg, Germany: Institute of Psychology.

Lösel, F. & Bender, D. (2003). Resilience and protective factors. In D. P. Farrington & J. Coid (eds) *Prevention of adult antisocial behaviour* (pp. 130–204). Cambridge: Cambridge University Press.

Lösel, F. & Bliesener, T. (1999). Aggressive conflict behavior and social information processing in juveniles. In I. Sagel-Grande & M. V. Polak (eds) *Models of conflict resolution* (pp. 61–78). Antwerp: Maklu.

Lösel, F. & Bliesener, T. (2003). *Aggression und Delinquenz unter Jugendlichen* [Aggression and delinquency in adolescence]. Neuwied: Luchterhand.

Lösel, F., Bliesener, T., & Bender, D. (in press). Social information processing, experiences of aggression in social contexts, and aggressive behavior in adolescents. *Criminal Justice and Behavior*.

Maguire, M. (2004). The Crime Reduction Programme in England and Wales: reflections on the vision and the reality. *Criminal Justice*, *4*, 231–237.

McGuire, J. (2002). Integrating findings from research reviews. In J. McGuire (ed) *Offender rehabilitation and treatment: Effective programs and policies to reduce reoffending* (pp. 3–38). Chichester: John Wiley & Sons, Ltd.

Michelson, L., Mannarino, A. P., Marchione, K. E., Stern, M., Figueroa, J., & Beck, S. (1983). A comparative outcome study of behavioral social-skills training, interpersonal problem-solving and non-directive control treatments with child psychiatric outpatients. *Behavior Research and Therapy*, *21*, 545–556.

Mischel, W. (1973). Toward a cognitive social learning reconceptualization of personality. *Psychological Review*, *80*, 252–283.

Moffitt, T. E. (1993). Adolescence-limited and life-course-persistent antisocial behavior: A developmental taxonomy. *Psychological Review, 100,* 674–701.

Nagin, D. S. & Pogarsky, G. (2003). An experimental investigation of deterrence: Cheating, self-serving bias, and impulsivity. *Criminology, 41,* 167–193.

Patterson, G. R., Reid, J. B., & Dishion, T. J. (1992). *Antisocial boys.* Eugene, OR: Castalia.

Pellegrino, D. S. & Urbani, E. S. (1985). An evaluation of interpersonal cognitive problem-solving training with children. *Journal of Child Psychology and Psychiatry, 26,* 17–41.

Perry, D. G., Perry, L. C., & Rasmussen, P. (1986). Cognitive social learning mediators of aggression. *Child Development, 57,* 700–711.

Prinz, R. J. & Miller, G. E. (1994). Family-based treatment for childhood antisocial behavior: Experimental influences on dropout and engagement. *Journal of Consulting and Clinical Psychology, 62,* 645–650.

Rose, G. (1992). *The strategy of preventive medicine.* Oxford: Oxford University Press.

Rubin, K. H., Bream, L. A., & Rose-Krasnor, L. (1991). Social problem solving and aggression in childhood. In D. J. Pepler & K. H. Rubin (eds) *The development and treatment of childhood aggression* (pp. 219–248). Hillsdale, NJ: Lawrence Erlbaum.

Sanders, M. R., Markie-Dadds, C., Tully, L. A., & Bor, W. (2000). The Triple P-Positive Parenting Program: A comparison of enhanced, standard, and self-directed behavioral family interventions for parents of children with early onset conduct problems. *Journal of Consulting and Clinical Psychology, 68,* 624–640.

Shure, M. B. (1992). *I can problem solve. An interpersonal cognitive problem-solving program.* Champaign, IL: Research Press.

Slaby, R. G. & Guerra, N.G. (1988). Cognitive mediators of aggression in adolescent offenders: 1. Assessment. *Developmental Psychology, 24,* 580–588.

Spivack, G. & Shure, M. B. (1974). *Social adjustment of young children: A cognitive approach to solving real-life problems.* San Francisco: Jossey-Bass.

Spoth, R., Redmond, C., Hockaday, C., & Shin, C. Y. (1996). Barriers to participation in family skills preventive interventions and their evaluations. A replication and extension. *Family Relations, 45,* 247–254.

Sutton, J., Smith, P. K., & Swettenham, J. (1999). Social cognition and bullying: Social inadequacy or skilled manipulation? *British Journal of Developmental Psychology, 17,* 435–450.

Taylor, T. K., Eddy, J. M., & Biglan, A. (1999). Interpersonal skill training to reduce aggressive and delinquent behavior: Limited evidence and the need for an evidence-based system of care. *Clinical Child and Family Psychology Review, 2,* 169–182.

Tremblay, R. E. (2000). The development of aggressive behavior during childhood: What have we learned in the past century? *International Journal of Behavioral Development, 24,* 129–141.

Tremblay, R. E. & Craig, W. M. (1995). Developmental crime prevention. In M. Tonry & D. P. Farrington (eds) *Building a safer society: Strategic approaches to crime prevention.* Vol. 19 (pp. 151–236). Chicago: The University of Chicago Press.

Tremblay, R. E., Pagani-Kurtz, L., Vitato, F, Masse, L. C., & Pihl, R. O. (1995). A bimodal preventive intervention for disruptive kindergarten boys: Its impact through mid-adolescence. *Journal of Consulting and Clinical Psychology, 63,* 560–568.

Tremblay, R. E., Vitaro, F., Gagnon, C., Piché, C., & Royer, N. (1992). A prosocial scale for the Preschool Behavior Questionnaire: Concurrent and predictive correlates. *International Journal of Behavioral Development, 15,* 227–245.

Urbain, D. S. & Kendall, P. C. (1980). Review of social-cognitive problem-solving interventions for children. *Psychological Bulletin, 88,* 105–143.

Webster-Stratton, C. & Taylor, T. (2001). Nipping early risk factors in the bud: Preventing substance abuse, delinquency, and violence in adolescence through intervention targeted at young children (0-8 years). *Prevention Science, 2,* 165–192.

Wilson, S. J., Lipsey, M. W., & Derzon, J. H. (2003). The effects of school-based intervention programs on aggressive behavior: A meta-analysis. *Journal of Consulting and Clinical Psychology, 71,* 136–149.

Winstok, Z. & Enosh, G. (in press). Exploring the intention to react to aggressive action among Israeli youth. *Journal of Research on Adolescence.*

Zelli, A., Dodge, K. A., Lochman, J. E., Laird, R. D., & Conduct Problems Prevention Research Group (1999). The distinction between beliefs legitimizing aggression and deviant processing of social cues: Testing measurement validity and the hypothesis that biased processing mediates the effects of beliefs on aggression. *Journal of Personality and Social Psychology, 77,* 150–166.

Chapter 8

THE DEVELOPMENT OF SOCIAL PROBLEM-SOLVING INTERVENTIONS IN YOUNG OFFENDER MENTAL HEALTH SERVICES: A FOCUS UPON SELF-HARM AND SUICIDE RISK

FIONA H. BIGGAM[1] and KEVIN G. POWER[2]

[1]Glasgow Caledonian University, and State Hospital, Carstairs UK
[2]University of Stirling, and NHS Tayside UK

INTRODUCTION

In recent years, empirical studies have indicated that the specific conditions of imprisonment such as overcrowding, or long-term incarceration do not consistently show any detrimental effect *per se* upon the psychological health of prisoners (Bonta & Gendreau, 1990) and that personal variables may have greater efficacy in predicting prison adjustment (Zamble & Porporino, 1988, 1990). The identification of such individual differences has potential ramifications for the development and implementation of intervention programmes that could assist the subsection of the penal population that displays considerable difficulties in coping with prison life. To date, there is growing evidence to suggest that social problem-solving ability may constitute a relevant personal factor, particularly in relation to the distress experienced by prisoners more at risk of developing mental health problems.

Young offenders are universally considered to be a group at risk of mental health problems, and this may be for several reasons as reviewed by Rutter, Gillen, & Hagell (1998) and also by Hagell (2002). First, the risk factors inherent in their offending are also risk factors for mental health difficulties among their peers in the general population. These factors include inconsistent and erratic parenting, childhood hyperactivity, trauma in childhood, and socio-economic

Social Problem Solving and Offending: Evidence, Evaluation and Evolution.
Edited by Mary McMurran and James McGuire © 2005 John Wiley & Sons, Ltd.

stresses on the family. Second, the risky and impulsive behaviours characteristic of many young offenders may in themselves cause mental health problems. Third, interaction with the criminal justice system can be stressful and can lead to anxiety and depression.

The vulnerability of young offenders to developing mental health problems has been an issue of considerable international concern (Alessi, McManus, Grapentine, & Brickman, 1984; Chiles, Miller, & Cox, 1980; Compas, Connor, & Hinden, 1998). To date, there have been a number of methodological difficulties associated with studies investigating the rates of mental health problems among young offenders but recent estimates indicate that young offenders are approximately three times more likely to develop mental health problems than their peers in the community, and up to 80% of incarcerated young offenders experience mental health problems of clinical concern (Hagell, 2002). The need for appropriate young offender mental health services has been emphasised in recent years, particularly in relation to growing international concern over the rates of young offender self-harm and suicide (Harris & Lennings, 1993; Kempton & Forehand, 1992; Liebling, 1993; Rhode, Mace, & Seeley, 1997).

Research from around the world has indicated that deliberate self-harm is an increasing and considerable problem among young people in general (Schmidtke et al., 1996; Davis & Kosky, 1991). This is reflected in the fact that the reduction of suicide and self-harming behaviour in the world community is now part of the 'Health for All' targets of WHO (World Health Organisation, 1992). Studies have indicated that around half of all people who kill themselves have histories of deliberate self-harm in the year prior to their death (Foster, Gillespie, & McClelland, 1997; Ovenstone & Kreitman, 1974). Self-harm must therefore be viewed as a significant risk factor for suicide.

Young offenders appear to be at significant risk in terms of self-harm and suicide. Liebling and Krarup's (1993) study of prisoners in the English system indicated that one-third of self-injuries and between one-fifth and one-quarter of suicides in prison occur among prisoners under the age of 21, even though this group represents less than one-fifth of the prison population. Among this group of prisoners, Liebling and Krarup suggested that the largest proportion of "poor copers" could be found. Vulnerable individuals are likely to have difficulties integrating into the prison regime, and are most likely to be victims of bullying and be at heightened risk of suicidal behaviour (Liebling, 1992; Power, Dyson, & Biggam, 1999). What is more, vulnerable young offenders are more likely to display signs of psychological distress (perhaps through hopelessness and a helpless outlook) rather than markers of a formal mental illness diagnosis (Inch, Rowlands, & Soliman, 1995). Vulnerable young offenders are also more likely to signal their distress through their behaviour, for instance through ingesting objects, overdosing, lacerating, or other self-damaging behaviour rather than through talking about their feelings to trusted individuals. The maladaptive behaviours of vulnerable young offenders often result from an inability to tolerate emotional distress long enough to pursue more adaptive solutions to problems. Their emotional dysregulation is often extreme, and they will respond to a host of complex emotional states such as anger, depression, anxiety, and irritability through violence and self-harming behaviour. Their impulsivity is often evident in their inability to tolerate stressful situations in the moment and their need to change aversive situations quickly. In essence, their emotions and behaviours are often out of proportion to the situation at hand. Helping vulnerable young offenders to change extreme noxious emotions and unhealthy behaviours is thus key to their adaptation.

It is appropriate and ethical to develop strategies for managing young offender mental health that are consistent with good practice as it is deemed in the research literature and models of service in the community. The aim of this chapter is to describe the stages required for such a development in offender mental health. First, we will consider the role of social problem-solving in relation to psychological distress and suicidal and self-harming behaviour in the general population and the implications for clinical intervention. Second, we will detail what we know from the literature to date about the problem-solving abilities of young offenders and the relationship with their mental health. Third, we will outline a recently completed intervention study which we piloted to develop, implement, and evaluate a brief problem-solving approach with young offenders identified as at risk of mental health problems and self harming or suicidal behaviour.

SOCIAL PROBLEM-SOLVING ABILITY AS A KEY MENTAL HEALTH DETERMINANT

Since the 1970s a general body of research has examined the importance of social problem-solving skills in moderating psychological and behavioural adjustment. From a mental health perspective, problem-solving serves as a general coping strategy that allows an individual to generate, select, and implement a whole host of effective behaviours which will enhance general well-being in psychological and social terms and protect the individual from possible maladaptation (D'Zurilla & Nezu, 1982; Lazarus & Folkman, 1984). Social problem-solving deficits have been demonstrated in a number of groups of clinical interest, including maladjusted children (Renshaw & Asher, 1982), emotionally disturbed adolescents (Siegal & Platt, 1976), male alcoholics (Intagliata, 1978); heroin users (Platt, Scura, & Hannon, 1973), diagnostically heterogeneous groups of adult psychiatric patients (Platt & Siegal, 1976), and individuals diagnosed with schizophrenia (Bellack, Sayers, Mueser, & Bennett, 1994). A host of studies have also examined problem solving in relation to particular clinical diagnoses such as depression (Marx, Williams, & Claridge, 1992; Nezu, Nezu, & Perri, 1989), or in relation to groups that warrant specialist clinical management, such as individuals engaging in self-harm or expressing suicidal ideation (Lerner & Clum, 1990; McLeavey, Daly, Ludgate, & Murray, 1994; Salkovskis, Atha, & Storer, 1990). Authors of many of these studies have argued that if limitations in respect of social problem-solving are partly responsible for adjustment problems, then the appropriate problem-solving training may not only enhance cognitive coping skills but also lead improvements in mental health.

PROBLEM-SOLVING INTERVENTIONS: THE OUTCOME STUDIES FOR MENTAL HEALTH IN THE GENERAL POPULATION

Over the past two decades, research has indicated the value of problem-solving interventions for a host of groups of clinical concern. Problem-solving training has been successfully used as a stand-alone clinical intervention for specific problems, as part of a comprehensive treatment package, a maintenance strategy, and as part of relapse prevention programmes (D'Zurilla & Nezu, 1999). Depression and deliberate self-harm are two issues of significant clinical concern where there is a growing body of evidence to suggest the value of problem-solving interventions for these groups.

There is a growing body of controlled trials that indicate the efficacy of problem-solving interventions in reducing clinical levels of depression (Arean, Perri, Nezu, Schein, Christopher, & Joseph, 1993; Dorwick et al., 2000; Hussian & Lawrence, 1981; Mynors-Wallis, Gath, Day, & Baker, 2000; Nezu, 1986; Nezu & Perri, 1989). The rationale behind these studies is that by developing social problem-solving abilities, an individual's self-efficacy is strengthened, which in turn enhances active coping and reduces the level of depression experienced. With the exception of three studies (Dowrick et al., 2000; Hussian & Lawrence, 1981; Mynors-Wallis et al., 2000), all the interventions have used small group formats. The research to date has indicated a reduction in psychopathology following a brief model of therapy (between 5-12 sessions, of 0.5-2.0 hours duration), and a significant proportion of the studies have demonstrated that treatment effects are maintained at follow-up periods ranging from six weeks to six months. Indeed, the *WHO Guide to Mental Health in Primary Care* (WHO, 1990) has advocated problem-solving interventions as an appropriate intervention for the treatment of depression.

Problem-solving interventions (in both individual and group therapy formats) have also been studied as a systematic intervention for suicidal and self-harming behaviour (Hawton et al., 1987; Lerner & Clum, 1990; McLeavey, Daly, Ludgate, & Murray, 1994; Salkovskis et al., 1990). The four studies published to date have indicated a reduction in psychopathology following a brief model of therapy (5-10 sessions of 1.0-1.5 hours duration), and there is some evidence that it may also reduce the incidence of self-harm (Salkovskis et al., 1990) with a significant proportion of the studies indicating that treatment effects are maintained at follow-up periods ranging from three–six months and that individuals who have had problem-solving training often describe better attitudes towards problem-solving and self-control (McLeavey et al., 1994).

The recent Cochrane Review and associated publications by Hawton and colleagues on psychosocial and pharmacological treatments for deliberate self-harm (Hawton, Arensman, Townsend, Bremner, Feldman, Goldney, et al., 1998, Hawton et al., 2004) indicate that there is currently insufficient evidence on which to make firm recommendations about the most effective interventions for deliberate self-harm, and that this is an issue of concern, given the size of the self-harm problem throughout the world, and its role in suicide prevention. Currently, the research is blighted by the fact that most of the interventions evaluated to date have been pilot investigations lacking in the statistical power to detect clinically significant changes. However, Hawton's team have argued that problem-solving interventions are a promising line of therapy, in that they are brief and easily taught. In terms of the UK, such a strategy is also in line with the NHS Health Advisory Service Thematic Review of Suicide Prevention (Williams & Morgan, 1994) wherein a problem-solving approach to intervention is advocated as best current practice. There is sufficient evidence from recent research on problem-solving and from the concerns about the mental health needs of young offenders to suggest that problem-solving training may be an important approach for intervention with young offenders who are vulnerable to mental health disturbance and deliberate self-harm.

THE SOCIAL PROBLEM-SOLVING ABILITIES OF OFFENDERS

Impoverished problem-solving abilities have also been considered to be a characteristic common among prisoners (Zamble & Porporino, 1988) with particular reference to avoidant and impulsive styles of problem-solving. Indeed, some researchers have gone as far as to suggest that problem-solving deficits may be a contributing factor to the impulsive behaviours that can lead to incarceration (Reeker & Meissner, 1977). To date, there has been a paucity of systematic studies examining problem-solving abilities of general adult prisoners (Grier, 1988; Higgins & Thies, 1982; Ivanoff et al., 1992; Pugh, 1993). The young offender population has received relatively little research attention with regard to problem-solving. In comparison to their non-offending peers, aggressive young offenders have been found to display a host of problem-solving deficits—including a reluctance to seek out information about a problem, an attributional bias towards inferring hostile intent in others, a difficulty in generating potential solutions, and a higher engagement in aggressive solutions (Akhtar & Bradley, 1991; Perry, Perry, & Rasmussen, 1986; Slaby & Guerra, 1988).

With particular reference to the important issue of self-harm and suicidal behaviour among young offenders, a review of the literature conducted by us in the late 1990s indicated that social problem-solving theories and models of intervention had not been adequately considered in this regard. Meanwhile, a growing body of evidence indicated the value of social problem-solving formulations in the understanding of suicidal and self harming behaviour in the general population. Consequently, in our research into the young offender population, we considered the three following issues:

1. What is the nature of problem-solving deficits among vulnerable and "at risk" sections of the young offender population, and how do such difficulties relate to their mental health?
2. In comparison to other young offenders, is there a difference in the problem-solving abilities and distress experienced by those with a past and/or present suicide risk?
3. What is the value of social problem-solving interventions for young offenders at risk of self-harm and/or suicidal behaviour?

Over recent years, we have conducted a series of studies that have attempted to consider each of these questions. We will present some of our main findings in this chapter with particular emphasis on the development, implementation, and evaluation of a social problem-solving intervention for these vulnerable prisoners.

In relation to our first question concerning the vulnerable and at-risk section of the young offender population, our initial series of studies (Biggam & Power, 1997, 1999a, 1999b) found that prisoners on suicide supervision showed the most marked problem-solving deficits as measured by the Means–Ends Problem Solving Procedure (MEPS; Platt & Spivack, 1975), followed by those removed from routine circulation and placed on a protection wing, and then victims of bullying in routine circulation. Suicidal prisoners showed the most marked deficits in terms of producing high levels of irrelevant problem-solving means that would not achieve adequate solutions to problems, along with the highest levels of "passive" problem-solving means, where they were more dependent on the actions of others to attain problem resolution. Although there were significant differences in the profiles of problem-solving deficits of these three groups, it was argued that all of them displayed highly impoverished problem-solving ability that could warrant intervention. Such deficits were not related to IQ. Furthermore, problem-solving deficits were found to correlate significantly with the psychological distress experienced by these prisoners, particularly in relation to depression and hopelessness, which are key risk factors for suicide (Beck et al., 1985).

Our second question concerned young offenders with a past and/or present suicide risk compared to young offenders with no such history (Biggam & Power, 1999c). First, we found that both prisoners who had previously been deemed "at risk" of suicide and those who were currently considered to be "at risk" showed higher levels of anxiety, depression, hopelessness, and more impaired problem-solving abilities as assessed by the MEPS (Platt & Spivack, 1975) when they were compared to young offenders with no history of mental health problems. Second, prisoners with a cyclical history of suicide risk (in that they were being currently viewed as a suicide risk, and had periods of high suicide risk and self-harm in their past) showed more marked levels of depression, anxiety, and a more hopeless style of problem solving when compared to their peers who had a history of self-harm or suicide risk but who were not currently experiencing a suicidal/self-harm crisis. One important finding was that prisoners who had a cyclical history of risk of repeated incidents of self-harming and suicidal behaviour continued to exhibit long-term psychological distress and impaired social problem-solving abilities. Periods of crisis appeared to further exacerbate these difficulties, making them more vulnerable to being deemed "at high current risk" of suicide and self-harm. The causal relationship between psychological distress and impaired social problem solving is difficult to tease out in this context. However, it could be speculated that those with a history of suicidal behaviour remain at heightened risk with respect to psychological distress and problem-solving vulnerability. During times of acute stress such as periods of imprisonment, or during episodes of interpersonal conflict or bullying, or when experiencing difficulties in adjusting to demanding environments in the lack of adequate social support, these individuals are vulnerable to a marked deterioration in their mental health accompanied by an exacerbation of their problem-solving difficulties. This, in turn, serves to heighten their suicidal risk.

Our work has drawn on the model linking problem-solving skills, depression, and hopelessness as risk factors for suicidal behaviour described in the work of Williams (1997). This model posits that the depressive thinking of vulnerable individuals acts as a key to their level of risk. Such individuals may become quickly despondent when problem-solving efforts fail, and engage in a series of cognitive distortions which exacerbate their distress—such as the "all-or-nothing thinking" that there are no other possibilities open to them; "arbitrary inference" where hard conclusions are drawn in the face of a lack of supporting evidence; or "overgeneralising" and "catastrophising" where the individual comes to expect the worst of a situation. Such distortions act as grist to the mill of the emotional distress of depression accompanied by a block in problem-solving efforts, which in turn foster a sense of hopelessness. Hopelessness is viewed as an integral factor, in that it disinhibits the course to drastic action such as self-harm or suicidal behaviour.

KEY COMPONENTS IN A PROBLEM-SOLVING PROGRAMME FOR MENTAL HEALTH

To date, most problem-solving training programmes (for both offender and non-offender groups) have been based on the prescriptive model of social problem solving originally described by D'Zurilla and Goldfried (1971) and refined by D'Zurilla and Nezu (1982). The works of D'Zurilla and colleagues delineate a five-stage model of problem solving and progressive training in the various stages of problem-solving is advocated as the basis of intervention. In essence, the five stages can be described as follows:

1. *Problem orientation.* The individual develops a problem-solving mindset, and is able to recognise when problem situations occur, to understand that social problems are part of everyday life, and to consider that action can be taken to alter the course of problems. The initial aim is to "stop and think" rather than go with the first (often impulsively) generated solution or become overwhelmed by problems. Some programmes have also included, as part of "problem orientation", consideration of stress (simple transactional model) and its effects upon emotions, using feelings to help recognise problem situations rather than treating feelings *per se* as the problem.
2. *Problem definition and goal setting.* The individual is encouraged to find out information about the problem situation and consider problems in terms of frequency, duration, complexity, and size. Participants identify specific problems experienced currently in their lives, separating "facts" from "opinions" through gathering information and reality testing. They also try to make problems more "specific" by using Who? What? Where? Why? When? Questioning, practising these tasks with personally relevant examples. They make problems more manageable in terms of setting realistic goals.

3. *Generation of alternatives.* This is where a range of potential solutions is developed. In this stage, participants are encouraged to be creative and not to censor their responses.
4. *Decision-making and action.* In this stage, individuals anticipate consequences and conduct cost–benefit analyses of proposed solutions, choosing the most appropriate. They practise means–end thinking, using personally relevant examples, by means of a progressive problem-solving approach (steps to solution). In the process, they become aware of obstacles and learn to tolerate or work through them.
5. *Evaluation.* The problem-solving strategy is reviewed after implementation. If the goals are achieved, then problem solving is deemed to be successful. If the goals are not achieved, the problem-solving process may be repeated in light of new information. The ongoing nature of problem-solving processes throughout life in response to new information, changing goals, and meeting obstacles is highlighted. Emotional well-being is also given special consideration.

The application of problem-solving training draws on a host of methods from the behavioural and cognitive therapies repertoire including the analysis of habitual reactions, skills practice, rehearsal, self-monitoring, analysis of thought patterns and distortions in thinking, Socratic questioning, guided discussion, and reflection. In group work, these skills are facilitated through instruction, active discussion, reflective listening, role play, and group and individual exercises to practise targeted skills. In some programmes, participants are provided with supplementary notes and exercises. A major benefit of problem-solving training is that it has been successfully implemented with people with learning disabilities (Loumidis & Hill, 1997), hence indicating that it can be a flexible and relevant intervention for individuals with low academic achievements, which will include many offenders.

PROBLEM-SOLVING INTERVENTIONS FOR MENTAL HEALTH AND SELF-HARM: THE FINDINGS OF PILOT INTERVENTION AMONG YOUNG OFFENDER GROUPS

In recent years, attention has been drawn to the clear need for mental health services for young people in prison (Nicol et al., 2000). Coupled with this, there has been a recognition that young offenders do not tend to use "primary health care services" to the same extent as other groups, and their needs are often responded to on a crisis basis which may become more apparent during periods of incarceration (Dolan et al., 1999). Indeed, time-limited, problem-solving based interventions may work very well as a form of "crisis-based" intervention for individuals at risk of self-harm or suicidal behaviour (Salkovskis et al., 1990). The third aim of our research was to consider the value of a controlled brief problem-solving intervention for vulnerable young offenders exhibiting mental health problems or self-harming and suicidal behaviour during imprisonment.

To investigate this, we implemented and evaluated a problem-solving intervention for mental health with vulnerable incarcerated young offenders in a Young Offenders institution (Biggam & Power, 2002). A total of 46 young males (aged 16-21) were selected due to their vulnerable status within prison. They were categorised as such because they had either been:

1. recently (in past four weeks), subject to the Scottish Prison Service's Act and Care Strategy as a result of being identified as a suicide risk due to recent emotional and behavioural indices;
2. victims of bullying in routine circulation in the prison (a group at high risk for mental health problems and suicidal behaviour); or
3. removed from routine circulation and placed on formal protection as a consequence of behavioural indications that they did not possess the adequate coping skills for dealing with life in routine circulation.

Strict inclusion/exclusion criteria were utilised in the study. Inclusion criteria included that participants had to belong to one of the above identified groups, be willing to participate in the study, and have a term of incarceration exceeding the research period (to allow the collection of follow-up data). Exclusion criteria included the presence of a psychotic illness, a physical illness of clinical significance, being a suspected or known bully, receiving psychotherapeutic assistance beyond the study, having highly impoverished literacy skills, and a liberation date prior to the collection of follow-up data.

Adequate therapeutic evaluations are dependent upon the selection of appropriate outcome measures. Our outcome assessments were selected in accordance with the findings of previous research which considered the relationship of the measures to the philosophical and empirical models of problem solving and the link with mental health, ease and clarity of use in forensic settings, and real-world validity in terms of outcome assessment. The measure of problem solving that most readily meets these requirements is the Social Problem-Solving Inventory-Revised (D'Zurilla et al., 2002) which has had its efficacy demonstrated in forensic populations as a measure of problem-solving skills (McMurran et al., 1999, 2001). The Hospital Anxiety and Depression Scale (HADS; Zigmond & Snaith, 1983) is considered to be a reasonable measure of levels of psychological distress of clinical concern in young offenders (Biggam & Power, 1997, 1999a, 1999b, 1999c); and the Beck Hopelessness Scale (BHS; Beck, Weissman, Lester, & Trexler, 1974) is an important measure of the lack of future-orientated thinking which is viewed as a key predictor of completed suicide and high suicidal ideation/intention (Beck, Steer, Kovacs, & Garrison, 1985) in both the general population (Greene, 1981) and prison populations (Liebling, 1992; Power & Beveridge, 1990).

The 46 participants were placed by means of alternating allocation to an intervention or comparison group; 23 prisoners took part in the problem-solving groups, and 23 were allocated to the no-intervention comparison group. A total of five problem-solving intervention groups ran, and were conducted by Fiona Biggam in the education room in the prison's formal protection hall or the group room in the prison surgery. A small group format was used to enhance therapeutic effectiveness and group cohesion, and to ensure the safety of participants. Given the evidence from community studies indicating the efficacy of brief interventions, the problem-solving training consisted of five sessions of $1-1\frac{1}{2}$ hours duration, and followed the prescriptive model of problem-solving training described earlier in this chapter. The social problem-solving skills training programme was devised specifically for the group based on the principles of the key elements of problem-solving described in the work of D'Zurilla and Nezu (1982, 1999), taking a session to explore and develop skills on each of the five stages of problem-solving. As the programme was being used to target mental health problems, educating participants to be aware of their feelings at each stage of the programme was an integral element, and in particular recognising the "thresholds" of distress wherein participants began to contemplate deliberate self-harm.

Along with weekly group sessions, the participants were offered the opportunity to engage in individualised "coaching" with the therapist, which focused entirely upon allowing the individual to practise their problem-solving skills in relation to homework exercises. This therapeutic adjunct has been increasingly utilised in interventions focusing upon self-harm, such as Dialectical Behaviour Therapy (Linehan, 1993). To ensure the integrity of the programme, the intervention conditions were monitored by strict adherence to the intervention manual and reflective discussions of the group processes with an experienced clinical psychologist.

We encouraged the participants in the study's intervention groups to consider the current social problems that they were facing. Problems were identified by means of a group process rather than by asking individuals to provide personalised lists of current concerns. In general terms, the problems provided by the prisoners could be grouped according to prison-based problems, concerns relating to family and friends, release issues, drugs and alcohol misuse, and offending behaviour. The scope of the problems indicated that these vulnerable young offenders not only had situational-specific problem-solving difficulties (pertaining only to life in prison), but also experienced significant problems in general, i.e., they had brought a significant amount of personal problems into the prison with them, which enhanced their vulnerability. However, around half of the problems identified by the participants were current, chronic, and related to life at present in prison.

Our controlled study adopted a three-month follow-up period and provided preliminary evidence that a brief problem-solving intervention can be effective in achieving clinically significant reductions of psychological distress, taking the participants' mental health status from an "at risk" to a "normal-mild" level in terms of depression, anxiety, and hopelessness as assessed by the HADS and BHS. Furthermore, the brief intervention enhanced the self-perceived problem-solving abilities of vulnerable young offenders in prison as assessed by the SPSI-R. Many of the improvements in mental health and social problem-solving functioning were still evident at three-month follow-up when compared to a non-intervention comparison group, who continued to display both levels of psychopathology which would be of clinical concern, and impoverished social problem-solving abilities.

Significant improvements in a number of self-assessed problem-solving abilities as measured by the SPSI-R subscales were noted among the intervention group at the three-month follow-up. Improvements were apparent on Negative Problem Orientation, Rational Problem Solving, and Avoidance Style. No statistically significant change was evident on three SPSI-R scales: the Solution Implementation subscale of the Rational Problem Solving Scale, the Impulsivity and Carelessness Style Scale, and the Positive Problem Orientation Scale.

Impulsiveness has been demonstrated to be a notable trait among young offenders (Daderman, 1999) and particularly those who engage in self-harm (Putnins, 1995). Community studies have also indicated that impulsiveness is associated with poor problem-solving ability among adults who engage in self-harm during times of significant life stress (Evans, Williams, O'Loughlin, & Howells, 1992), and more recently among self-poisoning adolescents (Kingsbury, Hawton, Steinhardt, & James, 1999). If impulsiveness could be considered to be a trait characteristic of young offenders, it is understandable that a brief intervention would not make an impact upon this. Clearly, impulsive problem-solving styles warrant further therapeutic attention with this group. Harris and Rice (1994) argue that interventions that attempt to consider impulsiveness as an isolated variable for treatment are likely to prove unsuccessful and it should be a component of an integrated treatment package.

Our failure to achieve change in the solution implementation and verification element of the problem-solving process is most likely to be due to the fact that the intervention focused entirely upon the cognitive elements of the problem-solving process, and paid little attention to the social skills competence of the participants. Young offenders have been previously demonstrated to be deficient in social skills and to benefit from appropriate social skills training (Henderson & Hollin, 1986; Spence, 1979, 1982). Like the cognitive elements of the problem-solving process, social skills training is multi-faceted and pays attention to non-verbal communication, listening and conversational skills, and assertive versus aggressive styles of responding. It is likely that in order to enhance overall problem-solving abilities and competence, the participants in our study would have benefited from concomitant social-skills training and that this should be an integral element of future interventions.

PROBLEM-SOLVING INTERVENTIONS FOR OFFENDER MENTAL HEALTH: IMPLEMENTATION ISSUES

While our study suggests that there may be a role for brief, problem-solving interventions for mental health with vulnerable young offenders in prison, the practical experience of the delivery of the programme indicated a number of issues that might be worthwhile for consideration in future developments. The programme deliverer (FB) noted that many of the young men were highly alexithymic, in that they often struggled to find the words to express their emotional states; they often experienced distress in a noxious, undifferentiated, somatic form and struggled to describe the concomitant emotion (e.g. angry, depressed, hopeless, agitated). In relation to this, they also experienced significant difficulties in differentiating "thoughts" from "feelings"—an ability which lies as the very heart of all cognitive-behavioural interventions. Given the difficulties the young men experienced with the "language" of emotions and therapy, there may be scope for the development of a "pre-therapy training" module to help them to identify and express emotions and cognitions. The young men in the current study were unusually compliant, but future studies may also need to consider the use of pre-intervention motivational interviewing with group participants to ensure their adherence to the programme and to enhance therapeutic outcomes.

Our study is reflective of most of the published studies to date on problem-solving interventions that have taken the form of "pilot" investigations, and all the therapeutic work has been delivered by a clinical psychologist or experienced mental health practitioner. Most programmes have been designed to allow them to be delivered by professionals other than psychologists—particularly prison officers with training in programme delivery. However, what is clear is that the provision and facilitation of many of the group-work skills in problem-solving interventions with self-harming and suicidal offenders are highly skilled and demanding tasks. First, group facilitators would have to have a good training in mental health issues, and particularly in understanding the aetiology and functions of self-harming behaviour. Group facilitators would also have to be aware of the importance of appropriate "pro-social modelling" in their own behaviour and be able to maintain and enforce the boundaries of the therapeutic group (McGuire, 2001). Vulnerable and self-harming prisoners can frequently engage in behaviours which interfere with the course of the therapeutic group, such as displaying hostility or a lack of commitment to the programme, or challenging boundaries, which in turn can disrupt the group dynamics. Competent facilitators should manage such disruptive behaviours by challenging them and also reinforcing the structure and objectives of the course. In order to maximise the effectiveness, future therapeutic work should consider the role of using co-therapists with appropriate clinical supervision.

CONCLUSION

To date, there is a growing body of evidence from both community and prison settings to indicate the value of problem-solving interventions for mental health problems and deliberate self-harm (Hawton et al., 1998). The continuing development of problem-solving interventions is an example of the value of the scientist-practitioner model at work. There has been a constant cycle of exchange between the development of theory and the testing of hypotheses in applied settings.

There is now preliminary evidence to suggest that problem-solving interventions with a mental health focus may assist in the prison's responsibilities to provide mental health services that are responsive to individual prisoners' needs. It could be argued that a problem-solving intervention for vulnerable individuals could be in line with a "Primary Care" service which could identify and assist those whose problems relate to more general difficulties in adjusting to prison life, and that such an intervention could be delivered by appropriately trained and experienced prison mental health staff. Future studies may find that by enhancing support as such a primary level, vulnerable prisoners may be able to remain in routine circulation in the prison.

However, it would be important to ensure that a brief problem-solving intervention for mental health issues is also integrated with other appropriate programmes, for example, detoxification or drug treatment programmes. A brief problem-solving intervention may also enhance the prisoner's ability to engage in future rehabilitation programmes. In the graded model of care promoted in Dialectical Behavior Therapy (Linehan, 1993), problem-solving modules precede more intensive and self-reflecting modules to ensure that at all times the patient has the skills and ability "to keep safe", to tolerate distress and ambiguity, and reduce self-harming behaviour. In some respects, problem-solving interventions for mental health may form an important building block for further programmed work relating to recidivism. Problem-solving therapy is also a brief, and relatively easily taught form of intervention (Hawton & Kirk, 1989), which may not require complex healthcare structures or expensive healthcare professionals (Dowrick et al., 2000) but nevertheless needs to be conducted by individuals with good mental health care skills in order to ensure that it can be delivered as an integral component of a good case management plan for vulnerable prisoners. The research to date indicates that much can be achieved through brief, focused intervention for vulnerable groups, who often find themselves debarred from formal accredited programmes in prisons on the basis that such programmes require the prisoner to be incarcerated for at least three months to complete them.

Evidence suggests that many vulnerable prisoners are in essence long-term prisoners in that they experience "revolving door" imprisonment, and there may be scope further to develop such a brief mental health intervention in order to get purchase on these individuals' mental health needs. Given that around half of all prisoners serve sentences of less than six months, and many may spend only a few weeks in jail, brief problem-solving interventions may assist in the prison's obligation to provide care for those in custody. Furthermore, given the research to date which indicates that many prisoners are at "higher risk" during remand periods, or the initial stages of imprisonment, there may be merit in bringing such brief interventions to these groups also.

Given the size of the potential population at risk, there is a requirement for larger randomised control trials to be conducted. To date, the literature considering interventions for self-harm both in the general population and offender populations is blighted by the fact that only small pilot studies have been conducted and hence they do not have the statistical power to detect clinically meaningful differences in the rates of repetition of deliberate self-harm or reduction in psychiatric morbidity. Most studies to date have relatively short follow-up periods (e.g., three months) and hence a longer follow-up period would be required to draw firmer conclusions regarding the maintenance of effective functioning, continued reduction in self-harming behaviour, and improvements of problem-solving abilities among young offenders. In order to assess the true efficacy of mental health programmes, further studies that examine whether their abilities transfer with the participants into the community should be considered. Future programmes would need to be extensive enough to demonstrate to offenders that the skills acquired in prison are generalisable to their complex lives in the community. Indeed, the goal of training should not be to teach problem solving in relation to specific problems associated with a specific context (e.g. prison), but to teach and appraise a general strategy that the individual would be encouraged to apply in any context.

Future studies also need to extend beyond the young offender population to other sections of the prison population (e.g. female prisoners, mentally ill adult male prisoners, difficult and disruptive prisoners). With the paucity of controlled studies to date, there is a need for further research into the efficacy and effectiveness of problem-solving interventions for offender mental health. In logistical terms, more rigorous studies may prove problematic due to the initial sample sizes required, the inherent difficulties in maintaining follow-up contact and the ultimate financial cost. Also, this form of research focuses upon offenders, many of whom have chaotic lifestyles and are thereby exceedingly difficult to monitor longitudinally in the community.

While by no means conclusive, there is growing evidence to suggest that brief, group-based problem-solving interventions could be effective in reducing the psychological distress experienced by vulnerable incarcerated young offenders and could have a positive impact upon their self-perceived problem-solving abilities. As the paradigm is an overt, objective intervention strategy, it appears suited to a group format within a prison setting and thus may act as an important component in therapeutic interventions with vulnerable young offenders. Future research which takes account of the methodological issues could add an important dimension to offender mental health services.

REFERENCES

Akhtar, N. & Bradley, E. J. (1991). Social information processing deficits of aggressive children. *Clinical Psychology Review, 11*, 621–644.

Alessi, N. E., McManus, M., Grapentine, W. L., & Brickman, A. (1984). The characterization of depressive disorders in serious juvenile offenders. *Journal of Affective Disorders, 6*, 9–17.

Arean, P. W., Perri, M. G., Nezu, A. M., Schein, R. L., Christopher, F., & Joseph, T. X. (1993). Comparative effectiveness of social problem-solving therapy and reminiscence therapy as treatments for depression in older adults. *Journal of Consulting and Clinical Psychology, 61*, 1003–1010.

Beck, A. T., Steer, A. R., Kovacs, M., & Garrison, B. (1985). Hopelessness and eventual suicide: A 10-year prospective study of patients hospitalised with suicidal ideation. *American Journal of Psychiatry, 142*, 559–563.

Beck, A. T., Weissman, A., Lester, D., & Trexler, L. (1974). The measurement of pessimism: The Hopelessness Scale. *Journal of Consulting and Clinical Psychology, 42*, 861–865.

Bellack, A. S., Sayers, M., Mueser, K. T., & Bennett, M. (1994). Evaluation of social problem-solving in schizophrenia. *Journal of Abnormal Psychology, 103*, 371–378.

Biggam, F. H. & Power, K. G. (1997). Social support and psychological distress in a group of incarcerated young offenders. *International Journal of Offender Therapy and Comparative Criminology, 41*, 213–230.

Biggam, F. H. & Power, K. G. (1999a). A comparison of the problem-solving abilities and psychological distress of suicidal, bullied, and protected prisoners. *Criminal Justice and Behavior*, 26, 196–216.

Biggam, F. H. & Power, K. G. (1999b). Social problem-solving skills and psychological distress among incarcerated young offenders: The issue of bullying and victimization. *Cognitive Therapy and Research*, 23, 307–326.

Biggam, F. H. & Power, K. G. (1999c). Suicidality and the state-trait debate on problem-solving deficits: A re-examination with incarcerated young offenders. *Archives of Suicide Research*, 5, 27–42.

Biggam, F. H. & Power, K. G. (2002). A controlled problem-solving, group-based intervention with vulnerable incarcerated young offenders. *International Journal of Offender Therapy and Comparative Criminology*, 26, 678–698.

Bonta, J. & Gendreau, P. (1990). Reexamining the cruel and unusual punishment of prison life. *Law & Human Behavior*, 14, 347–372.

Chiles, J. A., Miller, M., & Cox, G. B. (1980). Depression in an adolescent delinquent population. *Archives of General Psychiatry*, 37, 1179–1186.

Compas, B. E., Connor, J. K., & Hinden, B. R. (1998). New perspectives on depression in adolescence. In J. Jessor (ed.) *New perspectives on adolescent risk behaviour* (pp. 319–362). Cambridge: Cambridge University Press.

Daderman, A. M. (1999). Differences between severely conduct-disordered juvenile males and normal juvenile males: the study of personality traits. *Personality and Individual Differences*, 26, 827–845.

Davis, A. T. & Kosky, R. J. (1991). Attempted suicide in Adelaide and Perth: changing rates for males and females 1971–1987. *Medical Journal of Australia*, 154, 666–670.

Dolan, M., Holloway, J., Bailey, S., & Smith, C. (1999). Health status of juvenile young offenders: A survey of young offenders appearing before a juvenile court. *Journal of Adolescence*, 22, 137–144.

Dowrick, C., Dunn, G., Ayuso-Mateos, J. L., Dalgard, O. S., Page, H., Lehtinen, V., Casey, P., Wilkinson, C., Vazquez-Barquero, J. L., & Wilkinson, G. (2000). Problem solving treatment and group psychoeducation for depression: multicentre randomised controlled trial. *British Medical Journal*, 321, 1–6.

D'Zurilla, T. J. & Goldfried, M. R. (1971). Problem solving and behaviour modification. *Journal of Abnormal Psychology*, 78, 107–126.

D'Zurilla, T. J. & Nezu, A. M. (1982). Social problem solving in adults. In P. C. Kendall (ed.) *Advances in cognitive-behavioral research and therapy* Vol 1, (pp. 201–274). New York: Academic Press.

D'Zurilla, T. J. & Nezu, A. M. (1999). *Problem-solving therapy: A social competence approach to clinical intervention*. New York: Springer.

D'Zurilla, T. J. & Nezu, A. M. & Maydeu-Olivares, A. (2002). *Social problem-solving inventory–revised (SPSI-R): Technical manual*. North Tonawanda, NY: Multi-Health Systems.

Evans, J., Williams, J. M. G., O'Loughlin, S., & Howells, K. (1992). Autobiographical memory and problem-solving strategies of parasuicidal patients. *Psychological Medicine*, 22, 399–405.

Foster, T., Gillespie, K., & McClelland, R. (1997). Mental disorders and suicide in Northern Ireland. *British Journal of Psychiatry*, 170, 447–452.

Greene, S. M. (1981). Levels of measured hopelessness in the general population. *British Journal of Psychology*, 20, 11–14.

Grier, P. E. (1988). Cognitive problem-solving skills in anti-social rapists. *Criminal Justice and Behavior*, 15, 501–514.

Hagell, A. (2002). *The mental health of young offenders, bright futures: Working with vulnerable young people*. London: The Mental Health Foundation.

Harris, T. E. & Lennings, C. J. (1993). Suicide and adolescence. *International Journal of Offender Therapy and Comparative Criminology, 37*, 263–270.

Hawton, K., Arensman, E., Townsend, E., Bremner, S., Feldman, E., Goldney, R. et al. (1998). Deliberate self harm: Systematic review of the efficacy of psychosocial and pharmacological treatments in preventing repetition. *British Medical Journal, 31*, 441–447.

Hawton, K. & Kirk, J. (1989). Problem-solving. In K. Hawton, P. Salkovskis, J. Kirk, & D. Clark (eds) *Cognitive behaviour therapy for psychiatric problems: A practical guide.* Oxford: Oxford University Press.

Hawton, K., McKeown, S., Day, A., Martin, P., O'Connor, M., & Yule, J. (1987). Evaluation of out-patient counselling compared with general practice care following overdoses. *Psychological Medicine, 17*, 751–761.

Hawton, K., Townsend, E., Arensman, E., Gunnell, D., Hazell, P., House, A., & van Heeringen, K. (2004). Psychosocial and pharmacological treatments for deliberate self harm. *The Cochrane Library*, Issue 1. Chichester: John Wiley & Sons, Ltd.

Henderson, M. & Hollin, C. R. (1986). Social skills training and delinquency. In C. R. Hollin & P. Trower (eds) *Handbook of social skills training* Vol. 1: *Applications across the lifespan.* Oxford: Pergamon Press.

Higgins, J. P. & Thies, A. P. (1982). Social effectiveness and problem-solving thinking of reformatory inmates. *Journal of Offender Counseling Services and Rehabilitation, 5*, 93–98.

Hussian, R. A. & Lawrence, P. S. (1981). Social reinforcement of activity and problem-solving training in the treatment of depressed institutionalised elderly patients. *Cognitive Therapy and Research, 5*, 57–69.

Inch, H., Rowlands, P., & Soliman, A. (1995). Deliberate self-harm in a young offenders' institution. *Journal of Forensic Psychiatry, 6*, 161–171.

Intagliata, J. C. (1978). Increasing the interpersonal problem-solving skills of an alcoholic population. *Journal of Consulting and Clinical Psychology, 46*, 489–498.

Ivanoff, A., Smyth, N. J., Grochowski, S., Jang, S. J., & Klein, K. E. (1992). Problem solving and suicidality among prison inmates: Another look at state versus trait. *Journal of Consulting and Clinical Psychology, 60*, 970–973.

Kempton, T. & Forehand, R. (1992). Suicide attempts among juvenile delinquents: The contribution of mental health factors. *Behaviour Research and Therapy, 30*, 537–542.

Kingsbury, S., Hawton, K., Steinhardt, K., & James, A. (1999). Do adolescents who take overdoses have specific psychological characteristics? A comparative study with psychiatric and community controls. *Journal of the American Academy of Child and Adolescent Psychiatry, 38*, 1125–1131.

Lazarus, R. S. & Folkman, S. (1984). *Stress, appraisal, and coping.* New York: Springer.

Lerner, M. S. & Clum, G. A. (1990). Treatment of suicide ideators: A problem-solving approach. *Behavior Therapy, 21*, 403–411.

Liebling, A. (1992). *Suicide in prison.* London: Routledge.

Liebling, A. (1993). Suicides in young prisoners: A summary. *Death Studies, 17*, 381–409.

Liebling, A. & Krarup, H. (1993). *Suicide attempts and self injury in male prisons.* Report commissioned by the Home Office Research and Planning Unit for the Prison Service. London: Home Office.

Linehan, M. M. (1993). *Cognitive behavioural treatment of borderline personality disorder.* New York: Guilford Press.

Loumidis, K. & Hill, A. (1997). Training social problem-solving skill to reduce maladaptive behaviours in intellectual disability groups: The influence of individual difference factors. *Journal of Applied Research in Intellectual Disabilities, 10*, 217–237.

Marx, E. M., Williams, J. M. G., & Claridge, G. C. (1992). Depression and social problem-solving. *Journal of Abnormal Psychology, 101*, 78–86.

McGuire, J. (2001). What is problem solving? A review of theory, research and applications. *Criminal Behaviour and Mental Health, 11*, 210–235.

McLeavey, B. C., Daly, R. J., Ludgate, J. W., & Murray, C. M. (1994). Interpersonal problem-solving skills training in the treatment of self-poisoning patients. *Suicide and Life-Threatening Behavior, 24*, 382–394.

McMurran, M., Egan, V., Blair, M., & Richardson, C. (2001). The relationship between social problem solving and personality in mentally disordered offenders. *Personality and Individual Differences, 30*, 517–524.

McMurran, M., Egan, V., Richardson, C., & Ahmadi, S. (1999). Social problem solving in mentally disordered offenders: a brief report. *Criminal Behaviour and Mental Health, 9*, 315–322.

Mynors-Wallis, L. M., Gath, D. H., Day, A., & Baker, F. (2000). Randomised controlled trial of problem-solving treatment, antidepressant medication, and combined treatment for major depression in primary care. *British Medical Journal, 320*, 26–30.

Nezu, A. M., Nezu, C. M., & Perri, M. G. (1989). *Problem-solving therapy for depression: Theory, research and clinical guidelines*. New York: John Wiley & Sons, Ltd.

Nezu, A. M. & Perri, M. G. (1989). Social problem solving therapy for uniploar depression: An initial dismantling investigation. *Journal of Consulting and Clinical Psychology, 57*, 408–413.

Nicol, R., Stretch, D., Whitney, I., Jones, K., Garfield, P. Turner, K., & Stanion, B. (2000). Mental health needs and services for severely troubled and troubling young people including young offenders in an NHS region. *Journal of Adolescence, 23*, 243–261.

Ovenstone, I. M. K. & Kreitman, N. (1974). Two syndromes of suicide. *British Journal of Psychiatry, 124*, 336–345.

Perry, D. G., Perry, L. C., & Rasmussen P. (1986). Cognitive social learning mediators of aggression. *Child Development, 57*, 700–711.

Platt, J., Scura, W., & Hannon, J. (1973). Problem-solving thinking of youthful incarcerated heroin addicts. *Journal of Community Psychology, 31*, 278–281.

Platt, J. J. & Siegal, J. M. (1976). MMPI characteristics of good and poor problem-solvers among psychiatric patients. *Journal of Psychology, 94*, 245–251.

Platt, J. J. & Spivack, G. (1975). *Manual for the means–ends problem-solving procedure*. Philadelphia, RA: Department of Mental Health Services, Hahnemann Community Mental Health/Mental Retardation Center.

Power, K. G. & Beveridge, L. (1990). The effects of custody in a Scottish detention centre on inmates self-esteem. *International Journal of Offender Therapy and Comparative Criminology, 34*, 177–186.

Power, K. G. Dyson, G. P., & Biggam, F. H. (1999). *Bullying/victimisation in Scottish young offender institutions (YOIs)*. Edinburgh: Scottish Prison Service Occasional Paper No 1/99.

Pugh, D. (1993). The effects of problem-solving ability and locus of control on prisoner adjustment. *International Journal of Offender Therapy and Comparative Criminology, 37*, 163–176.

Putnins, A. L. (1995). Recent drug-use and suicidal-behavior among young offenders. *Drug and Alcohol Review, 14*, 151–158.

Reeker, G. T. & Meissner, J. A. (1977). Life skills in a Canadian federal pententiary: An experimental evaluation. *Canadian Journal of Criminology, 19*, 292–302.

Renshaw, P. D. & Asher, S. R. (1982). Social competence and peer status: The distinction between goals and strategies. In K. H Rubin & H. S. Ross (eds) *Peer relationships and social skills in childhood* (pp. 353–374). New York: Springer.

Rhode, P., Mace, D. E., & Seeley, J. R. (1997). The association of psychiatric disorders with suicide attempts in a juvenile delinquent sample. *Criminal Behaviour and Mental Health, 7*, 187–200.

Rutter, M., Gillen, H., & Hagell, A. (1998). *Antisocial behaviour by young people*. New York: Cambridge University Press.

Salkovskis, P. M., Atha, C., & Storer, D. (1990). Cognitive-behavioural problem solving in the treatment of patients who repeatedly attempt suicide: A controlled trial. *British Journal of Psychiatry*, *157*, 871–876.

Schmidtke, A., Bille-Brahe, U., Deleo, D., Kerkof, A., Bjerke, T., Crepet, P., & et al. (1996). Attempted suicide in Europe: rates, trends, and sociodemographic characteristics of suicide attempters during the period 1989–1992: Results of the WHO/EURO multicentre study on parasuicide. *Acta Psychiatrica Scandinavica*, *93*, 327–338.

Siegal, J. M. & Platt, J. J. (1976). Emotional and social real-life problem-solving thinking in adolescent and adult psychiatric patients. *Journal of Clinical Psychology*, *32*, 230–232.

Slaby, R. G. & Guerra, N. G. (1988). Cognitive mediators of aggression in adolescent offenders, 1: Assessment. *Developmental Psychology*, *24*, 580–588.

Spence, S. H. (1979). Social skills training with adolescent offenders: A review. *Behavioural Psychotherapy*, *7*, 49–56.

Spence, S. H. (1982). Social skills training with young offenders. In M. P. Feldman (ed.) *Developments in the study of criminal behaviour*, Vol. 1: *The prevention and control of offending*. Chichester: John Wiley & Sons, Ltd.

Williams, J. M. G. (1997). *Cry of pain: Understanding suicide and self harm*. London: Penguin.

Williams, R. & Morgan, H. G. (1994). *Suicide prevention: The challenge confronted: NHS Advisory Service thematic review*. London: HMSO.

World Health Organisation (1990). *WHO guide to mental health in primary care*. London: WHO Collaborating Centre for Mental Health Research and Training, Institute of Psychiatry.

World Health Organisation (1992). *Health for all targets: The health policy for Europe. Summary of the updated edition*. Copenhagen: World Health Organisation.

Zamble, E. & Porporino, F. J. (1988). *Coping, behavior, and adaptation in prison inmates*. New York: Springer.

Zigmond, A. S. & Snaith, R. P. (1983). Hospital anxiety and depression scale. *Acta Psychiatrica Scandinavica*, *67*, 361–370.

Chapter 9

THE *REASONING AND REHABILITATION* PROGRAM: OUTCOME EVALUATIONS WITH OFFENDERS

Daniel H. Antonowicz
Wilfrid Laurier University–Brantford, Canada

INTRODUCTION

Evidence of the efficacy of cognitive-behavioural programs in the rehabilitation of offenders has been found in several meta-analyses (e.g., Andrews et al., 1990; Pearson, Lipton, Cleland, & Yee, 2002). One of the earliest cognitive-behavioral programs and one of the most widely implemented is the *Reasoning and Rehabilitation (R&R)* program (Ross, Fabiano, & Ross, 1986). R&R has been delivered to an estimated 50,000 offenders in 17 countries and in almost every state in the USA. Based on the "cognitive model of offender rehabilitation and delinquency prevention" (Ross, 2004; Ross & Fabiano, 1985), R&R is a multi-faceted program designed to teach offenders social cognitive skills and values which are essential for prosocial competence.

R&R is also one of the most frequently evaluated programs. Its efficacy has been examined in a remarkable number of independent international evaluations not only in Canada where it was developed but also in California, Colorado, Georgia, Texas, Germany, Spain, Sweden and the United Kingdom. Each of the evaluations is reviewed in this chapter. Although limited in number, evaluations of the Enhanced Thinking Skills (ETS) program are also reviewed. Based on the R&R program, ETS includes the same targets as the R&R program but has adapted the R&R manualized training materials to provide a shorter program for the offender population in England and Wales.

Social Problem Solving and Offending: Evidence, Evaluation and Evolution.
Edited by Mary McMurran and James McGuire © 2005 John Wiley & Sons, Ltd.

PROGRAM DEVELOPMENT AND COMPONENTS

R&R is the outcome of a 40-year multi-stage, field-theoretical research project that began in 1964. The initial stages of the project involved field testing of a variety of intervention programs with institutionalized adolescent offenders which led to the development of a program that achieved success by training the offenders in problem solving and social skills by analyzing the antisocial behavior of their peers and persuading them to use these skills to help their peers (Ross & McKay, 1979). The findings from a later study in the project provided additional evidence of the value of training offenders in problem solving and social skills. The study involved an analysis of more than 100 programs that a narrative review of the rehabilitation literature had identified as effective in offender rehabilitation (Gendreau & Ross, 1979; Ross & Gendreau, 1980). The analysis indicated that effective programs differed from ineffective programs in terms of their inclusion of techniques which would foster the development of the offender's thinking and reasoning skills, their social skills, and their problem-solving skills (Ross, 1980). Subsequently, a component analysis (Ross & Fabiano, 1985) and a meta-analysis (Izzo & Ross, 1990) revealed that some technique designed to influence such skills was common to almost every treatment effort which had been successful in offender rehabilitation.

Effective programs included as a target of their intervention not only the offenders' behavior, feelings, vocational, or interpersonal skills, but their cognition. The research suggests that attending to how offenders think may be at least as important as focusing on how they feel or how they behave. Effective programs included some technique which could enhance the offenders' impulse control, increase their reasoning skills, improve their sensitivity to the consequences of their behavior, improve their ability to comprehend the thoughts and feelings of other people, increase their interpersonal problem-solving skills, broaden their view of the world, and help them to develop alternative interpretations of their environment, social rules, and social obligations.

The evidence that modifying offenders' thinking affects their recidivism led to the hypothesis that there might be something about the thinking of offenders that is associated with their antisocial behavior in the first place (Ross, 1980). Accordingly, in a later stage of the project, a search of four decades of research literature on the relation between cognition and crime revealed a considerable body of empirical evidence that many offenders have experienced developmental delays in the acquisition of a number of cognitive skills that are essential to social adaptation. Ross (2004) has summarized these as follows:

- *Impulsivity*. Many offenders fail to stop and think before they act. When they get an idea or a desire, they immediately respond without stopping to consider whether they should act or not. Many also fail to think *after* they act. They do not reflect back on their behavior and its consequences. Therefore, even when they experience punishment, they may not learn to modify their behavior.
- *Externality*. Many offenders believe that what happens to them depends on fate, chance, or luck. They believe that they are powerless, that they cannot control what happens to them, that they are controlled by other people and circumstances. Given the environments in which many of them have lived, this

is not surprising. However, such thinking makes them feel that there is no point in trying to succeed. Therefore, they may lack ambition and persistence.

- *Concrete thinking.* Many offenders are very concrete in their thinking. Their limited ability in abstract reasoning gives them major difficulties in understanding the concept of justice and the reasons for rules and laws. Moreover, it may give them difficulty in understanding the thoughts and feelings of other people. One cannot understand how other people are thinking or feeling just by their appearance; one must use abstract reasoning to consider what is going on inside their heads. Some individuals may lack an essential skill for successful interpersonal relations: an understanding of the thoughts and feelings of others (i.e., cognitive and affective empathy).

- *Conceptual rigidity.* The thinking of many offenders is inflexible, narrow, rigid, and intolerant of ambiguity. As a result, many continue to engage in behaviors which yield them few rewards and frequently get them into trouble.

- *Interpersonal cognitive problem-solving skills.* Many antisocial individuals have deficits in interpersonal cognitive problem-solving—the thinking skills which are required for solving problems in interacting with other people. In their interpersonal relations, offenders often fail to recognize that a problem exists or is about to occur. They fail to calculate the consequences of their behavior on other people, and they do not (or cannot) consider alternative solutions to such problems. They keep responding in their same old, ineffective way. Moreover, they may not understand the cause and effect relationship between their behavior and people's reactions to them.

- *Egocentricity.* Many offenders see the world only from their own perspective and may not have learned to consider how other people think or feel. As a result, they often misinterpret the actions and intentions of others. Their lack of awareness or sensitivity to other people's thoughts or feelings severely impairs their ability to form acceptable relationships with people. Offenders may lack an awareness or an appreciation of an important factor in the inhibition of illegal behavior: its effects on other people. Moreover, offenders encounter frequent interpersonal problems because they do not think about how others will feel. Their egocentricity may cause them to be ostracized and alienated.

- *Values.* Lacking social perspective-taking skills, they may fail to develop beyond egocentric, self-centered values. In deciding what is right, they may only consider how it affects themselves, not how it affects other people.

- *Critical reasoning.* The thinking of many offenders is often illogical and lacks self-criticism. As a result, they may be too easily influenced by thoughts which are presented to them not only by others, but by themselves.

Ross has pointed out that not all offenders have such cognitive difficulties, but a considerable number do. Some offenders have excellent cognitive skills—so good that they never enter the criminal justice system! It must be noted that the shortcomings described here occur in social (interpersonal) reasoning, and are not deficits in intelligence as measured by IQ tests. Such tests do not measure social intelligence. Many offenders have high IQs but are sadly lacking in social skills.

It must also be stressed that it is not only offenders who have such characteristics; they are common among many individuals who have difficulty in social adjustment. In fact, such inadequate reasoning may represent the thinking of all of us at times when we are tired, when we have consumed alcohol or drugs, when we are highly aroused or under-aroused or are experiencing interpersonal difficulties.

Ross has also made it clear that cognitive shortcomings are neither a necessary nor a sufficient cause of crime. However, he has argued that individuals who lack good cognitive skills may be "at risk". They may be unable to withstand the antisocial effects of living in a criminogenic environment of deprivation, parental criminality/substance abuse, chronic unemployment, parental discord, or authoritarian, abusive or neglectful parenting (Ross & Ross, 1989).

The foregoing research led Ross to develop a comprehensive, multi-faceted, manualized program for teaching these cognitive skills and values: R&R. The program was constructed by combining the best techniques from those rehabilitation programs which had been found to yield major reductions in recidivism, and added additional techniques which other research had indicated could teach social cognitive skills. Techniques and exercises were specifically selected which are enjoyable for antisocial individuals who are not easily motivated and often feel very negative toward school or "therapy". These were then modified and combined to form a 35-session (70-hour) group program. The following are the major components of the *Reasoning and Rehabilitation* program (Ross & Ross, 1995):

- *Self-control*. Offenders are taught to stop and think before they act; to consider all the consequences before making decisions; to formulate plans; to use thinking techniques to control their emotions and their behavior.
- *Meta-cognition*. Offenders are taught to tune into and critically assess their own thinking—to realize that *how* they think determines *what* they think, how they *feel* and how they *behave*. They are taught thinking strategies as a means of self-regulating their behavior.
- *Social skills*. Many offenders act antisocially because they lack the skills to act prosocially. Utilizing a modification of Goldstein's program (Goldstein, Sprafkin, Gershaw, & Klein, 1980), a large number of skills are taught which will help them achieve positive reinforcement rather than rejection in social situations (e.g., responding to criticism; apologizing; negotiating instead of demanding).
- *Interpersonal cognitive problem-solving skills*. Following Platt's work with heroin-abusing offenders (Platt, Perry, & Metzger, 1980), offenders are taught how to analyze interpersonal problems, how to understand and consider other people's values, behavior and feelings; how to recognize ways in which their behavior affects other people and why others respond to them as they do.
- *Creative thinking*. To combat their conceptual rigidity, a number of techniques developed by deBono (1981) are used to teach offenders alternative thinking; how to consider alternative, prosocial rather than antisocial ways of responding to the problems they experience.
- *Critical reasoning*. Offenders are taught how to think logically, objectively, and rationally without distorting the facts or externalizing the blame.
- *Social perspective-taking*. Throughout the program, with all of the techniques an emphasis is placed on teaching offenders to consider other people's views and feelings and thoughts. In effect, there is an emphasis on the development of empathy.

- *Values enhancement.* A number of group discussion techniques and a large number of commercially available games are used to teach values; specifically, to move the offender from his/her egocentric world-view to a consideration of the needs of others.
- *Emotional management.* An offender's success in social adjustment depends on his/her ability to avoid excessive emotional arousal. Ross adapted anger management techniques developed by psychologists so that they could be used by trainers who are not psychologists, and so that they could be applied to other emotions such as excitement, depression, fear, and anxiety which may be equally or more problematic for many offenders.
- *Helper therapy.* Ross has consistently encouraged R&R trainers to avoid limiting their program efforts to teaching the cognitive skills in the "classroom" but to encourage participants to practice using these skills outside of the training group. Based on the positive outcome of the early cognitive program with adolescent offenders (Ross & McKay, 1979), Ross has suggested that R&R trainers should encourage participants to be therapists or teachers for each other, and, whenever possible, to engage in helping those less fortunate than themselves. He has pointed out that by encouraging antisocial individuals to act in prosocial roles, they often come to appreciate the value of prosocial behavior, to recognize the rewards it can bring them, and to acquire social skills which can serve as alternatives to their antisocial behavior. Individuals who are placed in such roles often come to see themselves in a very different light and to attribute to themselves positive, prosocial characteristics which were previously foreign to them.

A basic assumption of Ross's research project was that in order to have a major impact on recidivism an effective rehabilitation program must be developed which can be delivered not only by highly specialized mental health professionals but also by line staff. Ross pointed out that there are simply not enough psychiatrists, psychologists, or social workers (or enough funds to support them) to enable a program which requires their services to be provided to enough offenders to have a major impact in reducing recidivism.

OUTCOME EVALUATIONS

The results of the large number of evaluation studies of R&R are presented in this section, which is organized in terms of the country where each study was conducted. A summary of the settings and the outcomes is presented in Table 9.1.

Canada

High-Risk Adult Probationers

The first experimental test of the efficacy of the R&R program in reducing recidivism was conducted with high-risk adult male probationers in two probation offices in Ontario, Canada (Ross, Fabiano, & Ewles, 1988). The probationers

Table 9.1 Evaluations of R&R and ETS

Authors	Setting	Recidivism Outcome
Ross et al. (1988)	Community	Positive
Fabiano et al. (1991)	Institutional	Positive
Porporino et al. (1992)	Institutional	Positive
Robinson (1995)	Institutional	Mixed
Johnson & Hunter (1995)	Community	Positive
Van Voorhis et al. (2001)	Community	Mixed
Van Voorhis et al. (2003)	Community	Positive
Austin (1997)	Community	Positive
Pullen (1996)	Community	Mixed
Murphy & Brown (1996)	Institutional	Positive
Kownacki (1995)	Community	Mixed
Raynor & Vanstone (1996)	Community	Mixed
Miles & Raynor (2004)	Community	Positive
Friendship et al. (2003)	Institutional	Positive
Falshaw et al. (2003)	Institutional	Mixed
Cann et al. (2003)	Institutional	Mixed
Berman (2005)	Institutional	Positive
Donnelly & Scott (1999)	Institutional	Pre/post only
Clarke et al. (2003)	Institutional	Pre/post only
Gretenkord (2004)	Institutional	Pre/post only
Martin & Hernandez (1995)	Institutional	Positive
Garrido (1995)	Institutional	Pre/post only

were randomly assigned to one of three groups: (1) regular probation (n = 23); (2) regular probation plus life skills training (n = 17); (3) regular probation plus cognitive skills training (R&R) (n = 22).

The regular probation group provided a "no treatment" control group to compare the outcome for the cognitive group while the life skills group was designed to serve as an attention-control group. Life skills training focused on such areas as money management, leisure activities, family law, criminal law, employment-seeking skills, alcohol and drug education.

The results indicated that only 18% of those trained in R&R were convicted of an offense during a nine-month follow-up period from program entry compared to 48% of the life skills group, and 70% of the regular probation only control group. Moreover, none of the R&R participants was incarcerated upon conviction, whereas the incarceration rates for life skills and regular probation individuals were 11% and 30%, respectively. Although the sample size in this study was modest, the data provided support for the view that cognitive skills training can lead to a major reduction in recidivism among high-risk probationers and that such training can be effectively delivered by line probation officers.

Adult Prisoners

A much larger test of the efficacy of R&R was conducted by the Correctional Service of Canada (CSC). CSC operates penitentiaries across Canada for offenders who are serving sentences from two years to life. In 1990, CSC adopted a version of the R&R program designed by Ross, Fabiano and Ross (1986) and have since implemented it in 47 penitentiaries and community residences across the country.

In a pilot study, the outcomes for program participants who had been randomly assigned to R&R (n = 50) were compared with those of prisoners who had been randomly assigned to a no-treatment (waiting list) comparison group (n = 26). In an average follow-up of 32 months, 35% of offenders who had completed R&R were reconvicted versus 55% of the comparison group. In addition, 70% of the offenders in the comparison group were re-incarcerated over the follow-up period compared with only 57% of the treated group. These data provided further evidence of the efficacy of the program and support for broader implementation (Fabiano, Porporino, & Robinson, 1991; Porporino, Robinson, & Fabiano, 1992).

A later study was conducted that stands out in the correctional literature in terms of the size of the sample. It examined the effectiveness of the R&R program with a sample of more than 4,000 CSC offenders who had completed the program between 1989 and 1994 (Robinson, 1995). A sub-sample of released offenders (n = 2,125) was followed up for a minimum period of a year and included 1,444 individuals who had completed the program, 379 offenders who were randomly assigned to a waiting list control group, and 302 program dropouts.

In terms of being readmitted into custody (following reconviction and/or technical violation), 45% of offenders who had completed the program were readmitted compared to 50% of waiting list control group members and 58% of program dropouts. The difference in readmission rates between the program completers and the control group represented an 11% reduction in recidivism.

Given the large sample size in this study, Robinson (1995) was able to examine differential treatment outcomes. Treatment effects were found to be stronger when the program was delivered in the community (e.g. half-way houses) as opposed to prison settings, and when it was delivered to offenders who evidenced medium to high levels on the social-cognitive deficit areas targeted by the program. Moreover, Robinson reported that R&R reduced the likelihood of recidivism by 19% for violent offenders, 29% for drug offenders, and 39% for sex offenders. In contrast, property offenders showed little response to the program. We shall return to this issue when we review the results of an evaluation conducted with prisoners in the UK.

United States

Colorado: Substance-Abusing Probationers

The efficacy of R&R was tested in Colorado in an experimental study with probationers with severe drug problems (Johnson & Hunter, 1995). Ninety-eight such offenders were assigned to the Specialized Drug Offender Program (SDOP) which provided more probation supervision than provided under regular probation conditions. Approximately half of the offenders in this intensive probation project were randomly selected to participate in the R&R program (n = 47); the other half received only intensive probation without R&R training (n = 51). Thirty-six other probationers, randomly selected from the same pool of offenders with severe drug/alcohol problems, served as controls. They received only traditional probation service without extra supervision or R&R programming.

An eight-month follow-up found that loss rates (i.e., absconsions, arrest warrants, revocations and revocations pending) for the intensive supervision groups (both with and without R&R) were lower than for the regular probation group. The loss rates for SDOP, R&R plus SDOP, and regular probation were 26%, 29%, and 42%, respectively.

Among the probationers receiving intensive supervision, loss rates were usually lower for those trained in R&R than for those not trained. This was particularly the case for probationers who were at least 30 years old and had low to average psychiatric, sociopathic, or employment problems. Moreover, for persons with extreme drug/alcohol problems, R&R training added to intensive supervision was found to yield the lowest loss rates among the three groups in the regular program (18% versus 43% for SDOP alone and 60% for regular probation).

During a one-year follow-up after the initial evaluation, the loss rate among those who were in good standing was substantially lower for probationers who received R&R training plus SDOP (19%) compared to the other two groups (30% for SDOP, and 35% for regular probation).

Georgia: Parolees

The R&R program has also been implemented on a large scale by the State of Georgia Board of Pardons and Parole. A two-phase evaluation was conducted with each phase utilizing an experimental design involving large sample sizes.

In Phase 1, offenders were randomly assigned to either the R&R program (n = 232) or to the control group (n = 236) which received regular parole supervision (Van Voorhis et al., 2001; Van Voorhis, Spruance, Ritchey, Johnson-Listwan, & Seabrook, 2004). Approximately half of the sample had at least one prior violent offense and approximately 70% were African-American. The participants who completed R&R performed better than either the comparison group participants or participants who did not complete R&R. Although no significant differences were found between experimental and comparison participants on technical violations, returns to prison were significantly lower for R&R program completers (27%) in relation to the comparison group (44%) and dropouts (66%) in the 30 month follow-up.

In Phase 2, a different sample of offenders was assigned to participate in R&R or in regular parole supervision (Van Voorhis et al., 2003). The large sample consisted of males and was again predominantly African-American. Recidivism results for program graduates (n = 280) were compared with those of the control group (n = 493) and program dropouts (n = 145). In the 30-month follow-up, the felony arrests/revocations for program graduates were significantly lower than for the control group and program dropouts (25% versus 36% and 35%, respectively). Similarly, the rates of return to prison were also significantly lower for the program graduates compared to the control group and the program dropouts (29% versus 41% and 43%, respectively). Parolees who achieved the most impressive treatment gains were Caucasian and between the ages of 28 and 32. On the other hand, neurotic offenders, as classified by the Jesness Inventory (Jesness, 1996), who participated in R&R had considerably higher recidivism rates than neurotic offenders who did not receive treatment.

California: Substance-Abusing Probationers

As reported in Robinson and Porporino (2001), Austin (1997), examined substance-abusing offenders on probation in California. Offenders participated in either R&R (n = 70) or in the Drug Aftercare Program (DAC) (n = 65). Rearrest rates for the R&R group and the DAC group were 25% and 32%, respectively. However, it is important to note that the author of this study was critical of the delivery because staff did not consistently follow the program procedures and there was insufficient implementation support within the program environment.

Colorado: Juvenile Probationers

In a study with juvenile offenders on probation in Colorado, Pullen (1996) examined 40 offenders who were randomly assigned to either R&R (n = 20) or to a control group (n = 20) and were followed up for 12 months after random assignment. Recidivism results during supervision revealed that 50% of the R&R program recidivated whereas only 35% of the control group did. However, in the post-supervision period, the recidivism rates for R&R participants and control group participants were 20% and 25% respectively. According to the author, implementation procedures were lacking in many respects and it was noted in the report that many of the program delivery staff failed adequately to prepare to deliver the training.

Georgia: Incarcerated Juvenile Offenders

Murphy and Brown (1996), as described in Robinson and Porporino (2001), examined an incarcerated sample of juvenile offenders who received R&R (n = 33) or were assigned to a control group (n = 16). Unfortunately, no information was provided on the random selection procedure. In a mean follow-up period of 16 months, the rearrest rate was 39% for the R&R group and 75% for the control group. Of those rearrested, 67% in the R&R group were reconvicted while 83% in the control group were reconvicted.

Texas: Probationers

Kownacki (1995) examined an abbreviated version of the R&R program in a probation setting in Texas. Offenders were randomly assigned to either R&R (n = 10) or to a control group (n = 10). However, five of the ten in the R&R group attended one or fewer sessions, two of the ten treatment members failed to attend any sessions and only three showed up for one of the sessions. Recidivism examined at six months post-intervention revealed that there were fewer viola-tion reports recommending probation revocation compared to the control group. Attendance is another issue that will be discussed further below.

Wales

A number of evaluations have also assessed the efficacy of R&R in Europe. Encouraging results were found with high-risk adult probationers in the eco-nomically deprived area of Mid-Glamorgan, Wales (Raynor & Vanstone, 1996). The *Straight Thinking on Probation (STOP)* project (as it is known in Wales) compared the results for 107 high-risk probationers who received the R&R program with the results for individuals who received correctional sanctions such as regular probation and incarceration (n = 548).

Using the "national risk of reconviction predictor" developed by the Home Office (1993), they found STOP completers had lower than predicted reconviction rates after 12 months of follow-up (35% vs. 42%). In contrast, those who received regular probation or incarceration had similar or higher rates of reconviction when their actual rates were compared with predicted rates. However, these results were not maintained at the 24-month follow-up. The predicted rate of recidivism was 61% while the actual rate was 63%.

Furthermore, compared with the combined sample of offenders who had received custodial sentences, those who had completed R&R while on probation were much less likely to have committed a further serious offense (8%) than those who had been incarcerated (21%) at 12 months. However, these effects were not maintained among those whom it was possible to follow up for 24 months (22% vs. 25%). In addition, upon reconviction, only 2% of STOP completers received a custodial sentence while 15% of those who had initially been incarcerated were reincarcerated.

It is interesting to note the similarity between the results of the Welsh project and the results of the earlier Canadian (Pickering) project. In the Welsh project, 27% of those on regular probation (no R&R) received a prison sentence for their subsequent conviction. In Canada's Pickering project this percentage was 30%. In both countries, the imprisonment rate for high-risk probationers completing R&R training was 0%.

Jersey

Another study of probationers was conducted in Jersey by Miles and Raynor (2004). It examined the impact of R&R (referred to as SMART—Self-Management and Rational Thinking in Jersey) as part of a larger risk and need assessment study on the Level of Supervision Inventory (LSI—Andrews & Bonta, 1995). Reconviction data within 12 months for SMART graduates (n = 37) was compared to SMART dropouts (n = 21). The results revealed that the re-conviction rate for SMART graduates was 36% while for SMART dropouts it was 88%.

England and Wales Prisons

A series of studies was also conducted in England and Wales in order to examine the effectiveness of prison-based R&R and Enhanced Thinking Skills (ETS) programs.

In the first study (Friendship, Blud, Erikson, Travers, & Thornton, 2003), adult males who participated in either R&R or ETS between 1992 and 1996 were examined in a retrospective quasi-experimental design. Program participants (n = 667) were matched to individuals in a comparison group (n = 1,801) on a number of relevant variables such as current offence and sentence length. All offenders were serving custodial sentences of two years or more. Program participants consisted of those who completed either R&R or ETS and those that dropped out of the program for various reasons (n = 66). In a two-year follow-up, there was a 14% reduction in reconviction among medium–low risk offenders and an 11% reduction among medium–high risk offenders for the combined group of R&R and ETS program participants. Furthermore, there was a 55% reduction in the chances of being reconvicted within two years for R&R participants and a 52% reduction for ETS participants. Unfortunately, the results for program completers and dropouts were combined, so we are unable to differentiate the findings.

In the second study, Falshaw, Friendship, Travers, and Nugent (2003) examined adult males who participated in either R&R or ETS between 1996 and 1998. Program participants (n = 649) were matched to a comparison group (n = 1,947) on a number of relevant variables. In this study, dropouts were not included in the treatment group results. Two-year reconviction rates were examined but no significant differences were found. One reason cited by Falshaw et al. (2003) for the lack of significant findings was that this study period involved a period of rapid expansion in the implementation of cognitive skills programs in prisons. There is little published evidence available on the effect of large-scale treatment program expansion but some experts suggest that treatment quality might be compromised in such projects (Gendreau, Goggin, & Smith, 1999).

In the third study, Cann, Falshaw, Nugent, and Friendship (2003) examined male adult and young offenders who participated in either R&R or ETS. One year and two year reconviction rates for male adult (n = 2,195) and young offender (n = 1,534) program participants were compared to matched groups who did not participate in the programs (n = 2,195 and n = 1,534, respectively). When program dropouts were excluded, the one-year reconviction rates were significantly lower for both R&R and ETS than for the matched comparison groups. There was a 2.5 percentage point difference in reconviction for adult male program completers and a 4.1 percentage point difference for young offender program completers. However, these effects were not maintained two years following release from prison. ETS had a greater impact on reconvictions than the R&R program. The authors suggest that the findings may be related to the fact that the ETS program was developed specifically for the prison population in England and Wales. The ETS program was also shorter which may have made it easier for the offenders to remain motivated. Shortened forms of R&R will be discussed later in this review.

A study by Wilson, Attrill, and Nugent (2003) examined the effect of completing either ETS or R&R while serving a prison sentence in England and Wales on reducing the cognitive deficits of male (n = 7,997) and female (n = 306) offenders. Participants who had no property offenses were compared to those with property offenses. The results of the pre- and post-intervention tests indicated that property offenders benefited just as much from cognitive skills training as did non-property offenders. However, future research would need to investigate whether similar results would be obtained using a measure of recidivism.

Sweden

Another outcome evaluation of the R&R was conducted with individuals incarcerated in a Swedish prison. Berman (2005) examined 339 male participants who were matched with a comparison group (n = 339). Program participants recidivated at a lower rate compared to the comparison group but this difference was not statistically significant. However, there was a significant difference in recidivism between those who completed the program (42%) and those who did not (58%). Further analysis of the data revealed that participants who had 9 to 20 previous convictions and those convicted of violent offenses had a lower level of reoffending compared to those with similar characteristics in the comparison groups. This held true for participants who completed the program and for those who dropped out.

Spain

Tenerife: Prison Inmates

In a study undertaken in Spain, Martin and Hernandez (1995) examined 57 male prison inmates in the Canary Islands who were under the age of 30 and had a history of prior convictions. Offenders were randomly assigned to either a group that received an abbreviated form of the R&R program or to a control group. Half of the R&R participants received social work intervention following the R&R program. In a two-year post-release follow-up, the success rate for the combined R&R and social work intervention group was the highest (67%) compared to 16% for R&R alone and 5% for individuals who received no form of intervention. Success was defined as not committing a new offense, not being imprisoned, and demonstrating an acceptable degree of readjustment.

Valencia: Institutionalized Juvenile Offenders

The effectiveness of R&R has also been examined with an incarcerated juvenile offender sample in Spain (Garrido, 1995). There were initially 14 R&R participants but only 7 completed the program; the comparison group was comprised of 17 individuals who were recruited from alternative custodial centres. R&R participants improved to a greater extent than the comparison group on measures of role-taking and problem-solving and on staff ratings of several behavioral measures.

Mentally Disordered Offenders

The R&R program has also been evaluated with mentally disordered offenders in three separate studies. All three evaluations assessed changes in pre- and post-measures of cognitive skills but no recidivism data are currently available for any of the studies. Unfortunately, all these studies were limited by their small sample size.

Scotland

In one study, Donnelly and Scott (1999) examined 12 male mentally disordered offenders in a Scottish state hospital who participated in the R&R program. Program participants were matched to a comparison group (n = 12); all study participants had at least one violent offense. R&R program completers demonstrated significant changes on two cognitive skill pre-/post-measures compared to the comparison group.

England

In the second study, Clarke, Walwyn, and Fahy (2003) examined inpatient mentally disordered offenders recruited from a medium security forensic unit in England who received R&R (n = 15). They were matched with a comparison group (n = 17) that received treatment as usual. The results revealed that the R&R group demonstrated significant improvements on several cognitive skills measures relative to the comparison group.

Germany

Another study was conducted with male forensic patients at a maximum security psychiatric hospital in Germany to examine the effectiveness of R&R (Gretenkord, 2004). Eleven individuals completed the program while the comparison group was comprised of five individuals. Ratings by the therapists were completed prior to and following the program for all participants in the study. The results revealed that the treatment group improved more than the comparison group in their ability to recognize problems and in their motivation to change one's behavior.

DISCUSSION

A number of evaluations of R&R have been conducted since the program's development in the 1980s. Evaluations have been conducted in institutional and community settings with a number of different subtypes of offenders. Some of the evaluations have been well controlled while others have not. Consistent with the substantial evidence of the success of a cognitive-behavioral approach to offender rehabilitation, the foregoing review of the studies indicates that the R&R program can yield significant reductions in recidivism. However, the research has also raised several issues that must be addressed in judging the efficacy of R&R:

1. *Program integrity.* The conflicting results of some programs raise serious questions about the degree to which program integrity has been compromised. No study report has indicated that a measure of program integrity was included in the research protocol and it is seldom possible to determine whether the well-articulated principles and practices that are detailed in the R&R program manuals have been followed. Failure to ensure program integrity may be the single most relevant factor that may account for the difference between the early success of R&R programs in British prisons and the lack of success of later implementations. The loss of program integrity in such cases may be a consequence of attempting to implement the program on a system-wide basis without ensuring that quality control is not compromised. This interpretation is in keeping with an emerging pattern across evaluations of cognitive programs - that the largest effects are for smaller programs (Wilson, Allen, & MacKenzie, 2000). Treatment personnel, program managers and researchers must identify and implement methods through which program integrity (as well as adequate staff selection, training, prolonged motivation and agency support) can be maintained when the agency attempts to extend R&R from a small, controlled intervention to a large-scale enterprise (cf. Gendreau et al., 1999; Van Voorhis, Murphy, & Johnson, 1999; Wilson et al., 2000). Unfortunately, when the honeymoon is over and the initial enthusiasm wanes, the program and its benefits suffer.

   It should be noted that since 1986 when the R&R program was first published, a considerable number of "look alike" cognitive programs have been produced. Unfortunately, many of these are "watered down" facsimiles of the R&R program that fail to provide all of the components of the original multifaceted program but are marketed by referring to the positive outcome evaluations of R&R. Few of these programs have been independently evaluated.

2. *Program completers vs. program dropouts.* The issue of program dropouts is very important for evaluation purposes. Some studies combined the recidivism results for both program completers and program dropouts and referred to the group as program participants. As a result, the beneficial effects that may have occurred for the program completers may be masked by the negative outcomes for program dropouts.

3. *Persistence of program effects.* The results of the evaluations of R&R in British prisons and Canadian penitentiaries indicate that the benefits of R&R in terms of reconvictions can be maintained over several years. However, other studies such as the evaluation of the STOP program for Welsh probationers indicated that the benefits eroded over time and suggest the need for continuing care or booster sessions.

4. *Treatment responsivity.* R&R has been successfully implemented with a wide variety of different types of offenders: adult and juvenile offenders; violent

offenders; substance-abusing offenders; property offenders; and sex offenders. Success has been achieved in both community and institutional settings. However, as it presently stands, R&R is a "shot-gun" program that fails to offer "different strokes for different folks". It does not enable trainers to provide differential treatment appropriate to the characteristics of the offenders it treats.

There have been a few attempts to determine who may be the most likely offenders to be impacted by the program, but some of this research has yielded contradictory results. Thus, whereas Robinson (1995) found that property (acquisitive) offenders did not respond as well to the program as did those that committed sexual, violent, and drug-related crimes, Wilson et al. (2003) found that property offenders who completed either R&R or ETS in UK prisons benefited from intervention. A large-scale and elaborate evaluation of R&R that is currently being conducted in Connecticut promises to yield more definitive information on the responsivity issue (Bogue, personal communication).

5. *Cognitive testing*. Research is also underway to develop a test battery that will enable trainers to identify the cognitive characteristics of program participants before they are involved in the program. Clearly offenders who do not evidence cognitive shortcomings should not be expected to benefit from R&R, however, at the moment only a rudimentary, *ad hoc* screening measure is being used in some settings – one that has never been subjected to adequate psychometric analysis.

PROGRAM DEVELOPMENT

The cognitive model of offender rehabilitation and the R&R program that it spawned were based on research published before 1985. Since then there has been a virtual explosion of interest in cognitive behavioral programs in the criminal justice field. There has also been a considerable number of empirical studies of the relationship between cognition and crime—particularly problem solving. Based on the post-1985 research and on the findings of evaluations of R&R, Ross and his colleagues have revised the cognitive model (Ross & Hilborn, 2004) and have developed or are currently constructing several new editions of R&R (dubbed "R&R2") that are both responsive to the new evidence and are specifically tailored to specific groups of offenders:

1. offenders who evidence symptoms of attention deficit (ADD) or hyperactivity disorder (ADHD);
2. antisocial drivers;
3. adolescent firesetters;
4. mentally disordered offenders;
5. offenders with learning disabilities.

Most social cognitive-behavioral programs that are designed to teach pro-social competence require 50 to 70 sessions. Some are extensive programs that require delivery over several years—unrealistically demanding for many agencies (and too expensive!). Based on the evidence reviewed above of the effectiveness of abbreviated R&R programs and in response to the concerns that many offenders are unable to be provided with the full R&R program because of the limited period of time that they are involved with agencies responsible for their treatment, a new short version of R&R has been developed and field tested: the *SHORT Version*. It is a brief, 18-hour program designed to teach basic social-cognitive skills and values to 13–16-year-old youth who are under supervision of juvenile justice agencies. Many such youth will benefit from their involvement in the *SHORT Version* and will not require additional training. However, the *SHORT Version* is intended to serve both as an "appetizer" and as a motivator for youths who require involvement in the more extensive program. Their involvement in the *SHORT Version* program will also provide the trainer with an opportunity to assess whether the individual requires and would likely benefit from a more extensive (24-hour) program that will also be available (Ross & Hilborn, 2003).

A new version of R&R has also been developed that specifically addresses an aspect of the offenders' social environment that is known to be critical in the etiology and persistence of antisocial behavior: the family. There is a substantial body of research that demonstrates the salience of family factors in the etiology of antisocial behavior, delinquency, and adult criminality. Rather than viewing such factors as symptoms of parental pathology, the *R&R2 SHORT Version for Families* is based on the assumption that individuals' difficulties may reflect a lack of prosocial competence in their parents (e.g., limited prosocial problem-solving skills, emotional management skills, negotiation skills, conflict management skills, reasoning skills, and underdeveloped prosocial values) (Ross, Hilborn, & Greene, 2004). The program is designed to empower the family by helping its members to acquire thinking, emotional, behavioral and interpersonal skills that will enable them to cope more effectively with the inevitable problems that are encountered in family life—particularly a family life that includes an antisocial child or adolescent. Moreover, the program is designed to teach family members specific social cognitive skills and values that can help them—and motivate them—to relate to one another in a way that will foster the development of prosocial competence in each family member. It is also designed to prevent delinquency in the offenders' siblings by improving interactions among family members that may have contributed to the development of antisocial behavior of such offenders.

It is clear that the cognitive model and the R&R program that it spawned have been well received in the criminal justice community for more than 18 years - a remarkable achievement given the typical short shelf-life of many, if not most, offender treatment programs (Ross & Hilborn, 2004). This review would indicate that the enthusiasm has been reinforced by evidence of its efficacy in a variety of settings, with a variety of types of offenders in a variety of countries. However, whereas its efficacy has been demonstrated in evaluation studies with unusually large numbers of offenders, enthusiasm for the program, which may be one key to its success, may have been jeopardized when the cost of training "Coaches" became exorbitant; the length of the program overtaxed agencies' human resources; program integrity was compromised by system-wide implementation, without system-wide quality control; and practitioners were unable to tailor the program to the particular characteristics of the program participants. The new (R&R2) specialized "family" of shorter editions of the original program based on the foregoing evaluations, on 20 years of research on the relation between cognition and offending behavior since 1985, and on the observations of R&R Trainers over more than 15 years of delivering R&R will enable agencies to implement R&R more economically and in keeping with the responsivity principle of effective correctional treatment. Hopefully, the evaluations of R&R will have sensitized program managers to the necessity for maintaining program integrity in delivering the new R&R2 programs.

REFERENCES

Andrews, D. A. & Bonta, J. (1995). *The Level of Service-Inventory-Revised Manual.* Toronto: Multi-Health Systems Inc.

Andrews, D. A., Zinger, I., Hoge, R. D., Bonta, J., Gendreau, P., & Cullen, F. T. (1990). Does correctional treatment work?: A clinically-relevant and psychologically-informed meta-analysis. *Criminology, 28,* 369–404.

Berman, A. H. (2005). The Reasoning and Rehabilitation Program assessing short–long-term out comes among male Swedish Prisoners. *Journal of Offender Rehabilitation, 40,* 85–103.

Cann, J., Falshaw, L., Nugent, F., & Friendship, C. (2003). *Understanding what works: Accredited cognitive skills programmes for adult men and young offenders.* Home Office Research Findings No. 226. London: Home Office.

Clarke, A., Walwyn, R., & Fahy, T. (2003). *A controlled trial of Reasoning and Rehabilitation with mentally disordered offenders.* Report prepared for South London and Maudsley NHS.

deBono, E. (1981). *CORT thinking program.* Toronto: Pergamon Press.

Donnelly, J. P. & Scott, M. F. (1999). Evaluation of an offending behavior programme with a mentally disordered offender population. *British Journal of Forensic Practice, 1,* 25–32.

Fabiano, E. A., Porporino, F. J., & Robinson, D. (1991). Canada's cognitive skills program corrects offenders' faulty thinking. *Corrections Today, 53,* 102–108.

Falshaw, L., Friendship, C., Travers, R., & Nugent, F. (2003). *Searching for "What works": An evaluation of cognitive skills programmes.* Home Office Research Findings No. 206. London: Home Office.

Friendship, C., Blud, L., Erikson, M., Travers, R., & Thornton, D. (2003). Cognitive-behavioral treatment for imprisoned offenders: An evaluation of HM Prison Service's cognitive skills programmes. *Legal and Criminological Psychology, 8,* 103–114.

Garrido, V. (1995). R&R with Spanish offenders and children "at risk". In R. R. Ross & R. D. Ross (eds) *Thinking straight: The Reasoning and Rehabilitation Program for delinquency prevention and offender rehabilitation* (pp. 359–382). Ottawa: AIR Training and Publications.

Gendreau, P., Goggin, C., & Smith, P. (1999). The forgotten issue in effective correctional treatment: Program implementation. *International Journal of Offender Therapy and Comparative Criminology, 43,* 180–187.

Gendreau, P. & Ross, R. R. (1979). Effectiveness of correctional treatment: Bibliotherapy for cynics. *Crime and Delinquency, 25,* 463–489.

Goldstein, A. P., Sprafkin, R., Gershaw, N. J., & Klein, P. (1980). *Skillstreaming the adolescent.* Champaign, IL: Research Press.

Gretenkord, L. (2004). *R&R treatment effects: Haina Pilot Study.* Unpublished report prepared for the Haina Forensic Psychiatric Hospital.

Home Office (1993). *The national risk of reconviction predictor.* London: Home Office Research and Planning Unit.

Izzo, R. L. & Ross, R. R. (1990). Meta-analysis of rehabilitation programs for juvenile delinquents: A brief report. *Criminal Justice and Behavior, 17,* 134–142.

Jesness (1996). *Jesness Inventory Computer Program Windows .* North Tonawanda, NY: Multi-Health Systems, Inc.

Johnson, G. & Hunter, R. M. (1995). Evaluation of the specialized drug offender program. In R. R. Ross & R. D. Ross (eds) *Thinking straight: The Reasoning and Rehabilitation Program for delinquency prevention and offender rehabilitation* (pp. 215–236). Ottawa, Canada: AIR Training and Publications.

Kownacki, R. J. (1995). The effectiveness of brief cognitive-behavioral therapy on the reduction of antisocial behavior in high-risk adult probationers in a Texas community. In R. R. Ross & R. D. Ross (eds) *Thinking straight: The Reasoning and Rehabilitation Program for delinquency prevention and offender rehabilitation* (pp. 249–260). Ottawa, Canada: AIR Training and Publications.

Martin, A. M. & Hernandez, B. (1995). The effectiveness of a multifaceted program incorporating a cognitive component: The evolution of PEIRS. In R. R. Ross & R. D. Ross (eds.), *Thinking straight: The Reasoning and Rehabilitation Program for delinquency prevention and offender rehabilitation* (pp. 389–410). Ottawa, Canada: AIR Training and Publications.

Miles, H. & Raynor, P. (2004). *Community sentences in Jersey: Risk, needs and rehabilitation.* Unpublished report, Jersey Probation and Aftercare Service.

Pearson, F. S., Lipton, D. S., Cleland, C. M., & Yee, D. S. (2002). The effects of behavioral/cognitive-behavioral programs on recidivism. *Crime and Delinquency, 48,* 476–496.

Platt, J. J., Perry, G. M., & Metzger, D. S. (1980). The evaluation of a heroin addiction treatment program within a correctional environment. In R. R. Ross & P. Gendreau (eds) *Effective correctional treatment* (pp. 421–437). Toronto: Butterworths.

Porporino, F. J., Robinson, D., & Fabiano, E. A. (1992). *Application of the cognitive skills training approach in Canada's prisons.* Ottawa: Correctional Service of Canada.

Pullen, S. (1996). *Evaluation of the Reasoning and Rehabilitation cognitive skills development program as implemented in Juvenile ISP in Colorado.* Unpublished report, Colorado Division of Criminal Justice.

Raynor, P. & Vanstone, M. (1996). Reasoning and Rehabilitation in Britain: The results of the Straight Thinking on Probation (STOP) programme. *International Journal of Offender Therapy and Comparative Criminology, 40,* 272–284.

Robinson, D. (1995). *The impact of cognitive skills training on post-release recidivism among Canadian federal offenders.* No. R-41. Research Branch. Ottawa: Correctional Services of Canada

Robinson, D. & Porporino, F. J. (2001). Programming in cognitive skills: The Reasoning & Rehabilitation Program. In C.R. Hollin (ed.) *A handbook of offender assessment and treatment*(pp. 179–193). Chichester: John Wiley & Sons, Ltd.

Ross, R. R. (1980). *Socio-cognitive development in the offender: An external review of the UVIC program at Matsqui Penitentiary.* Ottawa: Ministry of the Solicitor General.

Ross, R. R. (2004). *Reasoning and Rehabilitation: Overview for participants.* Ottawa: Cognitive Centre of Canada.

Ross, R. R. & Fabiano, E. A. (1985). *Time to think: A cognitive model of delinquency prevention and offender rehabilitation.* Johnson City, TN: Institute of Social Sciences and Arts.

Ross, R. R., Fabiano, E. A., & Ewles, C. D. (1988). Reasoning and rehabilitation. *International Journal of Offender Therapy and Comparative Criminology, 32,* 29–35.

Ross, R. R., Fabiano, E. A., & Ross, R. D. (1986). *Reasoning and Rehabilitation: A handbook for teaching cognitive skills.* Ottawa: Centre for Cognitive Development.

Ross, R. R. & Gendreau, P. (eds) (1980). *Effective correctional treatment.* Toronto: Butterworths.

Ross, R. R. & Hilborn, J. (2003). *R&R 2: SHORT Version for Youth.* Ottawa: Cognitive Centre of Canada.

Ross, R. R. & Hilborn, J. (2004). *Time to think again: A prosocial competence model for the treatment of antisocial behavior.* Ottawa: Cognitive Centre of Canada.

Ross, R. R. & Hilborn, J., & Greene, R. (2004). *R&R 2: SHORT Version for Families and Support Persons.* Ottawa: Cognitive Centre of Canada.

Ross, R. R. & McKay, H. B. (1979). *Self-mutilation.* Lexington, MA: Lexington Books/D.C. Heath Co.

Ross, R. R. & Ross, R. D. (1988). *Cognitive skills: Training manual for living skills—Phase 1.* Ottawa: Correctional Service of Canada.

Ross, R. R. & Ross, R. D. (1989). Delinquency prevention through cognitive training. *Educational Horizons, 67,* 124–130.

Ross, R. R. & Ross, R. D. (eds) (1995). *Thinking straight: The Reasoning and Rehabilitation program for delinquency prevention and offender rehabilitation.* Ottawa: AIR Training and Publications.

Van Voorhis, P., Murphy, L., & Johnson, S. (1999). *Process evaluation of the Georgia cognitive skills program: Phase one.* Cincinnati, OH: University of Cincinnati.

Van Voorhis, P., Spruance, L. M., Johnson-Listwan, S., Ritchey, P. N., Pealer, J., & Seabrook, R. (2001). *The Georgia cognitive skills experiment: Outcome evaluation—Phase one.* Cincinnati, OH: University of Cincinnati.

Van Voorhis, P., Spruance, L. M., Ritchey, P. N., Johnson-Listwan, S., & Seabrook, R. (2004). The Georgia cognitive skills experiment: A replication of Reasoning and Rehabilitation. *Criminal Justice and Behavior, 31,* 282–305.

Van Voorhis, P., Spruance, L. M., Ritchey, P. N., Johnson-Listwan, S., Seabrook, R., & Pealer, J. (2003). *The Georgia cognitive skills experiment: Outcome evaluation—Phase two.* Cincinnati, OH: University of Cincinnati.

Wilson, D., Allen, L., & MacKenzie, D. (2000). *Quantitative review of cognitive behavioral programs.* College Park, MD: University of Maryland.

Wilson, S., Attrill, G., & Nugent (2003). Effective interventions for acquisitive offenders: An investigation of cognitive skills programmes. *Legal and Criminological Psychology, 8,* 83–101.

Chapter 10

THE *THINK FIRST* PROGRAMME

James McGuire
University of Liverpool, UK

INTRODUCTION

As described in Chapter 1 of this volume, the use of problem solving as a focus
for helping individuals to change has taken two major forms. One of them is
closer to what most people would recognise as therapy, while the other bears a
stronger similarity to what most would call training. It is difficult to draw a hard-
and-fast line between the two ways of working. To make the picture more
complex, problem-solving methods have also been used in a third domain, that of
education. Within the latter field, the methods and materials used to engender
some type of change (usually the acquisition of knowledge or understanding) are
typically organised in a planned sequence which educators call a *curriculum*. In
individual change and the solving of personal problems, the idea has progres-
sively taken hold that some of the methods that are employed can also be ordered
into a format that makes them suitable for replication. In current terminology, the
intervention can be "manualised".

Problem-solving therapy or training lends itself readily to this, as there is an
inherent progression in the process of acquiring cognitive or social/interpersonal
skills. In criminal justice facilities such as prisons, in community-based supervision, and in secure mental health settings, there can be important advantages in
establishing standardised forms of intervention (McMurran & Duggan, 2005).
Such methods can draw on the available evidence base, and the ways in which
they do so can be made clear and explicit. Also, the use of a manual can allow
agencies to implement procedures for the preservation of treatment integrity.
Manualisation is sometimes criticised for the apparent assumption that "one size
fits all", and for producing intervention strategies that are too rigid. However, it
is possible to design manuals that incorporate sufficient flexibility to circumvent

Social Problem Solving and Offending: Evidence, Evaluation and Evolution.
Edited by Mary McMurran and James McGuire © 2005 John Wiley & Sons, Ltd.

this, by allowing practitioners scope for making certain adaptations and innovations in the way they deliver sessions.

The present chapter describes a multi-modal group programme, *Think First*, designed with those objectives in mind. Probably its most distinctive feature, however, is the specific focus within sessions on the analysis by participants of their own offending behaviour: the criminal acts that have led to their being imprisoned, placed on probation, or detained in secure mental health units. The programme depicts such behaviour as a problem that can be solved.

BACKGROUND TO PROGRAMME DEVELOPMENT

The *Think First* programme had its distant origins in a research project begun in the 1970s with the aim of providing pre-release training courses for offenders about to be discharged from prison (Priestley, McGuire, Flegg, Hemsley, Welham, & Barnitt, 1984). The primary objective of that project was to "develop, test and evaluate a training package which will equip selected offenders with skills relevant to keeping them out of trouble. This will include work, survival and social skills" (ibid., p. 12). The participants were 224 male prisoners in two experimental prison sites, and 123 male offenders sentenced to a probation-based alternative to custody, which required them to attend a Day Training Centre for a period of up to 60 days. Their tutors in each case were volunteer prison and probation officers who were offered special training for the purpose.

The activities those staff provided took the form of a series of group training sessions based largely on a "life skills" model, focused on the problems of finding work or a place to live, managing money, asserting rights, dealing with officialdom, and relating to others in both public and more private encounters. Some of the ideas were based on work that had been done by the *Saskatchewan Newstart* project, a large-scale initiative addressing the needs of marginalised groups in that Canadian province (Saskatchewan Newstart, 1973). The methods thus developed were then formulated as a four-stage model of the helping process, deploying the application of social skills training within a problem-solving framework (Priestley, McGuire, Flegg, Hemsley, & Welham, 1978). This led to numerous requests to provide short-in-service training events for staff of a wide range of agencies. There were no manuals as such, but collections of loose-leaf materials only partially "packaged", which could be assembled in diverse forms for use according to the needs of client groups or the types of work in which practitioners were involved. Some were arranged in a format that could be used as a curriculum to prepare school-leavers for entry to the adult world (McGuire & Priestley, 1981), others for the acquisition of helping skills by counsellors and allied practitioners (Priestley & McGuire, 1983).

Participant feedback within this project was overwhelmingly positive. There was evidence that programme "graduates" had greatly improved work records, and follow-up reports suggested they had applied their new skills to good effect in solving a number of difficulties with which they were faced. Probation supervisors as third-party corroborators endorsed the claim that programme participation had been highly beneficial. Regrettably, however, none of this had any impact on the subsequent recidivism rates of the programme members. When compared with offenders who applied for the programmes but were not selected to take part, and with a matched control group of non-applicants, there was no difference in re-offence rates at a two-year follow-up (McGuire & Priestley, 1983; Priestley et al., 1984).

There was, however, one exception to what was otherwise seen as a disappointing set of outcome statistics. At one of the experimental prison sites, where many of the prisoners referred for training had previous records of violent offending, prison staff included within the programme a number of activities designed to address the problem of personal violence. For this group of prisoners, there was a different pattern of offending after release, with a significant reduction in violent reconvictions not apparent among the comparison samples. There appeared to be an association between directly addressing a problem behaviour and success in making its recurrence less likely. While many other issues, including work, accommodation, family, money and similar problems were presumed to be associated with offending – an assumption drawn from the dominant criminological theories of the day – it nevertheless did not follow that tackling them led to a reduction in the antisocial behaviour of which individuals had been convicted in the criminal courts.

The logic of this seemed straightforward, almost compellingly so, to the extent that it was difficult to envisage how activities with offenders had taken the shape they had done in the past. Traditionally, direct work with those who had broken the law rarely if ever focused on the law-breaking activity itself. In social casework, offenders and their supervisors discussed the former's job prospects, housing needs, money management, marital discord, conflicts with authority, and so on. Indeed, the agenda seemed to include almost anything *but* the actions which had brought the individual to the attention of the law and which furnished the rationale for engaging him or her in discussions that would (it was hoped) bring about a change in behaviour. For a period after 1980, the very possibility of doing the latter was all but abandoned. The ethos of probation practice was heavily influenced by the critical reviews of outcome research, which had contributed to the emergence of a "non-treatment paradigm" (Bottoms & McWilliams, 1979).

The proposition thus emerged that the most likely way to bring about a change in offending was to address the actions that constituted it. Such a suggestion fitted with what was known about the acquisition of skills and the problem of "transfer of learning". Surprisingly given the then ascendant doctrine that "nothing works", a narrative review of research suggested that this proposal was supported by a number of previous findings (McGuire & Priestley, 1985). It was during that same year that the first meta-analytic review of offender treatment was also published (Garrett, 1985). Within a few years, based on the later highly influential review by Andrews, Zinger, Hoge, Bonta, Gendreau and Cullen (1990), it was possible to argue that those approaches more likely to yield an effect in decreased recidivism among repeat offenders probably had some features in common. The expanding evidence base since then has gradually elaborated our understanding of this (Antonowicz & Ross, 1994; Hollin, 1999; McGuire, 2002, 2004).

During the early 1990s, several colleagues and I developed a 12-session social problem-solving programme which was used with groups of patients detained in a high-security hospital (McGuire, 1999). The largest portion of the materials contained within this was based on the *Interpersonal Cognitive Problem-Solving* (ICPS) model of Spivack, Platt and Shure (1976) which I had observed in use on a study visit to (what was then) Hahnemann University, Philadelphia, and to a number of public elementary schools in that city where the methods were used with children from age 4 upwards (Shure, 2001; Shure & Spivack, 1979). In 1992-93, an extended version of these materials was developed for use in one of the English probation areas, and given the title *Problem-Solving Training and Offence Behaviour*. It consisted of 21 sessions, each lasting two hours, and in addition to problem-solving also included materials on social skills and self-management. At a later stage, a longer version was developed for use in prisons, incorporating further material on conflict resolution and attitude change.

In a parallel development, at the request of one of the Scottish Social Work Departments a series of sessions was devised to impart the key concepts of cognitive social learning theory, and of cognitive-behavioural therapies, using a combination of instruction and self-administered practical exercises. The "theory manual" thus produced became a resource for familiarising practitioners with the concepts on which programme materials were based, and a revised version was subsequently published as support material in initiatives towards probation *Pathfinder* programmes (McGuire, 2000).

The production of these methods in the form of a ready-made training or treatment manual was also influenced by the advent of the *Reasoning and Rehabilitation* (R&R) programme in British probation settings (see Antonowicz, present volume, Chapter 9; and McGuire, 1995). As the first manualised programme for working with offenders, R&R had an inspirational effect on the creation of structured activities in this field.

There are two principal forms of the *Think First* programme. The most widely used is applied in probation and other community corrections settings, and in its current version it consists, first, of four pre-group sessions, three conducted on an individual basis and one as an introductory group meeting. This is followed by 22 two-hour group sessions, and six individual post-group sessions. Some of the latter are designed to take place immediately after the group programme and to set the scene for individual supervision by case managers. Others occur after a gap of approximately three months, as a form of relapse prevention. The design of the prison version is much simpler, entailing group sessions only (30 of two hours each). The latter version has also been employed in a secure mental health unit yielding favourable impressions of its potential usefulness in that context (Fleck, Thompson, & Narroway, 2001).

THEORETICAL RATIONALE

The *Think First* programme is essentially a synthesis of two main elements. One is a cognitive-social-learning model of change, applying specific methods of problem solving, self-management and social skills training. The second is a focus on offending behaviour, analysis of crime events, enabling individuals to address and plan behaviour change and maintenance of gains. The overall objective is to help individuals acquire, develop and apply a series of social problem-solving and allied skills that will enable them to manage difficulties in their lives, and to avoid future re-offending.

The design and content of the programme and accompanying materials were informed by the accumulating findings of systematic surveys of research on the outcomes of work with offenders. Interventions most likely to accomplish the objective of reducing recidivism are generally agreed to have several distinguishing features (Andrews, 2001). In general, more effective programmes are structured, clearly conceptualised, theoretically driven, and empirically based; and more likely to involve the application of cognitive-behavioural and affiliated methods. They incorporate assessment of risk of re-offending and allocation of individuals to different levels of service according to their likely future risk. Individuals who, based on their previous histories of offending, appear more at risk of offending in future are offered more intensive services. They focus on aspects of individuals' lives that are conducive to or supportive of offence acts, such as specific patterns of social interaction, cognitive skills deficits, or anti-social attitudes. These and other difficulties can be described as criminogenic and may need to change if offending is to be reduced. The methods used and the manner of interaction between staff and offenders are designed to reflect the learning styles of participants; a feature known as responsivity. Finally, effective services possess programme integrity in that they are delivered by enthusiastic, empathic, appropriately trained, and adequately resourced staff who adhere to pre-decided methodological principles in undertaking the work.

As already outlined, another important feature of the manual contents is that they are based on the guiding principle that the individual's offence itself should be a prime focus of interest in any work undertaken with him or her. The alteration of any specific type of behaviour is more likely to be achieved if it is approached directly and attention is focused on it than if it is addressed only by indirect means. Beginning from an analysis of the offence, and the discovery of factors established to be contributory causes of it, subsequent work may (subject to the offender's agreement) depart from this area as appears necessary. Moreover, it is reasonable that in criminal justice services, a person's offences should be at least a starting-point for working with him or her, as its occurrence has provided the grounds for the individual's contact with the penal system.

None of this implies that individuals should be coerced into considering aspects of their offence behaviour in a confrontational or punitive manner. It is possible to combine a firm and rigorous approach which motivates individuals to take responsibility for their actions, with a positive and empathic interactive style of the kind established as fundamental in effective personal counselling. This is a highly skilled process and the difficulty of accomplishing it has often been underestimated. *Think First* was based on the assumption that, through personal qualities, selection, or professional training, such skills were already present in the tutors who would deliver the programme.

The main components of the programme were drawn from four principal areas of cognitive-behavioural intervention: (1) problem solving; (2) self-management; (3) social interaction training; and (4) values education.

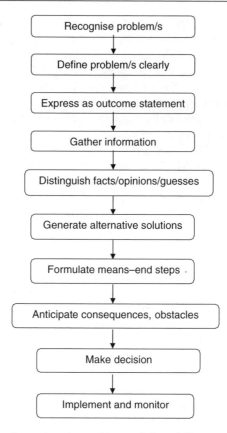

Figure 10.1 Sequence of exercises in problem-solving skill sessions

Problem Solving

Using a range of cognitive training exercises, this is designed to teach a number of "thinking skills" that have been isolated through research. The process of solving interpersonal problems has been analysed by a number of researchers who have reached a general consensus concerning the skills involved. The specific sequencing of skills training incorporated within *Think First* sessions is shown in Figure 10.1. Earlier studies supported the hypothesis that developing these skills could lead to sizeable reductions in rates of re-offending (Platt, Perry & Metzger, 1980; Ross, Fabiano & Ewles, 1988).

Self-Management

Research with a wide range of groups has demonstrated the importance of cognitive self-instructions in the management (or mismanagement) of behaviour. Self-statements of particular kinds are thought to be associated with a number of specific types of offences. Extensive work has shown the possibility of improving individuals' abilities to secure control over aspects of their feelings and behaviour that are causing difficulties for themselves or others. Problem-solving training is used as a basis for introducing offenders to the possibility of strengthening their skills of self-management, especially where ineffective self-management is an obstacle to solving other problems. Of particular importance here was the seminal work of Novaco (1975) and the development of anger control training.

Social Interaction Training

Most offences occur in an interpersonal context and some of them result from individuals' limited skills in dealing with certain encounters in an effective yet socially acceptable way. The programme is not designed to impart a full range of social skills are such, but to illustrate to participants the role of social problem solving in social interaction difficulties they have experienced. Association with criminal peers has repeatedly emerged as a cardinal risk factor for involvement in crime (see McGuire, 2004). A prime source of methods to address this in the pre-release training outlined above was the work of Goldstein, Sprafkin and Gershaw (1976) on preparing individuals for transfer from hospital into the community.

Values Education

Another set of factors now shown to have a significant influence on offences resides in specific beliefs or attitudes which are conducive to certain forms of anti-social behaviour (Simourd & Olver, 2002). Some individuals may hold more deeply embedded views or thinking patterns which reflect a disregard for the needs of others. These issues can be approached through moral-reasoning training aimed at a broad spectrum of thinking patterns, or specific attitude-change methods which have been used in relation to several types of offences. This strand is represented in only a small proportion of the community programme materials, though more time is devoted to it in the prison programme. Its inclusion was influenced by studies showing the impact of role-reversal and allied techniques in reducing the intensity of anti-social attitudes (Chandler, 1973; Culbertson, 1957; McDougall, Thomas, & Wilson, 1987).

The organisation of the above areas is such that the training in problem solving forms a kind of spine to which the other ingredients are methodologically interconnected. This conceptual scheme is depicted in Figure 10.2. Using the terminology of D'Zurilla, Nezu, & Maydeu-Olivares (2004), in trying to promote effective functioning, it is useful to distinguish two phases, of problem-solving and solution-implementation respectively. Based on the model of McFall (1982), in addition to learning how to solve problems, the development of competence also requires training in other social and behavioural performance skills. In *Think First*, acquisition of problem-solving skill is seen as underpinning the changes that are then applied in practice in other segments of the work. That

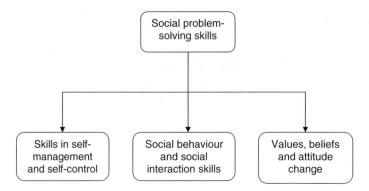

Figure 10.2 Conceptual structure of the programme

starting-point also offers users a framework for comprehending the overall shape of the experience.

Either a lack of, or repeated failure to apply, problem-solving skills may contribute to risk of offending in a number of ways. Similarly, limited self-management skills, social interaction skills, or specific types of beliefs may also do so. Figure 10.3 illustrates these dynamic risk factors with reference to the construction of *Think First*.

DESIGN AND DELIVERY

The delivery of this programme involves a range of personnel. When sentenced to probation, an offender's overall supervision is the responsibility of his or her case manager. The pre-group and group sessions, however, are provided by group tutors at designated programme sites. The pre-group sessions were introduced for induction purposes, to prepare individuals for participation in the programme, and retain their motivation until the date of commencement of the groups. The post-group sessions are intended to facilitate the transfer of activity from programme tutor to case manager, and to help develop an agenda for ongoing supervision. A further two sessions are provided to sustain learning at a point approximately three months after the end of the second phase. These sessions are delivered by case managers themselves, and designed to act as a "booster" for individuals at risk of re-offending. Both these sets of activities build on the principles of relapse prevention, presented here in a form known as self-risk management, influenced by the work of Bush (1995).

The frequency and timing of delivery of sessions have been varied to some extent to meet local service requirements. The commonest modes of delivery to date have been frequencies of between two and four sessions per week. However, there is evidence from outcome research that the latter, the achievement of a minimum of eight hours of group sessions per week, was associated with superior results in terms of both attendance and reduced rates of reconviction (Ong, Al-Attar, Roberts, & Harsent, 2003). This may be because a higher intensity

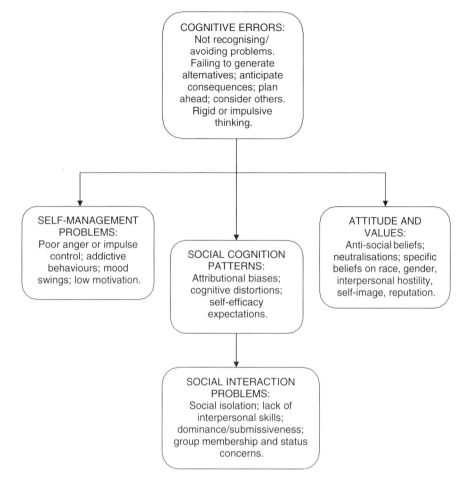

Figure 10.3 Relationship of components to criminogenic factors

of effort builds a momentum in participation and individual change, but this must remain speculative in the absence of more detailed research.

TARGETING AND SELECTION

In its use in probation services in England and Wales, *Think First* is classified as a generic cognitive skills/offending behaviour programme. This means that its designated "target group" consists of criminal recidivists likely to have committed a variety of previous offences, including property crimes and crimes against the person, and whose offence pattern suggests they might benefit from training in problem solving, self-management, or social skills. Problems in these areas are assessed by means of a semi-structured interview administered at the referral stage. The programme is reserved for those who present medium to medium/high risk in terms of potential future recidivism (National Probation

Service, 2002). This is assessed by means of the Home Office's standard actuarial prediction instrument for recidivism risk, the *Offender Group Reconviction Scale* (OGRS-2; Copas & Marshall, 1998). The OGRS-2 has also been shown to be a valid predictor for use with offenders who have mental disorders (Gray, Snowden, MacCulloch, Phillips, Taylor, & MacCulloch, 2004). For persons who have been convicted of sexual offences, domestic violence, drink-and-drive offences, or a marked pattern of substance-related offending, separate, more specialised programmes are available.

The contents of the programme are appropriate for both male and female offenders and for members of different ethnic groups. Provision is made within the materials for specific items of content to be varied by altering language, illustrative examples, and other aspects of session content to maximise relevance and responsivity and accommodate diversity among potential participants. The programme was designed for use within the context of an agency's policies concerning equal opportunities and anti-discriminatory practice. As stated in the *Delivery Guidelines* for the programme. It is essential that all staff involved in delivering the programme be familiar with and endorse the principles contained in those policies.

PROGRAMME DELIVERY AND TREATMENT INTEGRITY

Research findings on effectiveness suggest that criminal justice programmes work best when they involve action, participation, skills learning, and discussion linked to these activities, rather than either a didactic approach, on the one hand, or an unstructured, experiential/therapeutic approach, on the other. Sessions therefore incorporate a combination of some information-giving with active, practical exercises, opportunities for skills practice, and discussions focused on the assigned tasks. Elements of each of these ingredients are repeated sequentially across sessions to optimise learning. In addressing most problems and skills, a sequence is used in which the tutor gives an example of a familiar, everyday problem which the group first discusses in general terms. The tutor then invites group members to volunteer personal instances. The focus narrows further by examining situations in which such a problem was associated with committing a crime. When specific skills are being developed with reference to particular tasks, component skills learnt previously are repeated and practised in an integrated chain of activity.

An element of "pro-social modelling" is also important in delivering any programme of this kind. This means that as far as possible facilitators adopt and display a positive, constructive interactional style between themselves and the participant group. Sessions are oriented towards engendering an active, problem-solving frame of mind and a search for socially acceptable and feasible solutions.

Session Ingredients and Offence Focus

The opening sessions of the group programme develop essential skills of problem awareness and recognition, expressing problems in words, and gathering information. This phase also enables group members to become accustomed to working together and to foster a level of trust and collaboration. Session 6 (7 in the prison programme) consists almost in its entirety of an extended self-assessment by participants of their own current problems. This is done using a specially designed Problem Checklist, which participants complete and score during the session, yielding a problem profile, which they then discuss collectively. In the following session participants' attention is then focused on offending behaviour as a problem. Group members analyse offence incidents, focusing first on a single incident in some detail using the "5-WH" format (What, Who, When, Where, Why), then surveying a series of such incidents to detect patterns. In effect, they engage in a type of functional analysis of their own crime histories. Individuals present analyses of their own offending to the other members of the group. Later sessions use familiar cognitive-behavioural exercises such as A-B-C diaries, thinking reports, and tension thermometers (a variant of subjective units of distress) to examine different factors that may have contributed to their actions. Ensuing sessions are designed to allow practice of alternative ideas, actions and skills that can be used to avoid offending, and to solve other ongoing problems in individuals' lives.

Treatment Integrity

This is a highly structured programme with a specified sequence of themes, session objectives, and component exercises. As the preceding discussion indicates, however, some degree of flexibility is important in how issues are introduced; in the concrete, everyday examples used; and in specific facets of language or references to lifestyle that will reflect the composition of each new group. Thus, the question of treatment integrity or fidelity of delivery has been a particularly challenging one. This refers to the process by which the conceptual model on which a programme is based is recognisable in the process through which service users are offered assistance and expected to change (Hollin, 1995). The objective is to achieve a balance between adherence to that model while accommodating the range of needs and perspectives of participants.

For *Think First* and other accredited offending behaviour programmes, integrity is monitored through two main mechanisms. First, sessions are videotaped and a random selection of them viewed by independent observers using specially devised rating scales. Ratings are made of tutors' treatment adherence, style of delivery, and group-work skills. Scores are converted into a composite index, the *Implementation Quality Ratio*, part of a comprehensive audit process yielding annual "performance indicators". Second, tutors are allocated planning and debriefing time linked to delivery of sessions. Their work is also supervised by treatment managers according to a guideline whereby there should be, on average, a ratio of one session of supervision time to every 6-7 sessions of delivery time. In terms of the overall structure of the community programme, this indicates that there would be a total of four supervision sessions per staff member per programme. Records are kept of all these activities. For the prison programme, participants are asked to state personal goals after the 10th, 20th, and 30th (final) session of the programme, and their progress is discussed and reviewed with their Personal Officers.

ACCREDITATION AND DISSEMINATION

Provision of a structured, accredited programme involves a formidable array of documentation. The full set of materials consists of:

1. theory manual;
2. programme manual;
3. session supplements, the majority of them exercise work-sheets, with others containing explanatory notes;
4. a set of delivery guidelines;
5. staff training manual;
6. a monitoring and evaluation package consisting of selected psychometric instruments, and a range of observational and other checklists;
7. an accreditation manual designed for further refinement and appraisal of tutor skills;
8. a management manual designed by Home Office staff, though this is not unique to *Think First* but applies generically across all cognitive skills programmes.

The prison-based format was submitted to and approved by the then General Accreditation Panel within HM Prison Service in March 1997. While initially it was planned that the programme might be disseminated to a sizeable number of prison sites, in the event, it was implemented in only three. However, it was also used in two establishments of the Scottish Prison Service, and subsequently in a number of prisons in the state of Victoria, Australia.

The direct forerunner of *Think First*, entitled *Problem-Solving Training and Offence Behaviour*, was initially used in three probation service areas in England: Devon, Greater Manchester, and Teesside.[1] It was selected by the probation service as a *Pathfinder* programme when the associated policy initiative was announced in 1998. The present format of the community variant of the programme owes much to the advice of the Correctional Services Accreditation Panel (formerly the Joint Prison-Probation Accreditation Panel) who scrutinised the programme and validated it in January 2000. To be considered suitable for implementation, programmes are judged according to a set of 11 accreditation criteria (Home Office, 2002). Now entitled *Think First*, the programme was revised to address issues of enhancement and engagement, and to strengthen

---

[1]The work reported in this chapter spans a period when both the probation and prison service in England and Wales have undergone considerable organisational change. The National Probation Service was established in 2000 and entailed the centralisation of management structures across the previously partially autonomous probation areas. In a further change in 2004, the prison and probation services were merged to form the National Offender Management Service.

the focus on relapse prevention and risk management. This resulted in the introduction of the pre-group and post-group individual sessions, plus a single additional group session. In that form, the programme has been widely disseminated in England and Wales, delivered in 31 of the 42 probation service areas. In the three-year period from April 2001 to March 2004, a total of 11,624 offenders completed it. This version too is used at a number of locations in the community-based sector of Corrections Victoria, and is also being piloted by correctional services in South Australia and New South Wales.

EVALUATION

Regrettably there does not yet exist any randomised controlled trial of outcome effectiveness for either the community-based (probation) or institutional (prison) versions of the programme. It has been much more common to find probation programmes evaluated using quasi-experimental designs (McGuire, Broomfield, Robinson, & Rowson, 1995). Encouragingly, the proportion of outcome studies that employ controlled experimental designs included within meta-analyses has been increasing over the years. While, in the review by Gottschalk, Davidson, Gensheimer & Mayer (1987), only 38% of the studies involved randomised trials, in that by Lipsey & Wilson (1998) the corresponding figure was 45%, and in that by Farrington & Welsh (2003) 73%.

Short-Term Impact

A few studies have provided data on the short-term impact of the programme, using repeated measures designs with those who have completed it. McGuire & Hatcher (2001) reported pre-to-post psychometric data for 225 offenders who completed the programme in the three initial probation areas. This was based on a fairly limited set of measures and there was no untreated comparison group. The measures were *Crime-PICS* (Frude, Honess, & Maguire, 1994), a combined problem checklist and attitude scale, the *Impulsiveness-Venturesomeness-Empathy Scale* (Eysenck & Eysenck, 1991), the *Multidimensional Locus of Control Scale* (Levenson, 1973) and the *Self-Esteem Inventory* (Rosenberg, 1965). Significant changes in predicted directions were found for total scores and most sub-scales of *Crime-PICS*, and on measures of impulsiveness, empathy and self-esteem. A fuller version of these results is given by Hatcher & McGuire (2001).

Ong, Al-Attar, Roberts & Harsent (2003) found a mixed, but predominantly positive set of results in a separate study of another sample from the initial three *Pathfinder* areas. These data are all based on the earlier version of the programme that contained group sessions only. The authors used a series of measures of social problem solving, impulsiveness, locus of control, social reflection, criminal attitudes, perspective-taking, and situational response assessments. Pre- and post-test data were available on 120 offenders, 109 of whom had completed the programme. Of 30 sub-scale scores obtained, 22 changed in the expected direction with 10 being statistically significant. The remaining eight changed in the opposite direction and one was statistically significant. The authors noted a number of scoring problems with some sub-scales that may have compromised the analysis. They also proposed that a number of the scales required further validation studies before they could be used more extensively for this type of research. Nevertheless they also identified 15 variables which they considered could be valid and reliable candidates for measuring intermediate change on variables relevant to *Think First*.

Steele (2002a) has analysed a set of pre-to-post psychometric data from a sample of probationers who completed the programme in the Merseyside probation area during 2002. Unfortunately there were very few cases on which both pre-test and post-test data were available. Nevertheless, all scores showed changes in predicted directions and several were statistically significant, most notably that on the *Social Problem-Solving Inventory—Revised* (D'Zurilla, Nezu, & Maydeu-Olivares, 2002).

For the prison programme, a sizeable volume of pre-to-post psychometric data has been analysed and is being prepared for publication. As yet, however, no comparison sample exists against which to evaluate the patterns observed. The prison service has carried out short-term evaluation of all cognitive skills pro- grammes using a common set of self-report scales and structured interview assessments. This includes measures of impulsiveness, socialisation, locus of control, empathy, self-esteem, alternative thinking, and in some prisons, the *Psychological Inventory of Criminal Thinking Styles* (Walters, 1998). In addition, as part of a semi- structured interview, prisoners are asked how they would respond to a series of problem scenarios. Their responses are scored according to numbers of solutions, and to whether their actions can be classed as assertive, passive, or aggressive.

Pre-to-post scores have been analysed for a total of 405 prisoners who have completed the 30-session programme. The results show positive and highly significant changes on 12 out of the 15 measures. Data are also available from a proportion of these prisoners who were available for further evaluation approxi- mately 10 weeks after completion of the programme. This shows that the gains were maintained. Figures 10.4 and 10.5 show these results for a sample of prisoners tested at three time-points (commencement, completion, and short- term follow-up) on measures of impulsivity (n = 127) and socialisation (n = 129). The measures used were respectively the *Barratt Impulsivity Scale* (BIS-II; Barratt, 1994) and the *Gough Socialisation Scale* (Gough, 1960). Similar patterns were found for all other measures.

It was also hypothesised that participation in the programme would lead to a reduction in aggressive responses, and an increase in assertive responses, but no change in passive responses. These hypotheses were statistically confirmed.

Reconviction Studies

Findings of the first follow-up study of the pre-accredited version of the pro- gramme were not encouraging. The Probation Studies Unit at Oxford University conducted an outcome evaluation of programme completers from the three initial

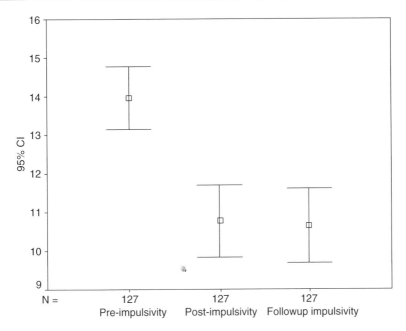

Figure 10.4   Impulsivity scores at three time-points: prison programme

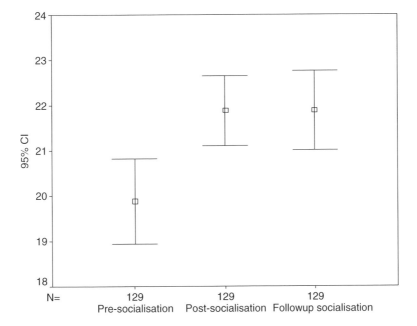

Figure 10.5   Socialisation scores at three time-points: prison programme

probation areas, comparing their progress with a group of prisoners. Not only did the programme participants re-offend at a higher rate than predicted, their recidivism rate was poorer than for the prisoner group, whose re-offence rate was surprisingly low. The latter is an anomalous finding, and was well below the rates generally seen amongst discharged prisoner samples. In addition, the two samples were rather poorly matched (Stewart-Ong, Harsent, Roberts, Burnett, & Al-Attar, 2003, cited in Debidin and Lovbakke, 2005).

Three recidivism outcome studies have been reported for *Think First* with more positive results. In the first, working at a local level, Steele (2002b) reported a one-year follow-up of the programme in the Merseyside Area of the National Probation Service. The sample consisted of 45 programme completers, 29 non-completers and 40 comparison group members placed on other community sentences. Completers had a significantly lower re-conviction rate than non-completers but while their rate was below that of the controls, the latter difference was not statistically significant. However, when attention was focused only on those offenders who met selection criteria for *Think First*, the reconviction rate for completers was considerably below that for controls (33% as against 53%).

Stewart-Ong, Harsent, Roberts, Burnett and Al-Attar (2004) carried out a further evaluative study in the three *Pathfinder* probation areas where the programme was originally piloted. They reported outcomes at six, nine and 12 months, for three groups: those who attended the programme in its entirety (completers), those who began but dropped out (non-completers), and those who were allocated but failed even to begin (non-starters). They examined reconviction rates, the proportions committing more serious offences, and the proportion receiving custodial sentences. The following are the data for 12 month follow-up. The respective rates of reconviction for the three groups were 44%, 77% and 74%; the proportions committing more serious offences, 18%, 32% and 29%; and the proportions given a sentence of imprisonment 3%, 16% and 24%. All of these differences were highly statistically significant ($p < 0.0005$) as between the completers and the other two groups.

Roberts (2004) has described a longer follow-up of the same samples. From an initial population of 267 offenders allocated to the programme, it proved possible to collect 18- and 24-month reconviction data on 223, consisting of 110 completers and 113 non-completers/non-starters. The two groups differed somewhat in risk level, obtaining OGRS-2 scores of 0.66 and 0.76 respectively. When these prior differences in risk level were taken into account, there were significant differences in reconviction rates at an 18-month follow-up, and a small but non-significant difference at 24 months.

More detailed analysis comparing completers, non-completers and non-starters showed that the association between completion and reconviction rates was moderated by risk level.

Amongst lower-risk offenders (OGRS-2 scores of 40 or less) there was no significant difference in reconviction rates between completers, non-completers and non-starters. In relation to medium risk offenders (OGRS-2 scores of 41-75) and higher risk offenders (OGRS-2 scores of 76 plus) there were significant differences with lower rates for completers than non-completers and non-starters. (Roberts, 2004, p.136)

The possibility that the differences obtained were due to a self-selection effect, in that completers of the programme were more motivated to avoid re-offending, even had they not attended the programme, cannot be ruled out as an explanation of these findings. There was no untreated comparison group in this evaluation. However, the non-starter group in effect received no intervention and the differences in outcome between that group and completers, controlling for prior risk level, suggests the presence of a significant "treatment effect".

Hollin, Palmer, McGuire, Hounsome, Hatcher, Bilby, & Clark (2004) have conducted a retrospective evaluation of the impact of probation *Pathfinder* programmes on re-conviction rates. Their experimental group was composed of offenders sentenced to a Probation Order (now called a Community Rehabilitation Order) between January 2000 and December 2001, with a requirement to attend one of five *Pathfinder* offending behaviour programmes (*Think First, R&R, Enhanced Thinking Skills, One-to-One*, or *Addressing Substance-Related Offending*). Hollin, McGuire, Palmer, Bilby, Hatcher, & Holmes (2002) give general descriptions of the latter programmes and their implementation. There was unfortunately a sizeable loss of data due to inaccuracies of recording within probation services: while initial data were provided by 26 Probation Areas in England and Wales, after data cleaning, only 16 areas were included in the final analysis. Nevertheless this is the largest evaluative study of its kind so far reported, incorporating a total sample of over 5,000 offenders.

As the objective of this research was to evaluate the effectiveness of the programmes, data for those who completed them and those who did not do so were analysed separately. A comparison group was assembled by taking a random group of offenders sentenced to a Probation Order during 2001 without a requirement to attend an offending behaviour programme. These offenders were drawn from the Probation Index database and came from eight probation areas. Information about the offenders' reconvictions over a period of between 12 and 18 months was obtained from the Home Office Offenders' Index: this included data relating to offence type, date of reconviction, and OGRS-2 scores.

In the study 1,262 offenders had been allocated to *Think First*, which thus contributed the largest single portion of the participants (56%) in the overall evaluation. At this stage, however, only 480 (38.03%) of those sentenced had completed the programme. A similar pattern of findings was obtained across all programmes and was reproduced for *Think First*. Programme completers showed the lowest reconviction rate, and non-completers the highest ($\chi^2 = 59.59$, $p < 001$), with the comparison group between the two. However, the raw data were difficult to interpret owing to prior differences between the samples in risk levels for future offending. The latter variables were taken into account by the use of multivariate analysis.

A sequential logistic regression was carried out to examine the effect of *Think First* in the prediction of group membership with respect to reconviction outcome. Age, OGRS-2 score, sex, and offence type were entered as predictors as these variables are known to be related to re-offending, followed by the treatment group (completer, non-completer, comparison). This resulted in a good model fit and the resultant model was significantly better than a constant-only model.

The addition of treatment group led to a significant improvement in the model provided by age, OGRS-2 score, sex, and offence type alone with correct

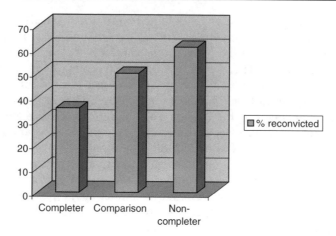

Figure 10.6   Reconviction rates by group status, controlling for risk level

classification of cases overall being 71.8%. The resultant odds ratios for the variables in this logistic regression indicated that the significant variables were age, OGRS-2 scores, offence type, and treatment group. With respect to treatment group, completing the programme made an offender 29.3% less likely to be reconvicted (as compared to non-completers and the comparison group), while being a non-completer made an offender 22.3% more likely to be reconvicted (as compared to completers and the comparison group). These findings are displayed in Figure 10.6 where the comparison group reconviction rate is set at 50%. Thus when risk levels and other variables known to have an impact on re-offending rates are taken into consideration, completion of *Think First* is associated with a highly significant reduction in subsequent rates of re-conviction.

Once again, in this study it was not possible to take account of self-selection and motivation as possible factors influencing the outcome. It could still be that those participants who complete programmes possess some feature, such as determination to succeed, that differentiates them from others and that this factor rather than programme participation accounts for their reduced offending. It is nevertheless arguable that the programme is also a factor. It may be that even where individuals were motivated to avoid offending, they would have failed to do so without the programme; or that their adherence illustrates that they found it helped them achieve their goals, which is part of its objectives. The result reported by Roberts (2004), of differential effects by risk-bands, also argues against a straightforward explanation in terms of self-selection alone. However, only further studies with randomised designs, and involving detailed examination of the factors influencing participation and non-participation will clarify and resolve these questions.

ATTRITION

A major problem encountered by all criminal justice programmes, particularly in community settings, is that of attrition. For the period covered by the *Pathfinder* evaluation just described, the completion rate of all the programmes evaluated was appallingly low. These difficulties have led to criticisms of the policy of introducing the requirement to attend, the setting of targets for throughput, and of the pace and scale of the entire implementation process (Ellis & Winstone, 2002).

On one level it is perhaps not surprising that compliance with community sentences poses a difficulty in the criminal justice system. It is more or less intrinsic to the relationship between persistent offenders and the legal system that the two are at odds with each other. Further, many offenders are beset with numerous problems, and may have very disorganised lives. These issues form part of recurrent debates about "law and order" and the call for heavier penalties, greater use of imprisonment or of other means of punishment or stricter control in the community.

Attrition occurs in two stages: despite being sentence by the court to attend, some offenders simply never arrive for the first session. Others start sessions but then drop out. It appears likely that a proportion of the attrition may be due to the literacy demands of the programme, which, like others of its type, have been found to be in excess of the attainment levels of many of those required to attend (Davies, Lewis, Byatt, Purvis, & Cole, 2004). This applied to skills in the area of speaking and listening as much as to written material. In response to these messages a number of modifications have been made to the language used in the manuals, and further guidance given concerning adaptations of the material.

Westmarland, Reid, Coulson, Hughes, & Hester (2002) carried out a unique study of the factors associated with attrition among offenders allocated to *Think First* in the Northumbria probation area. Their objectives were to investigate why so many offenders failed to commence or complete the programme, and to identify any steps that could be taken to improve this situation. Their study included several elements. The first was an analysis of 100 pre-sentence reports and assessments of individuals who had been recommended to attend the programme. The second involved a comparative study of the previous criminal records of non-starters, non-completers, and completers, respectively. The third entailed analysis of comments made on evaluation forms by 100 participants who completed the programme. Fourth, they conducted a series of interviews with case managers (n = 22), programme completers (n = 27) and non-completers (n = 9).

Some differences emerged between those likely to complete or not complete the programme. The former tended to have longer criminal records; they had committed an average of 33 previous offences across a 13-year period. They identified stress as a current major problem; were less likely to have poor self-esteem identified as a problem; and more likely to accept responsibility for their offending. Case managers typified those more likely to complete as being "ready" or motivated to stop offending, and less likely to have a personal crisis that would prevent them from attending. This study also highlighted the pivotal role of the case manager and the relationship he/she had established with the offender. Supplementing these findings, feedback concerning the programme was generally positive. Among those who completed, 63% reported finding the programme useful, only 9% saying it was "not very" or "not at all" useful. A large majority (82%) thought it was well organised and 62% considered that it would help them avoid re-offending. None of the evidence suggested that individuals with significant drug or alcohol problems were less likely to complete

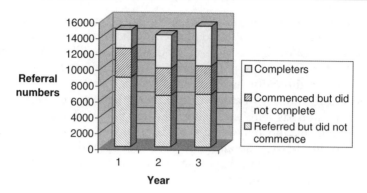

Figure 10.7 Programme referrals 2001–2004

the programme. Some offenders found the prospect of being in a group aversive and a majority took a very negative view of being asked to complete psychometric scales.

Encouragingly, there has been a steady increase in completion rates for *Think First* during the period 2001–4 (Skyner, personal communication, 2004). Across the three years, total numbers of referrals rose slightly from 14,785 to 15,283; commencements from 6,012 to 8,605; and completions from 2,374 to 5,037. Expressed as a fraction of referrals, the completion rates across the three years rose from 16.0 to 32.9%; expressed as a fraction of commencements they increased from 39.5 to 58.5%. These data are displayed in graphical form in Figure 10.7.

In Victoria, Australia, where the overall scale of implementation is more limited, completion rates have risen more steeply. Whereas during 2002-3 they were 55%, in 2003–4 they were 76% (Birgden, personal communication). A process evaluation of the dissemination of the programme has yielded generally very positive feedback (Bartholomew, Carvalho, & James, 2004).

CONCLUSION

The programme described in this chapter is derived directly from an application of concepts of social problem-solving and allied methods of training to the question of reducing offence-related behaviour. *Think First* has gone through several phases of evolution and is currently one of the most widely used cognitive skills programmes. In its present format it is the result of feedback and comments from a large number of "stakeholders", and it is likely that still further modifications will be made in the future. Preliminary evaluative information, both short-term and follow-up, is predominantly positive and encouraging, but there are competing hypotheses regarding the observed results and studies have not yet firmly demonstrated the programme's effectiveness. Further research is needed both to test its efficacy in more tightly controlled designs, and to examine the possible contribution of a range of other variables on participation, and on the types of change it is designed to engender.

REFERENCES

Andrews, D. A. (2001). Principles of effective correctional programs. In L. L. Motiuk & R. C. Serin (eds) *Compendium 2000 on Effective Correctional Programming*. Ottawa: Correctional Service Canada.

Andrews, D. A., Zinger, I., Hoge, R. D., Bonta, J., Gendreau, P., & Cullen, F. T. (1990). Does correctional treatment work? A clinically relevant and psychologically informed meta-analysis. *Criminology, 28*, 369–404.

Antonowicz, D. & Ross, R. R. (1994). Essential components of successful rehabilitation programs for offenders. *International Journal of Offender Therapy and Comparative Criminology, 38*, 97–104.

Barratt, E. (1994). Impulsiveness and aggression. In J. Monahan & H. J. Steadman (eds) *Violence and Mental Disorder: Perspectives on Risk Assessment*. Chicago: University of Chicago Press.

Bartholomew, T., Carvalho, T., & James, M. (2004). *A process evaluation of the implementation of the Cognitive Skills Program in Corrections Victoria*. Unpublished Summary Report. Deakin University, Melbourne.

Bottoms, A. & McWilliams, W. (1979). A non-treatment paradigm for probation practice. *British Journal of Social Work, 9*, 159–202.

Bush, J. (1995). Teaching self-risk-management to violent offenders. In J. McGuire (ed.) *What works: Reducing reoffending guidelines from research and practice*. Chichester: John Wiley & Sons, Ltd.

Chandler, M. J. (1973). Egocentrism and anti-social behavior: the assessment and training of social perspective-taking skills *Developmental Psychology, 9*, 326–332.

Copas, J. & Marshall, P. (1998). The offender group reconviction scale: a statistical reconviction score for use by probation officers. *Applied Statistics, 47*, 159–171.

Culbertson, F. M. (1957). Modification of an emotionally held attitude through role playing. *Journal of Abnormal and Social Psychology, 54*, 230–233.

Davies, K., Lewis, J., Byatt, J., Purvis, E., & Cole, B. (2004). *An evaluation of the literacy demands of general offending behaviour programmes*. Findings 233. London: Home Office Research, Development and Statistics Directorate.

Debidin, M. and Lovbakke, J. (2005). Offending behaviour programmes in prison and probation. In G. Harper and C. Chitty (eds) *The Impact of Corrections on Reoffending: A Review of 'What Works'*. Home Office Research Study 291. 2nd edition. London: Home Office Research, Development and Statistics Directorate.

D'Zurilla, T. J., Nezu, A. M., & Maydeu-Olivares, A. (2002). *Social problem-solving inventory– revised (SPSI-R)*. North Tonawanda, NY: Multi-Health Systems.

D'Zurilla, T. J., Nezu, A. M., & Maydeu-Olivares, A. (2004). Social problem solving: Theory and assessment. In E. C. Chang, T. J. D'Zurilla & L. J. Sanna (eds) *Social problem solving: Theory, research, and training*. Washington, DC: American Psychological Association.

Ellis, T. & Winstone, J. (2002). The policy impact of a survey of programme evaluations in England and Wales. In J. McGuire (ed.) *Offender rehabilitation and treatment: Effective programmes and policies to reduce re-offending*. Chichester: John Wiley & Sons, Ltd.

Eysenck, H. J. & Eysenck, S. B. G. (1991). *Manual of the Eysenck Personality Scales (EPS adult)*. London: Hodder and Stoughton.

Farrington, D. P. & Welsh, B. C. (2003). Family-based prevention of offending: A meta-analysis. *The Australian and New Zealand Journal of Criminology, 36*, 127–151.

Fleck, D., Thompson, C. L., & Narroway, L. (2001). Implementation of the Problem-Solving Skills Training Programme in a medium secure unit. *Criminal Behaviour and Mental Health, 11*, 262–272.

Frude, N., Honess, T., & Maguire, M. (1994). *Crime PICs II: Manual*. Cardiff: Michael and Associates.

Garrett, C. G. (1985). Effects of residential treatment on adjudicated delinquents: A meta-analysis. *Journal of Research in Crime and Delinquency, 22*, 287–308.

Goldstein, A. P., Sprafkin, R. P., & Gershaw, N. J. (1976). *Skill training for community living*. New York: Pergamon Press.

Gottschalk, R., Davidson, W. S., Gensheimer, L. K., & Mayer, J. P. (1987). Community-based interventions. In H. C. Quay (ed.) *Handbook of juvenile delinquency*. New York: John Wiley & Sons, Ltd.

Gough, H. G. (1960). Theory and measurement of socialization. *Journal of Consulting and Clinical Psychology, 24*, 23–30.

Gray, N. S., Snowden, R. J., MacCulloch, S., Phillips, H., Taylor, J., & MacCulloch, M. (2004). Relative efficacy of criminological, clinical and personality measures of future risk of offending in mentally disordered offenders: A comparative study of HCR-20, PCL:SV and OGRS. *Journal of Consulting and Clinical Psychology, 72*, 523–530.

Hatcher, R. & McGuire, J. (2001). *Report on the psychometric evaluation of the Think First programme in community settings*. Research report to the Home Office Probation Unit. London: Home Office.

Hollin, C. R. (1995). The meaning and implications of program integrity. In J. McGuire (ed.) *What works: Reducing reoffending: guidelines from research and practice*. Chichester: John Wiley & Sons, Ltd.

Hollin, C. R. (1999). Treatment programmes for offenders: Meta-analysis, 'what works', and beyond. *International Journal of Law and Psychiatry, 22*, 361–371.

Hollin, C. R., McGuire, J., Palmer, E. J., Bilby, C. Hatcher, R., & Holmes, A. (2002). *Introducing Pathfinder programmes into the probation service: An interim report*. Home Office Research Study 247. London: Home Office.

Hollin, C. R., Palmer, E. J., McGuire, J., Hounsome, J., Hatcher, R., Bilby, C., & Clark, C. (2004). *Pathfinder programmes in the probation service: A retrospective analysis*. On-Line Report 66/04. London: Home Office Research, Development and Statistics Directorate.

Home Office (2002). Joint Prison/Probation Services Accreditation Panel. *Performance standards manual for the delivery of accredited individual programmes*. London: National Offender Management Service.

Levenson, H. (1973). Multidimensional locus of control in psychiatric patients. *Journal of Consulting and Clinical Psychology, 41*, 397–404.

Lipsey, M. W. & Wilson, D. B. (1998). Effective intervention for serious juvenile offenders: A synthesis of research. In R. Loeber & D. P. Farrington (eds) *Serious and violent juvenile offenders: Risk factors and successful interventions*. Thousand Oaks, CA: Sage Publications.

McDougall, C., Thomas, M., & Wilson, J. (1987). Attitude change and the violent football supporter. In B. J. McGurk, D.M. Thornton & M. Williams (eds) *Applying psychology to imprisonment: Theory and practice*. London: HMSO.

McFall, R. M. (1982). A review and reformulation of the concept of social skills. *Behavioral Assessment, 4*, 1–33.

McGuire, J. (1995). Reasoning and Rehabilitation programs in the UK. In R. R. Ross & B. Ross (eds) *Thinking straight: The Reasoning and Rehabilitation Program for delinquency prevention and offender rehabilitation*. Ottawa: Air Training & Publications.

McGuire, J. (1999). Problem solving training: Pilot work with Secure Hospital patients. In D. Mercer, T. Mason, M. McKeown & G. MacCann (eds), *Forensic mental health care planning: A case study approach*. Edinburgh: Churchill livingstone.

McGuire, J. (2000). *Cognitive-behavioural approaches: An introduction to theory and research*. London: Home Office.

McGuire, J. (2002). Integrating findings from research reviews. In J. McGuire (ed.) *Offender rehabilitation and treatment: Effective practice and policies to reduce re-offending*. Chichester: John Wiley & Sons Ltd.

McGuire, J. (2004). *Understanding psychology and crime: Perspectives on theory and action*. Buckingham: Open University Press/McGraw-Hill Education.

McGuire, J., Broomfield, D., Robinson, C., & Rowson, B. (1995). Short-term impact of probation programs: An evaluative study. *International Journal of Offender Therapy and Comparative Criminology*, *39*, 23–42.

McGuire, J. & Hatcher, R. (2001). Offence-focused problem-solving: Preliminary evaluation of a cognitive skills program. *Criminal Justice and Behavior*, *28*, 564–587.

McGuire, J. & Priestley, P. (1981). *Life after school: A social skills curriculum*. Oxford: Pergamon Press.

McGuire, J. & Priestley, P. (1983). Life skills training with offenders in prisons and the community. In S. Spence & G. Shepherd (eds) *Developments in social skills training*. London: Academic Press.

McGuire, J. & Priestley, P. (1985). *Offending behaviour: Skills and stratagems for going straight*. London: Batsford.

McMurran, M. & Duggan, C. (2005). The manualisation of offender treatment. *Criminal Behaviour and Mental Health*, *15*, 17–27.

National Probation Service (2002). *Think First: Information for sentencers*. London: National Probation Directorate.

Novaco, R. W. (1975). *Anger control: The development and evaluation of an experimental treatment*. Lexington, KY: D. C. Heath.

Ong, G., Al-Attar, Z., Roberts, C., & Harsent, L. (2003). *Think First: An accredited community-based cognitive-behavioural programme in England and Wales. Findings from the prospective evaluation in three Probation Areas*. Oxford: Probation Studies Unit, Centre for Criminological Research, University of Oxford.

Platt, J. J., Perry, G., & Metzger, D. (1980). The evaluation of a heroin addiction treatment program within a correctional environment. In R. R. Ross & P. Gendreau (eds) *Effective correctional treatment*. Toronto: Butterworths.

Priestley, P. & McGuire, J. (1983). *Learning to help: Basic skills exercises*. London: Tavistock.

Priestley, P., McGuire, J., Flegg, D., Hemsley, V., & Welham, D. (1978). *Social skills and personal problem solving: A handbook of methods*. London: Tavistock.

Priestley, P., McGuire, J., Flegg, D., Hemsley, V., Welham, D., & Barnitt, R. (1984). *Social skills in prison and the community: Problem-solving for offenders*. London: Routledge and Kegan Paul.

Roberts, C. (2004). An early evaluation of a cognitive offending behaviour programme ('Think First') in probation areas. *Vista: perspectives on probation*, *8*, 130–136.

Rosenberg, M. (1965). *Society and the adolescent self-image*. Princeton, NJ: Princeton University Press.

Ross, R. R. & Fabiano, E. A. (1985). *Time to think: A cognitive model of delinquency treatment and offender rehabilitation*. Ottawa: Institute of Social Sciences and Arts.

Ross, R. R., Fabiano, E. A., & Ewles, C. D. (1988). Reasoning and rehabilitation. *International Journal of Offender Therapy and Comparative Criminology*, *20*, 165–173.

Saskatchewan Newstart (1973). *Life skills coaching manual*. Prince Albert: Training Research and Development Station, Department of Manpower and Immigration.

Shure, M. B. (2001). I can problem solve (ICPS): An interpersonal cognitive problem-solving program for children. *Residential Treatment for Children and Youth*, *18*, 3–14.

Shure, M. B. & Spivack, G. (1979). Interpersonal cognitive problem solving and primary prevention: Programming for preschool and kindergarten children. *Journal of Clinical Child Psychology*, *8*, 89–94.

Simourd, D. J. & Olver, M. E. (2002). The future of criminal attitudes research and practice. *Criminal Justice and Behavior, 29*, 427–446.

Spivack, G., Platt, J. J., & Shure, M. B. (1976). *The problem-solving approach to adjustment.* San Francisco, CA: Jossey-Bass.

Steele, R. (2002a). *Psychometric features of Think First participants pre and post programme.* Merseyside: Research and Information Section, National Probation Service.

Steele, R. (2002b). *Reconviction of offenders on Think First.* Merseyside: Research and Information Section, National Probation Service.

Stewart-Ong, G., Harsent, L., Roberts, C., Burnett, R. & Al-Attar, Z. (2004) *Think First prospective research study: Effectiveness and reducing attrition.* London: National Probation Service.

Walters, G. D. (1998). *Changing lives of crime and drugs: Intervening with substance-abusing offenders.* Chichester: John Wiley & Sons, Ltd.

Westmarland, N., Reid, P., Coulson, S., Hughes, J., & Hester, M. (2002). *An investigation into the factors associated with attrition in the Northumbria Probation Think First Programme.* Sunderland: International Centre for the Study of Violence and Abuse, University of Sunderland.

Chapter 11

STOP & THINK!
SOCIAL PROBLEM-SOLVING THERAPY WITH PERSONALITY-DISORDERED OFFENDERS

MARY MCMURRAN,[1] **VINCENT EGAN,**[2] **and CONOR DUGGAN**[3]

[1]*Cardiff University, UK*
[2]*Glasgow Caledonian University, UK*
[3]*University of Nottingham, UK*

INTRODUCTION

The work we describe in this chapter was developed in Arnold Lodge, a secure forensic unit in Leicester, UK, housing offenders detained under mental health legislation. In 1998, Arnold Lodge was commissioned to provide a service for men with personality disorder; that is, male offenders who are not only classifiable as suffering from at least one personality disorder but are additionally considered to be treatable and to require secure provision. The Personality Disorder Unit (PDU) was opened in 1999 with 10, later increasing to 12, places.

The PDU treatment programme is broad-based and aims to develop and maintain therapeutic relationships, teach people skills for appropriate containment of their behavioural disturbance, and address some of the interpersonal difficulties that are at the core of personality disorder. These therapeutic tasks are addressed in all stages of treatment, by all disciplines, and in various ways, including a therapeutic milieu, structured individual work, structured group treatment, and a range of individual therapies. The components of the PDU programme are shown in Figure 11.1.

Central to the PDU treatment programme, and the topic of this chapter, is *Stop & Think!*, a social problem-solving intervention. Before moving on to describe this aspect in detail, we will provide a brief description of the other structured treatment components to set *Stop & Think!* in context. These components have

Social Problem Solving and Offending: Evidence, Evaluation and Evolution.
Edited by Mary McMurran and James McGuire © 2005 John Wiley & Sons, Ltd.

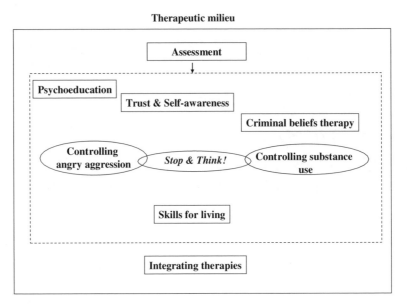

Figure 11.1   The Arnold Lodge PDU treatment programme

been documented in a set of treatment manuals, whose evolution we have described elsewhere (McMurran & Duggan, 2005).

Psychoeducation is where the patient's personality disorder diagnosis is clarified and core schemas related to the patient's problems are identified in a collaborative dialogue. This component developed from information that few patients had been informed of their diagnosis, and most of those who did know their diagnosis had picked up the information from reports rather than been informed by a clinician (D'Silva & Duggan, 2002). Even less common among patients was any understanding of how their diagnoses related to their emotional and behavioural problems. The Psychoeducation component not only informs patients of their diagnoses and helps clarify how their problems link with the diagnoses, but in the process also builds a therapeutic alliance.

The *Trust and Self-Awareness* group is based upon experiential therapy approaches and aims to build an atmosphere of trust in which group members will be better able to communicate with staff and with each other. *Criminal Thinking/Belief Therapy* aims to correct the maladaptive thinking styles that permit criminal behaviours. Based on the work of Walters (1995), thinking styles such as rationalisation, entitlement, and incongruity are identified and challenged in a structured treatment programme. *Controlling Angry Aggression* and *Controlling Substance Use* are structured group treatments targeting aggression (McMurran, Charlesworth, Duggan, & McCarthy, 2001) and drug and/or alcohol use for those identified with specific problems in these areas. *Skills for Living* is a social skills training group, covering a range of personal and interpersonal skills, such as positive thinking, communication, negotiation, and stress management.

Stop & Think!, the social problem-solving component, is based upon the premise that personality disorder is partly a deficit in interpersonal problem solving, hence all PDU residents participate in this part of the programme. In this chapter, we will present evidence for the assertion that people with personality disorder, particularly those who offend, are deficient in social problem solving, and we will describe our working model of social problem solving and personality disorder. We will then go on to describe the practice of *Stop & Think!*, which is a variant of D'Zurilla and Goldfried's (1971) well-known problem-solving therapy. We will present evidence of the effectiveness of *Stop & Think!* from the evaluation to date with PDU patients. Finally, we will describe the future directions planned for our research and practice.

PERSONALITY DISORDER, OFFENDING, AND SOCIAL PROBLEM-SOLVING

Good social problem-solving consists of the ability to recognise a problem when one arises, define the problem clearly and accurately, produce a diversity of possible solutions, anticipate outcomes, formulate an effective action plan that has stepwise stages, and carry out the action plan effectively. There is evidence from our own and others' research that people who offend, have personality disorders, or both, experience difficulties in these aspects of the problem-solving process.

In our research, we have examined social problem-solving abilities using the Social Problem-Solving Inventory-Revised (SPSI-R; D'Zurilla, Nezu, & Maydeu-Olivares, 2002). The SPSI-R gives a total Social Problem Solving (SPS) score plus scores on five main sub-scales: Positive Problem Orientation (PPO), Negative Problem Orientation (NPO), Rational Problem Solving (RPS), Impulsive/Careless Style (ICS), and Avoidant Style (AS). We have SPSI-R data for male personality disordered offenders, sentenced male prisoners (Sellen, 2004), and male mature students (McMurran, Blair, & Egan, 2002), which are presented in Table 11.1.

Table 11.1   Mean SPSI-R scores for personality disordered offenders and mature students

SPSI-R Scale	Personality disordered offenders (n = 42)	Prisoners (n = 39)	Mature students (n = 70)
Positive problem orientation	11.36 (14.50)*	9.23 (5.21)	12.82 (4.14)
Negative problem orientation	24.93 (14.45)	18.50 (12.49)	10.95 (6.79)
Rational problem solving	29.44 (21.14)	36.74 (19.10)	44.78 (12.60)
Impulsive/careless style	24.90 (14.89)	16.97 (11.32)	10.97 (5.84)
Avoidant style	17.80 (14.45)	12.67 (8.11)	8.25 (5.42)
Social problem solving total	10.45 (14.65)	10.33 (4.39)	13.39 (2.51)

Note: *Standard deviations in parentheses

Table 11.2 Correlations between NEO-FFI factors and SPSI-R scales for mentally disordered offenders (n = 52)

	PPO	NPO	RPS	ICS	AS	SPS
Neuroticism	−0.53***	0.77***	−0.33**	0.56***	0.39**	−0.69***
Extraversion	0.47***	−0.43**	0.21	−0.24	−0.20	0.40**
Openness	0.17	−0.24	0.30*	−0.32*	−0.32	0.36**
Agreeableness	0.15	−0.26	−0.02	−0.34*	−0.27	0.29*
Conscientiousness	0.42	−0.39**	0.21	−0.28*	−0.24	0.40**

Source: Reprinted from McMurran, M., Egan, V., Blair, M., & Richardson, C. (2001) The relationship between social problem-solving and personality in mentally disordered offenders. *Personality and Individual Differences, 30*, 517–524. Copyright © 2001, with permission from Elsevier.

Personality disordered offenders, in comparison with the other two groups, have the least desired scores on all but the PPO scale and the total SPS score.

When considering why a person might be poor at problem solving, a number of explanatory factors come to mind, one of these being personality. Very little research has been conducted into problem-solving abilities in people with specific personality disorders, but in one study, researchers found ineffective problem-solving to be associated most with Cluster C personality disorders, i.e., anxious, fearful traits, and Cluster A, i.e., odd, eccentric traits, but not Cluster B, i.e., erratic, flamboyant traits, although there was a possibility that Cluster B respondents overestimated their problem-solving abilities (Herrick & Elliott, 2001). We have investigated the relationships between personality traits and social problem solving.

We studied a combined sample of personality disordered offenders (n = 14) and mentally ill offenders (n = 38), these two groups being combined because there were no significant differences between them on SPSI-R scores (McMurran, Egan, Blair, & Richardson, 2001). The instrument used in this research to assess personality traits was the NEO-Five Factor Inventory (NEO-FFI; Costa & McCrae, 1992), which measures the 'Big Five' personality traits: Neuroticism (N), Extraversion (E), Openness (O), Agreeableness (A), and Conscientiousness (C). Correlations between the Big Five and SPSI-R scales are presented in Table 11.2. We investigated whether the Big Five predicted total SPS scores in a multiple regression, and found that a significant model emerged (Adjusted $R^2 = 0.555$, $F_{5,46} = 13.59$, $p < 0.0001$). Significant predictor variables were O (Beta = 0.340, $p < 0.001$) and N (Beta −0.539, $p < 0.0001$). We will examine the effects of O and N in turn.

Openness predicts good social problem-solving and O also correlates highly with intelligence (Harris, 2004); more intelligent individuals are better at social problem-solving. Specifically, looking at the correlations in Table 11.2, those who score high on O are more rational and less impulsive/careless in their approach to problem-solving. In our mature students' data, RPS also correlated significantly and negatively ($r = −.36, p < 0.01$) with ICS (McMurran et al., 2002). Thus, intelligence is associated with rational problem-solving, which is incompatible with an impulsive/careless style. This accords with other research where Openness has been shown to correlate with planful problem solving (Bouchard, 2003).

High levels of Neuroticism predict poor social problem solving. The facets of N are anxiety, hostility, depression, self-consciousness, impulsiveness and vulnerability (Costa & McCrae, 1992), and these facets are clearly not conducive to effective problem-solving. In our correlations (see Table 11.2), N relates positively to both the Impulsive/Careless Style and the Avoidant Style. Further investigation of this sample shows a significant correlation between ICS and AS ($r = 0.63, p < 0.001$). This relationship was also evident in our student sample, AS correlating significantly with ICS ($r = 0.58, p < 0.001$) (McMurran et al., 2002). These relationships indicate that any one person uses both maladaptive styles.

One aspect of N that we have investigated further is impulsiveness. Using our mature students' data, we investigated the relationship with impulsiveness, measured by the Barratt Impulsiveness Scale (BIS; Patton, Stanford & Barratt, 1995). All scales of the SPSI-R correlate significantly and in the expected direction with the BIS (PPO $r = -0.31$, $p < 0.01$; NPO $r = 0.31$, $p < 0.01$; RPS $r = -0.31$, $p < 0.01$; ICS $r = 0.43, p < 0.001$; AS $r = 0.38, p < 0.001$; SPS $r = -0.47, p < 0.001$). Impulsivity may, therefore, be a core feature of poor problem solving. Impulsivity is an underlying feature of antisocial and borderline personality disorder, and is a strong predictor of aggression and violence (Brennan & Raine, 1997; Hawkins, Herrenkohl, Farrington, et al., 1998; Links, Heslegrave, & van Reekum, 1999).

Looking back over the developmental pathway, it is probable that inherent traits and capabilities, in conjunction with the social context of a child's upbringing, set the scene for the development of particular problem-solving styles and behavioural responses to interpersonal problems. Impulsiveness presents an obstacle to the acquisition of good social problem-solving skills, a process that may be exacerbated in conjunction with low intelligence and poor verbal skills. Barratt and colleagues (1997) have found poor verbal skills to mediate the impulsivity–aggression relationship. Poor interpersonal problem solving may then lead to aggression and violence, since the person does not possess the thinking and behavioural skills to avoid or defuse problematic situations. Poor social problem solving has been shown to exert a mediating effect between impulsivity and aggression in adults (McMurran et al., 2002).

Persistent aggression will lead to core beliefs about the self as being aggressive. Serin and Kuriychuk (1994) have proposed just such an information-processing framework to explain aggression, whereby impulsivity, i.e., acting without thinking, and hostile attributional biases act synergistically to cue attention to provocation, thus leading to faster aggressive responses and to a more entrenched self-schemas relating to aggression. Schema-concordant information processing biases have also been identified in people with avoidant personality types, where information is selected to fit with avoidant beliefs (Dreessen, Arntz, Hendriks, Keune, & van den Hout, 1999).

McMurran, Fyffe, McCarthy, Duggan, and Latham. (2001) have suggested that poor social problem-solving may be both a cause and a consequence of dysfunction, as shown in the risk factor model represented in Figure 11.2. Poor cognitive abilities and adverse personality traits are likely to militate against the acquisition of good social problem-solving skills through information-processing limitations

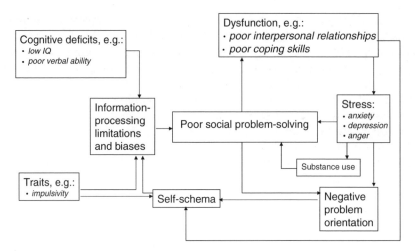

Figure 11.2 A social problem-solving model of personality disorder

and biases. Poor social problem-solving skills lead to interpersonal dysfunction, causing stress and associated moods (e.g., anxiety, depression, anger) which further impair social problem-solving abilities. Drink and drugs may be used as means of coping, and these would exacerbate problem-solving impairments. Personality traits are represented in self-schemas, i.e., core beliefs about the self. These schemas influence information processing and social problem solving, and are in turn influenced by social outcomes. Poor social problem-solving abilities and stress combine to produce a negative problem orientation which militates against change.

STOP & THINK!

Problem-solving interventions have been devised for offenders (Bourke & van Hasselt, 2001; McGuire, 2000; Ross, Fabiano, & Ross, 1986), with some evidence of their effectiveness (Lipsey, Chapman, & Landenberger, 2001; McGuire and Hatcher, 2001; Robinson, 1995). Here, we describe social problem-solving therapy applied with personality disordered offender inpatients.

Based upon the work of D'Zurilla and colleagues (D'Zurilla and Goldfried, 1971; D'Zurilla and Nezu, 1999), *Stop & Think!* addresses the seven problem-solving steps:

1. *Orientation*: Cueing in to bad feelings as a trigger for the problem-solving process and encouraging the belief that problems that can be solved.
2. *Problem definition*: Accurate definition of the problem, without relying on inferences or suppositions.
3. *Goal setting*: Setting goals as a basis for action planning.
4. *Generation of alternatives*: Creative identification of possible ways that goals might be achieved.

5. *Decision-making*: Examination of the advantages and disadvantages of each potential solution to assist with the choice of action.
6. *Action*: Using one or more of the viable options in a logically arranged means-end action plan.
7. *Evaluation*: After the action plan has been implemented, the outcomes are evaluated.

In *Stop & Think!*, these steps are translated into six key questions that the client group can understand and remember: (1) Bad feelings? (2) What's my problem? (3) What do I want? (4) What are my options? (5) What is my plan? (6) How did I do? or How am I doing? These key questions are used in each session, without variation, to teach people the *strategy* for solving problems. Repetition of the questions leads to overlearning, and hence increases the likelihood that the person will remember and use the strategy independently when problems actually arise. Although the questions are used without variation in each session, the problem addressed is whatever concerns the participant at the time, and so *Stop & Think!* is responsive to the client's needs.

The rationale behind *Stop & Think!* is explained to participants, and the six key questions are introduced. Although repeatedly working through the questions systematically may seem contrived and repetitive, this is explained as necessary in drawing the problem-solving process from unconscious to conscious processing in order to correct bad habits. An analogy is drawn with driving to clarify this point. As a learner driver, every operation of the driving process is conscious and deliberate, but, with practice, driving becomes automatic and fluent. The automatic process is more efficient and is generally safer, except when bad habits have developed. To correct bad habits, a person has to start thinking about the process again and make corrections. Once bad habits have been corrected, the new style of driving then becomes automatic. So it is with social problem solving, where the steps involved are brought into conscious processing, new skills are developed, and eventually the new problem-solving style becomes automatic.

Our experience is that personality-disordered offenders are poor at recognising their feelings and thus fail to cue into the problem-solving process. Often, the learning process occurs in reverse, with the problem stated first, and then the bad feelings associated with the problem are explored. Generic "bad feelings" are dismantled, differentiating the emotions to permit more effective problem-solving (Feldman Barrett, Gross, Conner Christensen, & Benvenuto, 2001), and identifying physical sensations improve emotion recognition.

Defining the problem clearly and accurately is given care and attention, since this is crucial in determining an effective solution. Often, personality-disordered offenders present compound, life problems that are too large to tackle. These are broken into constituent components, prioritised, and addressed one at a time. A clear problem definition permits a clear goal statement. Antisocial goals are not accepted, although antisocial options are not ruled out in the next stage.

Generation of alternatives is the stage in which change is most evident in treatment. In early sessions, personality disordered offenders generate few ideas for solving problems. Creativity is encouraged by example, where group leaders suggest alternatives, and by praising all options generated regardless of their quality. As sessions progress, the ability to generate a range of potential solutions to a problem increases, and, as this happens, negativity decreases. Participants begin to develop optimism about their ability to solve problems. After option generation, each option is revisited and its advantages and disadvantages are considered. None is ruled out at this stage, to prevent discarding an option which is not acceptable on its own but may be useful in conjunction with other options. Once the pros and cons of each option have been considered, the list is pruned of those that are rejected, leaving the accepted ones to be formulated into an action plan.

In the options stage, antisocial options are not censored, since their inclusion permits examination of the adverse consequences set against the gains in a cost–benefit analysis. Their inclusion also allows antisocial attitudes to be challenged. Facilitators can, in fact, be the ones to add antisocial options specifically so that they may be examined; participants are often wary of producing solutions they know to be socially unacceptable in case this is taken as an indication of risk or poor response to treatment. Usually, antisocial options are rejected by the participant, but if, after examining the consequences, a participant does wish to include an antisocial option, the group leader will normally express a moral or legal objection to its inclusion.

The selected options, of which there may be several, are grouped into themes, translated into specific, actionable tasks, and listed in a logical means–end sequence. The action plan aims to move participants on from expressing concern to taking action to solve problems, and participants are taught that the action plan must consist of items that they can leave the session and begin *doing*. Thus, "improve my self-esteem" is not an actionable item, whereas activities designed to lead to improved self-esteem are, for example "sign up for literacy classes". Help may be needed with the skills necessary to carry out the tasks in the action plan. *Stop & Think!* does not include social skills training, but it can include brief, *ad hoc*, skills training relevant to an action plan, for example, rehearsing a conversation.

On the PDU at Arnold Lodge, *Stop & Think!* is run in groups. Each session consists of one patient working through a problem and another patient giving feedback on the implementation of an action plan devised in a previous session. The emphasis is on personal and interpersonal problems. Practical problems, such as negotiating leave, finding accommodation, and accessing benefits are not ruled out, since they frequently have an interpersonal component, but they are not the main focus of group sessions. To assist with problem identification, nurses may suggest problems that they observe from the patient's behaviour on the unit. Problems raised in groups are passed on to key workers for follow-through. Key workers use *Stop & Think!* in individual work with patients, in order to reinforce the procedure. This avoids the logical inconsistency of one problem-solving procedure being taught in groups, yet a different procedure being used in individual work. Patients are also encouraged to use the *Stop & Think!* process independently, using a work sheet.

Patients are required to log all their problem-solving work in a single file, including work from *Stop & Think!* sessions and individual work. Group facilitators review this work monthly, following up and rationalising actions plans for consistency, reduction of overlap, and prioritisation. Occasionally, a group session may be spent reviewing problem-solving plans and individual work. Progress is reported at the patient's ward round and case review.

Regular audits of both group and individual practice are undertaken to enable managers to examine practice and take corrective action if problems are spotted. Annual audits of *Stop & Think!* include information on group take-up rates, staff involvement in running groups, examining patients' files for completed individual *Stop & Think!* forms, seeking staff views on *Stop & Think!*, and assessing patients' opinions of *Stop & Think!*

EVALUATION

Progress in *Stop & Think!* is evaluated using the SPSI-R (D'Zurilla et al., 2002). We first conducted a pilot study of *Stop & Think!* in Arnold Lodge with nine male patients, six of whom were diagnosed as mentally ill but were not floridly so at the time of the pilot study, and three of whom were classified as suffering from a personality disorder (McMurran, Egan, Richardson, & Ahmadi, 1999). Just six sessions of $1\frac{1}{2}$ hours' duration at weekly intervals produced a statistically significant improvement in patients' overall problem-solving scores, and significant reductions in impulsivity (ICS) and negative problem orientation (NPO). Although the number of patients treated was small, we took this to be an indication that *Stop & Think!* was a promising intervention.

Subsequent to this pilot study, *Stop & Think!* was implemented in the PDU. Information collection is ongoing, and SPSI-R information is currently available for 42 patients at baseline, 26 at nine months after admission to the PDU, 15 at 15 months, and 11 at 21 months. The baseline is taken during the first three months on the PDU, which is an assessment period, and thereafter tests are repeated at six monthly intervals. At baseline, this group of patients showed a poorer overall problem-solving profile than the samples described in Table 11.1.

Comparisons of SPSI-R scores over 21 months are presented in Table 11.3, showing that significant improvements were recorded on overall social problem solving and on RPS, ICS, and AS subscales. Scores on PPO and NPO were in the right direction, but statistical significance was not reached. Paired t-tests between baseline and 9 months, 9 months and 15 months, and 15 months and 21 months indicate that there is significant change only between baseline and 9 months ($t = 4.06$, $df = 25$, $p < 0.001$). This confirms our earlier finding that gains are rapid in the early stages of treatment and are maintained over time (McMurran, Fyffe, et al., 2001). The SPSI-R is administered annually after discharge and gains appear to be reasonably maintained for as long as three years.

FUTURE DEVELOPMENTS

The improvements shown in our treatment study are merely changes on a psychometric test, and actual behaviour change requires investigation. The literature suggests that improving social problem solving reduces dysfunction

Table 11.3. SPSI-R Scores for personality disordered patients in treatment

SPSI-R	Baseline N = 42	9 months N = 26	15 months N = 15	21 months N = 11	F (3,27)
Positive problem orientation	11.36 (14.50)†	12.92 (4.08)	14.40 (3.04)	13.82 (4.07)	1.32
Negative problem orientation	24.93 (14.45)	16.88 (10.42)	12.80 (7.82)	15.09 (10.29)	1.60
Rational problem solving	29.44 (21.14)	47.50 (18.69)	54.00 (16.84)	61.09 (14.49)	5.50**
Impulsive/Careless style	24.90 (14.89)	12.81 (12.01)	9.20 (9.28)	5.73 (7.27)	3.79*
Avoidant style	17.80 (14.45)	10.31 (7.05)	9.07 (6.70)	9.45 (6.95)	3.81*
Social problem solving	10.45 (14.65)	12.47 (4.54)	14.12 (3.37)	14.39 (3.46)	5.02**

Notes: †Standard deviations in parentheses; $*p < 0.05$; $**p < 0.01$

and improves behaviour (Herrick & Elliott, 2001; Robinson, 1995; Townsend, Hawton, Altman, et al. 2001), but in respect of this population the issue of behaviour change remains as yet unanswered. The PDU patients are being followed to see how they have progressed in terms of rehabilitation and recidivism.

The *Stop & Think!* programme on the PDU is also under development. One move is to promote patients who are sure of the basic principles to an advanced group, using the problem-solving process to tackle more challenging issues. Another direction is further examination of the self-schemas associated with maladaptive problem solving and linking *Stop & Think!* with schema-focused therapy.

A major limitation of the PDU treatment study is that there is no control or comparison group, without which it is impossible to account for change. Currently, the effectiveness of *Stop & Think!* is being examined in a randomised control trial – the Landscaped Project. This is an acronym for Local Agency Network for Dangerously Severe Community-living Adults with Personality Disorder. The Landscaped Project treatment is a combination of individual Psychoeducation (D'Silva & Duggan, 2002) and *Stop & Think!* groups, conducted by clinical psychologists, nurses, and social workers at various sites across the East Midlands of England. Men and women in both general adult and specialist forensic mental health services may be referred for treatment. Assessments include personality disorder using the IPDE (Loranger et al., 1994) and social problem solving using the SPSI-R (D'Zurilla et al., 2002). In due course, we will have information from this project not only on the effectiveness of *Stop & Think!* but also on social problem-solving profiles for different personality-disorder types.

One other area of concern in research is how problem-solving abilities are measured. Problem solving is a complex cognitive process that is hard to specify and articulate, and additionally it is a process that may operate outside conscious awareness. The SPSI-R is a self-report measure of how the respondent perceives him or herself to go about problem solving, and may be unsuited to the groups we wish to assess, given their limited verbal intelligence and psychological problems. Other methods of assessing social problem-solving skills typically examine a person's responses to problem vignettes, as in the Means–End Problem Solving (MEPS) procedure (Spivack, Platt, & Shure, 1976). Such methods also have their limitations, such as dubious external validity and poor reliability in rating responses (House & Scott, 1996). At Cardiff University, we are currently developing a comprehensive assessment of social problem-solving skills, using well-validated tasks developed by cognitive psychologists. These tasks will look more closely at stages of the problem-solving process, namely problem recognition, information gathering, causal analysis, and perspective-taking (Pakaslahti, 2000). As we have noted from other research, specific deficits differ according to diagnosis (Herrick & Elliott, 2001; Matthys, Cuperus, & van Engeland, 1999), and problem-solving profiles according to diagnoses are worthy of investigation. If there are significant differences between patients with regard to problem-solving skills, it may be too simplistic to apply the same problem-solving intervention to all. It may be important to refine problem-solving procedures accordingly, better to suit the needs of the person.

CONCLUSION

Social problem-solving therapy has proved a success with personality-disordered offenders. The procedures have been made explicit, thus facilitating the training staff in their application. At face level, the intervention appeals to common sense, both for practitioners and patients, and so it has been embraced enthusiastically. This communality of approach engenders a sense of cohesion among staff of different disciplines and between staff and patients. Furthermore, experience suggests that the clarity of the approach contains the chaotic feelings and behaviour of people with personality disorders. After a period of induction, patients quickly grasp the value of *Stop & Think!* and develop a sense of empowerment.

Although simple in structure, *Stop & Think!* is a procedure that addresses those cognitive functions that are linked with a range of psychological and behavioural problems. Indeed, the problem-solving process has been identified as a framework for understanding a variety of clinical disorders associated with executive functioning difficulties, that is the higher-order brain functions of attention, information organisation, forward planning, and self-control (Zelazo et al., 1997).

Stop & Think! is not restrictive; other interventions may be incorporated within the problem-solving framework or alongside it. Patients at later stages in the treatment process are encouraged to look for patterns to their problems – patterns that ultimately have their genesis in the individual's personality, and, as described at the outset, *Stop & Think!* is one component of a range of treatments. *Stop & Think!* is a non-anxiety-provoking entry route to the identification and treatment of complex issues.

ACKNOWLEDGEMENTS

The research upon which this publication is based has been supported by funding from the NHS National Programme on Forensic Mental Health R&D, the Home Office, and Nottinghamshire Healthcare NHS Trust. The views expressed in this publication are those of the authors and not necessarily those of the Forensic Mental Health Programme, the Department of Health, the Home Office, or the Trust. Thanks are due to clinical staff, patients, and researchers who have ben involved in *Stop & Think!* They have contributed immensely to practice development.

REFERENCES

Barratt, E. S., Stanford, M. S., Kent, T. A., & Felthous, A. (1997). Neuropsychological and cognitive psychophysiological substrates of impulsive aggression. *Biological Psychiatry, 41*, 1045–1061.

Bouchard, G. (2003). Cognitive appraisals, neuroticism, and openness as correlates of coping strategies: An integrative model of adaptation to marital difficulties. *Canadian Journal of Behavioral Science, 35*, 1–12.

Bourke, M. L. & van Hasselt, V. B. (2001). Social problem-solving skills training for incarcerated offenders. *Behavior Modification, 25*, 163–188.

Brennan, P. A. & Raine, A. (1977). Biosocial basis of antisocial behavior: Psychophysiological, neurological, and cognitive factors. *Clinical Psychology Review, 17*, 589–604.

Costa, P. T. & McCrae, R. R. (1992). *Revised NEP Personality Inventory (NEO PI-R TM) and NEO Five Factor Inventory (NEO-FFI)*. Odessa, FL: Psychological Assessment Resources, Inc.

Dreessen, L., Arntz, A., Hendriks, T., Keune, N., & van den Hout, M. (1999). Avoidant personality disorder and implicit schema-congruent information processing bias: A pilot study with a pragmatic inference task. *Behaviour Research and Therapy, 37*, 619–632.

D'Silva, K. & Duggan, C. (2002). The development of a psycho-educational programme for personality disordered patients. *Psychiatric Bulletin, 26*, 268–271.

D'Zurilla, T. J., & Goldfried, M. R. (1971). Problem solving and behaviour modification. *Journal of Abnormal Psychology, 78*, 107–126.

D'Zurilla, T. J., & Nezu, A. M. (1999). *Problem solving therapy: A social competence approach to clinical intervention.* 2nd edn. New York: Springer.

D'Zurilla, T. J., Nezu, A. M., & Maydeu-Olivares, A. (2002). *Manual for the Social Problem Solving Inventory-Revised.* North Tonawanda, NY: Multi-Health Systems, Inc.

Feldman Barrett, L., Gross, J., Conner Christensen, T., & Benvenuto, M. (2001). Knowing what you're feeling and knowing what to do about it: Mapping the relation between emotion differentiation and emotion regulation. *Cognition and Emotion, 15*, 713–724.

Harris, J. A. (2004). Measured intelligence, achievement, openness to experience, and creativity. *Personality and Individual Differences, 36*, 913–929.

Hawkins, J. D., Herrenkohl, T., Farrington, D. P., Brewer, D., Catalano, R. F., & Harachi, T. W. (1998). A review of predictors of youth violence. In R. Loeber & D.P. Farrington (eds) *Serious violent and juvenile offenders: Risk factors and successful interventions.* Thousand Oaks, CA: Sage.

Herrick, S. M., & Elliott, T. R. (2001). Social problem-solving abilities and personality disorder characteristics among dual-diagnosed persons in substance abuse treatment. *Journal of Clinical Psychology, 57,* 75–92.

House, R. & Scott, J. (1996). Problems in measuring problem-solving: The suitability of the Means-Ends Problem Solving (MEPS) procedure. *International Journal of Methods in Psychiatric Research, 6,* 1–9.

Links, P. S., Heslegrave, R., & van Reekum, R. (1999). Impulsivity: Core aspect of borderline personality disorder. *Journal of Personality Disorders, 13,* 1–9.

Lipsey, M. W., Chapman, G. L., & Landenberg, N. A. (2001). Cognitive-behavioral programs for offenders. *The Annals of the American Academy of Political and Social Science, 578,* 144–157.

Loranger, A. W., Sartorius, N., Andreoli, A., Berger, P., Buchheim, P., Channabasavanna, S. M., et al. (1994). The International Personality Disorder Examination. *Archives of General Psychiatry, 51,* 215–224.

Matthys, W., Cuperus, J. M., & van Engeland, H. (1999). Deficient social problem solving in boys with ODD/CD, with ADHD, and with both disorders. *Journal of the American Academy of Child and Adolescent Psychiatry, 38,* 311–321.

McGuire, J. (2000). *Think first.* London: National Probation Directorate.

McGuire, J. & Hatcher, R. (2001). Offense-focused problem solving: Preliminary evaluation of a cognitive skills program. *Criminal Justice and Behavior, 28,* 564–587.

McMurran, M., Blair, M., & Egan, V. (2002). An investigation of the correlations between aggression, impulsiveness, social problem-solving, and alcohol use. *Aggressive Behavior, 28,* 439–445.

McMurran, M., Charlesworth, P., Duggan, C., & McCarthy, L. (2001). Controlling angry aggression: A pilot group intervention with personality disordered offenders. *Behavioural and Cognitive Psychotherapy, 29,* 473–483.

McMurran, M. & Duggan, C. (2005). The manualisation of a treatment programme for personality disorder. *Criminal Behaviour and Mental Health, 15,* 17–27.

McMurran, M., Egan, V., Blair, M., & Richardson, C. (2001). The relationship between social problem-solving and personality in mentally disordered offenders. *Personality and Individual Differences, 30,* 517–524.

McMurran, M., Egan, V., Richardson, C., & Ahmadi, S. (1999). Social problem-solving in mentally disordered offenders: A brief report. *Criminal Behaviour and Mental Health, 9,* 315–322.

McMurran, M., Fyffe, S., McCarthy, L., Duggan, C., & Latham, A. (2001). 'Stop & Think!': Social problem-solving therapy with personality disordered offenders. *Criminal Behaviour and Mental Health, 11,* 273–285.

Pakaslahti, L. (2000). Children's and adolescents' aggressive behavior in context: The development and application of aggressive problem-solving strategies. *Aggression and Violent Behavior, 5,* 467–490.

Patton, J. H., Stanford, M. S., & Barratt, E. S. (1995). Factor structure of the Barratt Impulsiveness Scale. *Journal of Clinical Psychology, 51,* 768–774.

Robinson, D. (1995). *The impact of cognitive skills training on post-release recidivism among Canadian federal offenders.* Ottawa: Correctional Services of Canada.

Ross, R. R., Fabiano, E. A., & Ross, R. D. (1986). *Reasoning and rehabilitation: A handbook for teaching cognitive skills.* Ottawa: University of Ottawa Press.

Sellen, J. L. (2004). Unpublished data, University of Wales Institute, Cardiff.

Serin, R. C. & Kuriychuk, M. (1994). Social and cognitive processing deficits in violent offenders: Implications for treatment. *International Journal of Law and Psychiatry, 17,* 431–441.

Spivack, G., Platt, J., & Shure, M. (1976). *The problem solving approach to adjustment.* San Francisco, CA: Jossey-Bass.

Townsend, E., Hawton, K., Altman, D. G., Arensman, E., Gunnell, D., Hazell, P., et al. (2001). The efficacy of problem-solving treatments after deliberate self-harm: Meta-analysis of randomised controlled trails with respect to depression, hopelessness, and improvement in problems. *Psychological Medicine, 31,* 979–988.

Walters, G. D. (1995). The Psychological Inventory of Criminal Thinking Styles: Part I. Reliability and preliminary validity. *Criminal Justice and Behavior, 22,* 307–325.

Zelazo, P. D., Carter, A., Reznick, J. S., & Frye, D. (1997). Early development of executive function: A problem-solving framework. *Review of General Psychology, 1,* 198–226.

PART III

EVOLUTION AND EXPLORATION

Chapter 12

SOCIAL COGNITION AND SEX OFFENDERS

THERESA A. GANNON, DEVON L.L. POLASCHEK, and TONY WARD
Victoria University of Wellington, New Zealand

INTRODUCTION

Explaining why men offend sexually, and how best to rehabilitate them is always a "work in progress". Many pieces make up this fascinatingly complex jigsaw. Sex offenders' social cognition is recognised as a corner piece, and one that has received increasing research attention over the past decade.

Social cognition is concerned with how each of us uniquely experiences and makes sense of our social world (Fiske & Taylor, 1991). It is surely common sense that how sex offenders think, reason, and perceive their social world will have direct bearing on why they offend. How else could a man sexually abuse a child, or force sex on a woman, unless he views and experiences the world somewhat differently from others who do not sexually offend? In support of this view, clinicians and researchers frequently provide examples of sex offenders' offence-supportive statements made when they recount their offences (e.g., Abel, Becker, & Cunningham-Rathner, 1984; Hartley, 1998; Polaschek & Gannon, 2004; Saradjian & Nobus, 2003; Scully, 1988; Scully & Marolla, 1984; Ward, Louden, Hudson, & Marshall, 1995). For example, child molesters may argue that children are willing participants, or even initiators of sex (Abel et al., 1984; Neidigh & Krop, 1992) and rapists state that their victim really "wanted it", or eventually started to enjoy the rape (Scully, 1988, 1990; Scully & Marolla, 1984). The consistency and frequency of these statements have persuaded treatment providers that in order for sex offenders to be successfully rehabilitated, they must change their ways of talking about, and by inference, perceiving the social world. In fact, restructuring sex offenders' pro-offending thinking has become a core priority for most cognitive-behavioural treatment programmes (Beech & Mann, 2002; Marshall, Anderson, & Fernandez, 1999).

Social Problem Solving and Offending: Evidence, Evaluation and Evolution.
Edited by Mary McMurran and James McGuire   © 2005 John Wiley & Sons, Ltd.

How do sex offenders see their social world, and themselves? Do they view the social world in an offence-supportive manner, and if so, does this perception help to explain their sexual offending? How best can we use current knowledge of sex offenders' cognition to rehabilitate them? To help answer these questions, we have structured this chapter in the following manner. First, we outline the main tenets of a social cognitive perspective. Second, we review theory and research on social cognition with sex offenders, identifying the major findings, but also the knowledge gaps that remain. Finally, we draw some conclusions about how we can best use current research and theory to guide the rehabilitation of sex offenders.

SOCIAL COGNITION

As its name suggests, *social cognition* refers to the study of social actions using the knowledge and methods of cognitive psychology (Augoustinos & Walker, 1995; Fiske & Taylor, 1991). At its heart, this approach assumes that in order to understand social behaviour, we must examine the cognitive constructs associated with that behaviour (Ostrom, 1994). Particular emphasis is placed upon the *subjective* experience of the individual (Fiske & Taylor, 1991): each person's unique experience of the world, his or her own actions, and the actions of others.

The Basic Principles

Sherman, Judd, and Park (1989) argued that in order to understand a given behaviour, the field of social cognition should answer three major questions. First, what knowledge content is stored and structured in memory? Second, how does this organised knowledge affect the processing of social information, and the formulation of responses and behaviours? And, finally, how can these existing knowledge structures be changed or restructured?

Knowledge Content and Structure

Individual differences in behaviour and experience are hypothesised to result from each individual's unique pre-existing knowledge, and how this knowledge is organised in memory (i.e., cognitive *content* and *structure* respectively; Hollon & Kriss, 1984; Kendall, 1992). Knowledge structures contain units of information that, through life experience, are joined by associative links to form large networks of information (Collins & Loftus, 1975). Units of information with similar meaning and units that are frequently activated together develop strong connections, forming a structure known as a *schema* (Anderson & Bushman, 2002). Once activated, schemas guide us in predicting, explaining, and understanding our social world (Mann & Beech, 2003). So, when dealing with a social situation that has similarities to a previous one, individuals refer back to their schema of what usually happens in such circumstances (Fiske & Taylor, 1991;

Williams, Watts, MacLeod, & Mathews, 1997). It is important to note here that stored knowledge is thought to exist at several different levels of abstraction or scope, with general and more abstract knowledge at the top of the hierarchy (i.e., the general core beliefs), and more focused knowledge tapering down towards the bottom (Augoustinos & Walker, 1995; Sherman et al., 1989; Ward, 2000).

Processing Social Information

Given unlimited time and resources, individuals can, if motivated, interpret their own actions and those of others in a careful, methodical, and somewhat rational manner (i.e., the *naïve* scientist approach; Fiske & Taylor, 1991). More often than not, however, individuals are instead motivated to behave as *cognitive misers:* to perceive their complicated world in a relatively manageable way by relying on information that is readily available in the form of schemas (Augoustinos & Walker, 1995; Fiske & Taylor, 1991).

Life experience may provide many opportunities to rehearse a schema. Rehearsal results in increased linkage strength between knowledge units, providing a rich and complex body of knowledge (Anderson & Bushman, 2002), and also increases that schema's accessibility. When a particular schema has been repeatedly activated, it becomes *chronically* accessible, and is thought to be even more likely to guide subsequent information processing (Pettit, Polaha, & Mize, 2001).

However, schema activation may fluctuate, and research suggests that highly accessible schemas are particularly prone to situational priming (Bargh, 1982; Bargh, Lombardi, & Higgins, 1988). In fact, recently, researchers have found that motivation and affect play an important role in social information processing and the individual's use of processing shortcuts (e.g., Tiedens, 2001). For example, affective states (positive or negative) have been found to increase the probability that schemas will be used to guide information processing (see Bodenhausen, Kramer, & Susser, 1994; Bodenhausen, Sheppard, & Kramer, 1994; Tiedens, 2001), most probably because they reduce both the cognitive ability and the motivation to perceive the world in a careful and methodical manner (Kardes, 1994; Pettit et al., 2001). Besides affect, sexual arousal and alcohol or drug intoxication are also hypothesised to increase reliance on processing shortcuts using schemas (Pettit et al., 2001).

So how does a reliance on schemas ultimately affect the processing of social information? Schemas direct attention towards encoding schema-congruent stimuli, while schema-incongruent material is ignored or minimised (Kindt & Brosschot, 1997). When information is ambiguous or scant, research has also shown that schemas provide a basis for interpreting the likely causes and mechanisms behind such ambiguities (Dodge, 1980; Dodge & Frame, 1982). In other words, schemas are self-fulfilling knowledge bases that search for schema-congruent information, disregard incongruent information, and impose meaning upon events when they are unclear (Fiske & Taylor, 1991; Hollon & Kriss, 1984). Because schemas shape experience this way, individuals' perceptions, interpretations, and recall of information can be used to infer the content and structure of the knowledge that guides them.

More clues about individuals' cognitive structures and the content stored in them can be obtained by asking about their *cognitive products* (Hollon & Kriss, 1984; Kendall, 1992). Cognitive products are accessible thoughts, attributions, decisions, or beliefs that are produced from the general workings of the cognitive system (Ingram & Kendall, 1986). They are the spoken or unspoken outputs of social perception but may be unreliable in that they may easily be tainted by social desirability bias, and their accuracy is limited by how well individuals are informed about their own cognitive functioning.

Managing and Altering Dysfunctional Schemas

Clearly, pre-existing schemas are useful for helping us sift through and organise the vast quantity of perceivable social stimuli in any interaction, without using too many cognitive resources. However, schemas can contribute to distress and socially dysfunctional behaviour (e.g., when they are based on racial prejudice or misogyny; see Johnston & Hewstone, 1992; Pettit et al., 2001; Skov & Sherman, 1986). Because they are also strengthened by use, they can become very difficult though not impossible to alter. Sensible ways of revising problematic schemas have been suggested by researchers based on the principles of *assimilation* (when new information is fitted into existing cognitive structures) and *accommodation* (when cognitive structures adjust to accommodate new information).

Social cognitive psychologists generally agree that to make successful schema adaptation (i.e., to change the fundamental core beliefs governing a schema), individuals should be presented with many pieces of disconfirming evidence that challenge the fundamental principles of the underlying schema (see Weber & Crocker, 1983). If individuals are faced with only small amounts of schema-incongruent information, then schema revisions may be small and unremarkable (Augoustinos & Walker, 1995; Weber & Crocker, 1983). Schemas may also resist change by *subtyping* information (Weber & Crocker, 1983). When this happens, cases that appear to contradict the underlying principles of a schema may be stored as a specific *subtype*, posing no real threat to the underlying schema's "correctness" (see Hewstone, Johnston, & Aird, 1992; Johnston & Hewstone, 1992, for empirical evidence). Existing schemas may be altered drastically through presenting a piece of particularly prominent and memorably schema-contradictory information (Fiske & Taylor, 1991).

People can be taught ways of monitoring their information processing so that they are less influenced by pre-existing knowledge. For example, research suggests that when asked, people can process information thoroughly, without using cognitive shortcuts (Neuberg & Fiske, 1987). People can also inhibit self-talk from activated schemas (Johnston, Ward, & Hudson, 1997); however, successfully avoiding automatic thoughts is dependent upon certain criteria (Wegner, 1994). In brief, Wegner's research suggests that thought suppression involves two main processes of *monitoring* and *operating*. During the monitoring process, people locate unwanted thoughts (or thoughts that they wish to avoid in order to achieve a certain goal). Then the operating process can suppress the unwanted thought by substituting a more appropriate and goal-consistent thought (Johnston & Ward, 1996). However, individuals are only able to suppress unwanted thoughts successfully when they have enough cognitive resources available (ibid.). Ironically, when inadequate cognitive resources are available (e.g., during highly affective states or sexual arousal), the operating process (i.e., the *substitution* of thoughts) can break down, leaving the already located and unwanted thoughts highly accessible. This phenomenon is known as the *rebound effect* (see Macrae, Bodenhausen, Milne, & Jetten, 1994). Of course, the greater the number of unwanted thoughts located during monitoring, the more cognitive resources will be needed to substitute and replace them. To succeed at thought suppression then, people need to rehearse and automatise the process of substituting goal-congruent distractor thoughts (Johnston et al., 1997; Wegner, 1994).

The Benefits of a Social Cognitive Perspective of Sexual Offending

The application of a social cognitive framework has been very helpful in previous reviews of sex offender cognition (see Johnston & Ward, 1996; Segal & Stermac, 1990; Ward, Hudson, Johnston, & Marshall, 1997). The framework provides a clear organisational structure for existing theory and research, making the cognitive task of evaluating the contributions of disparate studies much easier. Structuring existing knowledge into a basic social cognitive framework helps provide a better understanding of how conceptually distinct cognitive constructs interact to produce sexually abusive behaviour. It also enables quick identification of gaps and inconsistencies, giving valuable direction for future theory development, research, and treatment design. However, it is just a framework, and determining where to place studies in that framework is itself sometimes an ambiguous task.

SEX OFFENDERS' COGNITION: WHAT WE KNOW

Beginning with Cognitive Distortions

Abel et al. (1984) were among the first researchers to investigate the content of sex offenders' cognition with child molesters in their clinical practice. They argued that child molesters develop atypical beliefs (or *cognitive distortions*) about sex and children that minimise the guilt experienced when they commit their offences, allowing them to continue their antisocial behaviour without distress. They observed that child molesters commonly sexualised the child and perceived the child to be a willing sexual partner (e.g., if the child didn't resist the assault or tell another adult, or if the child asked questions about sex). Child molesters also suggested that their abuse was acceptable for various reasons (e.g., it was educational for the child, it would cause no long-term harm, it would eventually be seen by society as appropriate behaviour). Over the next few years, researchers compiled extensive lists of sex offenders' offence-supportive content (e.g., Neidigh & Krop, 1992; Pollock & Hashmall, 1991). However, these lists were of limited value because they were primarily descriptive and thus of limited utility in research or treatment.

Developing a Theoretical Basis for Offence-Supportive Cognition

Work in other domains of cognitive psychopathology suggests that the concept of schemas offers a way of organising and explaining offence-supportive statements (e.g., Beck, Freeman, et al., 1990). Ward (2000) proposed a detailed conceptualisation of how the offence-related beliefs of sex offenders could be organised and generated. He chose a specific form of schemas, *implicit theories* (ITs) as the primary guiding structure in this theory. In brief, the concept of ITs comes from observations in developmental psychology (e.g., theory of mind; Wellman, 1990) in which children are hypothesised to gain knowledge by generating theories and testing them rather as a scientist does. Maladaptive ITs are hypothesised to develop in response to events that require explanation, often during childhood. For example, a child may develop the underlying belief that the world is a dangerous and hostile place due to experiences of physical abuse from family members. These pervasive theories are usually only revised when they fail to explain and predict behaviour (Drake, Ward, Nathan, & Lee, 2001).

ITs are thought to be used by offenders to make inferences about the beliefs, desires, and future intentions of victims (Ward & Keenan, 1999). In other words, these theories provide a context that offenders can use to interpret the social world in offence-supportive ways. There are three levels at which ITs can operate. First, there are general beliefs about people and their environment; second, there are middle-level beliefs about categories or classes of people (e.g., children); and third, there are more finely grained beliefs about, for example, a particular victim. The most important, or *core* beliefs are those held at the general and middle level, because they frame the interpretation of the social world in general.

A number of ITs have been proposed to describe the typical offence-supportive beliefs of both child molesters (Ward & Keenan, 1999) and rapists (Polaschek & Ward, 2002). Some of these are victim-class focused: theories that have particular relevance for understanding the intentions, desires, and behaviours of women or children. Others are more general theories about the world that may be shared by a wide range of individuals, especially those who are antisocial (ibid.). In the section that follows, we use each of these theories to organise a review of the main research findings on victim-class focused and then more general offence-supportive cognition.

Victim-Focused Knowledge

The first IT proposed to guide offence-supportive information-processing in child molesters is the *children as sexual beings* IT (Ward & Keenan, 1999). Men who hold this theory believe that children can only benefit from sexual contact with adults, since it helps to develop their inherent sexual nature. A similar IT, *women as sexual objects* has been proposed for rapists (Polaschek & Ward, 2002). Men who hold this theory see women as highly sexually preoccupied; sexual interest dominates their lives and they are always receptive to sexual approaches. In both cases, potential victims are viewed as unlikely to be harmed by sexual activity, unless excessive physical force is used.

In support of this theory is a body of research demonstrating that sex offenders often over-perceive sexual intent in their victims, and minimise or deny victim harm created by their offences (Abel et al., 1984; Beech, Fisher, & Ward, 2004; Hanson, Gizzarelli, & Scott, 1994; Hartley, 1998; Neidigh & Krop, 1992; Polaschek & Gannon, 2004; Saradjian & Nobus, 2003; Stermac & Segal, 1989; Scully, 1990; Scully & Marolla, 1984; Swaffer, Hollin, Beech, Beckett, & Fisher, 1999). For example, Saradjian and Nobus (2003) found that paedophile priests tended to view their child victims as desiring sex, or as one priest put it, "full of sex" (p. 912). Relatedly, Stermac and Segal (1989) have also found that child molesters tend to overestimate the child's responsibility for sexual abuse and under-estimate the harm resulting from that abuse.

Scully (1990) found that rapists sexualised their victims also, viewing their clothing as provocative, and perceiving women as constantly desiring sex, even if their words or actions blatantly contradicted this view. For example, even in the presence of a weapon, victims were often perceived as "wanting" the sexual contact, and as eventually succumbing to the sexual pleasures of rape. In relation to victim harm, Hamilton and Yee (1990) found that men who reported a high likelihood of raping were less likely to see the consequences as upsetting for a rape victim, and showed less knowledge about both the short- and long-term trauma associated with rape.

Polaschek (Polaschek & Gannon, 2004; Polaschek & Ward, 2002) argues that rapists also hold a *women are dangerous* IT. Men with this theory tend to perceive women as alien, unknowable beings who are impossible to understand, and who intentionally deceive, manipulate, and set out to destroy men by, for example, "crying" rape to put them in prison. Research with rapists indicates that they view their own victims, and women more generally, with suspicion. Malamuth and Brown (1994) found evidence for a *suspiciousness schema* in sexually aggres-sive men. These men perceived the overt intent portrayed by women in experi-mental vignettes as misleading, almost regardless of what that intent was. However, Malamuth and Brown did not describe the content of that schema. Polaschek and Gannon (2004) have found that a large proportion of rapists interviewed about their offences described women as being not only deceptive, but intentionally malevolent and manipulative individuals who go out of their way to get men into trouble. Beech et al. (2004) have reported a similar theme underlying the beliefs of some sexual murderers (most with adult victims).

The existence of this theory in rapists also has the potential to explain research suggesting that sexual aggression is linked to a variety of other constructs such as hostility towards women, dominance as a motive for sex, and a preference for impersonal sex (e.g., Malamuth, Heavey, & Linz, 1993), as well as the perception of male–female relationships as being exploitative (Check, Malamuth, Elias, & Barton, 1985).

General Beliefs and Knowledge

Several general ITs have been proposed to guide sex offenders' social-cognitive behaviour. Ward and Keenan (1999) and Polaschek and Ward (2002) suggest that both child molesters and rapists hold an *entitlement* IT, characterised by generally self-focused and controlling attitudes. Men who hold this theory are likely to believe that their needs are more important than those of others, and that they are within their rights to demand of others that these needs be met.

A number of researchers and clinicians have observed that sex offenders are self-focused individuals who concentrate predominantly on their own needs, goals, and desires (Beech et al., 2004; Gilgun & Connor, 1989; Hanson et al. 1994; Hartley, 1998; Polaschek & Gannon, 2004; Saradjian & Nobus, 2003). In terms of sexual needs, child molesters have been found to endorse more statements advocating male entitlement to sex than non-sex offending controls (e.g., "Men need sex more than women do"; Hanson et al., 1994). Incestuous molesters have been reported as perceiving their molesting to be some type of patriarchal right (Hartley, 1998). Both child molesters and rapists report feeling "entitled" to sexually aggress against their victim to control them (Neidigh & Krop, 1992; Polaschek & Gannon, 2004). The need for power, or a controlling and patronising attitude towards victims may be a particularly common theme in rapists' offence descriptions (e.g., Polaschek & Gannon, 2004).

Feeling superior in relation to women is, of course, a way of expressing traditional sex role stereotyping, and, at least in anonymous surveys of non-incarcerated samples, sexually aggressive men have endorsed these traditional attitudes. Check and Malamuth (1983) reported that almost half of the sex role stereotyping males they studied indicated some propensity to rape, and Muehlenhard (1988) showed that men who endorsed conservative and traditional sex role attitudes were more likely to perceive rape as being justified than those who were low on this dimension. Mosher and Anderson (1986) found that male students who endorsed attitudes indicating that they valued masculine toughness were more likely to indicate that they had been sexually aggressive.

In a rare experimental study investigating the organisation of knowledge structures in sex offenders, Pryor and Stoller (1994) presented undergraduate males with various word pair combinations of dominant, control, and sex-related words. They found that men who indicated a high likelihood of sexually harassing (high LSH) made higher estimates of the frequency of presentation of sexuality-dominance word pairs, and were more sure that they recognised these pairs than low LSH men. In other words, the performance of men with a higher LSH suggests the presence of a structural link between dominance and sexuality. Bargh, Raymond, Pryor, and Strack (1995) found that this link also existed for men reporting a high likelihood of committing rape, although for them, the relationship only functioned one way (i.e., power concepts primed sex, but sex did not prime power).

Perceiving other adults as socially dominant appears to be an underlying theme for some child molesters. Research suggests that child molesters view children as less threatening socially compared to adults (Howells, 1979), and that they are attracted to children's innocence (Elliott, Browne, & Kilcoyne, 1995;

Wilson & Cox, 1983). These types of perceptions have been hypothesised to stem from a general *dangerous world* IT, in which all adults are viewed with suspicion and mistrust. A generalised wariness of others (not just women) has also been noted in rapists; although the available evidence is not yet substantial.

Finally, Ward and Keenan (1999) argued for an *uncontrollability* IT that views humans as being unable to influence their own behaviour in the face of more powerful urges and emotions. As evidence, they note that many sex offenders who talk about the reasons underlying their offence place the blame on factors that seem to be out of their control by appealing to recent emotional disturbances, situational states such as intoxication or extreme sexual arousal, or even distant emotional disturbances from childhood (e.g., Beech et al., 2004; Neidigh & Krop, 1992; Polaschek & Gannon, 2004; Pollock & Hashmall, 1991). However, some of these cognitions may simply be excuses used by sex offenders to negate social disapproval.

To conclude, the hypothesis that sex offenders are guided by differing ITs is very useful for organising the disparate themes noted in the early cognitive distortions literature. ITs can also explain how offence-supportive statements are generated. Further, they may explain differences in cognition noted in subtypes of sex offenders. For example, experienced, extra-familial child molesters are hypothesised to be most likely to hold chronically accessible offence-related ITs because their longer criminal history has afforded much more opportunity for rehearsal (Ward, 2000). Beech (1998) has indirectly supported this hypothesis; he found that child molesters who endorsed significantly more distorted beliefs about children and sexuality on self-report measures tended to have many more previous victims than child molesters who displayed less deviant attitudes.

Comparing Sex Offenders with Others on Belief Questionnaires

In the previous section we reviewed studies that appeared to support the contention that sex offenders' social cognitive functioning is distinctly offence-supportive. However, closer examination reveals that this literature consists almost exclusively of two types of studies: (1) investigations of men who are willing to report that they are "at risk" of offending, a variable with an unknown relationship to sexual assault conviction; and (2) identified offenders who have spontaneously made offence-supportive statements during a discussion of their own offending.

To argue that such cognition may actually be etiological, one essential step is for research to demonstrate that there are genuine differences between identified offenders and non-offenders. This research requires the use of cognitive measures that are highly related to sex offending but can also be responded to by men who have not offended. These studies are reviewed below. Most have used questionnaires containing lists of belief-type items (i.e., cognitive products).

For rapists, such research has been surprisingly unsuccessful. Bumby (1996) and Marolla and Scully (1986) have obtained the most promising results. Bumby gave rapists, child molesters, and offender controls the RAPE scale (a measure of rape-supportive attitudes), and found that although rapists endorsed significantly more items than the offender controls, they could not be statistically differentiated from child molesters. Marolla and Scully found that rapists could not be distinguished statistically from offender controls on their more general attitudes (i.e., the Short Attitudes Towards Women Scale: ATWS; Spence Helmreich, & Stapp, 1973, the Hostility Towards Women Scale, or the Acceptance of Interpersonal Violence Scale; Burt, 1980). However, they were statistically different on their acceptance of rape myths (Rape Stereotype Scale; Marolla & Scully, 1986), although the actual mean difference was small, and therefore of questionable aetiological significance.

Segal and Stermac (1984) attempted to differentiate rapists, and two control groups of similar socio-economic status (offender and community controls) on the ATWS but could not statistically discriminate the three groups, all of whom showed quite liberal attitudes towards women. Other researchers have reported similar results with Sattem, Savells, and Murray (1984) finding that rapists displayed more liberal attitudes towards women than offender controls and non-offender controls; and Harmon, Owens, and Dewey (1995) reporting that rapists and non-offender controls held similar views about women, and that both groups were significantly less conservative than offender controls.

On the face of it, similar research with child molesters has been more successful in obtaining statistically significant differences when compared to controls on questionnaire measures of beliefs (see Segal & Stermac, 1990). For example, researchers using the popular Abel and Becker Cognition Scale (Abel et al., 1989), that assesses a range of offence-supportive beliefs, have found that child molesters endorse significantly more items than rapists (Hayashino, Wurtele, & Klebe, 1995; Stermac & Segal, 1989), offender controls (Hayashino et al., 1995) or community controls (Abel et al., 1989; Stermac & Segal, 1989; Tierney & McCabe, 2001). Researchers using the newer but similar MOLEST Scale (Bumby, 1996) have reported significantly higher scores for child molesters than rapists (Arkowitz & Vess, 2003; Bumby, 1996) and offender controls (Bumby, 1996; Marshall, Marshall, Sachdev, & Kruger, 2003). Still, some studies have not found differences on cognitive distortion questionnaires (e.g., Tierney & McCabe, 2001).

When found, are significant differences between groups clinically meaningful? On average, even in successful studies the child molesters still disagree with the offence-supportive items, just not as strongly as controls (e.g., Arkowitz & Vess, 2003). Several studies that didn't use control groups have also found that child molesters strongly disagree with offence-supportive beliefs (Langevin, 1991; Gannon, in press; Kolton, Boer, & Boer, 2001). The most frequent explanation for such findings is that child molesters are answering in a socially desirable fashion, facilitated by the transparent nature of the questionnaires (i.e., child molesters are *hiding* their antisocial beliefs from researchers; see Langevin, 1991).

However, in a series of recent studies designed to minimise the influence of social desirability on social cognitive measures, we found more evidence that child molesters primarily disagree with offence-supportive questionnaire items. Gannon (2002, in press) connected to a fake lie detector child molesters who had already demonstrated strong disagreement on a sexual offence-supportive beliefs scale. She then asked them to complete a second, parallel version of her scale. She hypothesised that if child molesters were intentionally trying to hide their beliefs on the first scale administration, then they would endorse more offence-supportive beliefs when attached to the fake lie detector. Yet despite child molesters indicating that they were quite convinced by the lie detector, the hypothesis was not supported; they did not endorse more offence-supportive beliefs in the lie detector condition, suggesting that they had not been disagreeing with the items simply to make a prosocial impression.

Gannon and Polaschek (2005) asked child molesters, non-sex offender controls, and male students, to complete a questionnaire about sex offence-supportive beliefs, and measured their response times for each item. Child molesters scored similarly to the control groups by disagreeing with beliefs. The response time measures were used to assess whether the child molesters were faking good. Research in personality has suggested that when faking good, participants tend to reject statements faster than when responding honestly, presumably because the shallow processing involved in faking is quicker than honest and reflective deep processing (Hsu, Santelli, & Hsu, 1989). However, our results showed that child molesters' response times could not be statistically differentiated from the other groups (who were presumably answering honestly), even after speed of motor responses and reading speed were controlled for. Taken together with the results from the fake lie detector study, this finding suggests that researchers should be cautious when interpreting low endorsements as being caused by impression management.

In summary, then, although sex offenders commonly discuss their own offences in ways that seem to indicate the existence of supportive knowledge content (e.g., Saradjian & Nobus, 2003; Hartley, 1998), it is often not possible to reliably differentiate sex offenders from others on questionnaire measures of their beliefs, and when such differences are found, still most sex offenders may disagree with most items. There are a number of possible explanations for this discrepancy. One may be that when sex offenders recount their own offences, they may be unwittingly giving us an inside view of how they originally perceived, interpreted, and encoded offence relevant information. When asked to assess formalised belief statements, however, the task of accessing their implicit guiding structures may be more effortful, incomplete, and inaccurate. People are notoriously inaccurate in their conscious reports of their guiding mental constructs (see Nisbett & Wilson, 1977), and the correspondence between explicit and implicit (i.e., automatic) measures of cognition is far from perfect even under circumstances in which participants are not strongly motivated to fake good (Dasgupta, McGhee, Greenwald, & Banaji, 2000).

Alternatively the difference may arise because discussing offending may function as a form of priming, activating schemas that are not chronically accessible. To our knowledge, no-one has conducted a questionnaire study in which sex offenders have been primed. Doing so would establish whether low endorsements on belief questionnaires are simply a function of a lack of chronicity in the implicated schemas.

A third explanation for the discrepancy in the research findings may be that when sex offenders recount their crimes, their accounts are riddled with post-offence excuses and justifications that *look* like they stem from distorted beliefs, when in fact they are situationally-specific attempts to avoid social opprobrium.

At present, there is no reliable way of distinguishing post-offence excuses and justifications from the products of offence-supportive theories, or schemas about the world. However, for future researchers hoping to investigate sex offenders' ITs, it may be helpful to categorise sex offender statements as theory-supportive only if they provide evidence of a pervasive way of viewing the world (e.g., "All women are spiteful"). Statements linked to specific victims may simply be situational impression management techniques or even a fairly objective perception of their victim (e.g., "My victim was spiteful": see Polaschek & Gannon, 2004).

Socio-Cognitive Processing

Like all social perceivers, sex offenders are thought to experience the common pitfalls associated with everyday social perception. Social information is processed in a way that supports and strengthens pre-existing beliefs; so attention is preferentially allocated to belief-supportive information, inconsistent information is ignored or minimised, and ambiguous information is interpreted as belief-supportive.

Up until now, we have used the term *cognitive processing* to refer mainly to the first stage of social information-processing: the initial perception, interpretation, and encoding of social information. However, researchers interested in the social skills of sex offenders have pointed out that there are probably intervening processing steps between initial interpretations and social behaviour. For example, in his information-processing model of social interaction, McFall (1990) argued that as well as effectively perceiving, interpreting, and comprehending social cues, individuals must also formulate effective responses for social interaction (*decision skills*), and implement these behaviourally (i.e., monitoring and modifying behaviour when appropriate; *enactment skills*).

We outline research on each of these three stages in the sections that follow, although it turns out that actual investigations of how sex offenders' beliefs affect their social processing are few, especially for child molesters.

Stage One: Perception, Interpretation, and Comprehension of Social Cues

Most studies have focused on this first stage of information processing, presuming that sex offending is partly a consequence of inaccurate interpretations of social cues based on pre-existing knowledge. For example, a rapist may misperceive the neutral, or somewhat negative cues of his date to indicate that she is playing a sexual game with him: that she really "wants it". Similarly, a child molester may misinterpret the innocent cuddling of a child to mean that he is interested in more sexual encounters. And perhaps most worryingly, sex offenders may ignore social cues from their victims indicating that they are not enjoying the experience or wish for it to stop (Ward et al., 1997). Being unable to "see" cues that contradict pre-existing schemas means that the beliefs derived from these schemas are never subject to refutation (Craig, 1990; Hartley, 1998), leaving sex offenders with the faulty and long-lasting impression that victims enjoyed and willingly participated in their own abuse.

A series of studies has investigated Stage One cognitive processing with men at risk of sexual aggression against women, focusing primarily upon whether these men can effectively perceive, interpret, or *decode* women's social cues and communications. Murphy, Coleman, and Haynes (1986) asked men from the community to watch video clips of a friendly man initiating social interaction with a woman. The woman's response to this initiation was either clearly hostile, assertive, seductive, or positive. Men who reported a higher likelihood of raping were also more likely to mistakenly label assertive communications as hostile but did not mistakenly label positive cues as sexually seductive.

Lipton, McDonel, and McFall (1987) investigated rapists' interpretations of men and women's communications using the Test of Reading Affective Cues (TRAC). This test consists of a number of scenarios, all depicting heterosexual interactions during a first date, or relatively long-standing relationship. The participant's task is to identify the affect of the target actor from five possible cues. Compared with violent and non-violent offender controls, rapists appeared to have particular difficulty when they had to identify the woman's negative affect, especially in the presumably more ambiguous first date situations. McDonel and McFall (1991) found similar results using the TRAC (for first date situations only) with students who indicated a high rape likelihood. However, neither study reported the nature of the mistakes made by men who misidentified the women's negative cues (Polaschek & Ward, 2002), and a later study conducted by Stahl and Sacco (1995) failed to identify any deficit for rapists who were asked to take part in a modified version of the task.

A more rigorous investigation of social perception was provided by Malamuth and Brown (1994) who asked men in the community to watch video clips of a male trying to strike up a social interaction with a woman in a bar. As with previous studies of this type, the woman's responses to this encounter were manipulated and participants were asked to interpret her social cues. The results showed that when the female actor emitted cues of rejection (either hostility or assertiveness), sexually aggressive males tended to over-perceive seduction. More interesting though was that these men also tended to interpret her positive cues as indicating hostility, yet failed to perceive overt hostility as hostile. Based on these findings, Malamuth and Brown proposed that sexually aggressive men hold a suspiciousness schema that leads them to perceive women's communications as untruthful and dishonest, regardless of the nature of those communications. This observation supports the IT research discussed earlier, showing that rapists frequently perceive women to be unknowable, hostile entities who are out to get the better of men (Beech et al., 2004; Polaschek & Gannon, 2004). Viewing all women's social interactions with suspicion will itself generate hostility towards them, further increasing the likelihood of sexual aggression (Ward et al., 1997).

Few studies have investigated the social perceptions and attributions of child molesters, and they have been limited to line drawings of facial affect or written descriptions of children's behaviours, rather than the more realistic video and audio media used to present adult stimuli. Hudson et al. (1993; study 2) asked child molesters and community controls to identify the emotions expressed in a series of child and adult drawings. The child molesters were less accurate at identifying facial affect than the controls, but this deficit was not specific to children. Unfortunately, because there was no offender control group, it is hard to know how these processing deficits compare to the general offender population.

Perhaps the best-known study of child molesters' processing was conducted by Stermac and Segal (1989), who had child molesters, rapists, and community controls read vignettes describing child sexual abuse. When asked to indicate the child's experience of and responsibility for the sexual abuse, child molesters were more likely to perceive that it was the child rather than the adult who was responsible for the abuse, and that the abuse was a positive experience for the child. Interestingly though, when the child in the vignette was depicted as crying during the abuse, child molesters' responses were similar to the controls. If social processing is driven by pre-existing schemas or ITs, then crying may be so schema-incongruent that it cannot be reinterpreted to fit.

Processing is often divided into two types: explicit or effortful or *intentional*, where resources are allocated deliberately and responses can be consciously altered to make a particular impression: and *automatic* or implicit processing, which is considered less prone to such influences because the processes run without conscious oversight and monitoring. In the social world, much of our information processing is actually automatised (Bargh & Chartrand, 1999). However, the studies reported above all used designs that allow for the use of intentional processing, and so may be subject to pressures to fake good.

We have recently attempted to circumvent the social desirability problem by examining automatic processing. Two studies (with intrafamilial offenders; Gannon, Wright, Beech, & Williams, 2005; and extrafamilial offenders, Gannon & Williams, 2005) asked child molesters and offender controls to read a vignette of a social interaction between a child and an adult and then complete a series of distracter questions. This vignette contained a number of ambiguous descriptions about a child's desires and intentions prior to and during sexual abuse (e.g., the child was described "letting out a small whimper" during the abuse). A little while later, participants were unexpectedly asked to recall all that they could about the vignette. We expected that the content of the memory recall would differ for child molesters and controls, reflecting the operation of different schemas on the perception, interpretion, and subsequent encoding of the ambiguous parts of the offence. However, neither child molesters nor controls recalled ambiguous content in an offence-supportive manner. Offenders did misremember the vignette in other ways, and approximately two-thirds of child molesters did not appear to realise exactly what the study was about when later questioned. In other words, despite using a design that was more likely to draw on automatic processing, these two studies of child molesters' processing also provide no evidence that child molesters' beliefs or schemas affect their social perception.

Another automatic processing study of child molesters (Mihailides, Devilly, and Ward, in press) has found more positive results. Using Greenwald's Implicit Association Test paradigm (IATS: Greenwald et al., 2002), they examined whether child molesters have more or stronger associations between children and sexual words (i.e., the *children as sexual beings* IT), losing control and sexual words (i.e., the *uncontrollability* IT), and entitlement and sexual words (i.e., the *entitlement* IT) than offender controls and non-offenders. Mihailides et al.

hypothesised that if child molesters really did, for example, hold beliefs that children are inherently sexual, then their response times for these stimuli should be faster. The results were supportive. Child molesters showed a stronger connection between children and sex-related constructs, and between uncontroll-ability and sex-related constructs than both control groups. Child molesters were also faster than non-offenders in responding to entitlement and sex-related constructs, but did not differ from the offender controls. The results of this study are the first to demonstrate experimentally that child molesters hold sets of associated concepts that are ultimately offence-supportive. Now, research needs to investigate *how* these associated beliefs distort social information.

Stage Two: The Formulation of Responses: Social Problem Solving

At the response formulation stage, McFall (1990) hypothesised that people generate options for responding, select the best, and then establish whether they know how to carry it out and whether it will work for them. Published research on these processes is scant. Grier (1988) gave rapists and community controls the Means–Ends Problem Solving Procedure (MEPS; Platt & Spivack, 1975), a measure that presents respondents with the beginning and end of a social story, and then asks them to indicate what happens in the middle: What does the character in the story actually *do* to solve the problem? The results showed that rapists did not differ from the control group in their ability to identify the responses necessary for the character in the story to solve the problem, in their identification of core obstacles to problem-solving success, or in the time it took them to complete this task. However, a close examination of each separate story showed that rapists identified significantly less problem-solving steps for the vignette depicting a man and woman who were settling an argument, a finding that should stimulate further research.

An unpublished study by Barbaree, Marshall, and Connor (1988; cited in Beech & Fisher, 2002, and Stermac, Segal, & Gillis, 1990) found that, although child molesters can generate responses to social problems, they are typically poor at identifying the *best* solution. One of the most recent studies examining sex offenders' social problem solving (Nezu, Nezu, Dudek, Peacock, & Stoll, 2003; see Chapter 6 of this volume), tested child molesters' problem solving *styles* using a 52-item Social Problem-Solving Inventory- Revised (SPSI-R; D'Zurilla, Nezu, & Maydeu-Olivares, 2002). They found that child molesters were characterised by dysfunctional problem solving styles such as a *negative problem orientation* (view-ing problem solving as threatening, impossible, and frustrating), *avoidance* of problem solving, and *impulsivity* or *carelessness* of problem solving. This volume attests to the pervasiveness of problem-solving deficits with offenders. Clearly, more research should examine whether these deficits are typical of sex offenders, whether they distinguish them from other offenders, and whether they respond to treatment.

Stage Three: The Enactment of Social Behaviour

McFall (1990) suggested that Stage Three was concerned with carrying out the chosen actions competently, including monitoring and modifying performance as feedback is detected. To some extent, managing behaviour requires a degree of mental control or self-regulation (Johnston et al., 1997). Research on the offence processes of sex offenders (Polaschek, Hudson, Ward, & Siegert, 2001) and Ward, Hudson, and Keenan's (1998) self-regulation model, both demonstrate that there are important differences in individual offenders' goals during the offence process. Different goals create corresponding differences in the enactment of offence-related behaviour. For example, offenders with *avoidance* goals seek to avoid sexual assault if at all possible. When they find themselves in a high risk situation, they will attempt to behave prosocially and at the same time keep mental control of a growing urge to offend. The considerable cognitive demands of such a situation are likely to disrupt both behaviour and monitoring, facilitating offending because the offender's resources are overwhelmed and he abandons self-control altogether as a result. On the other hand, some offenders have *approach* goals. They openly seek to offend, and may even take an offence expertise-based view of the enactment phase (Ward, 1999), deriving satisfaction from monitoring and adjusting offence behaviour to both maximise their own sexual enjoyment and to avoid victim disclosure and detection. Clearly this research shows both the diversity of social processes that can be accommodated in the McFall (1990) model, and also, how broad may be the range of social problem-solving deficits experienced by sex offenders.

In summary, then, the research on socio-cognitive *processing* contains a plethora of gaps and contradictions. The results for rapists appear to show that they do perceive, interpret, and comprehend social cues in a manner that confirms the operation of toxic schema about women and sex. However, we would clearly benefit from being able to determine which rapists are most prone to making mistakes, and the specific nature of these mistakes. For child molesters, the existing research is insufficient for firm conclusions. There is a particularly strong need for more studies that draw on automatic processing. With respect to the staged problem-solving model, research should go beyond simply investigating the sense an offender makes of a situation, to understanding how the subsequent steps also can strengthen schema by providing inaccurate but self-fulfilling feedback.

TREATMENT IMPLICATIONS

Rehabilitative interventions with any offender should always be informed by empirical evidence rather than theoretical intuition (McGuire, 2001; McGuire & Hatcher, 2001), and based on this review of the social cognition research, we have identified a number of issues worthy of consideration by treatment providers.

Treating the Source, Not the Product: Schema Therapy

In current sex offender treatment, efforts are often made to modify victim-specific beliefs, and to intervene with beliefs one statement at a time (Thornton & Shingler, 2001). However, for sex offenders with deeply entrenched offence-supportive theories, restructuring individual beliefs may simply lead to *subtyping* (i.e., storing a schema-contradictory belief as an exceptional case, so that it poses no threat to the schema's fundamental principles). Instead, therapists should be advised to restructure and challenge the *core* theory or schema that may be generating these individual belief statements (Beech & Mann, 2002; Mann & Beech, 2003). Effective ways of modifying these core beliefs may include: (1) education on the basic principles of schema-driven processing and how it can lead to inappropriate behaviour; (2) providing alternative ways of viewing social information that offenders have previously assumed to be offence-supportive; and (3) providing offenders with salient affective information (e.g., victim suffering) that challenges the underlying principles of their guiding theory (Drake et al., 2001).

A related treatment-process issue needs to be addressed in the education phase. The social cognitive perspective suggests that sex offenders with offence-supportive beliefs or theories are in a "Catch-22" position early in therapy. They must accept on trust that their theories may be wrong, or at least wrong more often than they think. Because schemas bias processing, they will continue to "see" information that appears to support their knowledge of the social world, and experience contrary information as absent. Until they are willing to experiment with checking the accuracy of such information against external sources, they will be as reluctant as we all are to discard core beliefs about how the world works.

Positive initial steps in the use of schema-focused treatment with sex offenders have already been implemented in the UK. Here, offenders characterised by high levels of offence-supportive attitudes have received this treatment (the *Extended Sex Offender Treatment Programme*) in addition to their standard sex offender treatment package (see Beech & Mann, 2002). In an evaluation of this approach using self-report measures, Thornton and Shingler (2001) found that sex offenders who showed little improvement in the standard programme reported greater improvement when their schemas were targeted in the extended programme. These offenders are hypothesised to hold deeply entrenched offence-supportive theories, so this finding is very encouraging, if preliminary. Future research efforts need to be targeted at assessing the relative gains of this type of extended therapy for different treatment recipients, and understanding the process by which offenders make such cognitive changes in treatment.

Progress is being made regarding interventions for sex offenders using information from research focusing on the initial stages in cognitive processing. Yet there is insufficient socio-cognitive empirical evidence at present to guide intervention into sex offenders' social problem solving and behavioural monitoring difficulties. Both areas are urgent priorities for research.

Cognitive Management of High Risk Situations

In relapse prevention terms, the social cognitive literature suggests that treatment providers should pay careful attention to the advice they give to men concerning the avoidance of unwanted thoughts (i.e., sex-related thoughts) in high risk situations. In brief, although the literature suggests that thought suppression can be successful, it is also prone to failure when cognitive resources are limited (which is especially likely to occur around the time of the offence process due to the disruptive effects of high affect, and sexual arousal; Johnston et al., 1997). It may be helpful for treatment providers to make sex offenders aware of the difficulties inherent in this task, and to educate sex offenders on those circumstances in which cognitive control may be most likely to fall short, especially the circumstances in which rebound effects are most likely. It is important that sex offenders are encouraged and motivated to discover appropriate inhibitory thoughts that can be used to take the place of unwanted thoughts with relative ease. With practice, the substitution of unwanted thoughts may become more automatic, and less liable to break down around times of high cognitive load (Johnston et al., 1997).

Does One Size Fit All?

Although the social cognitive approach is a useful perspective from which to view sex offending, like many other approaches it reveals the heterogeneity of offenders, and certainly does not offer standardized intervention solutions (Ingram & Kendall, 1986). Currently, many cognitive-behavioural rehabilitation programmes for sex offenders are mainly manual-based, targeting the same issues in all sex offenders and enabling treatment of large groups when resources are limited (Ward, Nathan, Drake, Lee, & Pathe, 2000). Faulty beliefs are thus identified as a problem and targeted for restructuring in *all* sex offenders, an approach that we believe may be problematic for two main reasons.

First, for child molesters, we have little robust scientific evidence to suggest that offence-supportive theories *do* affect their social information processing, despite the appeal of the idea. Offence-related statements heard in therapy may seem to be concrete evidence of distorted beliefs, but instead they may simply be normative impression management strategies. On the face of it, teaching all sex offenders about their offence-supportive beliefs may appear to provide a sensible safety net; it means that all sex offenders learn the dangers of biased information processing based on faulty beliefs, even if they don't actually hold them. However, it is important to keep in mind that there is no actual proof that offence-supportive beliefs exist prior to, or even during offending (Beech & Mann, 2002), and even if there was, their causal status would still be unknown. An implicit assumption of manualised treatment packages is that delivering unnecessary components to offenders is at worst a neutral experience for the recipient. Recently, Beech and Mann (2002) have argued that an offender's motivation to engage in treatment can easily be compromised by factors such as "labelling" by the therapist. We suggest that framing relatively normal accounting strategies as "thinking errors", or "distortions" may compromise the relationship between offender and therapist, undermining therapist credibility and offender motivation alike. We suggest that particular emphasis should be placed upon searching for more reliable indicators of distorted beliefs (i.e., statements indicating a more pervasive way of seeing the world outside of the offence episode), and identifying which offenders are most in need of intervention on this basis, before proceeding with that intervention.

The second area that needs attention is recognition that there are important differences between child molesters and rapists. Beech and Fisher (2002) have noted that, although current Sex Offender Treatment Programmes in UK prisons are designed to address both rapists' and child molesters' needs, the vast majority of treatment recipients are child molesters, a state of affairs that appears to be common worldwide (Polaschek, Ward, & Hudson, 1997). Implementing programmes for both rapists and child molesters that, in practice, deal mainly with child molesters may result in the neglect of some of rapists' treatment needs (Polaschek & King, 2002). Earlier in this chapter, we outlined certain areas of overlap between rapists and child molesters. For example, some offenders from both groups may be characterised by offence-supportive ITs of entitlement, or uncontrollability. But clearly, there are also differences between these groups. For example, rapists seem more likely to feel superior to women, a characteristic rarely noted in child molesters. In a group comprised mainly of child molesters, it may be hard to find enough "air time" to address rapists' theories, especially if the child sex offenders think they are irrelevant to them (see Polaschek & Gannon, 2004). One consequence may be to inadvertently reinforce feelings of superiority in rapists, who already are more vulnerable to thinking that they don't need to change or be in treatment (Polaschek & King, 2002).

CONCLUSIONS

Since the last extensive review of sex offender cognition from a social cognitive perspective (see Ward et al., 1997), encouraging progress has been made in both research and theory. First, researchers have begun to focus on both the content and organisation of stored knowledge, creating a more coherent understanding of how interconnected beliefs may function to bias social information processing (i.e., Beech et al. 2004; Polaschek & Gannon, 2004; Polaschek & Ward, 2002; Mann & Beech, 2003; Ward, 2000; Ward & Keenan, 1999). Second, researchers have started to move away from a reliance on naïve self-report methods of measuring offender cognition, and have begun to develop other, more sophisticated, less corruptible methods (e.g., actively measuring automatic information processing; Gannon & Polaschek, 2004; Gannon et al. 2005; Mihailides et al., 2004).

For rapists, the value of a cognitive processing approach is already evident, though plenty of work remains. For child molesters, there is little evidence at present of biases in social information processing. From these findings we could infer that distorted schemas simply are not in operation for these men. However we believe this is premature; it is likely that that other studies, using priming techniques and more realistic social stimuli may present more definitive results. Regarding research methodologies, we believe that it is important that researchers continue investigating the unconscious, automatic processing of sex offenders, since this behaviour most closely parallels real-world cognitive functioning.

Based on the research information to date, we argue that treatment providers should remain aware of the potential dangers of tarring all sex offenders with the same brush. There are likely to be as many differences as there are similarities between sex offenders in the type of offence-related knowledge held and how extensive and rigid this knowledge is. Future research needs to be conducted to direct us more clearly on this issue.

The social cognitive approach is only one piece in the fascinatingly complex jigsaw of sex offending but one that has great potential for increasing under-standing of sex offending as a highly malignant social problem. We hope that we have demonstrated convincingly the fruitfulness of the social cognitive approach over the past 15 years, and that researchers will be inspired to address the gaps in our current knowledge that still clearly need our attention.

REFERENCES

Abel, G. G., Becker, J. V., & Cunningham-Rathner, J. (1984). Complications, consent and cognitions in sex between children and adults. *International Journal of Law and Psychiatry, 7*, 189–203.

Abel, G. G., Gore, D. K., Holland, C. L., Camp, N., Becker, J. V., & Rathner, J. (1989). The measurement of the cognitive distortions of child molesters. *Annals of Sex Research, 2*, 135–153.

Anderson, C. A. & Bushman, B. J. (2002). Human aggression. *Annual Review of Psychology, 53*, 27–51.

Arkowitz, S. & Vess, J. (2003). An evaluation of the Bumby RAPE and MOLEST scales as measures of cognitive distortions with civilly committed sexual offenders. *Sexual Abuse: A Journal of Research and Treatment, 15*, 237–249.

Augoustinos, M. & Walker, I. (1995). *Social cognition: An integrated introduction.* London: Sage.

Barbaree, H. E., Marshall, W. L., & Connor, J. (1988). The social problem-solving of child molesters. Unpublished manuscript, Queen's University, Kingston, Ontario, Canada.

Bargh, J. A. (1982). Attention and automaticity in the processing of self-relevant information. *Journal of Personality and Social Psychology, 43*, 425–436.

Bargh, J. A. & Chartrand, T. L. (1999). The unbearable automaticity of being. *American Psychologist, 54*, 462–479.

Bargh, J. A., Lombardi, W. J., & Higgins, E. T. (1988). Automaticity of chronically accessible constructs in person × situation effects on person perception: It's just a matter of time. *Journal of Personality and Social Psychology, 55*, 599–605.

Bargh, J. A., Raymond, P., Pryor, J. B., & Strack, F. (1995). Attractiveness of the underling: An automatic power → sex association and its consequences for sexual harassment and aggression. *Journal of Personality and Social Psychology, 68*, 768–781.

Beck, A. T., Freeman, A., et al. (1990). *Cognitive therapy of personality disorders.* New York: Guildford Press.

Beech, A. R. (1998). A psychometric typology of child abusers. *International Journal of Offender Therapy and Comparative Criminology, 42*, 319–339.

Beech, A. R. & Fisher, D. (2002). The rehabilitation of child sex offenders. *Australian Psychologist, 37*, 206–214.

Beech, A. R., Fisher, D., & Ward, T. (2004). Sexual murderers' implicit theories. Manuscript submitted for publication.

Beech, A. R. & Mann, R. (2002). Recent developments in the assessment and treatment of sexual offenders. In J. McGuire (ed.) *Offender rehabilitation and treatment: Effective programmes and policies to reduce re-offending* (pp. 259–288). Chichester: John Wiley & Sons, Ltd.

Bodenhausen, G. V., Kramer, G. P., & Susser, K. (1994). Happiness and stereotypic thinking in social judgement. *Journal of Personality and Social Psychology, 66,* 621–632.

Bodenhausen, G. V., Sheppard, L. A., & Kramer, G. P. (1994). Negative affect and social judgement: The differential impact of anger and sadness. *European Journal of Social Psychology, 24,* 45–62.

Bumby, K. M. (1996). Assessing the cognitive distortions of child molesters and rapists: Developments and validation of the MOLEST and RAPE scales. *Sexual Abuse: A Journal of Research and Treatment, 8,* 37–54.

Burt, M. R. (1980). Cultural myths and supports for rape. *Journal of Personality and Social Psychology, 38,* 217–230.

Check, J. V. P. & Malamuth, N. M. (1983). Sex role stereotyping and reactions to depictions of stranger versus acquaintance rape. *Journal of Personality and Social Psychology, 45,* 344–356.

Check, J. V. P., Malamuth, N. M., Elias, B., & Barton, S. A. (1985). On hostile ground. *Psychology Today, 19,* 56–61.

Collins, A. & Loftus, E. (1975). A spreading-activation theory of semantic memory. *Psychological Review, 82,* 407–428.

Craig, M. E. (1990). Coercive sexuality in dating relationships: A situational model. *Clinical Psychology Review, 10,* 395–423.

Dasgupta, N., McGhee, D. E., Greenwald, A. G., & Banaji, M. (2000). Automatic preference for white Americans: Eliminating the familiarity explanation. *Journal of Experimental Social Psychology, 36,* 316–328.

Dodge, K. A. (1980). Social cognition and children's aggressive behaviour. *Child Development, 51,* 162–170.

Dodge, K. A. & Frame, C. L. (1982). Social cognitive biases and deficits in aggressive boys. *Child Development, 33,* 620–635.

Drake, C., Ward, T., Nathan, P, & Lee, J. (2001). Challenging the cognitive distortions of child molesters: An implicit theory approach. *Journal of Sexual Aggression, 7,* 25–40.

D'Zurilla, T. J., Nezu, A. M., & Maydeu-Olivares, A. (2002). *Social problem-solving inventory-revised (SPSI-R): Technical manual.* North Tonawanda, NY: Multi-Health Systems.

Elliott, M., Browne, K., D., & Kilcoyne, J. (1995). Child sexual abuse: What offenders tell us. *Child Abuse and Neglect, 19,* 579–594.

Fiske, S. T. & Taylor, S. E. (1991). *Social cognition.* 2nd edn. New York: McGraw-Hill.

Gannon, T. A. (2002). *Cognitive distortions in child sexual offenders: Fact or fiction?* Unpublished doctoral dissertation, University of Sussex, Brighton, UK.

Gannon, T. A. (in press). Increasing honest responding on cognitive distortions in child molesters: The bogus pipeline procedure. *Journal of Interpersonal Violence.*

Gannon, T. A. & Polaschek, D. L. L. (2005). Do child molesters deliberately fake good on cognitive distortion questionnaires? An information processing based investigation. *Sexual Abuse: A Journal of Research and Treatment, 17,* 183–200.

Gamon, T. A., & Williams, S. E. (2005). Distortions are in the eye of the beholder: What do child sexual offenders see? Manuscript in preparation.

Gannon, T. A., Wright, D. B., Beech, A. R., & Williams, S. E. (2005). Do child molesters hold distorted beliefs? What does their memory recall tell us? Manuscript submitted for publication.

Gilgun, J. F. & Connor, T. M. (1989). How perpetrators view child sexual abuse. *Social Work, 34,* 249–251.

Greenwald, A. G., Banaji, M. R., Rudman, L. A., Farnham, S. D., Nosek, B. A., & Mellott, D. S. (2002). A unified theory of implicit attitudes, stereotypes, self-esteem, and self-concept. *Psychological Review, 109,* 3–25.

Grier, P. E. (1988). Cognitive problem-solving skills in antisocial rapists. *Criminal Justice and Behavior*, *15*, 501–514.

Hamilton, M. & Yee, J. (1990). Rape knowledge and propensity to rape. *Journal of Research in Personality*, *24*, 111–122.

Hanson, R. K., Gizzarelli, R., & Scott, H. (1994). The attitudes of incest offenders: Sexual entitlement and acceptance of sex with children. *Criminal Justice and Behavior*, *21*, 187–202.

Harmon, G. A., Owens, R. G., & Dewey, M. E. (1995). Rapists' versus non-rapists' attitudes toward women: A British study. *International Journal of Offender Therapy and Comparative Criminology*, *35*, 269–275.

Hartley, C. C. (1998). How incest offenders overcome internal inhibitions through the use of cognitions and cognitive distortions. *Journal of Interpersonal Violence*, *13*, 25–39.

Hayashino, D. S., Wurtele, S. K., & Klebe, K. J. (1995). Child molesters: An examination of cognitive factors. *Journal of Interpersonal Violence*, *10*, 106–116.

Hewstone, M., Johnston, L., & Aird, P. (1992). Cognitive models of stereotype change (2): Perceptions of homogeneous and heterogeneous groups. *European Journal of Social Psychology*, *22*, 235–249.

Hollon, S. D. & Kriss, M. R. (1984). Cognitive factors in clinical research and practice. *Clinical Psychology Review*, *4*, 35–76.

Howells, K. (1979). Some meanings of children for pedophiles. In M. Cook & G. Wilson (eds), *Love and attraction*. Oxford: Pergamon press.

Hsu, L. M., Santelli, J., & Hsu, J. R. (1989). Faking detection validity and increment validity of response latencies to MMPI subtle and obvious items. *Journal of Personality Assessment*, *53*, 278–295.

Hudson, S. M., Marshall W. L., Wales D., McDonald E., Bakker L. W., & McLean, A. (1993). Emotional recognition skills of sex offenders. *Annals of Sex Research*, *6*, 199–211.

Ingram, R. E. & Kendall, P. C. (1986). Cognitive clinical psychology: Implications of an information processing perspective. In R. E. Ingram (ed.) *Information processing approaches to clinical psychology: Personality, psychopathology, and psychotherapy series* (pp. 4–22). San Diego, CA: Academic Press.

Johnston, L. & Hewstone, M. (1992). Cognitive models of stereotype change (3): Subtyping and the perceived typicality of disconfirming group members. *Journal of Experimental Social Psychology*, *28*, 360–386.

Johnston, L. & Ward, T. (1996). Social cognition and sexual offending: A theoretical framework. *Sexual Abuse: A Journal of Research and Treatment*, *8*, 55–80.

Johnston, L., Ward, T., & Hudson, S. M. (1997). Deviant sexual thoughts: Mental control and the treatment of sexual offenders. *The Journal of Sex Research*, *34*, 121–130.

Kardes, F. R. (1994). Consumer judgement and decision processes. In R. S. Wyer Jr. & T. K. Srull (eds) *Handbook of social cognition* (pp. vii–xii). 2nd edn. Hillsdale, NJ: Erlbaum.

Kendall, P. C. (1992). Healthy thinking. *Behavior Therapy*, *23*, 1–11.

Kindt, M. & Brosschot, J. F. (1997). Phobia-related cognitive bias for pictorial and linguistic stimuli. *Journal of Abnormal Psychology*, *106*, 644–648.

Kolton, D. J. C., Boer, A., & Boer, D. P. (2001). A revision of the Abel and Becker Cognition Scale for intellectually disabled sexual offenders. *Sexual Abuse: A Journal of Research and Treatment*, *13*, 217–219.

Langevin, R. (1991). A note on the problem of response set in measuring cognitive distortions. *Annals of Sex Research*, *4*, 287–292.

Lipton, D. N., McDonel, E. C., & McFall, R. M. (1987). Heterosocial perception in rapists. *Journal of Consulting and Clinical Psychology*, *55*, 17–21.

Macrae, C. N., Bodenhausen, G. V., Milne, A. B., & Jetten, J. (1994). Out of mind but back in sight: Stereotypes on the rebound. *Journal of Personality and Social Psychology*, *67*, 808–817.

Malamuth, N. M., & Brown, L. M. (1994). Sexually aggressive men's perceptions of women's communications: Testing three explanations. *Journal of Personality and Social Psychology*, 67, 699–712.

Malamuth, N. M., Heavey, C. L., & Linz, D. (1993). Predicting men's antisocial behavior against women: The interaction model of sexual aggression. In G. N. Hall, R. Hirshman, J. Graham, & M. Zaragoza (eds) *Sexual aggression: Issues in etiology, assessment, and treatment* (pp. 63–97). Washington, DC: Hemisphere.

Mann, R. E. & Beech, A. R. (2003). Cognitive distortions, schemas, and implicit theories. In T. Ward, D. R. Laws, & S. M. Hudson (eds) *Sexual deviance: Issues and controversies* (pp. 135–153). Thousand Oaks, CA: Sage.

Marshall, W. L., Anderson, D., & Fernandez, Y. M. (1999). *Cognitive behavioural treatment of sexual offenders*. Chichester: John Wiley & Sons, Ltd.

Marshall, W. L., Marshall, L. E., Sachdev, S., & Kruger, R. (2003). Distorted attitudes and perceptions, and their relationship with self-esteem and coping in child molesters. *Sexual Abuse: A Journal of Research and Treatment*, 15, 171–181.

Marolla, J. A. & Scully, D. (1986). Attitudes toward women, violence, and rape: A comparison of convicted rapists and other felons. *Deviant Behavior*, 7, 337–355.

McDonel, E. C. & McFall, R. M. (1991). Construct validity of two heterosocial perception skill measures for assessing rape proclivity. *Violence and Victims*, 6, 17–30.

McFall, R. M. (1990). The enhancement of social skills: An information processing analysis. In W. L. Marshall, D. R. Laws, & H. E. Barbaree (eds) *Handbook of sexual assault: Issues, theories and treatment of the offender* (pp. 311–330). New York: Plenum Press.

McGuire, J. (2001). What works in correctional intervention? Evidence and practical implications. In G. Bernfeld, A. W. Leschied, & D. P. Farrington (eds) *Offender rehabilitation in action: Implementing and evaluating effective programs* (pp. 25–43). Chichester: John Wiley & Sons, Ltd.

McGuire, J. & Hatcher, R. (2001). Offense-focused problem solving: Preliminary evaluation of a cognitive skills program. *Criminal Justice and Behavior*, 28, 564–587.

Mihailides, S., Devilly, G. J., & Ward, T. (2004). Implicit cognitive distortions and sexual offending. *Sexual Abuse: A Journal of Research and Treatment*, 16, 333–350.

Mosher, D. L. & Anderson, R. (1986). Macho personality, sexual aggression, and reactions to guided imagery of rape. *Journal of Research in Personality*, 20, 77–94.

Muehlenhard, C. L. (1988). Misinterpreted dating behaviors and the risk of date rape. *Journal of Social and Clinical Psychology*, 6, 20–37.

Murphy, W. D., Coleman, E. M., & Haynes, M. R. (1986). Factors related to coercive behavior in a nonclinical sample of males. *Violence and Victims*, 1, 255–278.

Neidigh, L. & Krop, H. (1992). Cognitive distortions among child sexual offenders. *Journal of Sex Education and Therapy*, 18, 208–215.

Neuberg, S. L. & Fiske, S. T. (1987). Motivational influences on impression formation: Outcome dependency, accuracy-driven attention and individuating processes. *Journal of Personality and Social Psychology*, 53, 431–444.

Nezu, C. M., Nezu, A. M., Dudek, J. A., Peacock, M., & Stoll, J. (2005). Social problem-solving correlates of sexual deviancy and aggression among adult child molesters. *Journal of Sexual Aggression*, 11, 27–36.

Nisbett, R. E. & Wilson, T. D. (1977). Telling more than we can know: Verbal reports on mental processes. *Psychological Review*, 84, 231–59.

Ostrom, T. M. (1994). Foreword. In R. S. Wyer Jr. & T. K. Srull (eds) *Handbook of social cognition* (pp. vii–xii). 2nd edn. Hillsdale, NJ: Erlbaum.

Pettit, G. S., Polaha, J. A., & Mize, J. (2001). Perceptual and attributional processes in aggression and conduct problems. In J. Hill & B. Maughhan (eds) *Conduct disorders in childhood and adolescence* (pp. 292-319). Cambridge: Cambridge University Press.

Platt, J. J. & Spivack, G. (1975). *Manual for the means–ends problem-solving procedure (MEPS): A measure of interpersonal cognitive problem-solving skill.* Philadelphia, PA: Hahnemann Community Mental Health/Mental Retardation Center.

Polaschek, D. L. L. & Gannon, T. A. (2004). The implicit theories of rapists: What convicted offenders tell us. *Sexual Abuse: A Journal of Research and Treatment, 16,* 299–315.

Polaschek, D. L. L., Hudson, S. M., Ward, T., & Siegert, R. J. (2001). Rapists' offence processes: A descriptive model. *Journal of Interpersonal Violence, 16,* 523–544.

Polaschek, D. L. L. & King, L. L. (2002). Rehabilitating rapists: Reconsidering the issues. *Australian Psychologist, 37,* 215–221.

Polaschek, D. L. L. & Ward, T. (2002). The implicit theories of potential rapists. What our questionnaires tell us. *Aggression and Violent Behavior, 7,* 385–406.

Polaschek, D. L. L., Ward, T., & Hudson, S. M. (1997). Rape and rapists: Theory and treatment. *Clinical Psychology Review, 17,* 117–144.

Pollock, N. L. & Hashmall, J. M. (1991).The excuses of child molesters. *Behavioral Sciences and the Law, 9,* 53–59.

Pryor, J. B. & Stoller, L. M. (1994). Sexual cognition processes in men high in likelihood to sexually harass. *Personality and Social Psychology Bulletin, 20,* 163–169.

Saradjian, A. & Nobus, D. (2003). Cognitive distortions of religious professionals who sexually abuse children. *Journal of Interpersonal violence, 18,* 905–923.

Sattem, L., Savells, J., & Murray, E. (1984). Sex role stereotypes and commitment to rape. *Sex Roles, 11,* 849–860.

Scully, D. (1988). Convicted rapists' perceptions of self and victim: Role taking and emotions. *Gender and Society, 2,* 200–213.

Scully, D. (1990). *Understanding sexual violence: A study of convicted rapists.* Boston: Unwin.

Scully, D. & Marolla, J. A. (1984). Convicted rapists' vocabularies of motive: Excuses and justifications. *Social Problems, 32,* 530–544.

Segal, Z. V. & Stermac, L. E. (1984). A measure of rapists' attitudes towards women. *International Journal of Law and Psychiatry, 7,* 437–440.

Segal, Z. V. & Stermac, L. E. (1990). The role of cognition in sexual assault. In W. L. Marshall, D. R. Laws, & H. E. Barbaree (eds) *Handbook of sexual assault: Issues, theories and treatment of the offender* (pp. 161–172). New York: Plenum Press.

Sherman, S. J., Judd, C. M., & Park, B. (1989). Social cognition. *Annual Review of Psychology, 40,* 281–326.

Skov, R. B. & Sherman, S. J. (1986). Information-gathering processes: Diagnosticity, hypothesis-confirmatory strategies, and perceived hypothesis confirmation. *Journal of Experimental Social Psychology, 22,* 93–121.

Spence, J. T., Helmreich, R., & Stapp, J. (1973). A short version of the Attitudes toward Women Scale (AWS). *Bulletin of the Psychonomic Society, 2,* 219–220.

Stahl, S. S. & Sacco, W. P. (1995). Heterosocial perception in child molesters and rapists. *Cognitive Therapy and Research, 19,* 695–706.

Stermac, L. E. & Segal, Z. V. (1989). Adult sexual contact with children: An examination of cognitive factors. *Behavior Therapy, 20,* 573–584.

Stermac, L. E., Segal, Z. V., & Gillis, R. (1990). Social and cultural factors in sexual assault. In W. L. Marshall, D. R. Laws, & H. E. Barbaree (eds) *Handbook of sexual assault: Issues, theories and treatment of the offender* (pp. 143–159). New York: Plenum Press.

Swaffer, T., Hollin, C., Beech, A., Beckett, R., & Fisher, D. (1999). An exploration of child sexual abusers' cognitive distortions with special reference to the role of anger. *The Journal of Sexual Aggression, 4,* 31–44.

Thornton, D. & Shingler, J. (2001). *Impact of schema level work on sexual offenders' cognitive distortions.* Paper presented at the 20th Annual Research and Treatment Conference for the Treatment of Sexual Abusers, San Antonio, USA.

Tiedens, L. Z. (2001). The effect of anger on the hostile inferences of aggressive and nonaggressive people: Specific emotions, cognitive processing, and chronic accessibility. *Motivation and Emotion, 25*, 233–251.

Tierney, D. W. & McCabe, M. P. (2001). An evaluation of self-report measures of cognitive distortions and empathy among Australian sex offenders. *Archives of Sexual Behavior, 30*, 495–519.

Ward, T. (1999). Competency and deficit models in the understanding and treatment of sexual offenders. *The Journal of Sex Research, 36*, 298–305.

Ward, T. (2000). Sexual offenders' cognitive distortions as implicit theories. *Aggression and Violent Behavior, 5*, 491–507.

Ward, T., Hudson, S. M., Johnston, L., & Marshall, W. L. (1997). Cognitive distortions in sex offenders: An integrative review. *Clinical Psychology Review, 17*, 479–507.

Ward, T., Hudson, S. M., & Keenan, T. (1998). A self-regulation model of the sexual offense process. *Sexual Abuse: A Journal of Research and Treatment, 10*, 141–157.

Ward, T. & Keenan, T. (1999). Child molesters' implicit theories. *Journal of Interpersonal Violence, 14*, 821–838.

Ward, T., Louden, K., Hudson, S. M., & Marshall, W. L. (1995). A description of the offense chain for child molesters. *Journal of Interpersonal Violence, 10*, 452–472.

Ward, T., Nathan, P., Drake, C. R., Lee, J. K. P., & Pathe, M. (2000). The role of formulation-based treatment for sexual offenders. *Behavior Change, 17*, 251–264.

Weber, R. & Crocker, J. (1983). Cognitive processes in the revision of stereotypic beliefs. *Journal of Personality and Social Psychology, 45*, 961–977.

Wegner, D. M. (1994). Ironic processes of mental control. *Psychological Review, 101*, 34–52.

Wellman, H. M. (1990). *The child's theory of mind*. Cambridge, MA: MIT Press.

Williams, J. M. G., Watts, F. N., MacLeod, C., & Mathews, A. (1997). *Cognitive psychology and emotional disorders*. 2nd edn. Chichester: John Wiley & Sons, Ltd.

Wilson, G. & Cox, D. (1983) *The child-lovers: A study of paedophiles in society*. London: Peter Owen Publishers.

Chapter 13

SOCIAL COGNITION IN PSYCHOPATHS: IMPLICATIONS FOR OFFENDER ASSESSMENT AND TREATMENT

RALPH C. SERIN[1] AND SHELLEY L. BROWN[2]

[1]*Carleton University, Canada*
[2]*Correctional Service Canada*

INTRODUCTION

> *I always know damn well I shouldn't do these things, that they're the same as what brought me to grief before. I haven't forgotten anything. It's just that when the time comes I don't think of anything else. I don't think of anything but what I want now. I don't think about what happened last time, or if I do it just doesn't matter. It would never stop me. (Grant, 1977, p. 60).*

Grant's description of a 22-year-old psychopath's insight into problem-solving is illuminating. Further, this particular individual's "intelligence was beyond question to anyone who knew him" (p. 60). Central, then, to the dilemma of understanding psychopaths' social interactions and problem solving is an apparent capacity for competency, but an inherent inability to convert that capacity into actions when required. It is this feature that has led to Cleckley's (1976) poignant title, *The Mask of Sanity*, in describing individuals who appear engaging and competent in social situations, but whose actions cause untold grief and harm to those who interact with them. The purpose of this chapter is to explore the contemporary conceptualization and measurement of psychopathy in offenders, with a view to understanding its implications for problem solving as it relates to criminality and violence.

Social Problem Solving and Offending: Evidence, Evaluation and Evolution.
Edited by Mary McMurran and James McGuire © 2005 John Wiley & Sons, Ltd.

SOCIAL COGNITION

Social cognition, by its very description, implies the manner in which individuals think about social situations. By extension, it is anticipated that such thought informs emotion and behaviour in a somewhat additive and symbiotic manner (Beck, 1976). Further, while not invariant, there should be some stability within individuals and to a much lesser degree, across specified situations. For our purposes, social cognition underlies social information processing and social problem solving. Of particular interest is whether certain diagnostic strategies (i.e., psychopathy as defined by high scores on the Psychopathy Checklist-Revised (PCL-R; Hare, 2003) can provide increased precision regarding understanding the interaction between social situations, thinking, and behaviour. While the published literature is quite limited in this particular area, other research may prove to be relevant to increase our understanding of psychopathy and social processing. The first area relates to an extensive literature on social-information processing and aggressive behaviour (Bettman, 1998; Crick & Dodge, 1994). The second area relates to behavioural and emotional self-regulation in psychopaths (Newman & Lorenz, 2002; Newman & Wallace, 1993).

PSYCHOPATHY

The past two decades have seen an unprecedented explosion in research and clinical interest regarding the importance of psychopathy in offender populations (correctional and forensic mental health). This interest was aptly summed by Robert Hare (1996) in his paper, *Psychopathy: A clinical construct whose time has come*. Much of this research has been driven by the Hare's development of the Psychopathy Checklist (Hare, 2003) which began as an operationalization of Cleckley's (1976) conceptualization of psychopathy and has proved to be the preferred measure of psychopathy in correctional and forensic applications. The utility of this construct continues to be the focus for important developments in risk appraisal strategies and civil commitment assessments (Douglas, Webster, Hart, Eaves, & Ogloff, 2001; Hare, 1999). New versions of assessment instruments for both adults (PCL-R; Hare 2003) and juveniles (PCL-YV; Forth, Kosson, & Hare, 2003) are now available. Also, research continues to ascertain the most parsimonious model of psychopathy (Hall, Benning, & Patrick, 2004) in order to inform theory and practice. A recent review of PsycINFO further illustrates the prominence of psychopathy as a research issue with offenders. The search word "psychopathy" yielded 2,259 hits, whereas the search words "violent offenders" yielded 410 hits and "violence and offenders" in combination yielded 1,652 hits.

A brief overview of the evolution of nomenclature and assessment strategies for psychopathy should prove helpful in situating the PCL-R. Disappointment in self-report inventories (e.g., the Minnesota Multiphasic Personality Inventory) spurred initial efforts by Hare and his colleagues to operationalize Cleckley's (1976) influential description of psychopathy. This led to the development of a 22-item checklist (Hare, 1980). Research spanning two decades and incorporating data from numerous countries has yielded several iterations of this checklist, the most recent being the Psychopathy Checklist-Revised, a 20-item scale where total scores reflect the extent to which an individual reflects the prototypical psychopath. Also, while there is some debate regarding the advantages of a two- or three-factor solution for the PCL-R (Cooke & Michie, 2001), the manual continues to support a two-factor solution as the gold standard, meaning high scores on both factors (Factor 1-interpersonal/affective, and Factor 2-social deviance) are required to meet diagnostic cutpoints. These factors are moderately highly inter-correlated ($r = 0.70$, $n = 9{,}016$; Hare, 2003). The preferred assessment strategy involves conducting semi-structured interviews and reviewing collateral information prior to scoring the scale, although some research applications have utilized file-only ratings from very comprehensive case files. Each item has a detailed description and exemplars for scoring. Clinical cutpoints of 30 or greater are recommended in the PCL-R manual to identify individuals high in psychopathy. Cut-offs of 25 have been recommended for UK populations (Cooke & Michie, 1999) and cut-offs of 25 or 26 have proved useful for prediction and other applied purposes in Britain and Sweden (Hare, 2003). This is consistent with taxon cut-offs reported by Harris, Rice, and Quinsey (1994). Training and credentialling are required for clinical use and the manual provides considerable empirical support regarding the reliability and validity of the PCL-R. In short, the PCL-R is a psychometrically robust scale for measuring the construct of psychopathy with correctional and forensic mental health populations. Most important, its utility for correctional and forensic applications has been its demonstrated predictive validity of general, violent and sexual recidivism in criminals and mentally disordered offenders (Hemphill & Hare, 2004).

Regarding nomenclature, there is increasing specificity assigned to the term psychopath. While the terms "sociopath", "psychopath", and "antisocial personality disorder" (APD) have been often used interchangeably, the empirical evidence is that psychopathy is a more specific diagnostic category (Hare, 2003). That is, the prevalence of APD in the general population is estimated at 3% in males (APA, 1994, p. 648), compared to 1% for psychopathy (Hare, 2003). The impact of this specificity is even more pronounced when considering offender populations. The proportion of offenders estimated to meet the diagnostic criteria for APD are 60–80% compared to 15–25% for psychopathy using the PCL-R. Prevalence rates vary according to gender - women have lower rates (Vitale & Newman, 2001) and security level - there is a greater proportion of psychopaths at maximum security (Wong, 1984). Some authors have used the term sociopathy to distinguish individuals whose childhood difficulties and social situation contributed to their criminality (Lykken, 1995), rather than specific personality or temperamental deficits as depicted by the use of the term psychopathy. Clearly, the terms are not equal, and the psychometric advantages of the PCL-R have made it the contemporary choice for measuring psychopathy in correctional and forensic applications. Further, it should be noted that 90% of all psychopaths meet the criteria for APD, whereas only 20% of offenders meeting the criteria for APD also reach the cutpoint on the PCL-R. In addition, the majority of offenders with APD fail to have the affective characteristics of Factor 1 (Hare, 2003).

Interestingly, research by Harris, Rice, and Quinsey (1994) found that child-hood variables were important in the identification of a psychopathy taxon, whereas adult criminal history variables were continuously distributed in their population of forensic patients and thus did not detect a taxon. Implicit in such findings regarding prevalence and taxonomy is that psychopathy is not synon-ymous with adult criminality. Further, the serendipitous findings that psycho-pathy significantly predicts recidivism in general offenders, sexual offenders, and mentally disordered offenders has greatly contributed to its appeal (Hare, 2003). Finally, with respect to violence, psychopathic offenders appear unique in numerous ways that have further stimulated risk assessment research. In particular, psychopathic offenders commit more violence in and out of prison, show more persistence of violence across the lifespan, and their use of violence is qualitatively different in that it is more instrumental or goal-directed. Again, this does not mean that psychopathy is synonymous with criminal violence, but that the vast majority of criminal psychopaths have committed a violent crime. Within most offender populations, however, the majority of violent offenders remain nonpsychopaths.

In summary, psychopathy as defined by the PCL-R is clearly a clinical construct of great importance in forensic research and practice (Harris, Skilling, & Rice, 2001). As a final cautionary note, researchers are beginning to observe that in spite of the utility of the PCL-R, individuals identified as psychopathic may still be etiologically heterogeneous such that both personality theory and specific bio-psychological mechanisms may assist in explaining different psycho-pathic syndromes (Brinkley, Newman, Widiger, & Lynham, 2004). Of particular interest, then, is whether other research regarding social processing and cogni-tion in psychopaths enhances our understanding of their criminal behaviour and informs more effective intervention and supervision strategies.

SOCIAL-INFORMATION PROCESSING

The developmental literature on aggression highlights several key points. First, aggressive behaviour that starts in early childhood is quite persistent over the lifespan (Moffit, 1993). Second, aggressive children display processing deficits that are both temperamental and cognitive which predispose them to misinter-pret situations and act in a pre-emptive and aggressive manner, even to non-hostile events (Crick & Dodge, 1994). The social-information processing model (Crick & Dodge, 1994) identifies key components that may be related to violent behaviour (see Figure 13.1 for a simplified version). These include the encoding of situational cues (e.g., increases in arousal and anger), the interpretation of these cues (e.g., causal attributions), goal clarification (e.g., hostile goal such as getting even), response generation (e.g., impoverished menu of options), and response selection (e.g., competency issue). Obviously these components are highly inter-dependent so that deficits or errors early in the process greatly influence subsequent choices in terms of response selection.

Several authors have suggested that a central component of these deficits is a set of cognitive schemas that lead the aggressive individual to be predisposed to

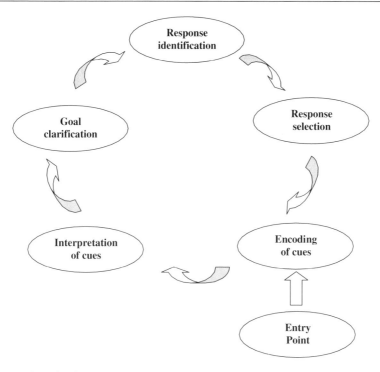

Figure 13.1   Social information processing model of aggression
Note: There is an interaction between components and an expected evaluation at each stage of the model.

interpret situations as hostile (Guerra & Slaby, 1990). Schemas are internal scripts that are related to behaviour (Novaco & Welsh, 1989). Research with juveniles has illustrated that behavioural expression of aggression is related to social-information processing biases and is present in males and females. Specifically, when faced with interpersonal problems, chronically aggressive children display processing biases and social cognitive deficits at every stage of the social information-processing model (Dodge & Schwartz, 1997). Aggressive children, when faced with real or hypothetical situations, tend to misinterpret social information, attribute hostility, select punitive and retaliatory goals, generate aggressive responses, and exhibit a preference for aggressive solutions. Dodge and Newman (1981) also creatively determined there was a developmental lag whereby aggressive youth requested less information prior to dealing with social interactions, in a manner similar to much younger children. Finally, aggressive children appear more likely to attend to less relevant social stimuli in determining the appropriate strategy for response. Clearly, these processing strategies serve to interfere with successful social interactions with others. In some respects, it is as if the cognitive schema of aggression pre-empts effective assimilation of relevant cues for effective social interactions and for resolving potential conflict situations. In a similar vein, Hare (2003) attributes psychopaths' use of violence to a hostile and self-centred view of the world.

For hostile individuals there has been an effort to utilize hypothetical vignettes as the stimulus set for appraising cognitive schemas (Dodge & Frame, 1982). Much of this research has utilized ambiguous situations to elicit the scripts presumed to be underlying the dysfunctional responding in chronically aggressive children. Vignettes have been employed in part because self-reports of dysfunctional behaviour are often influenced by response set and social desirability. Importantly, the methodology requires that the assessor provide a sufficient repertoire of salient situations to the offender in order for the vignettes to elicit responses.

The methodology entails the presentation of a situation (e.g., "You're at a party and someone walks by with a couple of drinks. They bump into you, spilling some drink in your lap. They continue to walk by and do not look your way."). Probing questions are then used to score or rate specific constructs such as hostile attributions, aggressive beliefs, problem definition, goal selection, anger, and empathy. Very preliminary data (Serin, Preston, Motiuk, & Brown, in preparation) from a violent offender programme indicates moderate inter-rater reliability ($r = 0.81$–0.93). Also, pilot research investigating the correlations with vignette-based constructs and psychological tests is encouraging. Vignette indices of anger correlated 0.38 with the Reactions to Provocation Scale (Novaco, 1994). Such a low correlation may be indicative that not all high-risk violent offenders have anger problems or that vignettes vary with respect to their valence for anger (Serin, 1991).

These hypothetical vignettes have also been applied to research with criminal psychopaths using the PCL-R as a diagnostic rating. Serin (1991) noted that incarcerated psychopaths report deficits in attributional biases and are more prone to instrumental aggression. Using similar vignette stimuli with a different offender sample, Vitale, Newman, Serin & Bolt (2005) reported that while Caucasian criminal psychopaths' attributions were related to hostility, explanations for African-American criminal psychopaths' attributions were depressogenic (a negative or pessimistic expectancy regarding the behaviour of others).

Perhaps the most exhaustive research investigating social cognition and psychopathy was conducted by Bettman (1998). This research was unique in several aspects. First, the sample was relatively large (n = 208) and highly criminal (mean number of convictions was 17.5). The majority (61.5%) were violent with 41.3% having at least two convictions for violent offences. Second, measures of social-information processing included a social problem-solving inventory utilizing open responses to four hypothetical situations; open and closed questions to reflect the components of the model described earlier; and self-report information regarding attitudes about violence. Third, various indices of violence were used from criminal history to self-reported number of physical fights. Fourth, psychopathy was measured using the PCL-R ($M = 21.2$, $SD = 8.9$). Finally, standardized indices of intelligence ($M = 96.2$), anger and social desirability were also available.

In general, the social information-processing model was supported. Offenders with encoding deficits were more likely to report a violent response preference. That is, offenders who reported a violent response indicated they would act immediately and would be angry. Notably these two encoding deficits were highly correlated ($r = 0.70$). Thus, appraisals of impulsivity (an intention to act immediately) and anger (high arousal component to a given situation) appear to be important aspects of a social information processing model of offender violence. Moreover, these two encoding deficits were significantly associated with frequency of self-reported fights ($r = 0.41$ and 0.57, respectively) and frequency of violent criminal convictions ($r = 0.31$ and 0.36, respectively). Finally, psychopathy was significantly associated with these encoding deficits ($r = 0.43$ and 0.52, respectively). Equally interesting is that psychopathy had no relation to offenders' likelihood of requesting additional information in order to respond to a particular situation. In combination, these findings provide additional empirical support for a social information processing model of understanding violence and the importance of the construct of criminal psychopathy in such a model.

In addition to encoding deficits, interpretative deficits also contributed to a preference for a violent response. Offenders who expressed a preference for a violent solution were more likely to blame the antagonist for causing the problem (causal attribution, $r = 0.49$) and more likely to attribute hostile intentions (hostile attribution, $r = 0.50$). Further, these two interpretative deficits were also significantly and positively correlated with self-reported fights ($r = 0.37$ and 0.49, respectively), violent convictions ($r = 0.22$ and 0.26, respectively), and psychopathy ($r = 0.25$ and 0.38, respectively). In addition, consistent with prior research, hostile attributions were correlated with psychopathy ($r = 0.38$).

The next component of the social information-processing model that Bettman (1998) considered was that of goal clarification. His hypothesis was that offenders with deficits would be more likely to select hostile goals. Consistent with the model, anger appraisals were significantly correlated with hostile goal selection ($r = 0.53$). Moreover, violent response preference was significantly correlated with hostile goals ($r = 0.67$).

According to the model, after appropriate goal identification, effective social problem solving necessitates the generation of alternatives. Bettman (1998) coded alternatives as being effective (e.g., withdrawal, negotiation) or hostile (e.g., threats, intimidation) and determined that those offenders who selected a violent response generated more hostile solutions ($r = 0.77$) and fewer effective solutions ($r = -0.37$). Furthermore, offenders estimated the anticipated efficacy of their given solution. Appraisal of response efficacy was significantly associated with choice of a violent response ($r = 0.76$). Notably, violence efficacy was also significantly correlated with psychopathy ($r = 0.40$), meaning that psychopaths were more likely to perceive a violent response as being more effective.

In sum, correlation analyses suggest that the components of the social information processing model are highly associated with each other and with a final response selection of violence. Notably, psychopathy was significantly related to each stage of the model, highlighting its importance in understanding social problem solving, particularly for situations that potentially lead to violence.

Importantly, Bettman (1998) also investigated the contribution of all stages of the model in predicting violent response selection. In combination, the social information processing variables (violent beliefs, encoding of cues, interpretation of cues, goal clarification, response identification and response selection) yielded an adjusted $R^2 = 0.72$ ($F (9,198) = 60.91$, $p < 0.001$). In addition, the model of social cognition accounts for a significant amount of the variance in predicting self-reported physical fights (adjusted $R^2 = 0.53$) and postdicting number of prior violent convictions, excluding robbery (adjusted $R^2 = 0.21$, F $(7,200) = 8.60$, p <0.01). Finally, given that antagonistic processing is associated with psychopathy, it was of interest to determine the extent to which social cognition might predict psychopathy. The linear combination of social processing distortions accounts for only 33.6% of the variance in the total PCL-R score. While the broad stages of the model were predictive, some aspects such as the endorsement of violence as the best solution were not. Overall, these findings suggest that psychopathy is associated with social processing deficits relating to violence and that specific cognitions account for differences in psychopathy ratings. Equally important, psychopathy is not synonymous with social information-processing deficits and its measurement includes elements beyond the model.

BEHAVIOURAL AND EMOTIONAL SELF-REGULATION

Increasingly, the experimental literature is indicating that the psychopath's inability to achieve stable, prosocial adjustment may involve information-processing deficits rather than simple deficits in morality or motivation. The research most germane to this perspective has been that of Joseph Newman and his colleagues (Newman, 1998; Newman & Lorenz, 2002; Newman & Wallace, 1993). The advantages of considering this applied laboratory research to the clinical syndrome of psychopathy are multiple. First, it is positivistic, an emerging theme informing correctional practice (McGuire, 2004). Second, it provides potential entry points for engaging psychopathic individuals in behaviour change by providing an alternative explanation for their response choices. Third, this experimental research addresses the processes underlying psychopaths' behaviour, with the potential of ameliorating pejorative views about their motivations.

A specific conclusion of Newman's research is that, relative to nonpsychopaths, psychopaths appear to be less adept at allocating processing resources to secondary tasks while engaged in goal-directed behaviour. These secondary tasks are integral to problem-solving efficacy and may include aspects of self-monitoring, connecting the current situation with past experiences and outcomes, and decoding cognitive and emotional contextual cues. The result is a specific deficit in self-regulation attributable to impaired response modulation (Newman, 1998). Much of Newman's experimental research in this area has been in the development of laboratory tasks to determine the parameters that influence response modulation in psychopaths.

Early work by Patterson and Newman (1993) translated the response modulation concept into cognitive/attentional terms which bears directly on social problem-solving efficacy. They suggested that response modulation deficits imply a failure to interrupt maladaptive approach behaviour, so that processing of secondary information or contextual cues fail to influence ongoing, goal-directed behaviour (Wallace, Vitale, & Newman, 1999). These researchers also suggest that different pathways may lead to such deficiencies. As such, "deficient response modulation short-circuits the processing that would otherwise inform (i.e., provide perspective on) ongoing behaviour" (Newman & Lorenz, 2002). Individuals can show cross-situational deficits or emotionally significant cues can increase non-specific arousal which exacerbates the dominant response preoccupation. Accordingly, they proposed that this behavioural self-regulation deficit also informs emotional processing strategies in psychopaths. This is consistent with Cleckley (1976) who noted:

> My concept of the psychopath's functioning postulates a selective defect or elimination which prevents important components of normal experience from being integrated into the whole human reaction, particularly an elimination or attenuation of those strong affective components that ordinarily arise in major personal and social issues. (p. 374)

As noted earlier, a hallmark of psychopaths is a callous and unemotional interpersonal style. Clinical descriptions and empirical evidence support this position (Hare, 2003). Affective characteristics that have been used to describe psychopaths include shallowness and profound lack of remorse or empathy. Of interest is whether applied research can explain these deficits in ways other than amorality and egocentrism. Derived primarily from physiological measures (e.g., electromyograph, event-related potentials, and blink-startle responses), researchers are increasingly demonstrating that psychopaths not only process emotional stimuli differently than controls but that they evidence emotional processing deficits that are both linguistic (Williamson, Harpur & Hare, 1991) and non-linguistic (Patrick 2001) in nature. Moreover, these deficits have been mainly related to elevations in Factor 1 scores.

For instance, in contrast to nonpsychopaths, reaction times for psychopaths are slower to negative affect words, in particular the callous, unemotional traits. Further, startle reflex to emotional slides was differentiated in controls but absent in psychopaths (Patrick, Bradley, & Lang, 1993). More recently, offenders high on the PCL-R emotional-interpersonal factor (Factor 1) showed diminished skin conductance to both pleasant and unpleasant sounds (Verona, Patrick, Curtin, Bradley, & Lang, 2004). As well, a Psychopathy Screening Device employed with children demonstrated that the ability to recognize sad and fearful expressions (but not happy, angry, disgusted or surprised expressions) was inversely related to level of affective-interpersonal disturbance (Blair, 1999). Given that emotion involves readiness for adaptive action and that psychopathy is highlighted by affective deficits, an understanding of the manner in which psychopaths process emotional content could have significant implications for developing treatment strategies.

Obviously, emotional processing will be influenced by experience. Scherer (1994) provides a stimulus-evaluation-check five-stage model for understanding how a person's behavioural reaction to a stimulus context develops with experience. He proposes that emotions act as an interface, mediating between environmental input and behavioural output. As in effective problem solving, when working well, emotions facilitate the generation and implementation of adaptive responses. Emotional and cognitive processing are then inextricably linked. Albeit at times an automatic process, emotions signal the need for *controlled* processing which involves the deliberate monitoring, evaluation and correction of behavioural responses. Automatic processing, perhaps prompted by intense emotions, results in a breakdown in self-regulation in a manner analogous to psychopaths' failure to attend to secondary cues when invested in goal-directed behaviour.

Two issues are crucial to the suggestion that psychopaths have cognitive and emotional processing deficits that increase the probability of criminal and/or violent behavioural responses. First, are there strategies that can ameliorate these deficits? Second, what are the parameters that might exacerbate psychopaths' apparent paucity in affective processing? With respect to strategies to improve psychopaths' performance, experimental research has shown that psychopaths can mimic the more effective response modulation of nonpsychopaths when the punishers are distinct (i.e., monetary) or they are forced to stop and reflect on changing contingencies (Newman & Kosson, 1986). Hence, the passive-avoidance deficits noted in psychopaths are predictable and possibly preventable, under certain conditions. In terms of emotional processing, using the lexical task (using emotion cues to facilitate word recognition), Lorenz and Newman (2002) demonstrated that emotional cues appear to activate associate networks that aid performance in controls, but such cues have little effect on the performance of psychopaths. They conclude that psychopaths display normal emotional responses when they are instructed to attend to emotional stimuli (e.g., pictures) and when emotion stimuli are relevant to their dominant response set (e.g., avoidance of punishment). Further, it appears that psychopaths, unlike controls, are impaired when emotional processing depends on automatic shifts of attention from the dominant response set to other less relevant aspects of the associative network.

We can now use these findings to provide an example of their impact on criminal and violent behaviour. Consider the situation of an assault in a bar. Bill is drinking with a woman named Sarah he recently met and with whom he hopes to have sex (she has captured his attention and he has a goal). Sarah is flirting and getting increasingly drunk when her friend, Lisa arrives. Following some discussion Bill suggests he take Sarah home. Lisa makes disparaging remarks about Bill. Sarah subsequently rebukes his suggestion and they each begin yelling at each other. Bill's response is to preemptively assault the friend, Lisa. Sarah starts yelling at Bill and rejects his proposal that they go back to his place. In fact, Sarah is horrified that her friend has been hurt and she threatens to call the police. Bill starts arguing with Sarah and the bartender calls the police. Within this context, Bill fails: (1) to recognize Sarah may not wish to have sex with him after assaulting her friend: (2) to attend to the emotional cues; and (3) to modify his response as the incident evolves. Furthermore, he failed to achieve his goal. Improved response modulation and social problem solving cannot guarantee success, but impoverished skills certainly enhance the likelihood of failure.

IMPLICATIONS

Despite relative enthusiasm for cognitive-behavioural programming for offenders that target problem solving (e.g., Reasoning and Rehabilitation, Cognitive Skills), published effect sizes remain quite modest (Van Voorhis, et al., 2003). Recently it has been suggested that a failure to attend to fidelity and integrity

issues may attenuate treatment gains (Bernfeld, 2001). This is clearly a consideration, but our review suggests that it also is important to understand the
mechanisms underlying offender change and to incorporate more specialized
assessments of such change, if treatment gains are to be maximized.

In particular, if criminal justice settings are to benefit from laboratory-based
knowledge, appropriate assessment strategies must be utilized. For instance, it is
quite unlikely that using a self-report anger scale will yield the same discrimination among offenders as do hypothetical vignettes and computerized tasks. That
is, such a scale will not provide the same understanding about offenders'
processing deficits. Given that the social information-processing model is hierarchical with deficits at one stage informing performance at another stage, each of
these stages may be a viable entry point for intervention.

Additionally, much work is required to develop valid competency measures of
cognitive processing gains in offenders. For these reasons, despite the advances
in terms of the measurement of psychopathy, we believe further progress will be
impeded without the application of laboratory-based research to clinical issues.
Accordingly, measures that are not solely self-report and that relate to the
mechanisms underlying these specific cognitive and problem-solving deficits
are required to augment treatment programmes, especially those intended for
psychopaths.

While the "What Works" agenda has been relatively positivistic (McGuire,
2004), there remains serious debate regarding the treatability of psychopaths
(Rice, Harris, & Cormier, 1992; Hare, 2003). In addition to concerns regarding
treatment readiness (Serin, 1995) and high attrition rates (Ogloff, Wong &
Greenwood, 1990), it seems that high Factor 1 scores are inversely related to
outcome (Hare, 2003). Hare's (2003) view is that current programming does not
address the manipulative elements of psychopathy and that staff are lulled into
believing gains have occurred when they have not. Other reviewers (Salekin,
2002) argue that the issue of treatment effectiveness remains an empirical issue,
with much of the published research failing to meet methodological or clinical
rigour. It is difficult to disentangle the findings when early studies failed to use
the PCL-R or failed to provide contemporary programming. Our review suggests
the false negative rate with respect to treatment performance for psychopaths
might be reduced through the use of vignettes, laboratory measures or more
specific behavioural competency measures.

The social information-processing literature on psychopathy (Bettman, 1998)
suggests a kind of cognitive short-circuit that predisposes psychopaths to violent
solutions, even to non-violent situations. They react more quickly and with
greater levels of arousal (i.e., anger) to situations and fail to consider alternative
solutions. It has been suggested that social information processing is moderated
by psychopathy to result in violent behaviour (Bettman, personal communication, 24 June 2004). Moreover, Newman's work suggests that psychopaths'
response modulation deficit is autonomic and greatly impedes their ability (or
inclination) to attend to secondary and relevant contextual cues. Consequently,
treatment targets must focus on improving processing abilities. Interventions that
attempt to modify emotions such as empathy would appear less viable but for
different reasons than previously considered. Perhaps the inability to assimilate

the views of others into their dominant response set rather than a general callous and uncaring attitude towards others is more useful in understanding the underlying cause of their empathic deficits. For instance, research with sex offenders indicates that many have offence-specific empathy deficits, but not a generalized incompetence regarding empathy (Marshall, Anderson, & Fernandez, 1999). Perhaps, then, treatment strategies for psychopaths should focus on information-processing deficits rather than empathy training.

The application of the experimental literature is central to increasing our understanding of the processes underlying psychopaths' maladaptive and criminal behaviour. If we adopt the perspective that psychopaths are deficient in discernible ways regarding cognitive and emotion processing that leads to predictable difficulties in response modulation and problem-solving, then we are perhaps making progress. Additional gains could also be realized if psychopaths are viewed as high risk/high need offenders (Andrews & Bonta, 2003; Simourd & Hoge, 2000).

The risk/need approach is founded on a social psychological model of behaviour change (Andrews & Bonta, 2003; McGuire, 2004) that focuses on individual differences rather than social and economic factors in understanding crime (McGuire, 2004). The risk/need approach has several key tenets. Foremost, needs are considered risk factors. Needs that increase the likelihood of future criminal behaviour are termed criminogenic. Criminogenic needs are related to risk such that higher need offenders are higher risk for continued crime (i.e., recidivism). Accordingly, higher risk and higher need offenders (e.g., psychopaths) require more intensive intervention, and equally important, lower risk offenders warrant minimal intervention (i.e., the risk principle). Intervention, or appropriate human service delivery (Andrews & Bonta, 2003), should target criminogenic needs (i.e., the need principle) and be delivered in a manner that is responsive to offenders' learning styles (i.e., the responsivity principle). Thus, treatment interventions specifically tailored to be responsive to the learning styles of psychopaths should in theory, prove most promising (Gendreau, Goggin, & Smith, 2002; Serin, 1995). Additionally, Simourd and Hoge (2000) have demonstrated that psychopaths do in fact exhibit higher levels of need compared to nonpsychopaths. It is plausible that the personological model (i.e., psychopathy) informs understanding about the processes underlying problematic behaviour, whereas the risk/need model may inform contextual aspects regarding the antecedents to crime. Additionally, both approaches can inform how treatment should be tailored for criminal psychopaths in order to maximize responsivity.

A final question is whether because of these information-processing deficits that psychopaths desist from crime in ways similar to nonpsychopaths. The age–crime curve shows that as age increases from approximately 20 years onwards there is a steady and substantial decline in the proportion of the population committing crimes. Cross-sectional research regarding psychopathy and age, however, suggests that the crime–age function is not fully replicated (Harpur & Hare, 1994). Importantly, longitudinal studies are required to determine more fully whether psychopaths have unique trajectories of crime desistance, which would inform offender re-entry and supervision strategies.

As well, the evidence is that desistance is more like a journey than a sudden event. McGuire (2004) notes that similar to pathways into offending, it involves changes of speed and reversals of direction, as events in individuals' lives unevenly evolve. Implicit in this review on desistance is that psychopathy may be a factor that differentially influences desistance, yielding discrete pathways for desistance for nonpsychopaths and psychopaths.

CONCLUSION

This review of the cognitive processing of criminal psychopaths reveals that a stage model appears useful in explaining their use of violence and that a specific response modulation deficit is apparent. Notable is that these conclusions have been drawn from clinical and applied research and reflect diverse assessment methodologies (i.e., clinical ratings, hypothetical vignettes, and laboratory measures). These conclusions also highlight the importance of criminal psychopathy as a construct and not simply a risk factor. The evidence suggests that psychopaths display specific deficits in attending to and utilizing cognitive and emotional information to deal with interpersonal situations. This evidence is both clinical and experimental, providing explanations for psychopaths' demonstrated deficits.

Simply providing additional treatment (i.e., more intensive or longer duration) fails to target the relevant mechanisms that might lead to behaviour change and improved self-regulation. We are reminded of the difficulty in providing intervention to individuals with fetal alcohol syndrome or learning disability, and where poor treatment outcome is no longer viewed as solely a motivational issue. It remains to be seen whether more specific intervention can ameliorate psychopaths' criminal and violent responses to social situations, but interventions that fail to recognize these identifiable deficits appear unlikely to advance the field.

REFERENCES

American Psychiatric Association (1994). *Diagnostic and statistical manual of mental disorders.* 4th edn. Washington, DC: American Psychiatric Association.

Andrews, D. A. & Bonta, J. (2003). *The psychology of criminal conduct.* 3rd edn. Cincinnati, OH: Anderson Publishing.

Beck, A. T. (1976). *Cognitive therapy and the emotional disorders.* New York: International Universities Press.

Bernfeld, G. A. (2001). The struggle for treatment integrity in a "dis-integrated" service delivery system. In G. A. Bernfeld, D. P. Farrington and A. W. Leshied (eds) *Offender rehabilitation in practice: Implementing and evaluating effective programs.* Chichester: John Wiley & Sons, Ltd.

Bettman, M. D. (1998). Social cognition, criminal violence, and psychopathy. Unpublished thesis, Queen's University, Kingston.

Blair, R. J. R. (1999). Responsiveness to distress cues in the child with psychopathic tendencies. *Personality and Individual Differences, 27,* 135–145.

Brinkley, C. A., Newman, J. P., Widiger, T. A., & Lynham, D. R. (2004). Two approaches to parsing the heterogeneity of psychopathy. *Clinical Psychology: Science & Practice, 11,* 69–94.

Cleckley, H. (1976). *The mask of insanity,* 5th edn. St. Louis, MO: Mosby.

Cooke, D. J. & Michie, C. (1999). Psychopathy across cultures: North American and Scotland compared. *Journal of Abnormal Psychology, 108,* 58–68.

Cooke, D. J. & Michie, C. (2001). Refining the construct of psychopathy: Towards a hierarchical model. *Psychological Assessment, 13,* 171–188.

Crick, N. R. & Dodge, K. A. (1994). A review and reformulation of social information-processing mechanisms in children's social adjustment. *Psychological Bulletin, 1,* 74–101.

Dodge, K. A. & Frame, C. L. (1982). Social-cognitive biases and deficits in aggressive boys. *Child Development, 53,* 620–635.

Dodge, K. A. & Newman, J. P. (1981). Biased decision making processes in aggressive boys. *Journal of Abnormal Psychology, 90,* 375–379.

Dodge, K. A. & Schwartz, D. (1997). Social information processing mechanisms in aggressive behavior. In D. M. Stoff, J. Breiling, & J. D. Maser (eds) *Handbook of antisocial behavior* (pp. 171–180). New York: John Wiley & Sons.

Douglas, K. S., Webster, C. D., Hart, S. D., Eaves, D., & Ogloff, J. R. P. (eds) (2001). *HCR-20 violence risk management companion guide.* Mental Health, Law and Policy Institute, Simon Fraser University, Burnary, BC, Canada.

Forth, A. E., Kosson, D., & Hare, R. D. (2003). *The Hare psychopathy checklist: Youth version.* Toronto: Multi-Health Systems.

Gendreau, P., Goggin, C., & Smith, P. (2002). Is the PCL-R really the "unparalleled" measure of offender risk? A lesson in knowledge cumulation. *Criminal Justice and Behavior, 29,* 397–426.

Grant, V. W. (1977). *The menacing stranger: A primer on the psychopath.* Oceanside, NY: Dabor Science Publications.

Guerra, N. G. & Slaby, R. G. (1990). Cognitive mediators of aggression in adolescent offenders: Intervention. *Developmental Psychology, 26,* 269–277.

Hall, J. R., Benning, S. D., & Patrick, C. J. (2004). Criterion-related validity of the three-factor model of psychopathy: Personality, behavior, and adaptive functioning. *Assessment, 11,* 4–16.

Hare, R. D. (1980). A research scale for the assessment of psychopathy in criminal populations. *Personality and Individual Differences, 1,* 111–117.

Hare, R. D. (1996). Psychopathy: A clinical construct whose time has come. *Criminal Justice and Behavior, 21,* 25–54.

Hare, R. D. (1999). Psychopathy as a risk factor for violence. *Psychiatric Quarterly, 70,* 181–197.

Hare, R. D. (2003). *The Hare psychopathy checklist-revised,* 2nd edn. Toronto: Multi-Health Systems.

Harpur, T. J. & Hare, R. D. (1994). The assessment of psychopathy as a function of age. *Journal of Abnormal Psychology, 103,* 604–609.

Harris, G. T., Rice, M. E., & Quinsey, V. L. (1994). Psychopathy as a taxon: Evidence that psychopaths are a discrete class. *Journal of Consulting and Clinical Psychology, 62,* 387–397.

Harris, G. T., Skilling, T. A., & Rice, M. E. (2001). The construct of psychopathy. In M. Tonry & N. Morris (eds) *Crime and justice: an annual review of research* (pp. 197–264). Chicago: University of Chicago Press.

Hemphill, J. F. & Hare, R. D. (2004). Some misconceptions about the Hare PCL-R and risk assessment: A reply to Gendreau, Goggin, and Smith. *Criminal Justice and Behavior, 31,* 203–243.

Lorenz, A. R. & Newman, J. P. (2002). Deficient response modulation and emotion processing in low-anxious Caucasian psychopathic offenders: Results from a lexical decision task. *Emotion, 2*, 91–104.

Lykken, D. T. (1995). *The antisocial personalities*. Hillsdale, NJ: Erlbaum.

Marshall, W. L., Anderson, D., & Fernandez, Y. M. (1999). *Cognitive behavioural treatment of sexual offenders*. Chichester: John Wiley & Sons, Ltd.

McGuire, J. (2004). *Understanding psychology and crime*: Perspecties on theory and action Buckingham: McGraw-Hill/Open University Press.

Moffit, T. E. (1993). Adolescence-limited and life-course-persistent antisocial behavior: A developmental taxonomy. *Psychological Review, 100*, 674–701.

Newman, J. P. (1998). Psychopathic behavior: An information processing perspective. In D. J. Cooke et al. (eds) *Psychopathy: Theory, research, and implications for society* (pp. 81–104). Dordrecht: Kluwer Academic Publishers.

Newman, J. P. & Kosson, D. S. (1986). Passive avoidance learning in psychopathic and non-psychopathic offenders. *Journal of Abnormal Psychology, 95*, 257–263.

Newman, J. P. & Lorenz, A. R. (2002). Response modulation and emotion processing: Implications for psychopathy and other dysregulatory psychopathology. In R. J. Davidson, K. Scherer, & H. H. Goldmith (eds) *Handbook of affective sciences* (pp. 1043–1067). Oxford: Oxford University Press.

Newman, J. P. & Wallace, J. F. (1993). Psychopathy and cognition. In P. C. Kendall & K. S. Dobson (eds) *Psychopathology and cognition* (pp. 293–349). New York: Academic Press.

Novaco, R. W. (1994). Anger as a risk factor for violence among the mentally disordered. In J. Monahan and H. J. Steadman (eds) *Violence and mental disorder: Developments in risk assessment* (pp. 21–59). Chicago: University of Chicago Press.

Novaco, R. W. & Welsh, W. N. (1989). Anger disturbances: Cognitive mediation and clinical prescriptions. In K. Howells and C. R. Hollin (eds) *Clinical approaches to violence* (pp. 39–60). Chichester: John Wiley & Sons Ltd.

Ogloff, J. R. P., Wong, S., & Greenwood, A. (1990). Treating criminal psychopaths in a therapeutic community program. *Behavioral Sciences and the Law, 8*, 181–190.

Patrick, C. J. (2001). Emotional processes in psychopathy. In A. Raine & J. Sanmartin (eds) *Violence and psychopathy* (pp. 57–78). New York: Academic Press.

Patrick, C. J., Bradley, M. M., & Lang, P. J. (1993). Emotion in the criminal psychopath: Startle reflex modulation. *Journal of Abnormal Psychology, 102*, 82–92.

Patterson, C. J. & Newman, J. P. (1993). Reflectivity and learning from aversive events: Toward a psychological mechanism for the syndromes of disinhibition. *Psychological Review, 100*, 716–736.

Rice, M. E., Harris, G. T., & Cormier, C. A. (1992). An evaluation of a maximum-security therapeutic community for psychopaths and other mentally disordered offenders. *Law and Human Behavior, 16*, 399–412.

Salekin, R. (2002). Psychopathy and therapeutic pessimism. Clinical lore or clinical reality? *Clinical Psychology Review, 22*, 79–112.

Scherer, K. R. (1994). Emotion serves to decouple stimulus and response. In P. Ekman & R. J. Davidson (eds) *The nature of emotion: Fundamental questions*. New York: Oxford University Press.

Serin, R. C. (1991). Psychopathy and violence in criminals. *Journal of Interpersonal Violence, 6*, 423–431.

Serin, R. C. (1995). Treatment responsivity in criminal psychopaths. *Forum on Corrections Research, 7*, 23–26.

Serin, R. C. & Preston, D. L. (2001). Designing, implementing and managing treatment programs for violent offenders. In G. A. Bernfeld, D. P. Farrington, and A. W. Leischied (eds) *Offender rehabilitation in practice: Implementing and evaluating effective programs* (pp. 205–221). Chichester: John Wiley & Sons, Ltd.

Serin, R. C., Preston, D.L., Motiuk, L. L., & Brown, S. L. (in preparation). Psychopathy and social information processing programming: Outcome data.

Simourd, D. J. & Hoge, R. D. (2000). Criminal psychopathy: a risk-and-need perspective. *Criminal Justice and Behavior, 27,* 256–272.

Van Voorhis, P., Spruance, L. M., Ritchie, P. N., Johnson-Listwan, S., Seabrook, R., & Pealer, J. (2003). *The Georgia cognitive skills experiment outcome evaluation: Phase II.* Washington, DC: National Institute of Justice.

Verona, E., Patrick, C. J., Curtin, J. J., Bradley, M. M., & Lang, P. J. (2004). Psychopathy and physiological response to emotionally evocative sounds. *Journal of Abnormal Psychology, 113,* 99–108.

Vitale, J. E. & Newman, J. P. (2001). Using the Psychopathy Checklist-Revised with female samples: Reliability, validity, and implications for clinical utility. *Clinical Psychology: Science & Practice, 8,* 117–132.

Vitale, J., Newman, J. P., Serin, R. C., & Bolt, D. M. (2005). Hostile attributions in incarcerated adult male offenders: An exploration of diverse pathways. *Aggressive Behavior, 31,* 99–115.

Wallace, J. F., Vitale, J. E., & Newman, J. P. (1999). Response modulation deficits: Implications for the diagnosis and treatment of psychopathy. *Journal of Cognitive Psychotherapy, 13,* 55–70.

Williamson, S., Harpur, T. J., and Hare, R. D. (1991). Abnormal processing of affective words by psychopathic individuals. *Psychophysiology, 28,* 260–273.

Wong, S. (1984). *Criminal and institutional behaviour of psychopaths.* Ottawa, ON: Programs Branch User Report, Ministry of the Solicitor General.

Chapter 14

MORAL REASONING

ROBIN HARVEY

University of Western Australia, Australia

INTRODUCTION

The previous chapters of this book highlight links between social information processing, social problem solving and the emergence and treatment of behavioural difficulties, conduct problems and more serious offending behaviour. In particular we understand that aggression and other forms of antisocial behaviour are influenced by the ways in which individuals process information, interpret situational cues and utilise previous experience. We are also aware of research demonstrating attributional and response generation differences between aggressive children and their non-aggressive peers (e.g. Huesmann & Guerra, 1997; Quiggle, Garber, Panak, & Dodge, 1992) and identifying an association between social cognitive beliefs and the decision to engage in aggressive behaviour (e.g. Guerra, Huesmann, & Spindler, 2003). For example, we know that from a very young age children's beliefs about the benefits and acceptability of aggressive behaviour impact on the level of aggression displayed (e.g. Guerra and Slaby, 1990). Aggressive children also rate behaviours that result in physical harm to others positively and anticipate tangible and social rewards from their actions (Arsenio & Kramer, 1992; Perry, Perry, & Rasmussen, 1986). In addition, it has been found that social schemas associated with context and experience play a part in the development and maintenance of aggressive and antisocial behaviour (Guerra et al. 2003). Many of these children have a developmental trajectory that results in a very high percentage of them being rated as juvenile delinquents in their adolescent years and subsequently becoming involved in adult criminal offences (Kazdin, 1995).

Less well considered in this literature is the relationship between social information-processing patterns, moral development, aggression and delinquency in childhood and adolescence and between moral and social reasoning and more serious offending behaviour in adulthood. This is despite the consistent position espoused by many cognitive developmental psychologists that moral develop-ment is associated with children's social experiences and impacts on the way in which they perceive the world. Directly related to this is the proposal that moral thought, judgement, and decision-making impact either directly or indir-ectly on the social behaviour of individuals within a community. In addition, research conducted within the framework of age-stage models of moral devel-opment demonstrates an association between pro-social behaviour and higher levels of moral reasoning, and links delinquency, offending and lower levels of moral reasoning, and moral judgements (for a review, see Nelson, Smith, & Dodd, 1990).

As a result of the failure to consider this association, moral development has rarely been viewed alongside or within the broader framework of social informa-tion-processing models that describe cognitive influences on social behaviour and outline the cognitive processes individuals use to make decisions about behaviour in social situations. Consequently, current models of intervention grounded by this framework and aiming to change the cognitions and social problem solving of troubled individuals of all ages have been developed without considering the critical influence of moral development and, more generally, social reasoning, on cognition and decision making. Proposals highlighting this critical gap in both research and practice are relatively new (e.g. Guerra, Nucci, & Huesmann, 1994; Smetana, 1995) and are based on the hypothesis that both researchers and clinicians must understand more about the interaction between moral reasoning and other areas of social cognition and its impact on behaviour. As this understanding improves and yields more complex models which focus on the development of moral reasoning, social information processing and attitude formation within a social cognitive framework, it is hoped that there will be improved intervention outcomes for programmes aimed at changing the cognitive processing and problem solving of serious offenders and younger individuals who display milder forms of antisocial behaviour.

Recent work in the area of moral reasoning and development has focused on children's responses to aggressive events, such as violence and aggression towards others, which is generally accepted by both researchers and theorists as a key moral issue. The findings of this research have been placed within a developmental framework that provides predictions about the current and future patterns of such individuals' moral reasoning and behaviour. Although cognitive development theorists Piaget and Kohlberg are recognised as providing an underpinning framework for understanding moral development, the relationship between social information processing, moral reasoning, and such behaviour can be most fruitfully examined using Turiel's (1978, 1983) domain model of social reasoning, as it provides a broader context for evaluating individuals' social and more specifically, moral reasoning. At the most general level, research investigat-ing children's responses to aggressive incidents has confirmed that when con-sidering areas of social interaction that can be placed in the moral domain such as the welfare of others, inflicting harm, fairness and justice, aggressive individuals frequently make judgements about their own and others' behaviour differently from those who display socially acceptable behaviour (e.g. Crane-Ross, Tisak, & Tisak, 1998). Turiel's social domain model attempts to explain these differences by proposing that children construct different forms of social knowledge, including morality, through their social experiences with adults, peers, and siblings and that this developmental process influences their social behaviour over the lifespan. This proposal has not been discussed in any detail in previous chapters and after a brief review of the theories of Piaget and Kohlberg, the following sections of this chapter will first present the theoretical underpinnings of Turiel's proposals; then describe links between our current understandings of social information processing, social problem solving and the domain model of social reasoning with particular reference to moral development; and, finally, discuss the implications for increasing the effectiveness of social cognitive intervention strategies in the future by drawing from our knowledge of social and moral reasoning.

EARLY INFLUENTIAL THEORIES OF MORAL DEVELOPMENT

Until the 1930s there was little attempt to understand morality and moral decision-making within the context of a cognitive or developmental framework although it was much discussed by philosophers, religious leaders, psychologists, and anthropologists prior to this time. Cognitive psychologists became involved when Jean Piaget (1932) presented a structured developmental approach to moral judgement and reasoning in his book *The Moral Judgement of the Child*. Similarly, Lawrence Kohlberg was particularly influential in the 1960s, 1970s and 1980s as he rethought and extended Piaget's work using a more experimental context. The domain model of social reasoning (Turiel, 1983), which proposes a different developmental process for social and moral reasoning from that suggested by Piaget and Kohlberg, has emerged more recently. This theoretical work remains grounded in the belief that there is an orderly developmental process in the emergence of moral understanding and judgements that underpin individual decision-making in everyday life and this is modified by and influences social behaviour. Before looking at current research and theoretical work integrating our understanding of social reasoning and social information processing, it is important to reflect briefly on the work of both Piaget and Kohlberg and its implications for decision-making and social behaviour.

Both Kohlberg and Piaget proposed hierarchical models of moral development. Piaget influenced the thinking of many developmental and cognitive psychologists when he described two sequential stages in the development of moral reasoning as well as an intermediate transitional stage. In developing this model, Piaget probed children's thinking about transgressions and punishment, rules of conduct, intentionality, rights and authority, equality and reciprocity by presenting them with a range of scenarios to reflect on.

The first stage alternatively labelled by Piaget as the stage of *heteronomous morality*, *moral realism* or a *morality of constraint* is characteristic of younger children (usually below the age of 7 or 8 years) who are not yet thinking at the concrete operational stage of reasoning. Piaget suggests that heteronomous reality is based on the child's immature cognitive structures in that they believe that everyone shares their own view of events, making it difficult for them to consider differing viewpoints of the same action. During this stage children see rules, obligations, and commands as external to themselves and independent of the context in which they are placed. They are a "given", inflexible and unchanging with justice being imposed by the "ruling authority" (usually adults) or the "law" with rewards and punishment inflexible.

Children at this stage of moral development take a very literal view of rules and transgressions and do not appear to be open to the possibility of differing viewpoints or flexible rules depending on circumstances. The key element of thinking at this stage are the beliefs that transgressions will be "found out" by "authority" and in the absoluteness of the values promoted by rules, that is behaviours or responses are either totally right or totally wrong. Furthermore, behaviour is evaluated on the basis of the consequences of the action rather than on the basis of the individual's intentions or motivations. The more severe the consequences, the more punishment is deserved.

The transitional stage in the development of moral reasoning begins around the age of 7 or 8 and Piaget suggests that this is to some extent dependent on a child's increasing social interaction with peers in more equal, egalitarian or give and take relationships. A stronger sense of independence begins to emerge with equality beginning to take priority over authority in matters of distribution and a belief that punishment that is reciprocal or based on restitution is more appropriate than the severe punishment previously advocated.

Piaget labels mature moral reasoning, which usually emerges at the age of 11 or 12 years, as the stage of *autonomous morality*, *moral relativism*, or the *morality of co-operation*. In this mature stage children's moral judgements encompass intentions, motivations, and extenuating circumstances, with equity dominating their thinking about justice. Individuals gradually come to reject unquestioning obedience to authority, arbitrary punishment, and immanent justice with rules considered to be modifiable products of social interaction.

Piaget suggests that variations in children's cognitive maturity, collaboration with peers, role taking, moral education and discussion, and other environmental experiences will lead to differences in the rate at which children move towards autonomous morality. He concludes that the two moral stages are best thought of as two overlapping thought processes in which autonomous morality "gradually succeeds in dominating the first" (Piaget, 1932, p. 132).

Kohlberg also used analysis of interviews with both children and adults about moral dilemmas to develop a comprehensive theory of moral development. Like Piaget, he proposed a series of developmental stages which are universal, hierarchical, and invariant although he emphasises that the moral development of any individual may cease at any particular stage. He described six developmental stages (see Figure 14.1) which deal with changes in thinking about moral dilemmas that usually occur in middle childhood, adolescence, and adulthood. Through these stages, Kohlberg attempted to describe the underpinning structures of moral understanding. He suggested that each successive stage is qualitatively different from the others, each embracing a new, more comprehensive and more coherent cognitive organisation of moral thinking (Kohlberg, 1981,

Level One: Preconventional reasoning	*Stage 1:*	Moral reasoning is based on the avoidance of punishment and obedience to perceived authority figures.
	Stage 2:	Moral reasoning is egocentric and based on the needs of the individual after consideration of rewards and punishment.
Level Two: Conventional reasoning	*Stage 3:*	Moral reasoning begins to be grounded by recognition of the needs of others and recognition of the importance of relationships.
	Stage 4:	Moral reasoning becomes concerned with upholding society's rules and laws for the sake of maintaining society itself.
Level Three: Post- conventional reasoning	*Stage 5:*	The individual understands that under certain circumstances laws can be broken. This is underpinned by a belief that society's laws are a contract between each individual and society.
	Stage 6:	Self chosen ethical principles guide behaviour and these are consistent over situations and time. These principles may overrule society's laws when they come into conflict.

Figure 14.1   Kohlberg's stages of moral reasoning

1984). Kohlberg goes on to suggest the maturation of cognitive capacities is critical to the development of moral reasoning because he believed that judging and evaluating right and wrong are primarily active cognitive processes. In particular, he asserts that social role taking or perspective taking is of primary importance in moral development, as it enhances an individual's ability to empathise with others and to perceive things from others' points of view. By taking roles, individuals become aware of conflicts or discrepancies between their own and others' judgements and actions. The resolution of conflicts between differing points of view brings the individual to higher, more mature moral stages that are more stable than the lower ones.

These stage models have underpinned research that provides some evidence of links between delinquent and offending behaviour and moral development although the general pattern of findings is a little inconsistent and dependent on the age of the participant sample (Blasi, 1980; Hogan, 1973). In general terms, research has generally demonstrated that young violent offenders have delayed moral development, being fixed at the preconventional level. At this level of moral reasoning we can expect individuals to have an egocentric and pragmatic world-view with little understanding of the needs of others. For example, Palmer and Hollin (1996, 1997) found a strong association between immature levels of moral reasoning (in terms of Kohlberg's stages) and self-reported delinquency in young offenders. Similarly, Lee and Prentice (1988) found a significant correlation between the capacity to take the perspective of others and stages of moral reasoning among a group of male offenders. A meta-analysis by Nelson, Smith, and Dodd (1990) confirms this view, concluding that young aggressive offenders were delayed in social moral development, using preconventional reasoning as a basis for their moral decision making compared with matched non-offending peers (who used conventional reasoning).

In contrast, Stevenson, Hall, and Innes (2003) measured the moral development of both male and female violent adult offenders to be at the conventional level, although it must be emphasised that their scores on the measure of socio-moral reasoning were generally lower than those of non-offenders. This finding confirms earlier work by Griffore and Samuels (1978) who also obtained more mature than predicted moral reasoning scores when they assessed adult offenders.

In an attempt to explain the mixed findings in the literature, Veneziano and Veneziano (1988) classified male delinquents in terms of their social competence and found that those who were considered more socially competent scored more highly in terms of morality and level of internal control. In contrast, Leeman, Gibbs, and Fuller (1993) found no correlation between social competence and moral reasoning. Similarly, Palmer and Hollin (1999) examined the social competence and socio-moral reasoning of young offenders using a measure of moral judgement that did not involve the use of dilemmas to determine an individual's stage of moral development. The results of this systematic study demonstrated that young offenders showed immature moral reasoning equivalent to that which would be expected from children aged 11–12 years. However, there was no demonstration of an association between their social competence and moral reasoning.

In line with the general proposals to be developed in this chapter, Palmer and Hollin (1999) suggest that there is a need to target both the social competence *and* moral reasoning of young offenders in order to get real behavioural change. Unfortunately, as we are aware, most current standardised social cognitive interventions that reflect current knowledge of social information processing and social skills focus on improving social competence and problem solving and do not attempt to encourage in any systematic way change in moral reasoning. Similarly, socio-moral interventions aiming to increase the moral reasoning of offenders to at least Kohlberg's stage 3 or what is known as the conventional stage (e.g. Goldstein, 1998) have not been informed by social information processing models. In addition there continue to be concerns that this simplistic approach is not appropriate to many adult offenders in particular as it is not clear that the developmental delay in the moral reasoning of offenders is consistently observed when careful evaluation of adult violent criminals is undertaken (Stevenson et al., 2003).

Thus, it appears that the theoretical models of Piaget and Kohlberg do not provide clinicians with a way forward when attempting to integrate moral reasoning patterns into current social problem-solving intervention strategies as they describe a developmental progression somewhat isolated from such approaches and do not appear to adequately capture the ways in which people make socio-moral judgements in complex situations. These models do not account for findings that even very young children may respond to moral dilemmas by reasoning from a variety of perspectives including rules and authority or justice and human welfare. Nor can they explain why some offenders show mature moral reasoning and why not all individuals with immature moral reasoning commit offences. Thus we turn to the domain model of social reasoning to provide a broader framework which may allow social problem solving, social information processing, and moral reasoning to form part of a complex strategy for prevention and rehabilitation in the future.

THE DOMAIN MODEL OF SOCIAL REASONING

Although grounded in a developmental framework, Turiel's model (1978, 1983) takes a different perspective from that of Piaget and Kohlberg, suggesting that children as young as 3 and 4 are able to reason about social situations by incorporating "moral" information about justice, fairness or concern for others' welfare into their thinking. He goes on to hypothesise that this influences their behavioural choices in both the short and long term. More generally, he posits that there are three distinct conceptual domains that individuals access in the process of social reasoning and behavioural decision-making, no matter what their age or stage of development. The *Personal* domain is related primarily to an individual's interpretation of an issue or event in terms of its impact on the self; the *Social Conventional* domain accounts for an individual's understanding of a situation in terms of social norms and expectations; and the *Moral* domain reflects an individual's recognition of a situation or event in terms of issues of human rights, welfare and fairness. In an expansion of the model, Tisak and Turiel (1984) identified a further *Prudential* domain. This domain describes an individual's understanding of issues primarily relating to personal safety and self-harm. However, this domain has frequently been considered in the research literature as a specific area of reasoning encompassed more generally by the personal domain. Thus, morality (defined in terms of justice, welfare, and rights) can be distinguished from concepts of social conventions which are the consensually determined standards of conduct specific to a particular group. In addition, reasoning within each of the domains undergoes structural developmental change with age; however, each has a distinct conceptual form with an independent developmental course and framework.

Within this model, Nucci (1981) suggested that individuals vary in the actions and events they categorise as associated with specific domains and such categorisation influences both reasoning and behavioural choice. He proposed that such variation is dependent to a large extent on an individual's interpretation of their life experiences and actions. It is this concept that allows us to suggest a strong link between social information processing and domain theory and supports the contention that domain-based reasoning influences the ways in which individuals perceive and respond to specific situations and, more broadly, to community standards. For example, Berkowitz, Guerra, and Nucci (1991) found certain individuals regard particular actions or events (e.g. the recreational use of some types of illegal drugs) as matters of personal choice and illegitimately regulated by social rules, thus influencing their own use of drugs and their response to others' drug-taking behaviour. Similarly, Smetana (1982) demonstrated that women's judgements about abortion depended on their treatment of the issue as a matter of personal choice or as a moral issue involving the life of another person and not on their level of moral judgement as evaluated by a standard Kohlberg assessment. Most women who chose to have an abortion viewed it as a matter of personal choice and their reasoning was uncorrelated with moral reasoning when assessed with a Kohlberg interview. Thus, it can be seen that response decisions and social judgements made about such actions or events are dependent upon an individual's interpretation of the events and subsequent domain categorisation and the salience of the moral and non-moral elements of the situation, not simply on increasing maturity in terms of moral reasoning. Helwig, Tisak, and Turiel (1990) went on to propose that the developmental progression within each domain of reasoning is dependent on an individual's previous social interactions and experiences, and to suggest that each has a separate developmental framework and trajectory.

In summary, this model proposes that individuals make judgements that influence their thinking and behaviour by accessing and integrating knowledge across social reasoning domains. The salience of each domain will vary, depending on the prior experience and current social interactions of the individual and this will determine his/her final judgement and resultant behaviour (Helwig et al., 1990; for reviews, see Smetana, 1995; Tisak, 1995). In contrast to earlier views of moral development, it is thought that judgements about how to respond in a particular situation will reflect individual and situational biases implicit in that event which may increase or decrease the salience of each domain (Guerra et al., 1994). For example, individuals who feel threatened or focus on meeting their own needs will view social situations from within the framework of the personal domain and will make both a social judgement and behavioural response according to this perception. Another individual may place priority on the moral issues pertaining to the same social situation and make a different social judgement resulting in a different behavioural response according to this focus.

Using this framework, we can predict that juvenile delinquents and young offenders may interpret and respond to events leading to harm to others, property damage or other unfair outcomes using different domain priorities than may be expected from people functioning effectively in the community. That is, their reasoning does not encompass judgements from the moral domain to the same extent as most other young people and their social information processing, in terms of response selection and behavioural enactment, will be influenced by domain placement.

OVERVIEW OF RESEARCH FINDINGS

Most research in this area has involved the examination of the social and moral reasoning of various groups of children and adolescents with only a small number of research studies focusing on young offenders. Despite this, we can learn from such work as much of the more recent research has focused on the social reasoning of children with behavioural disorders. As suggested earlier, conduct problems in childhood have been identified as a key predictor of future juvenile delinquency and offending behaviour. By understanding more about the social and moral reasoning of young conduct-disordered children, we can begin to develop intervention strategies that may assist in changing the thinking and skills of delinquents and young offenders.

The common research paradigm used to investigate children's and adolescents' social reasoning has been to present subjects with *prototypical* situations, that is, situations identified as focusing on issues specific to individual domains. For example, prototypic moral items include situations where the child is questioned about one child hitting another child, or one child being unfair in some way to another. In contrast, social conventional items focus on situations such as wearing the "wrong" clothes to school or not complying with a context-specific rule. Participants then make criterion judgements about the generalisability (e.g. *Is this always the right/wrong thing to do?*), seriousness (e.g. *How serious is this inappropriate behaviour?*), and independence from rules or authority of the action sequence (e.g. *Is this behaviour right/wrong in the absence/ presence of a rule or authority figure – such as a teacher or parent?*). Finally, justifications or reasons for the answers given in their judgements of the social situation presented are sought, in order to confirm placement of a child's decision-making in a social reasoning domain (e.g. *"Hitting the other child was the wrong thing to do because it is mean to hurt other kids"* is a justification associated with the moral domain whereas *"You shouldn't hit other children because the teacher/ parent/police might see you"* is a justification associated with the social conventional domain).

Using variations of this paradigm, it is clear that from a very young age children consistently make judgements and classify actions and responses within the framework provided by the moral, social conventional, and personal domains (Nucci & Turiel, 1978; Smetana, 1984; Smetana & Braeges, 1990; Smetana, Schlagman, & Adams, 1993; Tisak & Turiel, 1988; Zelazo, Helwig, & Lau, 1996). For example, prototypic moral transgressions such a hitting another child in order to obtain a desired toy, or taking another child's food are consistently identified as wrong by normally developing children as young as 3, even when the context of the act is changed (e.g. is the act/behaviour still wrong at home? at another school/daycare? or in another country?), or the individuals and/or authority figures altered (e.g. is the act/behaviour wrong in the presence/absence of a teacher/parent?) and even in the absence of a rule prohibiting the behaviour (e.g. is the act/behaviour wrong when there is no rule to say children shouldn't do it?). This is in contrast to transgressions encompassed by the social conventional domain such as failing to say "please" or "thank you" in a range of situations or failing to wear the clothes considered appropriate to an event (such as a uniform at school). Normally developing children and adolescents identify these patterns of "wrong behaviour" as specific to context and the rule that is in place. For example, children may judge such behaviour as wrong in a school environment but "OK" at home; wrong if a teacher is present, but not if a parent is the authority figure or the teacher is absent; or wrong only if there is an explicit rule forbidding the behaviour (Nucci & Turiel, 1978; Sanderson & Siegal, 1988; Siegal & Storey, 1985, Smetana, 1981, 1984, 1985; Smetana et al. 1993; Zelazo et al., 1996). In general terms, we can conclude that transgressions involving the moral domain of social reasoning are consistently identified by children as young as 3 years as wrong in all contexts. In contrast, judgements about social conventional transgressions are context-specific and dependent on explicit rules.

Finally, children's reasoning about the seriousness of a transgression or the amount of deserved punishment for a transgression also appears to be contingent on social reasoning domains. For example, when children evaluate moral and social conventional transgressions that frequently occur in preschool settings, they judge moral transgressions as more deserving of punishment and, in general, "more serious" (e.g. Smetana et al. 1988; Smetana & Braeges, 1990). As predicted, there are some age-related differences in social reasoning that have implications within the social information processing framework. Older children (10 years) appeared to coordinate information on outcomes with domain distinctions to modify their judgements on seriousness. In contrast, 6- and 7-year-olds make more rigid decisions based on the domains of social reasoning tending to ignore the outcomes of the transgressions (Tisak & Turiel, 1988).

Research also confirms that consistent reasoning patterns are found when comparing situations encompassing the personal domain, and discussion presented later in this chapter suggests that this also has relevance when considering the reasoning and subsequent behavioural choices of young offenders. Nucci (1981) employed a sorting task to evaluate the judgements of both adolescents and children about the "wrongness" of rule violations within each domain. As expected, he found that these individuals ranked moral transgressions as "more wrong" than social conventional transgressions. In turn, social conventional transgressions were ranked as "more wrong" than transgressions of rules imposed on matters regarded as an individual's personal choice. The justifications provided by individuals to support their judgement also provided clear evidence of differential domain categorisation. There was a significant correlation between ratings of seriousness of the act and domain categorization with acts rated as "least wrong" located in the personal domain. At all ages justification of an act as "least wrong" either identified that the consequences of the act would affect only the individual committing the act, or indicated that the act was a personal matter and should not be subject to rule restrictions. In his conclusions, Nucci (1981) suggested that individuals employ a common set of criteria to make judgements about social situations but proposed that they vary in their interpretation of which events fit which criteria. Similar findings by Smetana (1988) and Stoddart and Turiel (1985) confirmed that children and adolescents develop a set of non-moral and non-conventional events that are considered matters of individual choice. Judgement criteria in this domain are commonly based on reasoning related to a lack of harm to others and personal prerogative.

SOCIAL INFORMATION PROCESSING AND SOCIAL REASONING

As stated in previous chapters, it is clear that that there is a strong relationship between unacceptable behaviour and specific cognitive processes and it can be suggested that our understanding of this relationship is enhanced if we also consider the influence of social reasoning within this process. The evidence suggests that domain categorisation, which underpins the process of social judgement and possibly also the behavioural response, will impact on the situational cues an individual attends to, and the use made of internal cues, scripts and past experiences to interpret a situation. It may also influence the priority an individual gives to particular goals and outcomes in terms of their desirability. The findings also suggest that social and, in particular, moral reasoning is developed through exposure to response outcomes, selective attention to cues, and the internalisation of values and standards. In turn, domain placement will influence an individual's current and future judgements, response choices and behaviour in a range of real-life events. In addition, Turiel (1987, 1998) concludes that social learning in terms of prior knowledge, experience, and the development of beliefs about expected standards of conduct will affect the knowledge base and development of social reasoning and categorisation of events within particular domains. For example, prior experience as a victim or consistent exposure to aggressive events may lead to developmental change in the priorities young children place on personal safety and protection of possessions when attempting to understand and respond to a wide range of social situations. This, in turn, may increase the likelihood that these individuals make social judgements that promote, for example, an aggressive response in these situations. In contrast, individuals who have past exposure to situations where expected standards are emphasised, or the consequences of actions in terms of harm or fairness to others are discussed, are likely to develop different priorities in their social and moral reasoning leading to more effective problem solving (Barret, Rapee, Dadds, & Ryan, 1996). Such proposals are confirmed by recent findings that abused and neglected children demonstrate different patterns of inappropriate behaviour, with physically abused children engaging more in stealing behaviour and neglected children demonstrating patterns of cheating and less compliance with general rules than their peers. Such behaviours were found to be associated with cognitive and affective deficits, and correlated with variations in domain placement for situations encompassing moral transgressions (Koenig, Cicchetti, & Rogosch, 2004). Similarly, Smetana (1997) highlights the role of parenting in the development of moral reasoning and the impact of providing domain-appropriate feedback to changes in children's social interactions and moral reasoning skills.

Observational studies by Nucci and Weber (1995) and Tisak, Nucci, and Jankowski (1996) make an important contribution to the proposal of links between domain categorisation, social judgements, social information processing, and experience. Nucci and Weber examined "in home" interactions between children aged 3 and 4 years and their mothers. In this research, interactions involving moral, conventional, personal and prudential events were recorded across different contexts in the home (morning, free play, evening, and bedtime). Observers reported that mothers were more willing to negotiate personal issues with their children than items from other domains, and children were rarely prepared to argue with their mother over moral or social conventional issues. In contrast, even very young children made frequent challenges to their parent over personal issues. Based on these findings, they concluded that the challenging behaviour was determined, to some extent, by the child's categorisation of an event within the personal domain and previous experience in negotiating with his/her parent. Thus, the processing of cues from the interaction, past experience and domain classification all contributed to the response decision and subsequent behavioural outcome.

Using a similar research strategy, Tisak, Nucci, and Jankowski (1996) observed preschool children in a school setting. In this study, observers focused on transgressions that occurred naturally in the school playground. They found that the majority of moral transgressions involved physical harm and property loss with very few relating to property damage and psychological harm. Tisak and her colleagues used this information to explain earlier research findings demonstrating that very young children used the consequences of an event to justify rating transgressions involving physical harm to be more serious than that involving property damage. They went on to propose that young children frequently experience physical harm and property loss (which often involves a negative interaction with another child) as victims and, as such, the level of consequence of such an event is particularly salient to them when making a social judgement or domain placement. However, as children grow older, other aspects of the experiences acquire salience and impact on their interpretation of the event, their social judgement, and subsequent response decisions.

Tisak and colleagues also observed that moral physical harm events (physical harm to another) and acts that lead to harm to self (prudential events) occur in the free play environment with equal frequency. If the simplistic view of a link between exposure to real-life events and the development of differential social reasoning is taken, we would expect similar judgements to be made about these two types of transgressions. This is not the case. There is strong evidence suggesting that children make differential judgements on the dimension of seriousness about events that occur in each of these two domains (Tisak, 1993; Tisak & Turiel; 1984). To explain this and other findings, Tisak and her colleagues (1996) suggest that children's judgements are based on a more complex interpretation of real-life events. For example, they consider the basis for the moral versus prudential distinction in social reasoning to be an individual's understanding of the social relational features of moral transgressions, which have an impact on others. In contrast, prudential events, which by definition only impact on the self, are interpreted as less serious. Again, behavioural outcomes are expected to vary with this judgement. These conclusions are congruent with Turiel's (1978, 1983) earlier proposition that:

> Responses are not unilaterally determined by stimuli and, therefore, knowledge does not stem directly from experience. The child obtains knowledge by acting upon and abstracting from events. In addition to experiencing events, individuals select, interpret and systematize elements of their experience. (Turiel, 1983, p. 33)

Thus, it can be hypothesised that the elements of an event that individuals select and interpret to use as the basis for domain placement and subsequent social judgement will also impact on the information individuals use in the first three stages of social information processing. On this basis, the relationship found between social information processing and aggressive behaviour (e.g. Dorsch & Keane, 1994; Quiggle et. al., 1992; Weiss, Dodge, Bates, & Pettit, 1992) can be extended by considering links between social reasoning and aggressive behaviour.

MIXED DOMAIN RESEARCH – A REAL LIFE VIEW

On reflection, most real-life situations are more complex than the prototypic social situations frequently utilised in social and moral reasoning research, although the consistent pattern of domain distinction has been made clear from this early work. This problem has been recognised and evaluation of reasoning associated with more complex social events has been attempted and may help to provide more realistic information, allowing a clearer understanding of how social reasoning may impact on aggression in young children and more serious offending behaviours in adolescence and adulthood. Again, mixed domain research with the "normal" population needs to be examined for clues, as there is a paucity of this type of research using aggressive or offender status as a variable.

By definition, mixed domain events contain elements from more than one social reasoning domain and, as such, mimic real-life experiences. Turiel, Hildebrand and Wainryb (1991) concluded that most real-life situations require an individual to undertake the conceptual task of coordinating and prioritising different types of domain judgements in order to develop what he or she perceives as an effective response decision. Research findings support this conclusion as children's judgements about mixed domain events have been found to be influenced by the context within which an event takes place and the intentions and affect of the participants (Helwig, Hildebrand, & Turiel, 1995; Killen, 1990; Turiel, Hildebrand, & Wainryb, 1991).

Contextual factors in particular appear to influence social judgements and justifications of responses. For example, Crane and Tisak (1995) identify research evidence suggesting that the type of consequence, and children's familiarity with the events presented to them influence judgements about the seriousness of moral transgressions. They also highlight findings which suggest that judgements within the conventional domain are affected by which authority figure (e.g. peer, parent or teacher) is making and enforcing the rule. For example, children regard transgressions of mothers' rules as more serious than transgressions of teachers' rules. Crane and Tisak (1995) go on to suggest that the contextual variations found in judgements within social reasoning domains are linked to an individual's recognition that many events reflect aspects of more than one domain. Based on this premise, they investigated the social reasoning of young children (preschool, year one, and year three) and found that all groups of children identified both moral and conventional components of social events. In addition, they demonstrated developmental differences in the salience of the different domains. Older children drawn from the general population responded to the moral dimensions of the mixed domain tasks by making judgements that mixed domain transgressions were wrong, irrespective of whether an authority figure permitted or prohibited the event. This is in contrast to the younger children who more frequently focused on the social conventional aspects of the transgression, with judgements of permissibility being dependent on whether an authority figure permitted such an act. This suggests that, when making domain categorisations, there is a developmental progression in the way that children extract and interpret information from complex events.

Crane and Tisak (1995) link these findings to the ways in which adults and children interact when transgressions occur. That is, children learn to interpret what are the most important features of a transgression when making a social judgement. Earlier research (e.g. Dunn & Munn, 1985; Nucci, 1982; Turiel, 1983) concluded that young children's understanding of the underlying social judgements involved in transgressions from each domain is affected by the responses given by adults to children when transgressions occur. For example, when discussing a moral transgression with a child, teachers and parents tend to focus on issues of the resulting harm to others or on fairness. In contrast, when a social conventional transgression occurs, the authority figure primarily focuses on the rule prohibiting the behaviour. Nucci (1984) also found that older children were more responsive to teacher intervention after a transgression, when children perceive the intervention as congruent with their underpinning domain categorisation of the event. This finding is extended by Smetana (1997) who suggests that the results of a number of studies lead to the conclusion that children and adolescents actively evaluate social messages in terms of their domain appropriateness and reject messages that are domain inappropriate and inconsistent with the nature of the event. Given that in this chapter we are focusing on future directions, it is worth commenting that perhaps if aggressive children classify mixed domain events in atypical ways, then perhaps the responses of authority figures are not supporting the development of effective social reasoning skills. Similarly, if the social and moral reasoning of juvenile offenders and adult criminals does not reflect the expected categorisation and judgement patterns, then the standard interventions and offender rehabilitation approaches aimed at increasing maturity in moral reasoning may not be focused (in terms of domain categorisation) in a meaningful way that will encourage change.

LINKS BETWEEN MORAL DEVELOPMENT, SOCIAL REASONING AND AGGRESSION

In contrast to the theories of both Piaget and Kohlberg, social domain research suggests that from a young age children are developing a conceptual framework for internalised regulation about social situations that involve harm to others, property damage or fairness and this is the forerunner of self-regulatory behaviour in adolescence and adulthood. That is, moral reasoning and internalised control begins at as young as 3 years of age. It also appears that this type of internalised regulation is not as strongly associated with other events that are considered more dependent on external societal rules or specific contexts. Thus individuals' categorisation of events as "moral" or "non moral" is a key to their decision-making and subsequent behavioural choice and it appears that there is a wide variety of factors that will contribute to this categorisation in the long term.

Domain theory clearly has implications for understanding more about psychological mechanisms that underpin differences between the moral reasoning of aggressive children, delinquents, and young offenders when compared to individuals who are functioning effectively in the community, and has the potential to influence intervention approaches in the future. Do young children with behavioural problems and juvenile delinquents make the same judgements about transgressions or do they reason differently to their socialised peers? Do offenders make judgements about their criminal behaviour in terms of it being acceptable within particular contexts, or in the absence of police or security forces? For example do they perceive aggression towards others as universally unacceptable, as do most individuals, or do they believe this act is acceptable because they were being chased by a security officer or the police? Finally, do the early experiences of the delinquent or young offender impact on the framework within which domain judgements are made, in addition to forming biases in their social information processing and deficits in social skills, making the likelihood of hostile or antisocial behaviour more probable in a range of social situations?

The research presented thus far suggests that it may be possible to identify contrasts between the social reasoning of individuals who vary in their likelihood of acting aggressively. Is it possible to determine similar contrasts between the social reasoning of offenders and non-offenders? Remember, regulation of aggressive acts would generally be considered to fit into the moral domain of social reasoning as such acts involve issues of harm to others. Other property crimes would also be considered to fit this domain as they would be categorised by most community members as interfering with "others' welfare". We now understand how children as young as three consider issues and events pertaining to *harm* and interference with *others' welfare* to be wrong, independent of rules and authority, and worthy of more severe punishment than any other type of transgression. Knowledge of the links between social cognition and aggression, specifically social information-processing variations in terms of attributional biases, encoding of cues and response decisions, leads to the proposal that children who consistently display aggressive behaviour may also be interpreting and categorising events within social reasoning domains differently from children who display pro-social skills. That is, they may not be placing behaviours associated with harm to others, fairness or justice in the moral domain. This difference may lead to behavioural responses that seem appropriate to the child - given that individual's priorities in terms of social judgements about the event - but are inappropriate in terms of general behavioural expectations. Furthermore, the suggestion that the social experiences of aggressive children have led to different developmental trajectories within each of the domains, or interpretational biases in the way that they give priority in their social judgements to domain-linked facets of complex social situations, appears to have some validity. This in turn may lead to differences in the way these children respond to the social situations that they encounter, particularly those that might involve harm to others.

At this point in time we can only put forward hypotheses based primarily on findings from investigations of children's and adolescents' thinking but there certainly appears to be enough evidence to suggest that the social reasoning of offenders is likely to be different from that of their pro-social peers and may be influencing their social information processing in terms of their initial encoding of information, goal selection, and their behavioural choices. More work focused on the examination of the judgements and behavioural decision-making of juvenile delinquents and adult offenders within a framework of social domain theory is certainly a goal for future research and will clearly link to improvements in interventions.

As indicated earlier, it is believed that moral development plays a major role in behavioural regulation (Smetana, 1995) and research into the early developmental patterns of aggression (e.g. Fergusson, Lynskey, & Horwood, 1995; for reviews see Campbell, 1994; Keenan & Shaw, 1994; Landy & Peters, 1992; Offord, Boyd, & Racine, 1991) suggests that the development of social reasoning in young children can be linked to other measures of moral development and other cognitive skills that are linked to the self-regulation of behaviour. At an early age children begin to internalise values and standards (Beeghly & Cicchetti, 1994; Grusec & Goodnow, 1994; Kochanska, Aksan, & Koenig, 1995; Kochanska, DeVet, Goldman, Murray, & Putnam, 1994) and it is commonly accepted that child-rearing strategies have a major impact on this internalisation and the development of early moral cognition, with the young child using parental standards as a model for moral decision-making (Hoffman, 1984; Hoffman & Saltzstein, 1967; Zahn-Waxler, Robinson, & Emde, 1992). In particular, inductive parenting styles contribute to the development of empathic responses (Ijzendoorn, 1997; Smetana, 1997), and the emergence of empathy, commonly regarded as a first step in moral development, has been linked to the development of pro-social behaviour (e.g. Eisenberg, Fabes, Carlo, & Speer, 1993). As discussed earlier, domain categorisation requires the child to interpret information regarding social events using prior experience, expectations and beliefs and the integration of parental and societal standards are part of this internalisation process (Smetana, 1995). Children who are less empathic are more likely to make judgements that are not within the moral domain of social reasoning. That is, they will be less concerned with "others' welfare" and more likely to emphasise other considerations such as "personal need".

From a very early age, young children also begin to categorise actions as right or wrong (Smetana et al., 1993). Huesmann and Guerra (1997) examined the development of the self-regulatory beliefs of children aged between 7 and 10 years using a new scale specifically designed to assess normative beliefs about aggression. They found a developmental change in children's approval of aggression with some children considering the use of aggression as more acceptable as they grew older. This change in their approval of aggression correlated significantly with increases in aggressive behaviour. Of further interest was the finding that individual differences in the frequency of observed aggressive behaviour in older children were predicted by their normative beliefs at a younger age. Congruent with these findings, observational data suggests that children who develop strong self-regulatory patterns demonstrate consistent reductions in physically aggressive behaviour (Cummings, Iannotti & Zahn Waxler, 1989; Landy & Peters, 1992).

As described earlier, young children begin to make consistent social judge-ments based on the development of social reasoning skills at the same time that self-regulatory behaviour begins to emerge. By the age of 36 months, children consistently discriminate between social situations by suggesting that appropri-ate responses to some events are dependent on authority or social rules and are specific to that particular situation. Other responses are deemed appropriate by reflecting on more general concerns of harm, fairness, welfare or rights, and are not considered dependent on rules, or identified as specific to a particular environment (e.g. Nucci & Turiel, 1978; Smetana, 1981; Smetana et al., 1993). This age-related link suggests that a relationship exists between the development of social reasoning and the emergence of self-regulatory behaviour.

Turiel (1987) and Guerra and her colleagues (1994) were the first to make a more general theoretical link between aggressive behaviour and aspects of social reasoning. These researchers also proposed that there is a relationship between aggressive behaviour and moral reasoning with domain placement making an impact on behavioural decision-making. That is, they hypothesised that aggres-sive responses are dependent, to some extent, on an individual's understanding of the moral aspects of a situation or event and the priority they give to these understandings. Guerra and her colleagues went on to suggest that the extent to which an individual focuses on, and gives priority to, issues of harm or welfare in a given situation will have an influence on the judgement and response a person makes to that particular situation. For example, when a child is confronted with a social situation which has a moral dimension (e.g. wanting to take a desired toy from another child), the child who chooses to respond aggressively is more likely to have recognised the situation in terms of the personal domain (his/her right to have the toy) as opposed to a child who responds in pro-social way reflecting a greater emphasis on the moral domain of social reasoning (the importance of not hurting other children when attempting to obtain the desired toy).

In an extension of this proposal, it can be suggested that juvenile offenders may reason and respond differently to their age peers by virtue of the domain prioritics thcy place on complex events. For example, when confronted by the need to obtain funds to sustain a drug habit, the young offender is likely to place priority on personal aspects of the situation (the craving for the drug) rather than the moral aspects of purse snatching (that someone might be hurt or their property is taken), whereas another individual will place importance on the moral dimension even though he or she also may require funds for drugs. In a simplistic view it can be suggested that all individuals are likely to be able to identify both the moral and personal dimensions of the situation but it will be individuals who prioritise the personal domain who will make behavioural decisions that will lead to offending behaviour. Turiel reached a similar conclu-sion, suggesting that aggressive actions and the consequences of those actions should be placed in the "context of how individuals perceive and conceive the social world and social relationships" (1987, p. 98).

There have been relatively few studies directly investigating links between the domain model of social reasoning and aggressive behaviour, but those that have provide some evidence for such a relationship. For example, Guerra and Nucci's (1992) research (as cited in Guerra et al., 1994) examined the relationship between aggression and judgements of whether particular actions or events were primarily issues of morality, social convention, prudence, or personal choice. They found that adolescents who reported they indulged in frequent aggressive acts were more likely to identify prototypical moral situations, such as hitting or hurting another person, as matters of personal choice than were non-aggressive adolescents. They also reported that differences between aggressive and non-aggressive adolescents in terms of their judgements about non-moral issues were not significant. Based on this evidence, Guerra and her colleagues concluded that the "tendency to engage in aggressive or delinquent behaviour is a function of its domain placement, and that more aggressive individuals can be characterised by an overextension of the personal domain" (1194, p. 24).

Crane-Ross, Tisak, and Tisak (1998) also examined whether the social cognitive beliefs of adolescents were associated with moral and social conventional rule-violating behaviours. Results indicated a specific link between an adolescent's beliefs within each domain of social reasoning and the types and level of rule violating behaviour. Using self- and peer-ratings of social behaviour, the researchers found that adolescents' beliefs about moral and social conventional rule violations in terms of the legitimacy, the outcome value, and the impact on others of such actions, predicted both the level of peer- and self-rated aggression and social conventional rule violations, with ratings of aggressive behaviour best predicted by beliefs and values reflecting the moral domain. Similarly, self-reported beliefs within the conventional domain strongly predicted social conventional violations rather than the adolescent's beliefs and values associated with aggression.

Although not directly investigating whether displays of aggressive or convention-violating behaviour are related to the classification of an event in the personal domain, the findings of this research support the contention that variations in the patterns of domain classification influence behaviour and are linked to domain-specific social reasoning. For example, an important predictor of aggressive behaviour, as assessed by both peer- and self-rating scales, was the adolescents' belief that the act was legitimate in the circumstances presented. In the vignettes used to assess beliefs about aggression, peer provocation provided the context for aggressive acts. Under these circumstances, such events might invite consideration of both personal and moral domain criteria. Comparison of ratings between adolescents with high levels of aggression and their less aggressive peers suggested that judgements about the legitimacy of the event may have been dependent on whether priority was given to criteria within the personal domain or to those within the moral domain. Similarly, Roth (2002) found that differences in social reasoning patterns and domain classification were significantly associated with differences in risk behaviour in adolescents.

These findings confirmed earlier work by Tisak and Jankowski (1996) who demonstrated social reasoning differences between adolescents categorised as "severe" offenders (had committed violent crimes) as opposed to those who had committed minor offences. Of particular interest when considering the moral development of young offenders was their finding that the more violent individuals emphasised conventional rules over moral considerations in the justification of social decision-making suggesting there is a clear variation between aggressive and non-aggressive individuals in their application of explicit rules to decision-making and a lack of moral priorities implicitly guiding their judgements.

In an interesting finding that adds weight to the conclusion that there are social reasoning differences between aggressive individuals and their non-aggressive peers, Harvey, Fletcher, and French (2004) examined the social reasoning priorities 7-year-old boys utilised when they were faced with complex social events. The results clearly demonstrated that the children rated as either aggressive or non-aggressive had differing domain priorities in their decision-making when they were required to integrate information drawn from different social reasoning domains. In general terms, it appeared that aggressive boys identified social conventional and personal issues as of greater importance than moral considerations. Of particular interest was the finding that these children most frequently placed priority on an explicit social rule rather than an implicit value. That is, the majority of aggressive boys selected a response that demonstrated they placed priority on meeting the explicit situational rule contained in a complex social event rather than prioritising issues of harm to others. Aggressive and non-aggressive children also demonstrated contrasting responses for complex events requiring them to evaluate the moral/personal and social conventional/personal domain mix. In events containing both moral and personal domain considerations, a significant majority of aggressive children selected a behavioural response which demonstrated that personal needs were more salient to them than considerations drawn from the moral domain. Their social decision-making also appeared dependent on whether or not parents or teachers were present to witness their behavioural response (typical of reasoning associated with the social conventional domain). In contrast, all normally developing children placed priority on the moral domain. Congruent with the earlier findings of Tisak and Jankowski (1996), these researchers found that the aggressive boys continued to place priority on social rules even in situations that may be regarded as under their personal control.

In summarising the data, Harvey and colleagues (2004) suggest that aggressive children classify particular behaviours and events within the moral, social conventional and personal domains in the same way as non-aggressive children make similar social judgements about these events. For example, they will agree that "hitting is wrong" because it will hurt someone when they are presented with this simple scenario. However, in more complex social situations it appears they prioritise the competing demands of these domains differently from non-aggressive children. Explicit social rules that are regulated by authority figures present in the immediate environment are more meaningful than the implicit self-regulation of the moral domain. In addition, aggressive children appear to be somewhat "fuzzy" about which situations are appropriately within their personal control. The research suggests that they place priority on personal concerns when there are competing implicit moral considerations but overextend social rules to encompass situations that normally developing children consider matters of personal choice. These conclusions are congruent with those of other social domain researchers who suggest that social judgements frequently require coordination of information across knowledge systems which will be influenced by the context within which the event occurs and the individual's experiences and interpretive biases (e.g. Guerra et al., 1994; Turiel, 1983, 1987; Turiel and Smetana, 1984).

Early research by Nucci and Herman (1982) also provides information about links between behavioural disorders and social reasoning in children although their target group was somewhat younger than the previous work described. These researchers used prototypic events to examine social reasoning, and although there are some methodological problems with this study involving subject selection, it is worth discussing as it is one of the very few to focus specifically on the social reasoning of aggressive children. Using the familiar experimental paradigm and analysis, they found that both aggressive and "normal" children ranked moral transgressions as more serious than conventional transgressions. Similarly, social conventional breaches ranked as more serious than transgressions of rules that governed events generally considered as within the personal domain. However, when response justifications were examined within each domain classification, Nucci and Herman (1982) found that participants in the control group were significantly more likely to justify their response using an *unjust act* explanation than the aggressive group. The aggressive children were significantly more likely to use a *categorical wrong* justification than the controls. This type of justification involved statements that an act is "always wrong" or "always prohibited" with no further elaboration. Although not discussed by the authors of the paper, it can be hypothesised that this type of response would more logically fit into the rule-driven social conventional domain. That is, the act is wrong because an explicit rule says it is wrong.

These researchers also demonstrated that the aggressive children were more dependent on explicit rules when they found that this group did not identify all the prototypic moral transgressions presented to them as wrong irrespective of rules. They considered two transgressions, involving hitting and not sharing abundant goods, as appropriate if there was no specific rule in place to cover the event. This contrasts with the social reasoning of pro-social peers who identified all prototypic moral transgressions as wrong in the absence of rules or authority. Nucci and Herman (1982) explained this contrast by suggesting that the aggressive group justified their decision by taking a more personal perspective in their social reasoning rather than recognising the moral concerns intrinsic to the event. In addition, they suggested that the aggressive group was more dependent on the social conventional or *rule-driven* criteria of the events presented to them than the control group, who appeared to recognise that acts of aggression or not sharing were still not legitimate in the absence of specific rules or authority figures.

The final significant result of this study also demonstrates a clear contrast between the domain classification decisions made by aggressive children and the control group. In a finding that contrasts to the later work of Guerra and Nucci (1992) but has limited support in the results obtained by Harvey et al. (2004), Nucci and Herman (1982) determined that aggressive children were significantly less likely than their pro-social peers to judge prototypic personal items as matters within their personal control. That is, relative to normal subjects, aggressive children were less likely to consider that some actions were a matter of personal discretion. The contrast in findings between Guerra and Nucci (1992) and the latter work may be explained by age-related differences in the experimental groups. Nucci and Herman (1982) and Harvey and colleagues assessed the social reasoning of young children whereas Guerra and Nucci (1992) examined judgements made by adolescents. It can be hypothesised that the differences in the social reasoning patterns identified in these two pieces of research may be linked to developmental changes that have not yet been investigated experimentally.

Other more recent research by Blair and his associates (1997) has also provided evidence that children's responses on a measure that required children to make moral/social conventional domain judgements about a range of transgressions predicted the degree of behavioural disturbance in children previously identified with conduct problems. As would be predicted from the studies presented so far, the more aggressive individuals made domain judgements reflecting placements of events in the social conventional domain whereas more moral judgements and justifications were recorded for the children identified as less disturbed.

In summary, the evidence presented in this chapter suggests that consistent differential reasoning patterns are found between normally developing and aggressive peers. These are influenced by the individual's placement of social transgressions within the personal, social conventional, and moral domains, which in turn are influenced by the priorities given to situational cues and scripts based on past and current experiences of the individual. Children as young as 3 and 4 years and drawn from the normal population demonstrate consistent patterns of social reasoning reflecting their understanding of moral, social conventional, personal, and prudential considerations. It is also clear that children and adolescents make judgements about mixed domain events based on the priorities they give to each social reasoning domain, with, for the most part, moral considerations taking priority over social conventional and personal domain criteria. Personal considerations will also take priority over judgements reflecting the social conventional restrictions, if older children and adolescents decide that an event is within their personal control. These judgements, in turn, appear to have an impact on behavioural outcomes. It also appears that from a young age children who are developing aggressive patterns of behaviour and are on a developmental trajectory that predicts future delinquency and offending behaviour can discriminate between the moral, social conventional and personal domains (although their discrimination appears somewhat "fuzzy"). However, the priorities they place on various domains in behavioural decision-making contrasts with that of their normally developing peers. Notwithstanding the lack of extensive research in the area, the empirical findings in the areas of social reasoning and other facets of cognitive development provide enough evidence to consider the proposal that there are developmental differences in the way that aggressive children and adolescents make judgements about real-life and complex events when compared to the judgements expected from their pro-social peers. Specifically, it can be suggested that young aggressive children are likely to place transgressions involving aggression toward others within the social conventional domain, focusing on rule- and authority-based criteria. In certain circumstances, they will also identify personal considerations as very important in their decision-making. In contrast, their pro-social peers appear more likely to take account of criteria drawn from the moral domain. It can also be hypothesised that the research evidence indirectly indicates that aggressive children are less likely than their pro-social peers to categorise so-called "personal" events as within their control and are more likely to consider such acts as falling within the social conventional domain of social reasoning. That is, they are looking for fixed rules and authority figures to guide their decision making. In contrast, aggressive adolescents are more likely to consider events as within their own personal domain and focus on criteria from within this domain. If a developmental pattern within this framework can be confirmed through future research, then once more it can be suggested that intervention to change domain-based reasoning may be an effective tool in assisting in changing the behavioural decision-making of young offenders.

IMPLICATIONS FOR INTERVENTIONS

Given the relationship between social reasoning and behavioural decision-making, there are clear implications for social cognitive treatment approaches of aggression and other forms of antisocial and offending behaviour. Currently, links between aggressive behaviour and deficits and distortions in problem-solving skills, attributions of hostile intent (particularly in ambiguous situations) and negative self-statements, have led to the development of intervention programmes which have been quite popular in treatment approaches for young conduct disordered children and with older, antisocial individuals. These types of interventions have become known generically as "problem solving skills training" or PSST. In these programmes, intervention has commonly focused on addressing the cognitive deficits and biases that have been identified as contributing to displays of aggressive behaviour (e.g. Hudley, 1994; Pepler, King, & Byrd, 1991). Although often criticised for the outcome measures used, most treatment studies have suggested that this type of approach has the potential to reduce aggressive and antisocial behaviour in children and adolescents (e.g. Guerra & Slaby, 1990). However, for the most part, these intervention approaches have led to only small reductions in aggressive behaviour, and many individuals continue to remain outside the range of normative behaviour relative to peers of the same age and sex (e.g. Kazdin, Bass, Siegal, & Thomas, 1989; Kazdin & Crowley, 1997).

It can be hypothesised that one of the reasons for less than expected levels of improvement in antisocial behaviour patterns is that such programmes have not taken into account our understanding of the moral and social reasoning patterns of normally developing individuals and the findings that aggressive children and conduct disordered adolescents show deficits and biases in their use of social knowledge. When planning social cognitive interventions, programmes must also aim to improve the social reasoning skills of the participants, attempting to ensure that the moral domain of social reasoning becomes more salient in the behavioural decision-making of aggressive children, juvenile delinquents, and adult offenders. In particular, we must begin to work on changing the character-istic ways in which aggressive individuals make judgements about events and transgressions in terms of social domain membership. As presented earlier, such judgements will have a strong influence on the situational cues encoded, the ways in which these cues are interpreted and the identification of socially desirable outcomes. In addition, priorities established by antisocial individuals leading to domain placement in mixed domain or complex events must also be considered in any social cognitive treatment approach. Attempts to increase the saliency of the moral domain for aggressive children, juvenile delinquents, and adult offenders should have an impact on the ways in which they interpret the social events they confront and their behavioural response.

There have been numerous attempts to develop interventions with the primary aim of encouraging "more mature" moral reasoning in young offenders. These programmes have usually been framed within a Kohlbergian perspective and are based on the premise that offenders show patterns of "pre-conventional" or "immature" moral reasoning and an egocentric bias. Such interventions provide social perspective-taking opportunities to offenders in order to encourage more mature levels of moral reasoning (Gibbs et al., 1995). For the most part, programmes of this type can be placed in one of two categories. First, there has been some focus on community-based interventions where offenders are placed in environments that emphasise the importance of democracy and justice and are encouraged to participate in decision-making particularly in the area of making and enforcing "community rules" (e.g Higgins, 1995). However the outcomes of such projects are equivocal as objective evaluation has been very difficult with evidence of effectiveness largely anecdotal and without any comparative data with control populations. Second, session-based group inter-ventions have also attempted to change the moral maturity of offenders with mixed success. In this type of programme, offenders are presented with a range of moral dilemmas and problem situations. Through discussion with each other and group leaders, they are provided with alternative perspectives on various hypothetical situations and are challenged when they demonstrate immature reasoning or an egocentric focus. The results of such programmes are mixed with Arbuthnot and Gordon (1988) and Allen, MacKenzie and Hickman (2001) finding indications of more mature moral reasoning and improved behaviour after participation. In contrast, Gibbs (1984) and Niles (1986) found improvements in moral reasoning but no associated change in behaviour. Similarly, Putnins (1997) reported that a programme aiming to make offenders more aware of the impact of their crime on victims increased moral maturity but failed to indicate whether this led to subsequent changes to behaviour. As suggested earlier, it may be that using Kohlberg's model of moral development as a basis for intervention is limited, because unlike the social domain model, it was derived exclusively from analyses of prescriptive or deontic judgements about what hypothetical char-acters on Kohlberg's test should ideally do as opposed to people's actual moral judgements about their own and others' behaviour.

In an analysis of the literature Gibbs and colleagues (1995) found that such approaches generally had limited success in translating more mature moral reasoning into behavioural change although Allen, MacKenzie, and Hickman (2001) cite specific examples where behavioural improvements have been identi-fied for certain categories of offenders. It is suggested that most interventions focusing on improving the maturity of moral reasoning do not have the desired impact on behaviour because they do not tend to take account of other areas of social cognitive processing, nor do they frame moral development within the broader context of real-life or complex decision-making as reflected by the domain model of social reasoning.

There are some treatment strategies that are beginning to incorporate our knowledge of the impact of social information processing and other cognitive processes with work in the area of moral reasoning. A recent example is the programme known as "Aggression Replacement Training" (Goldstein, Glick, & Gibbs, 1998). This intervention focuses on developing anger management strategies, improving social skills and problem solving in addition to working with moral maturity. The findings have been quite positive in gaining behavioural change for both juvenile delinquents (for a review, see Goldstein et al., 1998) and adult offenders (Sugg, 2000, as cited in Palmer, 2003; see McGuire and Clark, 2004).

There are also some positive results from a pilot study completed by Harvey (2003), which is one of the first to use a domain-based approach to incorporate working to improve children's decision-making skills based on aspects of the moral domain (developing skills in using "inside rules") into a social cognitive intervention programme. Although not focused specifically on an offender population, Harvey demonstrated that including activities that focused on domain categorisation and internalisation of rules in a standardised social cognitive skills programme (The Dinosaur Programme, Webster-Stratton, 1994) resulted in additional improvement in behavioural outcomes for aggressive children in a school context when compared with the behaviour of aggressive children who were exposed to the standard social cognitive skills programme and a control group who simply received games-based activities.

The results of these two intervention studies provide systematic evidence that incorporating moral reasoning within a broader framework of social cognitive intervention does work to change behaviour and is a very promising area for intervention. However, it is important to emphasise that such work is only in its infancy and there remains much to do. In addition, such programmes and general management of offender populations also need to recognise that the current domain-based social reasoning of individuals will make a difference to the salience of specific interventions that are aiming to improve self-regulation and decision-making. Such a statement is grounded in the findings presented earlier that individuals are more responsive to directions by authority figures when the content of the direction is congruent with the domain classification of the event by that individual. In particular, the results of several studies suggest that children actively evaluate social messages in terms of their domain appropriateness and reject messages that are domain inappropriate and inconsistent with the nature of the event (Killen, Breton, Ferguson, & Handler, 1994; Nucci, 1984). For example, if a child classifies an event within the moral domain, then intervention and direction citing reasons of preventing harm or ensuring fairness to others have been shown as relevant to the child and effective in modifying behaviour. In contrast, if the direction or explanation is incongruent with domain classification, for example, a direction or explanation citing general implications for harm when the child perceives the transgression as related to social conventional rules, he/she is less likely to consider the direction/explanation relevant, reducing the effectiveness of any intervention to follow. If there are consistent patterns of difference in the domain classification of events between aggressive and antisocial individuals and their pro-social peers, perhaps the ongoing interventions that are made by a range of authority figures are often perceived as irrelevant or effective (or both) by the aggressive individual. To extrapolate to the offender population, it can be hypothesised that if the responses of the authority figures and therapists working with these individuals do not respond to an offence or inappropriate decision in ways that are relevant to the domain classification of that offence by the individual, then, in the short term at least, the discussion will be disregarded or ineffective. For example, when trying to engage a violent offender in an initial discussion about an aggressive act it may be more effective to acknowledge perpetrators' personal needs and/or to identify the act as a transgression against social/community rules; and to work in the longer term towards placement of such behaviour in the moral domain rather than the initial focus being on the welfare of the victim. This will become more meaningful once issues of domain placement become more salient. In addition, given the findings that aggressive children have developed a "fuzzy" understanding of personal entitlement, it may be important for standardised interventions and less formal interactions to begin to assist offenders to understand more about the facets of social interaction that in the arena of personal control and choice.

Of course, these types of strategies are currently in the realm of speculation but as this chapter is focusing on future directions for working with offending populations it seems appropriate to bring them forward. There is no research suggesting that such strategies are effective, but the work with aggressive children has certainly identified that they might be meaningful strategies to assist in changing the social cognitions of this very difficult population. In addition, similar work with young aggressive children may be effective in reducing the number of juvenile delinquents and adult offenders as we increase the effectiveness of social cognitive interventions. As discussed in this and previous chapters, response scripts, cognitive biases and other cognitive processes are less entrenched in the earlier years and self-image has not deteriorated to the same extent that it often has in adolescents and adult offenders (e.g. Loeber, 1991; Mize and Ladd, 1990).

CONCLUSION

It is clear from this review that there is a lot to be done in understanding the moral reasoning of aggressive and antisocial children, juvenile delinquents and adult offenders and developing appropriate intervention strategies. The cognitive-developmental theories of Kohlberg and Piaget are not particularly helpful in this regard as they explain moral development as a single developmental pathway along which individuals progress. This type of explanation may be appropriate when dealing with hypothetical dilemmas but does not explain the research evidence that suggests that young children are making "moral judgements'' about a range of hypothetical and real-life events from the age of 3 and 4. Nor do these theories explain the variations in moral reasoning by individuals in various offender categories. Finally, there is ongoing debate about the effectiveness of interventions based on these theories.

As discussed in this chapter, recent research suggests that the developmental pathways for moral reasoning of offenders are best understood within the framework of social domain theory, with social reasoning considered a key component in behavioural decision-making. This theory can be accommodated within a broader cognitive framework outlining the development of aggressive and antisocial behaviour which takes into account the cognitive distortions, social information processing variations, reduced problem-solving skills, problematic early-life experiences and limited social schema that have been identified in the research literature.

Unfortunately most researchers interested in the development of aggressive behaviour and those working with offender populations have focused on a stage approach to moral development and there have been few attempts to directly link moral reasoning, domain placement, and social cognition in the research literature or in treatment approaches. Thus, the links between social cognition, social reasoning, and the development of antisocial behaviour in individuals are theoretically understood but somewhat limited by the paucity of empirical evidence. However, we do know there are measurable differences in the social reasoning patterns of aggressive individuals when compared to their more pro-social peers, although most of the research has focused on children and adolescents and has not tracked developmental changes with time. We also know that young aggressive children tend to focus on explicit regulation in their explanations of responses to negative social events whereas their pro-social peers use internalised regulatory patterns. Antisocial adolescents have been found to categorise aggressive responses within the personal domain leading to behavioural decisions based on the legitimacy of the aggressive action and a lack of consideration about the impact of such a response on the welfare of others.

Juvenile delinquency and adult offending are social problems whose history of theoretical and therapeutic solutions represents a legacy of frustration. To this point, rehabilitation or control efforts provide mixed results although pathways utilising social cognitive approaches appear fruitful when considering the effectiveness of various interventions. Within this type of approach it is hoped that an additional focus on the reasoning of offenders based on social domain theory may assist in increasing the effectiveness of such programmes and improve the capacity of these individuals to make effective judgements about a range of social situations in the community.

REFERENCES

Allen, L., MacKenzie, D., & Hickman, L. (2001). The effectiveness of cognitive behavioural treatment for adult offenders: A methodological, quality based review. *International Journal of Offender Therapy and Comparative Criminology, 45,* 498–514.

Arbuthnot, J. & Gordon, D. (1988). Crime and cognition: Community applications of sociomoral reasoning development. *Criminal Justice and Behavior, 15*, 379–393.

Arsenio, W. & Kramer, R. (1992). Victimisers and their victims: Children's conceptions of the mixed emotional consequences of moral transgressions. *Child Development, 63*, 915–927.

Barret, P. M., Rapee, R. M., Dadds, M. M. and Ryan, S. M. (1996). Family enhancement of cognitive style in anxious and aggressive children. *Journal of Abnormal Child Psychology, 24*, 187–203.

Beeghly, M. & Cicchetti, D. (1994). Child maltreatment, attachment, and the self system: Emergence of an internal state lexicon in toddlers at high social risk. *Development and Psychopathology, 6*, 5–30.

Berkowitz, M. W., Guerra, N., & Nucci, L. (1991). Sociomoral development and drug and alcohol abuse. In J. L. Gerwitz & W. M. Kurtines (eds) *Handbook of moral behavior and development*: Vol. 3. *Applications* (pp. 35–53), Hillsdale, NJ: Erlbaum.

Blair, R. J. (1997). Moral reasoning and the child with psychopathic tendencies. *Personality & Individual Differences, 22*, 731–739.

Blasi, A. (1980). Bridging moral cognition and moral action: A critical review of the literature. *Psychological Bulletin, 88*, 1–85.

Campbell, S. B. (1994). Hard-to-manage preschool boys: Externalising behavior social competence and family context at two-year follow up. *Journal of Abnormal Child Psychology, 22*, 147–166.

Crane, D. & Tisak, M. S. (1995). Mixed-domain events: The influence of moral and conventional components on the development of social reasoning. *Early Education & Development, 6*, 169–180.

Crane-Ross, D., Tisak, M. S., & Tisak, J. (1998). Aggression and conventional rule violation among adolescents: Social reasoning predictors of social behavior. *Aggressive Behavior, 25*, 347–365.

Crick, N. R. & Dodge, K. A. (1994). A review and reformulation of social information processing mechanisms in children's social adjustment. *Psychological Bulletin, 115*, 74–101.

Cummings, E. M., Iannotti, R. J., & Zahn-Waxler, C. (1989). Aggression between peers in early childhood: Individual continuity and developmental change. *Child Development, 69*, 887–895.

Dorsch, A. & Keane, S. P. (1994). Contextual factors in children's social information processing. *Developmental Psychology, 30*, 611–616.

Dunn, J. & Munn, P. (1985). Becoming a family member: family conflict and the development of social understanding in the second year. *Child Development, 56*, 480–492.

Eisenberg, N., Fabes, R., Carlo, G., & Speer, A. (1993). The relations of empathy related emotions and maternal practices to children's comforting behaviour. (Special issue: Social context, social behaviour and socialization.) *Journal of Experimental Child Psychology, 55*, 140–150.

Fergusson, D. M., Horwood, L. J., & Lynskey, M. T. (1995). The stability of disruptive behaviors. *Journal of Abnormal Child Psychology, 23, 3*, 379–396.

Gibbs, J., Arnold, K., Ahlborn, H. & Cheesmena, F. (1984). Facilitation of sociomoral reasoning in delinquents. *Journal of Consulting and Clinical Psychology, 52*, 37–45.

Gibbs, J., Potter, G., & Goldstein, A. (1995). *The Equip program*. Champaign, IL: Research Press.

Goldstein, A., Glick, J., & Gibbs, J. (1998). *Aggression replacement training*. 2nd edn. Champaign, IL: Research Press.

Griffore, R. & Samuels, D. (1978). Moral judgements of residents of a maximum security correctional facility. *The Journal of Psychology, 100*, 3–7.

Grusec, J. E. & Goodnow, J. J. (1994). Impact of parental discipline methods on the child's internalization of values: A reconceptualization of current points of view. *Developmental Psychology, 30,* 4–19.

Guerra, N., Huesmann, L., & Spindler, A. (2003). Community violence exposure, social cognition, and aggression among urban elementary school children. *Child Development, 74,* 1561–1576.

Guerra, N. G., Nucci, L., & Huesmann L. R. (1994). Moral cognition and childhood aggression. In L. R.Huesmann (ed) *Aggressive behaviour: Current perspectives* (pp. 13–33). New York: Plenum Press.

Guerra, N. G. & Slaby, R. G. (1990). Cognitive mediators of aggression in adolescent offenders: 2. Intervention, *Developmental Psychology, 26,* 269–277.

Harvey, R. (2003). Towards responsive relationships: Enhancing social reasoning and social skills in young children. Unpublished pilot study, report to Healthway, Western Australia.

Harvey, R., Fletcher, J., & French, D. J. (2004 - submitted). Social reasoning: Mixed domain variations between aggressive non-aggressive boys. *Journal of Abnormal Child Psychology.*

Helwig, C. C., Hildebrand, C., & Turiel, E. (1995). Children's judgements about psychological harm in social context. *Child Development, 66,* 1680–1693.

Helwig, C. C., Tisak, M. S., & Turiel, E. (1990). Children's social reasoning in context. *Child Development, 61,* 2068–2078.

Higgins, A. (1995). Educating for justice and community: Lawrence Kohlberg's vision of moral education. In W. Kurtines & J. Gerwirtz (eds) *Moral development: An introduction* (pp. 49–81). Boston: Allyn and Bacon.

Hoffman, M. (1984). Empathy, its limitations and its role in comprehensive moral theory. In J. Gerwitz & W. Kurtines (eds) *Morality, moral development, and moral behaviour* (pp. 283–302). New York: John Wiley and Sons, Ltd.

Hoffman, M. & Saltzstein, H. (1967). Parent discipline and the child's moral development. *Journal of Personality and Social Psychology, 5,* 45–57.

Hogan, R. (1973). Moral conduct and moral character: A psychological perspective. *Psychological Bulletin, 79,* 217–232.

Hudley, C. (1994). Perceptions of intentionality, feelings of anger, and reactive aggression. In M. Furlong & D. Smith (eds) *Anger, hostility and aggression: Assessment, prevention, and intervention strategies for youth.* Vermont: Clinical Psychology Publishing Company Inc.

Huesmann, L. R. & Guerra, N. G. (1997). Children's normative beliefs about aggression and aggressive behavior. *Journal of Personality & Social Psychology, 72,* 408–419.

Ijzendoorn, M. (1997). Attachment, emergent morality and aggression: Toward a developmental socio-emotional model of antisocial behaviour. *International Journal of Behavioural Development, 21,* 703–727.

Kazdin, A. E. (1995). *Conduct disorders in childhood and adolescence.* 2nd edn. Thousand Oaks, CA: Sage Publications.

Kazdin, A. E., Bass, D., Siegal, T., & Thomas, C. (1989). Cognitive-behavioral treatment and relationship therapy in the treatment of children referred for antisocial behavior. *Journal of Consulting & Clinical Psychology, 57,* 522–535.

Kazdin, A. E. & Crowley, M. (1997). Moderators of treatment outcome in cognitively based treatment of antisocial behavior. *Cognitive Therapy & Research, 21,* 185–207.

Keenan, K. & Shaw, D. S. (1994). The development of aggression in toddlers: A study of low income families. *Journal of Abnormal Child Psychology, 22,* 53–77.

Killen, M. (1990). Children's evaluations of morality in the context of peer, teacher-child, and familial relations. *Journal of Genetic Psychology, 151,* 395–410.

Killen, M., Breton, S., Ferguson, H., & Handler, K. (1994). Preschoolers' evaluation of teacher methods of intervention in social transgressions. *Merrill-Palmer Quarterly, 40,* 399–416.

Kochanska, G. (1995). Children's temperament, mothers' discipline, and security of attachment: Multiple pathways to emerging internalization. *Child Development, 66,* 597–615.

Kochanska, G., Aksan, N., & Koenig, A. L. (1995). A longitudinal study of the roots of preschoolers conscience: Committed compliance and emerging internalisation. *Child Development, 66,* 1752–1769.

Kochanska, G., DeVet, K., Goldman, M., Murray, K., & Putnam, S. (1994). Maternal reports of conscience development and temperament in young children. *Child Development, 65,* 852–868.

Koenig, A., Cicchetti, D., & Rogosch, F. (2004). Moral Development: The association between maltreatment and young children's prosocial behaviours and moral transgressions. *Social Development, 13,* 1.

Kohlberg, L. (1981). *The philosophy of moral development.* San Francisco: Harper & Row.

Kohlberg, L. (1984). *Essays on moral development: The psychology of moral development.* San Francisco, CA: Harper and Row.

Landy, S. & Peters, R. (1992). Toward an understanding of a developmental paradigm for aggressive conduct problems during the preschool years. In R. D. Peters, R. J. McMahon, & V. L. Quinsey (eds) *Aggression and violence throughout the lifespan* (pp. 1–30). Newbury Park, CA: Sage Publications.

Lee, M. & Prentice, W. (1988). Interrelations of empathy, cognition and moral reasoning with dimensions of juvenile delinquency. *Journal of Abnormal Child Psychology, 16,* 127–139.

Leeman, L., Gibbs, J., & Fuller, D. (1993). Evaluation of a multi-component group treatment program for juvenile delinquents. *Aggressive Behaviour, 24,* 335–346.

Loeber, R. (1991). Antisocial behavior: more enduring than changing? *Journal of the American Academy of Child & Adolescent Psychiatry, 30,* 383–397.

McGuire, J. and Clark, D. (2004). A national dissemination programme. In A. P. Goldstein, R. Nensén, B. Daleflod and M. Kalt (eds) *New Perspectives on Aggression replacement Training: Practice, Research and Application.* Chichester: John Wiley and Sons.

Mize, J. & Ladd, G. W. (1990). A cognitive-social learning approach to social skills training with low status preschool children. *Developmental Psychology, 26,* 388–397.

Nelson, J., Smith, D., & Dodd, J. (1990). The moral reasoning of juvenile delinquents: A meta analysis. *Journal of Abnormal Child Psychology, 18,* 231–239.

Niles, W. (1986). Effects of a moral development discussion group on delinquent and pre-delinquent boys. *Journal of Counselling Psychology, 33,* 45–51.

Nucci, L. P. (1981). Conceptions of personal issues: A domain distinct from moral or societal concepts. *Child Development, 52,* 114–121.

Nucci, L. P. (1982). Conceptual development in the moral and social-conventional domains: Implications for social education. *Review of Educational Research, 52,* 93–122.

Nucci, L. P. (1984). Evaluating teachers as social agents: Students' ratings of domain appropriate and domain inappropriate teacher responses to transgressions. *American Educational Research Journal, 2,* 367–378.

Nucci, L. P., Guerra, N., & Lee, J. (1991). Adolescent judgements of the personal, prudential and normative aspects of drug usage. *Developmental Psychology, 27,* 841–848.

Nucci, L. P. & Herman, S. (1982). Behavioral disordered children's conceptions of moral, conventional and personal issues. *Journal of Abnormal Child Psychology, 10,* 411–426.

Nucci, L. P. & Turiel, E. (1978). Social interactions and the development of social concepts in preschool children. *Child Development, 49,* 400–407.

Nucci, L. P. & Weber, E. K. (1995). Social interactions in the home and the development of Development. *Child Development, 49,* 400–407.

Offord, D. R., Boyd, M. H., & Racine, Y. A. (1991). The epidemiology of antisocial behavior in childhood and adolescence. In D. J. Pepler and K. H. Rubin (eds) *The development and treatment of childhood aggression* (pp. 31–54). Hillsdale, NJ: Lawrence Erlbaum.

Palmer, E. (2003). An overview of the relationship between moral reasoning and offending. *Australian Psychologist, 38*, 165–174.

Palmer, E. & Hollin, C. (1996). Sociomoral reasoning, perceptions of own parenting and self-reported delinquency. *Personality and Individual Differences, 21*, 175–182.

Palmer, E. & Hollin, C. (1997). The influence of perceptions of own parenting on sociomoral reasoning, attributions for criminal behaviour, and self reported delinquency. *Personal and Individual Differences, 23*, 193–197.

Palmer, E. & Hollin, C. (1998) A comparison of patterns of moral development in young offenders and non-offenders. *Legal and Criminological Psychology, 5*, 201–218.

Pepler, D., King, G., & Byrd, W. (1991). A social-cognitively based social skills training program for aggressive children. In D. Pepler & K. Rubin (eds) *The development and treatment of childhood aggression* (pp. 361–379). Hillsdale, NJ: Lawrence Erlbaum.

Perry, D. G., Perry, L. D. & Rasmussen, P. (1986). Cognitive social learning mediators of aggression. *Child Development, 57*, 700–711.

Piaget, J. (1932). *The moral judgement of the child.* New York: Free Press.

Putnins, A. (1995). Victim awareness as a core program for young offenders. *Youth Studies Australia, 14*, 38–41.

Quiggle, N. L., Garber, J., Panak, W. F., & Dodge, K. A. (1992). Social information processing in aggressive and depressed children. *Child Development, 63*, 1305–1320.

Roth, N. (2002). Moral identity and moral sensitivity: A domain analysis of risk and prosocial behavior. *Dissertation Abstracts International: Section B: The Sciences & Engineering.* Vol 63(3-B), 1552. US: Univ Microfilms International.

Sanderson, J. A. & Siegal, S (1988). Conceptions of moral and social rules in rejected and non-rejected preschoolers. *Journal of Clinical Child Psychology, 17*, 66–72.

Siegal, M. & Storey, R. M. (1985). Day care and children's conceptions of moral and social rules. *Child Development, 56*, 1001–1008.

Smetana, J. G. (1981). Preschool children's conceptions of moral and social rules. *Child Development, 52*, 1333-1-336.

Smetana, J. G. (1982). Reasoning in the personal and moral domains: Adolescent and young adult women's decision making regarding abortion. *Journal of Applied developmental Psychology, 2*, 211–226.

Smetana, J. G. (1984). Toddlers' social interactions regarding moral and conventional transgressions. *Child Development, 55*, 1767–1776.

Smetana, J. G. (1985). Preschool children's conceptions of transgressions: The effects of varying moral and conventional domain related attributes. *Developmental Psychology, 21*, 18–29.

Smetana, J. G. (1988). Adolescents' and parents' conceptions of parental authority. *Child Development, 59*, 321–335.

Smetana, J. G. (1995). Morality in context: Abstractions, ambiguities and applications. In R. Vasta (ed.) *Annals of child development: a research annual* (Vol. 10, pp. 83–130) London: Jessica Kingsley.

Smetana, J. G. (1999). The role of parents in moral development: A social domain analysis. *Journal of Moral Education, 28*, 311–321.

Smetana, J. G. & Braeges, J. (1990). The development of toddlers' moral and conventional judgements. *Merrill-Palmer Quarterly, 36*, 329–346.

Smetana, J. G., Schlagman N., & Adams, P. W. (1993). Preschool children's judgements about hypothetical and actual transgressions. *Child Development, 64*, 202–214.

Stevenson, S., Hall, G. & Innes, J. (2003). Sociomoral reasoning and criminal sentiments in Australian men and women violent offenders and non-offenders. *International Journal of Forensic Psychology, 1*, 111–119.

Stoddart, T. & Turiel, E. (1985). Children's concepts of cross-gender activities. *Child Development*, 56, 1241–1252.

Sugg, D. (2000). *Wiltshire Aggression Replacement Training (ART): One year reconvictions and targeting.* Unpublished report, RDS. London: Home Office.

Tisak, M. (1995). Domains of social reasoning and beyond. *Annals of Child Development*, 11, 95–130.

Tisak, M. & Jankowski, A. M. (1996). Societal rule evaluations: Adolescent offenders' reasoning about moral, conventional and personal rules. *Aggressive Behavior*, 22, 195–207.

Tisak, M. S., Nucci, L., & Jankowski, A. M. (1996). Preschool children's social interactions involving moral and prudential transgressions: An observational study. *Journal of Early Education & Development*, 7, 137–148.

Tisak, M. & Turiel, E. (1984). Children's conceptions of moral and prudential rules. *Child Development*, 55, 1030–1039.

Tisak, M. & Turiel, E. (1988). Variation in seriousness of transgressions and children's moral and conventional concepts. *Developmental Psychology*, 24, 352–357.

Turiel, E. (1978). Mores, customs and conventions: Social regulations and domains of social concepts. In W. Damon (ed.) *New directions for child development: Social cognition* (pp. 45–74). San Francisco: Jossey-Bass.

Turiel, E. (1983). *The development of social knowledge: Morality and convention.* Cambridge: Cambridge University Press.

Turiel, E. (1987). Potential relations between the development of social reasoning and childhood aggression. In D. H. Crowell, I. M. Evans & C. R. O'Donnell (eds) *Childhood aggression and violence: Sources of influence, prevention and control. Applied Clinical Psychology* (pp. 95-114). New York: Plenum Press.

Turiel, E. (1998). The development of morality. In W. Damon (ed.), *Handbook of child psychology*, 5th edn. Vol 3: N. Eisenberg (ed.), *Social, emotional and personality development.* New York: Academic Press.

Turiel, E., Hildebrand, C., & Wainryb, C. (1991). Judging social issues: Difficulties, consistencies, and inconsistencies: 1. *Monographs of the Society for Research in Child Development*, 56, 1–103.

Turiel, E. & Smetana, J. G. (1984). Social knowledge and social action: The coordination of domains. In J. L. Gerwitz, & W. M. Kurtines, (eds) *Morality, moral development, and moral behavior* (pp. 261–282). Hillsdale, NJ: Lawrence Erlbaum.

Veneziano, C. & Veneziano, L. (1988). Knowledge of social skills among institutionalized juvenile delinquents: An assessment. *Criminal Justice & Behavior*, 15, 152 171.

Webster-Stratton, C. (1994). Advancing videotape parent training: A comparison study. *Journal of Consulting and Clinical Psychology*, 65, 93–109.

Weiss, B., Dodge, K., Bates, J., & Pettit, G. (1992). Some consequences of early harsh discipline: Child aggression and a maladaptive social information processing style. *Child Development*, 63, 1321–1335.

Zahn-Waxler, C., Robinson, J., & Emde, R. (1992). The development of empathy in twins. *Developmental Psychology*, 28, 1038–1047.

Zelazo, P., Helwig, C., & Lau, A. (1996). Intention, act and outcome in behavioral prediction and moral judgement. *Child Development*, 67, 2478-2-492.

Chapter 15

SOCIAL PROBLEM-SOLVING AND OFFENDING: REFLECTIONS AND DIRECTIONS

Mary McMurran

Cardiff University, UK

INTRODUCTION

Contributions to this book provide evidence of the usefulness of the social problem-solving framework in explaining offending behaviour, understanding how offending developed, and driving effective offender treatment. The aims of this concluding chapter are, first, to note lessons learned from research and practice in this field, and, second, to suggest possible developments in theory, research and practice that build upon the findings that have been described.

As noted by James McGuire in Chapters 1 and 10, there are two strands to the development of problem-solving interventions with offenders – the training strand, more typical in corrections psychology, and the therapy strand, more typical in clinical psychology. There are representations of both strands in this text, and each carries messages for the future of social problem-solving research and interventions with offenders.

The first correctional services programme significantly addressing social problem-solving was Ross and Fabiano's (1985; Ross, Fabiano, & Ewles, 1988) Reasoning and Rehabilitation (R&R). One of the most important features of R&R was that it had a theoretical rationale whose validity could be (and was) examined by research. R&R was based upon evidence of offenders' cognitive deficits, as described and updated by Daniel Antonowicz and Robert Ross in Chapter 5. The importance of this was revealed later when meta-analyses of offender outcome studies showed that, among other things, programmes with a conceptual underpinning focused on cognitive processes were most effective (Izzo & Ross, 1990).

Social Problem Solving and Offending: Evidence, Evaluation and Evolution.
Edited by Mary McMurran and James McGuire   © 2005 John Wiley & Sons, Ltd.

This ground-breaking treatment programme was significant in lending credence to the notion that offender treatment could work, thus countering the "nothing works" pessimism of the 1970s (Martinson, 1974). R&R has since been implemented with a variety of types of offender in many different jurisdictions, with generally positive outcomes, as described by Dan Antonowicz in Chapter 9. Where outcomes have been less positive, there arises the question of whether programmes have been implemented with integrity or if this may have been compromised. I will return to this point shortly.

One other intervention to have sprung from the R&R bedrock is Enhanced Thinking Skills (ETS; Clark, 2000), implemented originally in the Prison and Probation Services for England and Wales. This is highly similar to R&R in terms of the model of change and the range of treatment targets, including a focus on problem solving, but is considerably shorter at 21 sessions compared to R&R's 38 (Blud & Travers, 2001). In a study of 670 adult male prisoners to have participated in either ETS or R&R between 1992 and 1996, compared with retrospectively matched controls, initial outcomes with regards to reconviction at two years post-release were highly promising, with as much as a 14% reduction in reoffending for the treatment group over the untreated (Friendship, Blud, Erikson, & Travers, 2002). A later study, however, was less positive. A sample of 3,729 male prisoners who participated in ETS between 1998 and 2000 was compared with a matched control group at one and two years post-release, with the results showing no differences in reconviction between the two groups at either time (Cann, Falshaw, Nugent, & Friendship, 2003). What could be going wrong?

The later lack of a positive finding could, as Antonowicz suggests, be due to challenges to the quality of the programme. In the early days, when the numbers treated were fewer, results were favourable and consequently the programme was rolled out at speed across England and Wales. In the Probation Service, for example, targets set as part of the Government's Crime Reduction Programme in 1999 were to have 10,000 offenders on accredited programmes by 2001/2002, and 60,000 by 2003/2004, with a consequent 5% reduction in reconviction observed by 2003 (Crime Reduction website). Such a mass roll-out could possibly have impacted adversely on the quality of the programme. In striving to meet target numbers of offenders completing programmes, it is possible that less discernment may be exercised in the selection of offenders, with less suitable and less motivated offenders consequently being recruited into programmes. The second evaluation showed that, if drop-outs were excluded from the analyses, offending at one year post-release was lower for the treatment group by 2.5%, which supports the notion of less rigorous attention to selection criteria.

Mass roll-out carries with it other risks of compromise to quality. If less suitable offenders are recruited to groups, they may disrupt the therapy process and thus diminish the experience for others. It may be that criteria for staff selection are broadened to include as programme facilitators those who may not possess the best personal and professional skills. If services struggle to resource high-volume programmes, it may be that preparation and debriefing time are pared to the bare essentials, thus eroding the quality of sessions.

Compromise of treatment quality with mass roll-out has been observed by others. Eisenberg and Fabelo (1996) described a five-year programme in Texas to provide 14,000 new substance abuse treatment places. They commented on the difficulties in providing treatment on such a large scale, including difficulties meeting demands for staff training, problems in maintaining inmate selection procedures, challenges to maintaining programme consistency, increased numbers of drop-outs, and difficulties providing adequate post-release support.

Effective programmes can clearly be rendered ineffective by careless execution, and there needs to be some judicious control and restraint of the unmanageable treatment targets imposed upon programme providers. Loss of treatment integrity leads to less effective treatment which contributes unfairly to the evidence that offender treatment does not work. As Ogloff and Davis (2004) have observed, there is a great deal at stake in the recent resurgence of investment in rehabilitation activities. It would be regrettable if poor results were to be misinterpreted as a failure of intervention methods rather than due to contextual factors (as they more probably are), and lead to a decline in programmes. This needs to be guarded against.

With protection of treatment integrity as a solid basis, we can then move on to developing social problem-solving interventions. One place to look for ideas is the second social problem-solving strand, namely the therapy approach, which has its origins in D'Zurilla and Goldfried's (1971) seminal paper on social problem solving and behaviour modification. Social problem-solving therapy has a considerable track record in clinical psychology generally, due in no small part to the research and writings of Thomas D'Zurilla, Arthur Nezu, and Christine Maguth Nezu. It has effective application in problems of anxiety, depression, suicidality, anger, substance abuse, schizophrenia, and physical health problems (Nezu, D'Zurilla, Zwick, & Nezu, 2004). In Chapter 6 of this text, D'Zurilla, Nezu, and Nezu summarise their highly influential model of social problem-solving therapy and turn their attention to its utility in the treatment of sex offenders. It is on this model that Fiona Biggam and Kevin Power (Chapter 8) based their work with young offenders who self-harm, and I and my colleagues, Vincent Egan and Conor Duggan based the *Stop & Think!* programme for personality disordered offenders (Chapter 11).

The social problem-solving framework, as presented in Figure 15.1, has beauty in its simplicity. In this streamlined form, it draws attention to the principal cognitive and behavioural domains that may be underdeveloped or maladaptively developed, thus raising the likelihood of offending. The framework also provides a comprehensible and useful map for developing interventions with people who offend, as with others, and there is evidence in this text for the effectiveness of problem-solving approaches with different populations of offenders. However, the simplicity of the framework is deceptive. While it serves a useful purpose in clearly conveying the general problem-solving process, it conceals the detail of what the process entails. The social problem-solving model captures within it a range of psychological skills (Pakaslahti, 2000; Zelazo et al., 1997), some of which are listed in Table 15.1. This shows that in social problem-solving training and therapy an impressive number of skills are being promoted.

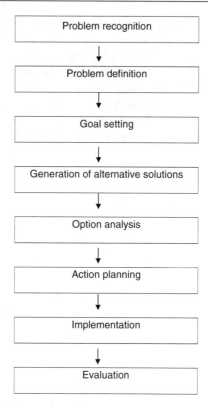

Figure 15.1 A social problem-solving framework

Table 15.1 The range of skills required for social problem solving

Recognising a problem exists	Problem-solving	Solution implementation
Self-awareness	Emotion control	Sustained attention
Emotion recognition	Attention	Impulse control
Social perception	Information gathering	Use of social rules
	Information filtering	Monitoring progress
	Causal analysis	Error detection
	Creative thinking	Error correction
	Consequential thinking	Perseverance
	Forward planning	
	Decision making	
	Memory	

INDIVIDUAL DIFFERENCES

Offenders, in all their variety, will have different social problem-solving profiles; strengths and deficits will not be uniform. The individual's personality traits may assist or impede social problem solving through their effect on information processing. Newman (1998) is one of the major researchers into cognitive processing deficits in those offenders designated as "psychopaths", and in this book Ralph Serin and Shelley Brown (Chapter 13) draw on this body of research to develop our understanding of social problem-solving in that group. However, other personality traits require attention in relation to information-processing, social problem-solving and offending.

Wallace and Newman (1998), for example, have suggested a model whereby three major personality traits affect attention, which in turn impacts information processing, self-regulation, behaviour, and affect. High neuroticism (N) facilitates the automatic orientation of attention, thus disrupting the controlled information processing that is necessary for self-regulation. Poor self-regulation is associated with negative affect and psychopathology. High extraversion (E) focuses attention on opportunities for reward, and high introversion (I) focuses attention on threat, with skewed information thus being entered into the process. More speculatively, high psychoticism (P) is thought to be associated with a focus on external circumstances rather than one's own actions in explaining events (i.e., blaming others), whereas low P is a focus on one's own actions rather than external events (i.e., blaming oneself). The series of questions requiring attention is: How do personality traits affect information processing? How do styles of information processing affect social problem-solving? And how do styles of social problem-solving link with offending? Identifying differences more clearly will enable the refinement of assessment and selection, and will assist with the rational development of interventions better to suit individual needs.

EMOTIONS

Closely linked with personality is the realm of emotions. Emotion regulation is important to effective problem-solving and this is an area that attracts much attention in offender treatment. Negative emotional states have been identified through longitudinal studies as risks for involvement in delinquency (Caspi & Silva, 1995). Studies of individuals' experiences and circumstances prior to committing new offences have also demonstrated the significance of dysphoric and other mood changes (Zamble & Quinsey, 1997). More specifically, negative mood states have been shown to be associated with relapse to certain types of offending (e.g., sexual offending; Hanson & Harris, 2000), and for relapse to behaviours associated with offending (e.g., heavy drinking and drug use; Bonta, Law, & Hanson, 1998; Harris, Rice, & Quinsey, 1993). Mood states as dynamic risk factors are widely attended to in treatments, such as anger interventions (e.g., Novaco, Ramm, & Black, 2001) and mood management modules within treatments (e.g., Ward, Hudson, & Keenan, 2001).

The perception and understanding of emotions in self and others are also essential to effective interpersonal problem-solving, and this aspect of problem-solving requires further study in offenders. First, recognition of one's own adverse emotions is key in triggering the problem-solving process. Barrett et al. (2001) studied emotion recognition in relation to emotion regulation. They examined emotion differentiation, that is, how specifically or generally an emotion is labelled. Specificity, they argued, is essential to successful social problem solving in that feelings give information about the current situation that is helpful in planning what to do next. They found that the ability to label negative emotional experiences more precisely was associated with better emotion regulation through use of a range of strategies, particularly when the emotional experience was intense. Information about offenders' emotion recognition skills would assist with developing ways of promoting the use of problem-solving skills. The skills may be there, but to have any effect they have to be used, and the initiation of the process requires scrutiny.

Second, emotional issues are features of many interpersonal problems and the emotions of others must be recognised and factored into the problem-solving process. There has been considerable research into emotion perception in clinical populations, for example, people with schizophrenia, autism, and anorexia. Recently, there have been studies of emotion recognition in psychopathic individuals, with deficits noted particularly in identifying fear and sadness (Blair, Colledge, Murray, & Mitchell, 2001; Blair et al., 2002). This line of research could usefully be extended to offenders more widely.

'Emotional intelligence' is a relatively new construct that addresses the skills relevant to interpersonal problem solving, namely the perception, expression, understanding, and regulation of emotions (Mayer, Caruso, & Salovey, 1999). In general, the relationship between emotional intelligence and social problem solving seems worthy of further exploration. This should be conducted with regard to some of the current concerns surrounding the construct. Researchers have questioned whether emotional intelligence adds anything over and above general intelligence and personality, with some finding no uniqueness in the construct (Schulte, Ree, & Carretta, 2004) while others are more supportive of its value (Warwick & Nettelbeck, 2004). There remains a need for further definitional refinement, for example, distinguishing trait from ability aspects of emotional intelligence, as well as a need to develop reliable and valid measures (Petrides, Furnham, & Frederickson, 2004).

Only one study to date is known to have examined emotional intelligence in offenders. In a sample of 118 male prisoners, contrary to expectation, offenders scored significantly *higher* overall than a normative sample on Bar-On's (1997) measure of emotional intelligence (Hemmati, Mills, & Kroner, 2004). The sample scored significantly higher on subscales measuring intrapersonal emotional intelligence, interpersonal emotional intelligence, and adaptability, but showed no difference on scales of stress management or general mood. The authors suggest that offenders may interpret items differently or may respond differently. Thus, the issue of measurement of emotional intelligence in offenders needs some attention to pave the way for further research. Even allowing for measurement idiosyncrasies, there was still a strong inverse correlation between emotional intelligence scores and psychopathology in this sample, suggesting that the area is worthy of consideration.

DEVELOPMENTAL PATHWAYS

In raising the issue of individual differences, the question arises of how an offender develops a specific problem-solving profile. The study of how personality traits contribute to the acquisition of problem-solving skills, how they later mediate the influence of traits on behaviour, how traits moderate the effectiveness of social problem-solving, and how social problem-solving skills and personality develop and change in a reciprocal and reflexive process over time are all issues that demand further study.

In tracing a developmental pathway, the reciprocity between individual characteristics and the social environment is explanatory. Traits must be seen in a process of dynamic interplay with situational and other contextual variables where behaviour is best understood as a product of person–situation interactions (Mischel, 2004). As observed by Rich and Bonner, "any variable can serve as an antecedent, a mediator, a moderator, or a consequence in the social problem-solving process" (2004, pp. 29–30). From an early age, personality traits may impact upon social problem-solving, but problem-solving skills develop in specific directions by courtesy of the actions of others in the individual's social environment. Liisa Keltikangas-Järvinen in Chapter 2, and Walter Matthys and John Lochman in Chapter 3 examined problem-solving in the early years, with particular reference to aggression. This line of enquiry has strong implications for prevention of later problems, particularly through the potential to enhance promising pre-school and parenting programmes (Farrington, 2003). Friedrich Lösel and Andreas Beelmann provide us with an example of an effective early intervention in Chapter 7.

BELIEFS, ATTITUDES, SCHEMAS, AND SCRIPTS

Over the lifespan into adulthood, the individual's learning experiences may be captured in the broader knowledge structures of beliefs, attitudes, schemas, and scripts. Once developed, these broad knowledge structures again in turn influence social information processing. The development of these constructs in relation to aggression has been the focus of considerable research (e.g., Crick & Dodge, 1994; Huesmann & Guerra, 1997). Some elements of this may be observable at a very basic level through processes such as the automaticity of responses (Bargh & Ferguson, 2000), and the routes by which this may channel activity into aggression require further and more detailed study (Todorov & Bargh, 2002). Additionally, an extension of this research to other areas of offending is warranted, and Theresa Gannon, Devon Polaschek, and Tony Ward in Chapter 12 extend the field in relation to sex offenders.

At this later stage in life, when beliefs, schemas, and scripts are entrenched, the label of personality disorder is frequently invoked to describe and explain abnormal social problem-solving. In Chapter 4, Laura Dreer and colleagues examine personality-disorder in relation to substance abuse, and in Chapter 9, my colleagues and I have reported some research findings in relation to personality disordered offenders. If scripts and schemas impinge on social problem-solving, then integrating aspects of schema therapy (Young, Klosko, & Weishaar, 2003) may advance social problem-solving interventions. This is supported by the findings of Salekin's (2002) review of interventions with people with psychopathic traits, a particularly difficult-to-treat client group. The most encouraging results came from approaches including cognitive-behavioural and personal construct therapies and related methods which "addressed patients' thoughts about themselves, others, and society. Thus, they tended directly to treat some psychopathic traits" (Salekin, 2002, p. 101). Salekin's comment shows clearly the relevance of broader issues, which are likely include moral reasoning, as comprehensively described by Robin Harvey in Chapter 14.

ASSESSMENT

One final issue relates to how offenders' problem-solving abilities are measured. In Chapter 1, James McGuire distinguished between process measures and outcome measures. Self-report questionnaires such as the Social Problem Solving Inventory - Revised (SPSI-R; D'Zurilla, Nezu, & Maydeu-Olivares, 2002) tap the internal, cognitive processes that people use to solve problems. These internal processes are complex and often automatic. Many offenders, and other clinical populations, may not have the capacity accurately to identify and articulate the cognitive processes of problem-solving. Furthermore, offenders' generally poor literacy and comprehension levels (Davies, Lewis, Byatt, Purvis, & Cole, 2004) militate against their understanding of and responding to questionnaires.

Outcome measures, such as in the Means–End Problem Solving procedure (MEPS; Spivack & Platt, 1980), provide problems and judge the respondent's problem-solving abilities by the range and quality of suggestions generated. These methods suffer from the problems provided having dubious external validity and the judgemental aspect of rating responses can lead to poor inter-rater reliability (House & Scott, 1996).

As in most fields of psychological measurement, continued work is required on improving validity and reliability. D'Zurilla, Nezu, & Maydeu-Olivares (2004) propose problem-solving self-monitoring, which permits a focus on real-life problems. My colleagues and I at Cardiff University are currently developing a comprehensive assessment of social problem-solving skills guided by knowledge from mainstream cognitive psychology.

CONCLUSION

James McGuire concluded in his review of meta-analyses of offender treatment studies that, "Those programmes and services that work best are founded on an explicit and well-articulated model of the causes of crime and criminal acts. This should be conceptually clear and based on sound, systematic empirical evidence" (2001, p. 34). Social problem-solving is one underpinning model that should be further articulated and tested in relation to offending. Contributors to this book have provided a solid platform on which to base further developments. Their innovative work is of great value, not only to researchers and practitioners, but also to offenders and members of society, all of whom should embrace theory-driven, empirically tested, and effective interventions to reduce crime.

REFERENCES

Bargh, J. A. & Ferguson, M. J. (2000). Beyond behaviorism: On the automaticity of higher mental processes. *Psychological Bulletin, 126*, 925–945.

Bar-On, R. (1997). *EQ-i Bar-On emotional quotient inventory*. Toronto: Multi-Health Systems, Inc.

Barrett, L. F., Gross, J., Christensen, T. C., & Benvenuto, M. (2001). Knowing what you're feeling and knowing what to do about it: Mapping the relation between emotion differentiation and emotion regulation. *Cognition and Emotion, 15*, 713–724.

Blair, R. J. R., Colledge, E., Murray, L., & Mitchell, D. G. V. (2001). A selective impairment in the processing of sad and fearful expressions in children with psychopathic tendencies. *Journal of Abnormal Child Psychology, 29*, 491–498.

Blair, R. J. R., Mitchell, D. G. V., Richell, R. A., Kelly, S., Leonard, A., Newman, C., & Scott, S. K. (2002). Turning a deaf ear to fear: Impaired recognition of vocal affect in psychopathic individuals. *Journal of Abnormal Psychology, 111*, 682–686.

Blud, L. & Travers, R. (2001). Interpersonal problem-solving skills training: A comparison of R & R and ETS. *Criminal Behaviour and Mental Health, 11*, 251–261.

Bonta, J., Law, M., & Hanson, K (1998). The prediction of criminal and violent recidivism among mentally disordered offenders: A meta-analysis. *Psychological Bulletin, 123*, 123–142.

Cann, J., Falshaw, L., Nugent, F., & Friendship, C. (2003). *Understanding What Works: Accredited cognitive skills programmes for adult men and young offenders*. Home Office Research Findings, No. 226. London: Home Office.

Caspi, A. & Silva, P. A. (1995). Temperamental qualities at age 3 predict personality traits in young adulthood: Longitudinal evidence from a birth cohort. *Child Development, 66*, 486–498.

Clark, D. (2000). *Theory manual for enhanced thinking skills*. London: Home Office.

Crick, N. R. & Dodge, K. A. (1994). A review and reformulation of social information-processing mechanisms in children's social adjustment. *Psychological Bulletin, 1*, 74–101.

Crime Reduction (undated). Crime reduction programme. <http://www.crime reduction.gov.uk/crpinit3.htm>. Accessed 16 November 2004.

Davies, K., Lewis, J., Byatt, J., Purvis, E., & Cole, B. (2004). *An evaluation of the literacy demands of general offending behaviour programmes*. Home Office Research Findings No. 233. London: Home Office.

D'Zurilla, T. J., & Goldfried, M. R. (1971). Problem solving and behavior modification. *Journal of Abnormal Psychology, 78*, 107–126.

D'Zurilla, T. J., Nezu, A. M., & Maydeu-Olivares, A. (2002). *Manual for the social problem solving inventory-revised*. North Tonawanda, NY: Multi-Health Systems, Inc.

D'Zurilla, T. J., Nezu, A. M., & Maydeu-Olivares, A. (2004). Social problem solving: Theory and assessment. In E. C. Chang, T. J. D'Zurilla, & L. J. Sanna (eds) *Social problem solving: Theory, research and training* (pp. 11–27). Washington, DC: American Psychological Association.

Eisenberg, M. & Fabelo, T. (1996). Evaluation of the Texas correctional substance abuse treatment initiative: The impact of policy research. *Crime and Delinquency, 42*, 296–308.

Farrington, D. P. (2003). Advancing knowledge about the early prevention of adult antisocial behaviour. In D. P. Farrington & J. W. Coid (eds) *Early prevention of adult antisocial behaviour*. (pp. 1–31). Cambridge: Cambridge University press.

Friendship, C., Blud, L., Erikson, M., & Travers, R. (2002). *An evaluation of cognitive behavioural treatment for prisoners*. Home Office Research Findings No. 161. London: Home Office.

Hanson, R. K. & Harris, A. J. R. (2000). Where should we intervene? Dynamic predictors of sexual offense recidivism. *Criminal Justice and Behavior, 27*, 6–35.

Harris, G. T., Rice, M. E., & Quinsey, V. L. (1993). Violent recidivism of mentally disordered offenders: The development of a statistical prediction instrument. *Criminal Justice and Behavior, 20*, 315–335.

Hemmati, T., Mills, J. F., & Kroner, D. G. (2004). The validity of the Bar-On emotional intelligence quotient in an offender population. *Personality and Individual Differences, 37*, 695–706.

House, R. & Scott, J. (1996). Problems in measuring problem-solving: The suitability of the Means–Ends Problem Solving (MEPS) procedure. *International Journal of Methods in Psychiatric Research, 6*, 1–9.

Huesmann, L. R., & Guerra, N. G. (1997). Children's normative beliefs about aggression and aggressive behavior. *Journal of Personality and Social Psychology, 72*, 408–419.

Izzo, R. L., & Ross, R. R. (1990). Meta-analysis of rehabilitation programs for juvenile delinquents. *Criminal Justice and Behavior, 17*, 134–142.

Martinson, R. (1974). What works? Questions and answers about prison reform. *The Public Interest, 10*, 22–54.

Mayer, J. D., Caruso, D. R., & Salovey, P. (1999). Emotional intelligence meets traditional standards for an intelligence. *Intelligence, 27*, 267–298.

McGuire, J. (2001). What works in correctional intervention? Evidence and practical implications. In G. A. Bernfeld, D. P. Farrington, & A. W. Leschied (eds) *Offender rehabilitation in practice: Implementing and evaluating effective programs* (pp. 25–43). Chichester: John Wiley & Sons, Ltd.

Mischel, W. (2004). Toward an integrative science of the person. *Annual Review of Psychology, 55*, 1–22.

Newman, J. P. (1998). Psychopathic behavior: An information processing perspective. In D. J. Cooke, A. E. Forth, & R. D. Hare (eds) *Psychopathy: Theory, research, and implications for society*. Dordrecht: Kluwer Academic Publishing.

Nezu, A. M., D'Zurilla, T. J., Zwick, M. L., & Nezu, C. M. (2004). Problem-solving therapy for adults. In E. C. Chang, T. J. D'Zurilla, & L. J. Sanna (eds) *Social problem solving: Theory, research and training* (pp. 171-181). Washington, DC: American Psychological Association.

Novaco, R. W., Ramm, M., & Black, L. (2001). Anger treatment with offenders. In C. R. Hollin (ed.) *Handbook of offender assessment and treatment.* (pp. 281-296). Chichester: John Wiley & Sons, Ltd.

Ogloff, J. R. P. & Davis, M. R. (2004). Advances in offender assessment and rehabilitation: Contributions of the risk-needs-responsivity approach. *Psychology, Crime & Law, 10*, 229–242.

Pakaslahti, L. (2000). Children's and adolescents' aggressive behaviour in context: The development and application of aggressive problem-solving strategies. *Aggression and Violent Behaviour, 5*, 467–490.

Petrides, K. V., Furnham, A., & Frederickson, N. (2004). Emotional intelligence. *The Psychologist, 17*, 574–577.

Rich, A. R., & Bonner, R. L. (2004). Mediators and moderators of social problem-solving. In E. C. Chang, T. J. D'Zurilla, & L. J. Sanna (eds) *Social problem solving: Theory, research, and training.* (pp. 29–45). Washington, DC: American Psychological Association.

Ross, R. R. & Fabiano, E. A. (1985). *Time to think: A cognitive model of delinquency prevention and offender rehabilitation.* Johnson City, TN: Institute of Social Sciences and Arts.

Ross, R. R., Fabiano, E. A., & Ewles, C. D. (1988). Reasoning and rehabilitation. *International Journal of Offender Therapy and Comparative Criminology, 32*, 29–35.

Salekin, R. T. (2002). Psychopathy and therapeutic pessimism: Clinical lore or clinical reality? *Clinical Psychology Review, 22*, 79–112.

Schulte, M. J., Ree, M. J., & Carretta, T. R. (2004). Emotional intelligence: Not much more than *g* and personality. *Personality and Individual Differences, 37,* 1059–1068.

Spivack, G. & Platt, J. J. (1980) *Measures of social problem-solving for adolescents and adults.* Philadelphia, PA: Preventive Intervention Research Center, Hahnemann University.

Todorov, A. & Bargh, J. A. (2002). Automatic sources of aggression. *Aggression and Violent Behavior, 7,* 53–68.

Wallace, J. F., & Newman, J. P. (1998). Neuroticism and the facilitation of the automatic orienting of attention. *Personality and Individual Differences, 24,* 253–266.

Ward, T., Hudson, S. M., & Keenan, T. R. (2001). The assessment and treatment of sexual offenders against children. In C. R. Hollin (ed.) *Handbook of offender assessment and treatment* (pp. 349–361). Chichester: John Wiley & Sons, Ltd.

Warwick, J. & Nettelbeck, T. (2004). Emotional intelligence is . . .? *Personality and Individual Differences, 37,* 1091–1100.

Young, J. E., Klosko, J. S., & Weishaar, M. E. (2003). *Schema therapy: A practitioner's guide.* New York: Guilford, Press.

Zamble, E. & Quinsey, V. (1997). *The criminal recidivism process.* Cambridge: Cambridge University Press.

Zelazo, P. D., Carter, A., Reznick, J. S., & Frye, D. (1997). Early development of executive function: A problem-solving framework. *Review of General Psychology, 1,* 198–226.

INDEX